Grassroots
Associations

For Helen and Karen

Grassroots
Associations

David Horton Smith

Sage Publications, Inc.
International Educational and Professional Publisher
Thousand Oaks ▪ London ▪ New Delhi

For information:

Sage Publications, Inc.
2455 Teller Road
Thousand Oaks, California 91320
E-mail: order@sagepub.com

Sage Publications Ltd.
6 Bonhill Street
London EC2A 4PU
United Kingdom

Sage Publications India Pvt. Ltd.
M-32 Market
Greater Kailash I
New Delhi 110 048 India

Printed in the United States of America

Library of Congress Cataloging-in-Publication Data

Smith, David Horton.
        Grassroots associations / by David Horton Smith
            p.   cm
        Includes bibliographical references and index.
        ISBN 0-8039-5992-3 (cloth: alk. paper)
        ISBN 0-8039-5993-1 (pbk.: alk. paper)
            1. Associations, institutions, etc.—United States.   2. Nonprofit
        Organizations—United States.   3. Voluntarism—United States.
        Social action—United States.   I. Title
        HN55.S54 2000
        361.7′63′0973—dc21   99-50814

This book is printed on acid-free paper.

00   01   02   03   04   05   06   7   6   5   4   3   2   1

Acquisition Editor: Jim Nageotte/Nancy Hale
Production Editor: Elly Korn
Editorial Assistant: Cindy Bear
Typesetter: Susan Selmer
Cover Designer: Michelle Lee

Contents

PART I:
TOWARD A ROUND-EARTH PARADIGM FOR
THE VOLUNTARY NONPROFIT SECTOR

PART II:
THE DISTINCTIVE NATURE OF GRASSROOTS ASSOCIATIONS

PART III:
THEORETICAL PARADIGMS AND CONCLUSIONS

Key Abbreviations in This Book

GAs = grassroots associations, which are significantly autonomous, formal nonprofit groups that use the associational form or structure, that are volunteer run and composed essentially of volunteers as analytical members, and that have a relatively small local scope (i.e., locally based). Hence, they are one important form of nonprofit group.

VGs = voluntary groups, which are nonprofit groups or any type, whether GAs or based on paid staff, and whether local, national, or international in scope. To be a VG, a significant proportion of a group's analytical members (regular service-providing affiliates) must be acting out of voluntary altruism, as defined in Chapter 1.

VNPS = voluntary nonprofit sector, which is the voluntary, independent, so-called "third sector" of society that manifests voluntary altruism and may be divided into the member benefit subsector and the nonmember benefit subsector. The other three sectors are the household/family sector, the business sector, and the government sector.

Foreword

David Horton Smith has studied and written about voluntary associations for more than 30 years. He founded the principal scholarly group (the Association for Research on Nonprofit Organizations and Voluntary Action) and the principal journal (*Nonprofit and Voluntary Sector Quarterly*) in the field. This book might well be his magnum opus. It distills his research and that of more than 2,000 other scholars who have studied what he calls "grassroots associations" (GAs), and it presents important new theoretical constructs for helping us understand these groups.

The book should help rebalance this scholarly field. Smith argues—correctly, in my view—that the past two decades of nonprofit sector scholarship have carried us away from an older, broader, and (in many ways) more accurate view of the organizational phenomenon that lies outside the family, the state, and the market. He claims that recent attention to large, visible "paid-staff nonprofits"—universities, hospitals, cultural organizations, and social service agencies such as the YMCA, the Salvation Army, and Catholic Charities—ignores perhaps 90% of the real voluntary or nonprofit sector, which he calls the "dark matter" of the nonprofit sector, just as physical dark matter constitutes about 90% of the mass of the universe.

In a perfect illustration of the principle that "whatever goes around comes around," this book brings us back to the larger sociological, anthropological, and historical vision out of which nonprofit studies originally came. It is a much-needed corrective. Although getting data on nonprofit hospitals and universities is easier than getting data on GAs, and although writing about the Ford

Foundation and the Metropolitan Museum often is more appealing than writing about self-help groups, book clubs, Bible study groups, choral groups, garden societies, and hobby clubs, the latter groups constitute the bulk of nonprofit effort. This large world of small public benefit organizations, mutual benefit organizations, and unincorporated associations has been largely ignored by mainstream nonprofit scholarship of the past 20 years. Smith's book brings much-needed attention to this dark matter of the nonprofit universe.

Public benefit is, in fact, a questionable term, Smith says. He prefers *nonmember benefit* to public benefit. Although that substitution probably does not have much of a political chance, it is a point worth pondering. Most "public benefit" or "charitable" nonprofits bring some benefits to the special groups served by the agencies as well as to the agencies' staffs, boards, and volunteers. Conversely, many "mutual benefit" or "noncharitable" nonprofits serve some charitable purposes.

An interesting contribution is Smith's attention in passing to socially deviant associations such as the Ku Klux Klan, witches' covens, paramilitary groups, gangs, and cults. He argues that just as the for-profit sector has its Mafia and other embarrassments, the nonprofit sector also has its unpleasant side that is too easily ignored.

The entire book is a critique of excessive attention to "establishment" nonprofits. Smith is particularly critical of the research work of Independent Sector, discussing in some detail its *Nonprofit Almanac,* giving and volunteering studies, National Taxonomy of Exempt Entities, and other products. He also criticizes the nonprofit academic centers for giving too much attention to paid-staff nonprofits and insufficient attention to GAs. Nor is he totally satisfied with the work of the organization and journal he founded or of the two other scholarly journals in the field (*Voluntas* and *Nonprofit Management and Leadership*). Too often, he claims, these promote "flat-earth maps" of the nonprofit sector, ignoring everything except paid-staff, formal, incorporated public benefit nonprofits.

Some of the most interesting parts of the book come in Smith's analysis of the fundamental concept of "voluntary altruism" as well as the organizational characteristics of GAs, such as the organizational life cycle of associations and the organizational effectiveness of associations.

Smith's book is an excellent introduction to a huge amount of research and theory, from many academic disciplines and professions, on voluntary associations. Both experienced scholars and students new to the field will find his long list of references valuable. At different points in the book, Smith says he has come across more than 2,000 references related to the topic, citing about 1,200 of them. He is deeply aware of this community of scholars on whose shoulders his work stands.

Readers will appreciate the short and lucid concluding sections at the end of each chapter.

This is a labor of love, the result of a 30-year love affair with what the author now calls *grassroots associations.* Smith is one of the relatively few nonprofit scholars who has given serious general attention to the smaller, more informal, often unregistered nonprofit groups. He criticizes people who, in their passion for "bigness and brightness," ignore the smaller groups. The important thing, he stresses throughout the book, is not the size, wealth, or power of particular nonprofit organizations but, rather, the *cumulative impact* of the millions of small nonprofit groups.

Readers will find things to like and dislike in this ambitious book. Some might be put off by the long list of references, others by the theoretical discussions. I would quibble with some of the categorization; it seems to me that Smith tends to "over-separate" paid-staff nonprofits and GAs, whereas the reality often is quite mixed. For example, I know of a choral society with a paid music director and a paid half-time assistant as well as 30 to 40 unpaid singers, a 10-person volunteer board, some program volunteers, and so on. This is technically a paid-staff nonprofit and might even fall into the 10% of "light matter" nonprofits, according to Smith, but such a group hardly compares with truly "establishment" nonprofits such as Stanford University and Massachusetts General Hospital.

This is both a general readership book and a serious technical book. It covers a very broad territory. Only a David Horton Smith could have attempted it. We are the beneficiaries of his daring.

Michael O'Neill
Professor and Director
Institute for Nonprofit Organization Management
University of San Francisco

Preface

What do the following groups have in common: an Alcoholics Anonymous local group, a Lions Club, a citizens' group organized to prevent siting a toxic waste incinerator in its town, a witches' coven, a Girl Scout troop, a Masonic Lodge, and a Bible reading group of a church? All are what many sociologists for decades have called *voluntary associations.* I choose to call them *grassroots associations* (GAs) to emphasize that I am concerned centrally here with voluntary associations that are local in scope, not with supralocal voluntary associations such as state, regional, national, or international associations.

GAs, as I deal with them here, are mainly volunteer in composition, with more volunteer work/activity hours per year than paid-staff hours serving the groups' goals. In very rough terms, GAs and supralocal volunteer groups have less than one paid-staff full-time equivalent (less than 1,700 hours of annual *paid* staff work for the group). I deal with these and other definitional characteristics of GAs briefly in Chapter 1 and at more length in another document with a colleague (Smith and Dover, forthcoming). Most of the book deals with empirical and theoretical GA characteristics.

I have tried to think of many of the important questions about GAs and then to answer them based on the theory and/or empirical research available including my own. In this process, I hope that I have asked some new questions. I have presented some new theory of my own and/or elaborations of earlier theories where I could and where I felt that it was potentially useful. The very analytical structure of the book's chapters gives an overview of the questions that I think are most important to ask and answer about GAs as groups and sometimes organizations (formal groups).

I weave together a quarter-century of hitherto widely scattered research and theory in this book. The result is a type of tapestry, with strands of research and strands of theory—the vast majority of it based on the period since the publication of an earlier overview work by C. Smith (no relation) and Freedman (1972; see also D. Smith, 1975, and Knoke, 1986, for overviews). I present and expand on some microtheories of GAs and develop inductively a broad theory of GAs of my own throughout the book. But most important, I have developed a general theoretical and empirical *critique* of the entire field of nonprofit research in this book. I present this critique briefly and generally here and in Chapter 1, with more detail on this "round-earth" paradigm in every substantive chapter of the book. I treat this metaphor and critique again at length in Chapter 10.

In essence, I argue in this book that there are many "flat-earth" voluntary nonprofit sector (VNPS) paradigms that are distorting the reality of the VNPS in related but different major ways. *I define a flat-earth VNPS paradigm as any general perspective on the VNPS that omits major "territories" of the sector.* So defined, flat-earth VNPS paradigms can be avoided only by studying VNPS phenomena with great balance and comprehensiveness.

The most widespread example of a flat-earth paradigm among mainstream VNPS scholars existing today is the paid-staff nonprofit flat-earth VNPS paradigm. It overemphasizes the larger, wealthier, older, more visible nonprofits in which most of the work is done by paid staff rather than by volunteers (Hodgkinson and Weitzman, 1992; Hodgkinson et al., 1992). This paradigm emphasizes (a) volunteers in service volunteer programs, which are nonautonomous "volunteer departments" of work organizations, or (b) informal volunteers, who have no organizational auspices for their volunteer activity. About 100 million associational volunteers participating in GAs in the United States circa 1990 are potentially ignored as such (Hodgkinson and Weitzman, 1992; see also Chapter 2).

* * *

Most of this book deals with GAs during the past 25 years or so, and for this period mainly GAs and their volunteers in the United States. This means that I am de facto falling prey to the distinctive nationalist focus flat-earth VNPS paradigm and the antihistoricism flat-earth VNPS paradigm in this book (but see Smith, 1997c).

I urge social science and social profession scholars in all countries to contribute to the study of GAs and voluntary action in those countries and in the world as a whole throughout human history and "prehistorical" anthropology and archaeology by making their own attempts at theoretical and empirical syntheses.

The field of nonprofit and voluntary action research (or "nonprofit research") generally has come a long way during the past 25 years or so since it was "aggregated" by the Association of Voluntary Action Scholars as the forerunner of the Association for Research on Nonprofit Organizations and Voluntary Action (ARNOVA) and by the *Journal of Voluntary Action Research* as the forerunner of *Nonprofit and Voluntary Sector Quarterly* (see Appendix A). Although still a fledgling field or "discipline," nonprofit research probably now has a "million-year future." What has been done during the past quarter-century or more in this nonprofit research field is *very tiny* relative to the research on nonprofits, including GAs, that is likely to be done during the 21st century or new millennium (Smith, forthcoming b). This field of interest is growing rapidly.

The VNPS, volunteer groups, other nonprofits, and individual volunteering are not likely to suddenly vanish in the future of humankind unless there is a world catastrophe or dictatorship of vast proportions. Hence, there probably *always* will be a significant and perhaps growing scholarly field that studies such correspondingly growing voluntary action phenomena. The scholarly discipline of economics is likely to still be around for the new millennium because presumably there always will be some significant degree of monetary exchange and other relevant economic phenomena of the business sector among humankind, wherever people live and for however long they live.

This very long future existence of major social science academic disciplines also is likely to be true with the discipline of political science because there presumably will still be forms and aspects of government, laws, and power for the new millennium if humankind survives that long. Seen in this very long future perspective, or even in the much briefer but still long-term perspective of the 21st century, nonprofit and voluntary action research is a strong contender for most future growth because the VNPS is likely to show the greatest relative growth among the four or five major sectors of human society.

In the final chapter, I predict that the 21st century will be the century of voluntary action and of volunteering as defined in Chapter 1. I see the 19th century as the century of the "industrial person" and the 20th century as the century of the "service/information person," to be followed by the new century of the "volunteer person" or *Homo Voluntas.*

* * *

I believe this book to be more comprehensive than any other so far published about GAs and their volunteers. I hope that the book will be interesting and instructive to readers of various types, but there is a great deal more to learn and a great deal more literature in sociology and other disciplines that needs to be reviewed and integrated.

- Perhaps some *scholars* might be influenced to look anew at their general research paradigms and their theoretical and empirical research questions concerning GAs because of the book.

- Perhaps some *practitioners* might find some useful nuggets of information about GAs in the book. This could be true for paid-staff nonprofit leaders as well as GA leaders because research on GAs has some significant implications for paid-staff nonprofits, especially with regard to volunteer programs located in work organizations such as paid-staff nonprofits, businesses (e.g., proprietary hospitals), and government agencies.

- Perhaps some *research funding organizations,* such as the National Science Foundation, the National Institute of Mental Health, the Aspen Institute Nonprofit Sector Research Fund, the Charles Stewart Mott Foundation, the Ford Foundation, the W. K. Kellogg Foundation, the Lilly Endowment, and other similar funders of some research on nonprofits and volunteer groups, might begin to see more clearly the overall cumulative importance of GAs as the "dark matter" of the nonprofit sector. If they do, then they might correspondingly provide more funds for needed research on GAs, especially comparative research on paid-staff and volunteer nonprofits now lacking, as noted earlier here and later in this book.

* * *

In addition to scholars listed in the References section of this book, I also have major intellectual debts owed to a variety of other social science scholars who have done little, if any, significant work in the *nonprofit* research field, especially Alex Inkeles, my graduate school mentor.

Although I have not had any grants for the literature reviewing or the writing involved, I am grateful for a small grant from the Project on Nonprofit Governance, directed by James R. Wood, of the University of Indiana at Bloomington and the Center on Philanthropy of the Indiana University at Indianapolis. This grant was of significant help in my research on GAs in one suburb (Appendix C), a study that I draw on repeatedly in this book.

I benefited from part-time research assistance from three graduate students in the sociology department at Boston College: Julie Boettcher, Aimee Marlow, and Marlene Bryant (who has been especially competent and helpful in securing documents and in the final stages of preparation of the references). Maureen Eldredge and Eunice Doherty, secretaries of the department, have been my principal long-distance liaisons with my department, sending to me in Florida regular shipments of mail coming to the office at Boston College. I am grateful for their help.

There are many people who I want to thank for helping me directly with the work of researching and writing this book including both professional colleagues and friends/relatives, some of whom are both. My friend, Michael

O'Neill, gave me encouragement to start another book project when I was uncertain whether I could or would ever write another book after a decade-and-a-half "dry spell" given personal and health problems. I now believe that he was right, and I thank him for the perspicacity to see that it was possible and for the kindness to tell me about it. Other close friends, such as Terry Adams, Burt R. Baldwin, Al Hogle, David Karp, Ce Shan, and John Yong, also have been very supportive, as has Gary Prince. Karen Fruzan has been particularly inspirational during the past year or so. I need all of them in my life to keep going and to "do my thing," as people used to say. I am very grateful that each of these persons exists and wants me in his or her life as well.

My sister, Helen Marie Smith, has made invaluable contributions in affection, moral support, and companionship at crucial times. She also has done a great deal of volunteer work on the extensive references. I could not have written this book without her help in these ways, and I will continue to be deeply grateful for all that she has done for me in my life. My daughter, Laura, also has been a treasure who helps me keep going via telephone calls, even though I see her less often than I would like. My former wife, Barbara, gave me needed moral support and companionship while some ideas for this book were percolating in my mind prior to our separation in 1995.

The two most recent former *Nonprofit and Voluntary Sector Quarterly* editors-in-chief, Jon Van Til and Carl Milofsky, have been exceptionally helpful, as have John Messer (former associate editor) and anonymous reviewers, in helping me make "silk purses out of sows' ears." They often have seen more value in my earlier related articles that I have written than I have been able to see initially myself. Their constructive style of criticism has helped me to feel like reworking my initial pieces for rerunning the gauntlet of peer reviewing.

In this same vein, I appreciate the useful and constructive criticism on articles that are related to, or are parts of, the present book from anonymous reviewers of other major nonprofit research/management journal. Dennis R. Young, editor of *Nonprofit Management and Leadership,* and Linda Serra, that journal's co-managing editor, have been very helpful in seeking to publish the best version that I was capable of writing for certain articles that are partly included in this book or are roots of present ideas in the book.

Michael A. Dover was of immense help in getting my references organized in computer-readable format. I also received helpful comments from various colleagues on one or more book chapters, and I wish to thank all of them for their time, their minds, and their generosity: Wolfgang Bielefeld, Thomasina Borkman, Mary Anna Caldwell, Justin Davis Smith, Julie Fisher, William Gamson, David Knoke, Mark Lyons, David Mason, Michael O'Neill, Susan Ostrander, Jone Pearce, Richard Sundeen, and Jon Van Til. Unfortunately, I cannot now recall some other colleagues who have commented on much earlier article forms of some chapters in this book. If I have left out some such people, then it is simply because of my bad memory, not meanness of spirit.

My Sage Publications editors also have been exemplary: James Nageotte, my editor at Sage, and Armand Lauffer, my substantive editor (a professor of social work at the University of Michigan). Nageotte, in particular, was astute enough to see the potential value of my book prospectus when many other publishers to whom I also sent the prospectus could "not find room for it" in their book lists. I could not ask for better editors. I especially appreciate their patience in letting me take the necessary time to do what I thought needed to be done so as to make this book as magnum an opus as I could under the circumstances.

PART I

TOWARD A ROUND-EARTH PARADIGM OF THE VOLUNTARY NONPROFIT SECTOR

Introduction

Briefly, grassroots associations (GAs) are local volunteer groups. Most readers will be familiar with at least some of the common types of GAs in the United States such as those noted in the first paragraph of the preface. To further arouse the reader's interest, here I present some examples of unusual GAs drawn mainly from the literature on GAs in less developed, but also from some modern, Western nations and one former Eastern Bloc nation:

- Among immigrant Japanese in Brazil after World War II, GAs have been very strong and active but split into two factions or sets of groups: those GAs accepting Japan's World War II defeat and those GAs insisting on *Japan's actual victory,* operating as deviant secret societies to maintain this fictive reality (Maeyama, 1979).

- Squatters' neighborhood associations (resident GAs in urban slums) in several Latin American nations, including Mexico, have been successful in generating high levels of squatter participation and in attaining major goals such as new services and other tangible benefits for their neighborhoods (Fisher, 1984).

- In India, caste associations aim at preserving and enhancing the benefits and prestige of a given Indian caste and its members. They are becoming GAs or supralocal volunteer associations as an urban intermingling of traditional and modern bases of interaction (Gandhi, 1978).

- Fisher (1993, p. 43) states that at least 40 developing nations have rotating credit GAs that allow poor people to borrow occasionally after they have contributed regularly to the GAs for a time (cf. Cope and Kurtz, 1980; Little, 1965; Soen and de Comarmond, 1971). These are partly economic and partly social GAs.

- A village improvement GA in Bolivia, with some help from a French development assistance paid-staff nonprofit, built a 14-kilometer (8.5-mile) road *by hand* across a mountain to improve the market for village-grown fruits and vegetables (Fisher, 1993, p. 37).

- The Tampa Bay Symphony is a 90-person volunteer orchestra (GA) that serves a seven-county Tampa Bay region of Florida (case study by author).

- Chonaikai or formal neighborhood organizations (GAs) in Tokyo collect dues from most residents and arrange many local activities as well as helping to mediate between the neighborhood and the city government on specific proposals (Bestor, 1985).

- Quasi-underground paramilitary "survivalists" have existed in the United States for decades as GAs, mostly in rural areas. They prepare for a final battle for control of "their" territory or area against the "Communists" and representatives of the national and other levels of government (Karl, 1995; Zellner, 1995).

- Hungary recently has seen the rise of self-help GAs for autistic children's parents, for alcoholics, and for cancer patients (Hegyesi, 1992).

NONPROFIT-TYPE CLASSIFICATIONS

There have been several major attempts at creating general *purposive* classifications of nonprofits: the National Taxonomy of Exempt Entities (NTEE) (Hodgkinson and Toppe, 1991), the International Classification of Non-Profit Organizations (ICNPO) (Salamon and Anheier, 1992b), and the Standard Industrial Classification (SIC) code categories for nonprofits specifically (Executive Office of the President and Office of Management and Budget, 1987; B. Smith, 1992). The National Opinion Research Center (NORC) also has long used a classification of most purposive types of GAs or supralocal associations (Davis and Smith, 1989; Verba and Nie, 1972). Smith (1996) deals with some of my critique and suggestions for improvements to include GAs better focused particularly on the ICNPO, which I believe is the best scheme (see also Gronbjerg, 1994; Turner, Nygren, and Bowen, 1993).

These various attempts at general purposive classification schemes involve a *purposive-type flat-earth paradigm,* in my view. The creators and users of these schemes tend to assume implicitly that such classifications are the most important if we are to understand nonprofits and how they work. Such an assumption is unwarranted, for such utility has not been proven. What we need is some "round-earth" research on the major purposive classifications to test their general comparative utility in relationship to analytical classification variables.

To do this, one must actually use a substantial number of *analytical* type classifications on a broad sample of nonprofits, including GAs, comparing their utility with the alternative use of purposive types in finding important similarities in the nature and operation of nonprofits (Amis and Stern, 1974; Cutler, 1980; Hougland, 1979; Politser and Pattison, 1980; Smith, 1995d, 1996; Smith, Baldwin, and White, 1988; Smith, Seguin, and Collins, 1973). Some examples of analytical type classifications might include age (e.g., large vs. small, or a continuous variable); size of annual revenues; size of membership (if any); size of staff (if any); and degree of internal democracy, power, prestige, and the like.

Not all nonprofits are of the conventional, mainstream, and law-abiding sort that most people, including scholars, think of as nonprofits. That view of the voluntary nonprofit sector as "angelic" is an ideology and another flat-earth paradigm, not a realistic description of nonprofits. Nonprofits can be basically, or even wholly, *deviant* from consensual societal norms (Smith, 1995c, forthcoming a). Such deviant nonprofits can cause or continue the most major types of individual deviance among their members (Smith, 1995c). The survivalist GAs noted earlier are one example. The Brazilian immigrant Japanese GAs insisting on Japan's actual victory in World War II are another example (Maeyama, 1979).

1

Definitions and Metaphors

This chapter begins with a connotative definition of grassroots associations (GAs) and then briefly discusses some broader theoretical background on the study of associations. The "dark matter" astrophysical metaphor and the map-making metaphor used in this book are then presented. Much of the chapter is devoted to a presentation of the definitions involved in my theory of voluntary altruism. The chapter conclusion details many reasons for the usefulness of this theory.

THE CONNOTATIVE DEFINITION
OF GRASSROOTS ASSOCIATIONS

Grassroots associations are locally based, significantly autonomous, volunteer-run, formal nonprofit (i.e., voluntary) groups that manifest substantial voluntary altruism as groups and use the associational form of organization and, thus, have official memberships of volunteers who perform most, and often all, of the work/activity done in and by these nonprofits. The dividing line between GAs and paid-staff voluntary groups (VGs) is not clear-cut, being a matter of gradation rather than a hard-and-fast cutting point on the all volunteers versus all paid-staff dimension of degree of market remuneration received by "analytical members" of nonprofits. If one has to make a cutting point, then it should be at 50% or more of the total work done in and for the group by volunteers. Analytical members are people who regularly provide services aimed at the operative goals of a group.

GAs are distinctive among volunteer nonprofits in having a relatively small local scope (i.e., locally based) in terms of some combination of member residences, member workplaces, or the territorial scope of group activities and goals if larger than the scope of member residences or workplaces (Smith, 1967, 1972c, 1981, 1994b, 1997d; Smith and Dover, forthcoming). The local territorial base or scope served by a GA can be a building (Lawson, 1983; McKenzie, 1994), a block (Unger and Wandersman, 1983), a housing development (McKenzie, 1994), a neighborhood (Davies, 1966; Milofsky and Romo, 1988), a community (Milofsky, 1988a), or a somewhat larger local area such as a metropolitan area or one or two adjacent counties (Lincoln, 1977).

This local base or scope and associational form of some volunteer nonprofits is why I use the term *grassroots associations* in labeling such groups. Volunteer nonprofits that serve a supralocal territory are not GAs, but they still are quite similar to GAs and important in their own right, although seldom studied among all voluntary associations. Supralocal volunteer associations are volunteer nonprofit groups for a region of a state, a state, a region of the country, a country, or a set of related (e.g., adjacent) countries.

In defining GAs, the *grassroots* part of the label is not defined narrowly to indicate only nonprofits seeking *sociopolitical change* through local citizen action and participation (Walker, 1975). GAs are not necessarily the local-level unit of a social movement (Lofland and Jamison, 1984). Perlman (1976), for example, turns *grassroots* from an adjective or a noun into a verb in her article, "Grassrooting the System," when speaking of VGs working for sociopolitical change from local levels. It must be recognized that every local association *type* has some GAs within it that get involved in some political or pressure group activity sometimes, according to two U.S. national representative samples of adults (Verba and Nie, 1972, pp. 178-79; Verba, Schlozman, and Brady, 1995, p. 63).

Table 1.1 might help the reader to quickly see the overall nature of my definition of GAs. There are six defining characteristics. In the first column of the table, the first three factors (1-3) characterize all nonprofits by my definition, whereas the latter three factors (4-6) characterize only GAs by my present definition (as a subtype of nonprofits). I include here the first three characteristics defining all nonprofits as a category, just as one would include some defining characteristics of all plants in defining trees or grass.

In Table 1.1, the second column gives an idea of the types of entities that are *excluded* from the category of GAs by my definition here. At the bottom of the table is a list of characteristics that are not part of the definition of GAs because they can vary widely among different GAs. These are included to make clear that I expect variation among GAs on these four important dimensions of groups, including nonprofit groups.

TABLE 1.1 Elements of the Definition of Grassroots Associations

Characteristic of Grassroots Associations	*Omitted From Grassroots Associations Category*
1. Group form	Individual, unorganized, amorphous behavior
2. Voluntary altruism based	Business, government, or household/family goals
3. Significantly autonomous of other groups (even if formally affiliated)	Completely controlled subunit of another group/organization
4. Association form (common interest, members elect officers, members pay dues, etc.)	Non-membership-dominated groups
5. Local (small in territorial base or scope)	Supra-local territorial base or scope (from several counties up to international scope)
6. Volunteer staffed (majority of work done by volunteers)	Paid-staff workers based (majority of work done by paid staff)

Characteristic included in grassroots associations but as a range, not as a defining characteristic

a. Member benefit versus mixed benefit versus nonmember (public) benefit goals (Smith, 1991)

b. Informal versus semiformal versus formalized structure and operations (Smith, 1992b)

c. Voluntary/uncoerced versus some pressure versus strong pressure/coercion to join, participate, and/or exit group (so long as some significant voluntariness remains)

d. Low to high degree of sociopolitical change orientation (present use of *grassroots* term includes *any* type of *locally based* nonprofit, volunteer-run association activity, political or nonpolitical)

Nonprofits exist or have existed with many different structural forms including not only associations but also foundations, fund-raising intermediaries, underground groups, federations, national franchises, loose networks, tight bureaucratic hierarchies, unique-unaffiliated groups (e.g., monomorphic GAs), amorphous-informal-fluid forms, tontines, burial societies, charismatic one-person dictatorship cults, rotating credit associations, and others. A non-profit might have more than one of these structural features at the same time and might vary in structure over time. Thus, I focus on only one form of nonprofit in this book, not on all forms.

SOME BROADER BACKGROUND
ON THE STUDY OF ASSOCIATIONS

The dark matter of the voluntary nonprofit sector (VNPS) that is GAs was what caught DeTocqueville's ([1845] 1945) eye when he visited America about 160 years ago. He thought, probably *incorrectly,* that such GAs were a peculiarly "American" type of group and activity. Brown (1973) argues to the contrary that, if DeTocqueville had come to America a half-century earlier, he would not have been so struck by voluntary associations. Brown sees such associations as related mainly to concurrent industrialization and modernization, which occurred on a broad scale in America during that period, especially in the Northeast (see also Smith, 1973c, 1997c).

Weber (1972), writing in 1910 or so, proposed a "sociology of associations" for these important phenomena. Harrison (1960) reanalyzes Weber, stating that voluntary associations represent a balance between the need for bureaucratic methods and the distrust of centralized authority. Meister (1972b) has written a book on the sociology of associations and proposes the latter as a new specialty within sociology. This suggestion never has been acted on effectively, to my knowledge.

GAs are the original organizational form of the VNPS, probably arising some 25,000 years ago (Anderson, 1973), with paid-staff nonprofits arising much more recently (about 5,000 years ago) (Smith, 1997c). Indeed, Billis (1993a) argues, "The core of the voluntary sector is the associational base out of which organizations [i.e., bureaucratic, often paid-staff organizations] grew" (p. 241). And Schuppert (1991) notes, "Associations [German *Vereine*] may be unjustly neglected in social science research" (p. 129). Other researchers have made similar comments (Milofsky, 1988a, p. 19), including myself in this book, and theory as well as in many earlier publications.

Sketching the nature of the nonprofit sector (NPS) in a book more than 25 years ago, Boulding (1973) presented two alternative economies to the usual market exchange economy. In the market economy, people usually exchange things of equal value (e.g., $30,000 for a car). In this usual case, the net worth of both parties usually is little affected by the transfer. But in unequal transfers, things are very different. Boulding notes that being robbed is a coercive transfer, as is having to pay taxes—the "economy of fear." One's net worth declines in either case relative to just prior to the coercive transfer.

But in the "economy of love" or charity, the philanthropic economy, the transfer also is unequal because the donor/giver loses material wealth, whereas the recipient/donee gains in net worth. Broadening Boulding's (1973) concept to include gifts of volunteer time makes his concept of the economy of love applicable generally to the VNPS including GAs and their associational volunteers. Wagner (1991) makes a similar distinction between (market) exchange relationships and sharing relationships. The latter corresponds to Boulding's economy of love and the VNPS. Sugden's (1984) concept of "reciprocity" and what Etzioni (1961) calls a "normative-voluntary compliance structure" also are alternative versions of the charitable economy or sharing. These are manifested in GAs and their volunteers as well as by volunteers in service programs run by work organizations and by stipended (partially remunerated) volunteers or quasi-volunteers.

A related distinction between two principles of human association has been suggested by Fuller (1969). He notes that, at the roots, there are only two key principles of human association: freely given shared commitment and legal principle/coercion. Boulding (1973) suggests the long obvious third principle of human association, market exchange, as would any economist. Market exchange *could* be seen as a form of exchange based on legal principle, but it is not coercive through the power of law unless parties somehow contract to create a binding market agreement for market exchange. I prefer to keep these two forms of transfer or exchange separate—coercive versus market exchange.

The business and government sectors consist *mainly* of fully remunerated paid staff associating on the basis of legal principle (explicit or implicit work contracts) and economic exchange for their respective goals. By contrast, the household/family sector contains unremunerated, nonvolunteer family workers (e.g., homemakers) and essentially nonworking family members (especially children, the ill or injured, and the elderly) associating on the basis of shared commitment and household/family unselfishness. (The latter is "altruism" with a special meaning for kindness/help for other household or family members.) Shared commitment to some goal(s) based on voluntary altruism characterizes the VNPS. Business and government altruism also exist, as does family/household altruism. And all of these motivations can coexist in the same individual at the same or different times in a given day or week of normal life in modern society.

A partly similar but different type of distinction is made by Alexander (1987). He contrasts nonprofit activity, which is altruistic and noncommercial, with profit-seeking or commercial activity, much of which is egoistic. Nonprofit activity generally is seen as having more "virtue" or as being more socially desirable in modern society.

Stebbins (1996) uses the concept of "serious" leisure to describe volunteering analytically. This roots GAs and volunteering solidly in people's leisure time, where they properly belong. But the notion of serious leisure also points up the fact that, unlike most leisure, these types of serious leisure are aimed at being productive and useful rather than merely enjoying oneself. Enjoyment can be present as well, but this is not essential for an activity to be serious leisure activity. Taking night school courses is another type of serious leisure, and there are others besides volunteering.

THE ASTROPHYSICAL
DARK MATTER METAPHOR

When I worked on this book intensively for a year or so, I hit on a metaphor for understanding GAs in the VNPS that I liked very much. This penultimate metaphor was the bright matter versus dark matter metaphor based on the astrophysical universe as currently understood by many astrophysicists. I still use this metaphor in this book from time to time, mainly because it includes an amusingly coincidental estimate of the dark matter to bright matter ratio in our astrophysical universe of 10 to 1. This ratio (Longair, 1996, p. 145) also roughly fits my own estimates of the 5-to-1 to 10-to-1 ratio of the estimated number of VGs in the United States circa 1990 not listed with the Internal Revenue Service (IRS) to the number of VGs so registered (see Chapter 2; Smith, 1997d). Something big clearly is missing in both realms.

As it turns out, there seems to be insufficient bright matter that we can "see" by various technologies and instrumentation in the "known" universe to account for how some huge chunks of such bright matter, such as certain galaxies and galactic clusters, seem to operate gravitationally, based on the work of Einstein and later astrophysicists. Bright matter in the universe includes stars, star clusters, and at one time various other interesting "bright stuff out there" that had not yet been figured out (e.g., quasars). Astrophysicists and astronomers are not yet sure what all the dark matter is. Some do not believe that much of it exists. Recently, some have suggested that very tiny particles called neutrinos might constitute most of the dark matter. *In the VNPS, we are much more certain that the dark matter exists and that it consists of GAs and associational volunteers.*

In studying the VNPS, many scholars have been concerned mainly with the bright or most visible nonprofits such as paid-staff nonprofits, especially larger ones such as colleges/universities and hospitals. O'Neill's (1989) book describes and discusses the major categories of paid-staff nonprofits and their origins in the United States. The book also has a chapter that treats mutual benefit nonprofits (most of which are voluntary associations) and, at their local levels, GAs. In my view, GAs often are ignored by mainstream "flat-earth" nonprofit scholars including many members of the major scholarly associations such as the Association for Research on Nonprofit Organizations and

Voluntary Action (Appendix A) and the International Society for Third Sector Research.

THE MAPMAKING METAPHOR AND
THE FLAT-EARTH VNPS PARADIGMS

In this book, I argue that there are several cognitive maps in common use by nonprofit scholars that are obscuring some important phenomena of the VNPS, particularly GA phenomena. Mapmakers are supposed to shed light on the nature of the territory they purport to map, not to purposely obscure or omit important parts of that territory supposedly covered by their map *when they know it exists.* Knowingly false maps created as misinformation or disinformation for some policy reason are *worse* than useless. Again metaphorically, they can lead us to stumble, crash, sink, or even die by hitting nothing where something should be or vice versa in the dark of territory not accurately mapped. There also are potentially great opportunity costs of not knowing about useful shorter routes, dead-end routes, and valuable resources one could access if one had an accurate map of a territory.

Before Columbus and other early European explorers such as Magellan demonstrated incontrovertibly that the world was essentially round, early pre-Columbian Eurocentric cartographers had egocentrically (and ignorantly) portrayed Europe as the center of, and essentially all of, the world that existed or mattered. Most of the earth's surface was unknown to these cartographers, and even the notion of a round earth was not widely accepted. Cartographers drew similarly distorted equivalent flat-earth maps in other ancient civilizations in other parts of the world where such civilizations flourished. *All* early societies, including preliterate societies, were pervasively egotistical and chauvinistic about the patches of earth where they lived even when nomadic—a persistent and deeply rooted human territoriality trait, as for other animals (Ardrey, 1966).

For early mapmakers, the earth was flat, as "everyone knew," and only strange and foolish people such as Columbus and Magellan (or their equivalents in other civilizations) believed otherwise. In the history of European cartography (Zerubavel, 1992), this issue was part of a long controversy over many centuries about the shape of the earth and the nature of its surface all over the world, especially land versus water and the height/depth of each.

Understanding these facts is basic to grasping the meaning of my flat-earth versus round-earth metaphor in regard to the VNPS and GAs in this book. I developed this metaphor as I wrote this book, especially in writing Chapter 2. I knew a good deal about what I saw as various problems with much VNPS research, but I sought a simple yet powerful metaphor that would synthesize my critique and also help convince other scholars, professionals, practitioners, and leaders concerned with this sector that many, but not all, of them were not looking at the VNPS correctly.

I discuss all of the major flat-earth paradigms I see in Chapter 10. In each case, some major VNPS phenomena are omitted. In several cases, the problem I identify is an overemphasis on one type of phenomenon and inadequate attention to the "opposite" type or some omitted type of VNPS phenomenon on some key dimension—paid-staff versus volunteer VGs, establishment versus social movement VGs, traditional service versus self-help or advocacy VGs, angelic/conventional versus "damned"/deviant VGs.

In addition, I see as flat-earth paradigms the views that the VNPS is unimportant, that there are only three sectors of society, that money is the key to understanding the VNPS, that one can understand the VNPS only in a distinctive nationalist way, that purposive-type classifications of VGs are the only important classifications or the most important ones, that the history of the VNPS can ever be ignored, that the less developed world can be ignored, that informal or semiformal VGs can be ignored, that religious VGs can be ignored, that only sociodemographic predictors of participation matter, and that VGs can be studied in isolation.

Thus, using my cartographic metaphor, *several "dark continents" or "dark territories" are missing from the usual flat-earth maps conceptually and empirically,* as just noted. And the way in which to "fix" this situation is not to tinker with the flat-earth paradigms but rather to discard them individually as incomplete cognitive maps of major aspects of the whole sector. It makes sense to retain the specific details of the flat-earth paradigms if accurate for some part of the VNPS but not the whole VNPS. Overall, one must replace such restricted paradigms with a better round-earth paradigm that does *more* justice to the accumulating facts on the VNPS all over the world and throughout history.

My proposed round-earth paradigm, sketched in Chapter 10, is more than just paying more attention to GAs and associational volunteers, as it sounds in some earlier versions when I was not so clear on what I am trying to do here. My friend and colleague, Thomasina Borkman of George Mason University, made comments on some chapters of this book in draft form that helped me to apply my flat-earth critique more broadly than just to VNPS magnitudes. I am especially grateful for her insight that the ignoring of self-help groups is another one of the flat-earth paradigms.

With my broader critique of flat-earth scholarship regarding VNPS phenomena, I am saying that we need, collectively as nonprofit and voluntary action scholars and practitioners, to look at a variety of phenomena in a new integrative and synthetic way that we have not done before because of *several limited, very limiting, and now outdated paradigms of the VNPS.*

The VNPS concept itself, beginning with Cornuelle (1965), was a step forward in synthesizing a large body of theory, research, and practice in a very loose and programmatic way (cf. Hall, 1992). I believe that what I am calling the round-earth VNPS paradigm is another step forward. The reader can judge for him- or herself.

The flat-earth paradigms of the VNPS are just outdated perspectives on facts that have accumulated about the sector during the past few decades (see Chapter 10). As Kuhn (1962) argues and demonstrates in his seminal work on scientific revolutions more generally, the old flat-earth VNPS paradigms are just barely limping along on a number of fronts. This entire book is really about how the older and narrower flat-earth VNPS paradigms, whatever we label them, are simply incorrect because they are so misleading and incomplete. They cannot any longer fit the accumulating facts about all the facets of the VNPS generally, particularly about GAs.

A new round-earth paradigm is required. This paradigm change will create some problems for people who cherish one or more of the flat-earth paradigms. It did for me, as I had to give up my cherished volunteer and membership VGs flat-earth paradigm. But, as consolation, it opens up new types of research dealing with hitherto ignored variables and relationships. One example is the percentage of volunteer dependence in a VG, which comes to the fore in this book as a crucial variable in understanding VGs.

Perhaps my flat-earth paradigm labels are unnecessarily pejorative, or perhaps not. I mean for these labels to alert many scholars and practitioners to alternative ways of viewing the accumulating facts about the VNPS as a whole. I have been writing and talking about GAs without as much effect as I would like to see sometimes. So, now I am trying to be more forceful in my argumentation here as contrasted with earlier attempts (e.g., Smith, 1981, 1991, 1992b, 1993b, 1994b).

TOWARD A THEORY OF VOLUNTARY ALTRUISM: KEY DEFINITIONS

My definition of a GA depends crucially on the term *voluntary altruism,* which this technical part of the chapter attempts to define, among other terms. In any useful theory, one must start with careful definitions of key terms and the concepts to which they refer, linking some of these terms, preferably key terms, to empirical reality as we know it using appropriate methodology for assessing the phenomena involved. Later, I try to do this for my *theory of voluntary altruism,* a phrase I use to refer to my general theory of the VNPS including all three main levels of abstraction: societal/territorial, grouplike/organizational, and individual. The theory is only partially presented here. A much more complete set of linked definitions can be found in Smith and Dover (forthcoming).

The concept of the voluntary, nonprofit, third, independent, or philanthropic sector (or VNPS) has been around for more than 30 years in the United States (Cornuelle, 1965; Etzioni, 1972; Shultz, 1972; Smith, Reddy, and Baldwin,

1972a). By the mid- to late 1970s, major policy study commissions on either side of the Atlantic had picked up the concept and studied it with research inputs from social scientists (in the United States: the [Filer] Commission on Private Philanthropy and Public Needs, 1975; in the United Kingdom: the Wolfenden Committee, 1978; see also Perri 6 and Leat, 1997). These two commissions gave the VNPS concept greater early visibility than would otherwise have been the case, perhaps, but both resulted from a new policy interest preceding the initiation of each that was relevant to VNPS concerns (Hall, 1992; Perri 6 and Leat, 1997).

The VNPS and its components subsequently have been defined by many people in different but usually related ways. Space limitations preclude my reviewing all of them (but see, e.g., Kendall and Knapp, 1995; Kramer, 1987; Lohmann, 1992; Salamon, 1992; Salamon and Anheier, 1992a, 1997; Perri 6 and Leat, 1997; Smith, 1981, 1991, 1992b, 1993b, 1997d; Van Til, 1988; Van Til and Carr, 1994; Wilderom and Miner, 1991). Kendall and Knapp (1995) refer to the VNPS as "a loose and baggy monster" (p. 66), an apt characterization. But I wish here to make some significant progress in making the VNPS construct more precise and readily usable.

Altruism: The Present Definition

My approach here is to begin by defining voluntary altruism. Then I define voluntary action in terms of voluntary altruism. After that, I define both volunteers and VGs simultaneously, seeing their cumulative activities as individual versus group voluntary action in some time period, based causally on voluntary altruism. *This is different from all other definitions, to the best of my knowledge.* I am able to take such an approach only because I have at last identified what I believe to be a common underlying factor in the VNPS, VGs, volunteers, and voluntary action. This is a major improvement on my various earlier attempts at defining voluntary action and voluntary groups (see especially D. Smith, 1975, 1981).

Voluntary altruism is the concept that underlies and supports all of my other key definitions here. Once it has been carefully defined anew, the other key concepts differ either in levels of abstraction from an act to an individual to a group or in degree of remuneration (nonremuneration vs. underremuneration).

First, I define **altruism** more generally as follows:

a. an internal disposition (goal, value, motivation) of

b. a group or an individual as an "entity" (see Smith, 1967, for my definition of a social group)

c. focused on providing a significant service or services to another entity beyond itself and beyond its corresponding household or immediate family (see Smith, Shue, and

Villarreal, 1992, who suggested reserving the philanthropy concept for transactions and situations beyond oneself and one's immediate household/family);

d. defining *service* as an action that is intended by the provider-entity to increase, maintain, or enhance the net satisfaction (or economic "utility") and, hence, as an attempt to help;

e. the "target of benefits" (Gamson, 1990) or "helpee" defined as the entity or population that the provider-entity is trying to help in some way.

In sum, *altruism in rough terms is an internal concept referring to the tendency or disposition of an entity to try to help others by satisfying such others in some way* (Batson, 1991). As such, altruism exists in all four main sectors of society. Kendall and Knapp (1995) note recently, in a similar vein, that "voluntarism is, of course, not the preserve of the voluntary sector" (p. 88). As I define it, altruism per se is not intrinsically voluntary in nature, nor is it intrinsically good or virtuous, unlike in many other definitions.

Needed Change From the Traditional Elitist View of Altruism

I differ sharply (Smith, 1981) with various other scholars in my theoretical view of altruism and philanthropy (Boulding, 1973; Bremner, 1960; Humphreys, 1995; Jordan, 1960; Salamon, 1992, p. 5). Such scholars take a more traditional, narrower, and idealized approach, tending to view altruism as identical with the total motivation for "charitable services" or philanthropy narrowly conceived. Even my concept of *voluntary* altruism is broader than the traditional view of altruism, as will be seen shortly.

Corresponding traditional "philanthropic interactions," or "charitable interactions" of a nonmonetary and nonphysical nature, between a provider-entity and a person have long been seen in terms of (a) an altruistic donor/provider-entity who (b) helps via interpersonal interaction (c) a needy recipient/client/ "case"/donee who is (d) a nonmember outside the provide-entity, (e) without the provider-entity gaining anything of significant value from the transaction and (f) with the recipient greatly benefited in one or more important ways as a consequence of the interaction (Bremner, 1960; Jordan, 1960). This characterization clearly is an exaggeration to some degree, presented as an ideal type for emphasis on key dimensions.

Thus, I define altruism as the cause of service and service as the result of altruism. With this version of altruism, there is no added, condescending, emotional baggage coming from the earlier history of philanthropy, charity, "noblesse oblige," "lady bountiful," or "personal social services" in the traditional sense (Bremner, 1960; Humphreys, 1995; Jordan, 1960). Gaylin et al. (1978) give a good overview of "the limits of benevolence" in their book, *Doing Good.*

In my theory of voluntary altruism, the *altruism itself involves at least a signifi-cant mixture of self-serving and other-serving dispositions for a provider-entity in any societal sector.* Not just empirically, but also theoretically, altruism never is a "pure" set of altruistic motivations or goals in human beings as entities (Smith, 1981), nor is it a pure set of selfish or self/entity-serving goals. This still fits with the origins of the word *altruism* from Latin "other-concern." Such a *significant mixture* is far better in terms of general human welfare than Hobbes's concept of "war of all against all." Where the traditional view of altruism goes astray, in my view, is that it believes its own "constructed" history and "press clippings," making altruism as the cause of service to others seem too virtuous. In fact, ser-vice is a normal and integral part of human life, for we are social animals.

Even when regular volunteers are the providers of services, being a *recipient* of helping services (especially from specific others in person) now is known to be far from an unalloyed set of satisfactions for such recipients. In nonmember/ "public" service-oriented VGs, there are potentially high costs to the recipients including making them feel inadequate, creating dependency in them (Gaylin et al., 1978), and harming their self-esteem that in turn affect their general sense of efficacy and then other aspects of their personalities and lives, especially aspects relating to aspirations and accomplishments (e.g., see the literature review in Gross, Wallston, and Piliavin, 1980).

In addition to the provision of money, goods, and services from provider to recipient, we must take account of potential *benefits* for provider-entities including wages for paid work by individuals, some possible psychic benefits for any type of service workers, and (for service groups) usually income from sales, fees, and interest as well as income from grants, contracts, and donations. We also must consider potential *costs* for recipients such as their relevant nega-tive "emotional work" performed (e.g., recipients faking gratitude to providers when being humiliated by providers given the implicit and explicit dependency involved) (Hochschild, 1983). The nature and degree of *reciprocity, sharing, or exchange* needs to be studied for all the parties (i.e., stakeholders) in any given volunteer transaction, not *assumed by definition.* This also is true for the nature and degree of *caring, social support, and positive emotional attachment/relationship* between providers and recipients (Duck, 1988).

Defining Voluntary Altruism

Having redefined altruism simply as the goal or motivation directly underly-ing attempted services to or the helping of another, I define **voluntary altruism** as the presence for an entity (person or group, using an average for groups) of a special form of altruism with a combination of all of the following elements, especially Elements 1 to 6 as core criteria:

1(a). more genuinely based on some significant mix of humane caring for (Jeavons, 1992; Lohmann, 1992; O'Neill and Young, 1988, p. 4), social support of (Clary, 1987; Powell, 1994; Wuthnow, 1994), and sharing of oneself and one's resources with other entities including co-members (Lohmann, 1989; Powell, 1994; Wagner, 1991) as three primary goals of the provider-entity deemed helpful to the helpee (Boulding, 1973; Lohmann, 1992; O'Neill, 1989, 1994; Smith, 1991, 1993b), not simply philanthropic, charitable, public benefit, public purpose, public welfare serving, or non-member serving in their traditional and narrow senses (Bowen et al., 1994; Bremner, 1960; Humphreys, 1995; Jordan, 1960; Nielsen, 1979; Salamon and Anheier, 1992a);

1(b). as a specification of Element 1(a), the provider-entity is "humane-core-value driven," defined as manifesting significantly one or more of the following seven positive social values discussed in the next subsection: civic engagement, sociopolitical innovation, social religiosity, sociability, social aesthetics, economic system support, and personal social service (the joint optimization of these seven values is seen as defining the public interest or general long-term welfare of a society or other sociopolitical territory) (Smith, 1977);

2. at least moderately freely chosen (Cnaan, Handy, and Wadsworth, 1996; Smith, Reddy, and Baldwin, 1972a, p. 162; Van Til, 1988, p. 9) by the provider-entity from among multiple options rather than being strongly influenced by the central concerns of the business, government, or household/family sectors (a new approach to the content of Smith et al., 1972a, pp. 161-62; see also Kendall and Knapp, 1995, pp. 86-87);

3. not coerced by biopsychic or biosocial factors (i.e., not based on a strong genetically induced compulsion such as the goal of breathing or excretion) or based on virtual social compulsions such as the goals of doing at least minimal personal grooming or wearing at least the minimum of proper clothing usually (Smith et al., 1972a, p. 161) (this criterion probably also differentiates voluntary altruism from household/family altruism, in which there is a more likely genetic basis for living together and "reciprocal altruism" [Dawkins, 1976]).

4. more sensitive to the specific nature of the helpee entity/population as the target of benefits and its probable needs, wants, and wishes over time, from the past to the future, rather than emphasizing mainly convenience to or benefits for the provider-entity (e.g., self-help health VGs are more sensitive to their members' emotional needs, generally, than other-helping social service VGs such as hospitals tend to be [Powell, 1994; Stanton, 1970], and any VG tends be more sensitive to helpee needs than are government agencies and many businesses, although not necessarily more sensitive than households/families);

5. expecting to be underremunerated or unremunerated relative to market prices for work done or for other valuables or property provided (e.g., no or relatively low remuneration for work done, for a monetary loan, for an object/equipment lent, or for a gift transfer) (Cnaan et al., 1996, p. 371; Hatch and Mocroft, 1979; Kendall and

Knapp, 1995, p. 87; Mirvis, 1992; Smith et al., 1972a, pp. 162, 168); more specifically, underremuneration refers to not having an expectation of direct, high-probability economic returns/benefits/wages at current market levels for the work or other valuable resources provided to some helpee as the target of benefits but receiving some remuneration, whereas nonremuneration refers to no economic returns at all (Smith et al., 1972a, p. 162);

6. expecting to receive some significant mix of entity (self)-serving and other-serving psychic income/satisfaction/"utility" for the valuable resource(s) provided (this requirement was in the Smith et al., 1972a, definition to a certain extent and more clearly in the Smith, 1981, definition; see also Badelt, 1987; Hodgkinson and Weitzman, 1992, chap. 6; Limerick and Burgess-Limerick, 1992; Majone, 1984; Mirvis, 1992; and Van Til, 1988, p. 8, focusing on the goals of volunteers as individuals); *primary satisfaction* or *direct satisfaction* might be defined as satisfaction that comes directly from some experience and that does not include increasing another's satisfaction; satisfaction from helping others get satisfaction might be termed *secondary satisfaction* or *indirect satisfaction* because it *must* be mediated by another's satisfaction, not just provided to oneself by oneself or provided to oneself *by another irrespective of that other's satisfaction in so doing.*

The forgoing six requirements are the core criteria in my definition of voluntary altruism. Following are some *additional factors* that must be kept in mind to have a proper understanding of, and to make proper use of, the concept of voluntary altruism:

7. specifically allowing helpees to be either official or analytical members (defining the latter as regular service-providing affiliates of a group attempting to contribute to the group's operative goals, whatever these affiliates are termed by the group [Smith, 1972c]) as well as the usually assumed case of helpees including nonmembers of a provider-entity that is a group or some mix of these (this provides for the specific inclusion of member benefit groups, mutual aid groups, social support groups, and self-help groups as well as the usual nonmember benefit groups (O'Neill, 1989, 1994; Powell, 1994; Salamon, 1992; Salamon and Anheier, 1992a; Smith, 1991, 1993b; Wuthnow, 1994);

8. specifically realizing that the degree of formalization of the auspices of the services can vary widely along a continuum, from very informal all the way to very formalized and complex;

9. specifically *including co-member altruism as the only altruism involved* in the small percentage of instances *when the voluntary altruism is defined as negative or deviant voluntary altruism for a group* (Smith, forthcoming a); the latter is termed negative or deviant altruism because it fits Elements 2 to 8 but comes *close* to not fitting Element 1, just barely fitting (see Smith, 1998b, on "deviant nonprofits" and "negative social capital").

Voluntary Altruism Versus
Altruism in Other Sectors

The other three sectors besides the VNPS manifest some nonvoluntary altruism, but each with a different "sector twist" or "sector spin." As a result, there is altruism and corresponding altruistic actions, interactions, and transactions in all four of the main sectors of society. Business altruism, government altruism, and household/family altruism all can be seen as based on their usual respective sector goals and means (Smith, 1991).

As contrasted with voluntary altruism, in nonvoluntary altruism, the altruism is more apparent than genuine—more secondary as an instrumental means to other ends than primary as an end in itself (O'Neill and Young, 1988, p. 4, suggest this type of differentiation of the VNPS and its groups from the other societal sectors). In genuine voluntary altruism, there is a *primary* focus on caring, social support, and sharing, whereas the altruism of businesses or government agencies, or the "unselfishness" of households/families, is more apparent in being based more on other underlying values or causes.

Apparent business altruism usually is based mainly on expectations by the business owners/managers/boards of directors for greater economic return by seeming to be altruistic toward (provide services to) customers and workers or by seeming to care for the general welfare of the customers or larger society. This apparent business altruism may or may not be rooted in genuine voluntary altruism, but usually it is not. The practice of providing services, or of being altruistic by my definition, has become one widespread hallmark of post-industrial service and information societies such as the United States and the United Kingdom.

Apparent government altruism, as in providing such "public goods" as national parks and nationally supported highways, is based mainly on the longer term expectations of government workers and leaders to fulfill the properly enacted laws and regulations of the government within a given sociopolitical territory so as to receive full remuneration for their paid work. Legislators who enact or repeal such laws have a variety of both self-serving and other-serving motivations. Basic government altruism in providing public goods, however, is enforced by the power to coerce compliance with such laws, including tax laws, using agents of social control.

Household/family unselfishness is a special form of "altruism," always with quotation marks around the "altruism" term in my theory. Unlike voluntary, business, or government altruism, household/family "altruism" differs in that the target of the benefits of one's relatively unselfish concern is one or more persons of the individual's *own immediate* household or family, *not beyond them,* as in the case of the other three types of sectoral altruism (i.e., altruism characteristic of a given societal sector). Some sociobiologists see much of this intrahousehold/family unselfishness as significantly rooted in human genetic programming (Dawkins, 1976). In this case, such action might not be altruism at all in any genuine sense, just as cooperating ants or bees are not being altruistic in their colonies or hives.

Voluntary Altruism and Seven Humane Core Social Values

The phrase *humane-core-value driven* is, in a sense, a detailed specification of what others might mean by "public purpose" or "the public interest." It relates most closely, perhaps, to the definition of the "commons" by Lohmann (1992). Be that as it may, I mean *humane-core-value driven* to refer to the presence of one or more of seven specific social values in an entity as an individual motivation or group goal that specifies, in further detail, the first criterion of voluntary altruism regarding caring/social support/sharing.

1. *Civic engagement values* are defined as an entity's tendency to manifest attitudes of citizen duty, civic pride, civic responsibility, community concern, concern for civil society, and general promotion of the public interest in some institutional area or activity type using socioculturally accepted means and other concerns relevant to the continued democratic political functioning and governance of some territory (Barber, 1984; Conway, 1991; Putnam, Leonardi, and Nanetti, 1993; Verba et al., 1995).

2. *Sociopolitical innovation values* are defined as an entity's tendency to manifest a concern to identify and define new social problems and unmet public needs; to provide responsible sociopolitical dissent and negative feedback in society regarding unmet public needs; to mobilize individuals and groups to seek social changes that will foster the public interest, the general welfare, and social justice; and to use new approaches to political action and social change in such a way that others beyond oneself and outside one's household/ family probably will be helped. Such improvements may be sought by interest groups, using conventional political means (Berry, 1997; Hrebenar, 1997), or by social movement groups, using unconventional sociopolitical action such as protest to achieve such change (Carter, 1974; McAdam and Snow, 1997, references).

3. *Social religiosity values* are defined as an entity's tendency to manifest one or more religion-based or faith-based concerns in a variety of life activity areas such as to "love thy neighbor generally"; to have compassion for and share available resources with the less fortunate; to support a church, mosque, or temple and its activities; to help by giving money or time to provide religious education by one's religious group for others outside one's household/family; to help

others "find God," "find Jesus," or relate closely to equivalent abstract principles; and so on (Stark and Glock, 1968; Johnstone, 1992).

4. *Sociability values* are defined as an entity's tendency to be concerned with creating and sharing positive, expressive, friendly interactions with other entities beyond the household/family for their own sakes as ends in themselves; with creating a sense of community and social integration among some set of people or population; with fostering positive social capital in informal interpersonal relationships; and with making sure that instrumental tasks of entities are not performed in such a way as to squeeze out all friendly and interpersonal feelings and interactions from such tasks (Duck, 1988; Mason, 1996).

5. *Social aesthetics values* are defined as an entity's tendency to be concerned with creating, performing, presenting, or preserving art, music, literature, mass media, physical performances, sport, acrobatics, or other creations in significant part for the enjoyment of others beyond oneself and outside the household/family (Kelly, 1996). Thus, social aesthetics activities, based on the relevant values, include the co-participant, self-help aspects of all amateur teams or multiperson sports and recreation (Kelly, 1996) as well as arts group activities (Blair, 1994). Solitary arts and recreation are not included here (Quarrick, 1989).

6. *Economic system support values* are defined as an entity's tendency to be concerned with providing auxiliary support for the economy and business sector through helping people beyond itself and outside the household/family of participating individuals alone or as group members (Estey, 1981; Krause, 1996; Morrison, 1970). The present social value type does not include either the economy itself (the business sector) or most of what is called "social economy" (Bruyn, 1977) because the latter is mainly part of the business sector per se.

7. *Personal social service values* are defined here as the residual individual (psychological) or group (social structural/purposive) tendencies to be concerned with satisfying the needs and wishes of others beyond oneself and one's household/family through direct in-person activities by provider-entities after having removed from the present category the six preceding types of voluntary social values. Specifically, personal social service values may refer to dealing with another's satisfaction in regard to physical health, mental health, education, information, housing, food, transportation, clothing, day care of children, and so on (Davis-Smith, 1993; Hodgkinson and Weitzman, 1992).

Each of these seven positive, humane, core social values defines a different subtype or (in subsets) combination of voluntary altruism and corresponding voluntary action, formal or informal, based on the principal type(s) of voluntary altruism involved. This specification of seven underlying, humane, core social values in a broad way as defining voluntary altruism differentiates the present approach to defining the VNPS from most others.

Defining the Other Principal Components of the VNPS

With a careful definition of voluntary altruism, it now is possible to define the terms referring to the other major components of the VNPS quite simply as follows.

1. Voluntary altruism has two subtypes: (a) **volunteer altruism** is defined as voluntary altruism that involves significant motivations/goals of a provider-entity for unremunerated activity; (b) **quasi-volunteer altruism** is defined as voluntary altruism that involves significant motivations/goals of a provider-entity for underremunerated activity, not just unremunerated activity or remunerated activity. These are ideal types, with reality being an underlying continuum of degree of individual remuneration in relation to market prices for services rendered.

2. Voluntary altruistic action, or more briefly, **voluntary action,** is defined as action that results in significant degree from the voluntary altruism of an entity aimed at a target of benefits beyond the entity's own immediate household or family. In the case of a group entity, the target of benefits for individual participants generally must be beyond themselves as individuals and beyond their own immediate households or families. *Action* is defined as externally observable changes in an entity. There are two subtypes of voluntary action: (a) **volunteer action** is significantly unremunerated voluntary action by an individual or a group and results significantly from volunteer altruism; (b) **quasi-volunteer action** is significantly underremunerated voluntary action and results significantly from quasi-volunteer altruism. These two types tend empirically to be a matter of degree, not a dichotomy as I present them here for simplicity of exposition. The key dimension involved again is degree of remuneration, as for Definition 1. Quasi-volunteer action is found among most of the paid staff of quasi-volunteer VGs.

3. A *volunteer* is defined as a person who does a significant amount of voluntary action in a specified time period (e.g., last week, last year). There are two main subtypes:

(a) **Pure volunteers** are essentially unremunerated for some of their voluntary action provided to a given VG during some time period. Alternatively, one can define pure volunteers as people who do some significant amount of volunteer action for a given VG during some specified time period. These are, in essence, identical definitions. In either case, pure volunteers perform an ephemeral or temporary role (Zurcher, 1978) or a secondary role (Warner, 1972). This definition fits with conventional definitions of volunteers (Cnaan et al., 1996). People become pure volunteers for many reasons (Smith, 1994a), but they basically receive psychic benefits whatever other benefits they get.

(b) **Quasi-volunteers** are essentially underremunerated for some of their voluntary action provided to a given VG during some time period. Alternatively, one can define quasi-volunteers as people who do some significant amount of quasi-volunteer action for a given VG during some specified time period. These are, in essence, identical definitions. Therefore, it is possible to be both a pure volunteer in regard to some voluntary action and a quasi-volunteer in regard to other, different voluntary action during the *same* time period because the voluntary action is done for different specific VGs. People who become quasi-volunteers also receive some psychic benefits in addition to monetary benefits. For example, Onyx and Maclean (1996) found that paid VG workers said their work offered personal challenges and social meaning (see also Mirvis, 1992; Steinberg, 1990).

4. Formal and informal volunteers refer to the auspices of volunteering. **Informal volunteers** are people who are doing volunteer activity to benefit one or more others beyond the household/family but are doing so outside any formal group context. By contrast, **formal volunteers** do their volunteer work in a group context as analytical members of some VG or service volunteer program.

5. A **voluntary group** is defined as a group that does a substantial amount of voluntary action during a specified time period. *Group* is defined carefully elsewhere (Smith, 1967). *Substantial amount* here means 50% or more of the cumulative hours of group action as performed by analytical members during the specified time period including both volunteers and quasi-volunteers each counted only once for the given group during a given time period. *Analytical members* were defined earlier and are roughly regular service-providing affiliates of a group (Smith, 1972c).

There are three main analytical types of voluntary groups so defined:

(a) **All-volunteer groups** are defined as voluntary groups, 95% or more of whose cumulative, group-related hours of actions by analytical members are volunteer action for the given VGs during a given time period. The GAs I study usually are VGs of the present type (Smith, forthcoming b).

(b) **Volunteer groups** are defined as voluntary groups, 50% or more of whose cumulative, group-related hours of actions by analytical members are volunteer action for the given VGs during a given time period. Thus, *volunteer groups* is a broader term including all-volunteer groups as an extreme or nearly pure type.

(c) **Quasi-volunteer groups** are defined as voluntary groups, 50% or more of whose cumulative, group-related hours of actions by analytical members are quasi-volunteer action for the given VGs during a given time period. These groups have been termed "paid-staff nonprofits," "voluntary agencies," or simply (and nondiscriminatingly) "nonprofit organizations" (Powell, 1987; Smith, 1981; Wilderom and Miner, 1991). A similar distinction is made by others (Klausen, 1995; Milofsky, 1988b).

In all three instances (a-c), the theoretical types defined here will tend to occur empirically as points on a continuum. Thus, these three types might be used theoretically as is or with somewhat changed cutting points in terms of cumulative, group-related hours of actions by analytical members for given VGs during a given time period. My theory of voluntary altruism argues that this dimension is of substantial importance in understanding the causal structure of the VNPS and its major components in relation to other individual characteristics and group structure and process variables. Not necessarily *all* action in quasi-volunteer VGs (let alone in all VGs) is quasi-volunteer action. Some action might simply be remunerated. For every hour of service provided to an organization, one might ask whether it is unremunerated, underremunerated, or fully remunerated.

In terms of larger aggregation of VNPS terms and components, **narrower voluntary groups** are defined as identical to volunteer groups, as defined previously. **Broader voluntary groups** are defined as the sum of volunteer groups and quasi-volunteer groups, as defined previously. These are used later to define the VNPS simply.

Quite distinct from the forgoing, theoretically, are pseudo-VGs. These are groups that claim themselves to be or are labeled by others to be VGs (nonprofits) but that, in fact, involve no significant voluntary altruism (Nikolov, 1992). Many organizations on the IRS tax-exempt list in the United States are thought by critics of the tax exemption system to be pseudo-VGs, although the term is mine (cf. Bennett and DiLorenzo, 1989, 1994; Gaul and Borowski, 1993).

It is assumed that, during any time period in any sociopolitical unit, there might be some people claiming to be volunteers or groups claiming to be VGs that are not, in fact, still (if ever) acting significantly out of voluntary altruism. Rose-Ackerman (1990) terms this a matter of whether or not a VG still is "fulfilling its charitable mission" (p. 21). In my view, this is an empirical question, not a classification resulting from their IRS or equivalent tax status elsewhere. Scholars, and not government bureaucrats, should decide on a case-by-case basis what group is or is not a VG for research purposes. Because of the importance of voluntary altruism in my definitional scheme, scholars also will have to decide on who is a volunteer and of which type in VGs or potential VGs. This all would be time-consuming if it had to be done for every potential VG. However, the task can be made far simpler by randomly sampling nonprofits in each territory of interest if one's interest is in research, not registration or taxation. Some shortcut will have to be found for taxation/tax-exemption decisions.

6. There are two related definitions of the VNPS in my theory of voluntary altruism:

(a) The *narrow definition* of the VNPS is the sum of all volunteer altruism, all volunteer action, all volunteers, and all volunteer groups. Thus, the VNPS defined should properly be termed the *voluntary sector* now because of the centrality of voluntary altruism in its definition here. This also is true for the broad definition given shortly. I will continue to use the longer term and the VNPS acronym until there is widespread acceptance of the present definitions or some reworking of them in the directions I suggest.

The term *voluntary* is used to qualify the term *nonprofit sector* here because my theory of voluntary altruism suggests that the negative definitions (nonprofit) or other, merely numerical designations (i.e., third sector) should be scrapped and replaced with the earlier, positive, and now carefully defined *voluntary sector*. Until that can be arranged, putting the *voluntary* before the *nonprofit* helps to convey some new meaning of my preferred term for the sector that we study. Weisbrod (1977) was one of the first to use the term *voluntary nonprofit sector,* which I am using as an interim label. This label captures the special strength of the VNPS—ideological commitment (Rose-Ackerman, 1990).

(b) The *broad definition* of the VNPS is the sum of the four components of the narrow definition of the VNPS plus all quasi-volunteer altruism, all quasi-volunteer action, all quasi-volunteers, and all quasi-volunteer groups. Alternatively, the broad definition of the VNPS may be given more simply as the sum of all voluntary altruism, all voluntary action, all broader volunteers, and all broader voluntary groups.

In either case, my theory of voluntary altruism makes a distinction between volunteer altruism and quasi-volunteer altruism, along with all their correlative terms as components of the VNPS. The narrow version of the VNPS may be termed the **narrow voluntary sector** (NVS). The broad version may be correspondingly termed the **broad voluntary sector** (BVS).

Simply put, the broad version includes quasi-voluntary altruism and its related components, whereas the narrow version includes only volunteer altruism and its related components. Although this might all be a matter of degree empirically, it still is quite useful theoretically to be able to refer rather precisely to the three sets of phenomena so defined: voluntary altruism generally (broad version of VNPS interest/definition), volunteer altruism more specifically (narrow version of VNPS interest/definition), or quasi-volunteer altruism as an alternative specific interest (paid-staff VGs, their program service volunteers, and their board volunteers).

CONCLUSION

I show in this chapter that it is possible to take a quite different precise approach to defining the VNPS than is taken by most, if not all, others in the field. In so doing, I focus central attention on the dispositional concept of voluntary altruism—as a motivational or goal-oriented tendency of an entity, whether an individual or a group. Although defining voluntary altruism is complex, once it has been done, the other definitions of the VNPS and its major components follow very simply. This is a substantial theoretical advance. The resulting definition has elements of similarity to prevailing definitions of voluntary nonprofit groups (Kendall and Knapp, 1995; Salamon and Anheier, 1992a, 1994, 1997) as well as to major definitions of volunteers (Cnaan et al., 1996; Van Til, 1988). There remain, as well, some key elements of similarity to the earlier definitions of voluntary action by Smith et al. (1972a) and D. Smith (1975, 1981), and of the commons (Lohmann, 1992). I also give a precise connotative definition of GAs, based on the definition of voluntary altruism.

In my theory of voluntary altruism, altruism is service to another—an action by a provider-entity attempting to increase the helpee's net satisfaction (i.e., utility). *Voluntary* altruism, then, is altruism that involves the six following *core criteria* simultaneously: (a) more genuine caring/social support/sharing as primary goals of the provider-entity such that the provider-entity is more humane-core-value driven; (b) at least moderate provider-entity autonomy from other sectors and groups; (c) non-biopsychosocial compulsion of the provider-entity; (d) more provider-entity sensitivity to helpee's needs, wants, and wishes; (e) expected underremuneration or nonremuneration of the provider-entity; and (f) expected significant mix of entity- and other-serving satisfactions for the provider-entity.

The present definitions differ from prior attempts by defining terms for individuals and groups at the same time generally, terming either one individual or a group to be an *entity*. This approach highlights some important similarities in the definitions at these two levels of abstraction. The present approach similarly differs from those of others in defining the VNPS in terms of a combination of goals (voluntary altruism), activities by entities (voluntary action), volunteers of two subtypes, and voluntary groups of two subtypes. In all cases, there are underlying *dimensions* or continua hypothesized to be existing empirically. Types distinguished here are ideal types in the Weberian sense, intended to ease exposition and memory of these definitions.

The present theory of voluntary altruism identifies the central importance of the dimension of percentage of analytical members of voluntary *groups* who are unremunerated versus underremunerated versus fully remunerated for a given group and time period. Analytical members are regular service-providing affiliates of the VGs, whatever they might be called by the VGs themselves. Even more precise is the related dimension of percentage of cumulative hours provided to the groups by pure volunteers or by regular volunteers. I argue that these two related dimensions will have great empirical statistical and qualitative importance in relation to other important aspects of VGs. I show this in part by the literature review in this book.

A third alternative way of viewing this same dimension of VGs is to compare as analytical types volunteer VGs versus quasi-volunteer VGs versus non-volunteer (paid-staff) groups, examining the relationship of ranked types to the other important characteristics (structures and processes) of these groups. One hopes that the Johns Hopkins Comparative Nonprofit Sector Project will do this (Salamon, Anheier, and Associates, 1998). If and when such research is properly done by any researcher, comparing VGs of such different major analytical types (vs. purposive types such as health, education, and advocacy), I argue that the results will show that the rank-ordered set of group categories given here will powerfully relate with statistical significance to more important group/organization variables in general than do purposive type VGs.

Similarly, I argue in my theory of voluntary altruism that the dimension of degree of remuneration of *individuals,* taking as rank-ordered categories pure volunteers versus quasi-volunteers versus paid-staff workers, is crucial in understanding the actions of such people in a given group or organization and particularly the voluntary action of people either in informal contexts or in voluntary groups. My theory suggests that there will be the largest differences in job/role/task attitudes between people at the extremes of this dimension, namely, pure volunteers versus paid-staff workers.

Pearce (1982) has studied this empirically in matched groups of all volunteers versus paid-staff workers. With four pairs of matched volunteer and paid-staff organizations of different types, she found that volunteers were more likely to work when and how they wanted, that volunteers reported more personal influence in the organization, and that leaders in volunteer organizations reported more dependence on volunteers than did leaders in paid-staff organizations. There are very few studies, to my knowledge, that have gathered such data on individuals in the same survey from different points on this dimension.

In the definitions of the VNPS here, one approach is a broad version including both volunteer and quasi-volunteer altruism and voluntary action. A narrow version includes only volunteer altruism and volunteer action. The narrow version has been my career-long central interest, and at the local level, it is the focus of this book. One can use either version of the VNPS definition, according to research or policy needs (or both) for a more restrictive or more inclusive type of measurement. Both approaches are real and valid in their own terms, although they are quite different in the theoretical and empirical magnitudes of their estimations. These two alternative approaches of broad and narrow definitions of the VNPS, VGs, and volunteers are unique to my theory of voluntary altruism, to the best of my knowledge.

A major implication of these VNPS definitions is that current attempts to measure the numbers of volunteers and VGs, and hence of the total size of the VNPS, need to be revised in a number of ways. Such revisions should particularly attempt to include member benefit VGs and their associational volunteers in a more adequate way (Smith, 1997d). This has not been done in some major existing attempts to describe the VNPS (Hodgkinson and Weitzman, 1992; Hodgkinson et al., 1992; Salamon, 1992).

When attempts are made to compare the VNPS in different nations, as in the Johns Hopkins Project (Salamon and Anheier, 1992a, 1994; Salamon et al., 1998), this needs to be done with attention to definitions given here. However, I see progress in the gradual broadening attention of that specific project to VGs (e.g., GAs) between the initial definitions (Salamon and Anheier, 1992a) and more recent definitions and data (Salamon and Anheier, 1994, 1997; Salamon et al., 1998). I hope this continues and expands in scope given the major funding for, researcher involvement in, and importance of this project.

My theory of voluntary altruism, as presented in part in this chapter, has a number of advantages. My definitions are centrally "operational" in the use of the construct of voluntary altruism. But there also are important "structural" components. Thus, there are important areas of overlap with, as well as differences from, earlier definitions of my own or others. The VNPS concept is retained as useful and carefully defined in an objective, nonnormative way, and it is hoped that this will lead to its "recapture" from elites (Perri 6 and Leat, 1997). There is some provision made for overlap among sectors. My approach adds volunteers more clearly and equally into the definition of the VNPS along with VGs.

A dimension of formalization of voluntary altruism, voluntary action, volunteers, and voluntary groups is recognized and allowed for theoretically. I suggest that empirical work at present should attempt to measure informal volunteering for individual volunteers but only semiformal and more formal volunteering for VGs. This avoids the worst problems of measurement with informal groups, although precise definitions of *group* and *formal group* exist and could be used empirically to identify informal versus formal groups (Smith, 1967, 1972c).

On the whole, the approach to definitions here is positive rather than negative. It differs from just saying "nongovernmental, nonbusiness, nondistribution constraint" and so on. This is done by grounding voluntary altruism definitionally in caring/social support/sharing as manifested in positive, humane, core social values in a unique way. The approach permits clear distinctions between volunteer VGs and quasi-volunteer VGs (which I term *paid-staff nonprofits* elsewhere [Smith, 1981, 1997d]). This is an important theoretical advantage given recent research showing major differences between the two major analytical types of VGs (Smith, 1997a, 1997c, 1997d).

The approach here is cross-national in scope and intention, and it is generally consistent with the Johns Hopkins Project data and many of its more recent definitions (Salamon and Anheier, 1994, 1997). Among other virtues, the present approach is consistent with the presence of large numbers of mutual aid and self-help groups around the world (Fisher, 1993; Lavoie, Borkman, and Gidron, 1994; Powell, 1994; Salamon and Anheier, 1994; Wuthnow, 1994). I suggest elsewhere (Smith, 1996) that the failure to include such groups clearly enough in the early definitions and the classification scheme of the Johns Hopkins Project needed remedying.

This approach explains the "nondistribution criterion" of Hansmann (1980) in terms of voluntary altruism, with the latter viewed as theoretically more basic around the world (Weisbrod, 1992). Nations give tax-exemption status to certain groups because such groups manifest more voluntary altruism in the judgment of legislators and government administrators. Founders of new groups tend to choose the VNPS/VG approach because of the voluntary altruism they believe is manifested in the new groups' values. The governments of the countries in which the new VGs are located tend to go along with this judgment.

The theory of voluntary altruism explains *why* the VNPS, VGs, and volunteers usually are respected and admired to a significant degree in societies around the world and have been so esteemed for centuries, even millennia (Smith, 1997c; Weisbrod, 1992). The current, largely negative approaches to definition of the sector and its components cannot explain such popular and governmental esteem or the tax exemptions that usually go with it in most countries (Weisbrod, 1992). Specifically, the nondistribution criterion does not explain the tax exemptions or popular esteem for VGs through time and space (Hansmann, 1980, 1987).

Without positive, humane-core-value-driven definitions based on voluntary altruism such as I offer, one cannot sensibly discuss the extent to which nonprofits are becoming commercialized and leaving behind their initial voluntary altruism (Starkweather, 1993). Similarly, only such a positive definition, independent of government classifications, permits us to question any given case of government tax exemption for particular VGs or category of such groups. And only this type of positive definition permits one to discuss how contemporary VGs are becoming quasi-governmental/quasi-statutory because of recent government downsizing and privatization—the contracting out to VGs and businesses of many paid services formerly provided by government agencies at some territorial level (Smith and Lipsky, 1993).

Finally, and not least of all, the present approach also is utterly crucial in understanding the attacks on U.S. quasi-volunteer VGs and their tax exemptions by various critics supposedly acting in the public interest (Bennett and DiLorenzo, 1992, 1994; Brody, 1996; Gaul and Borowski, 1993). Such attacks are broadly warranted, from my viewpoint, when groups that are "attacked" have formal tax exemptions in any nation or historical time period but have no significant voluntary altruism involved. Rose-Ackerman (1990) puts this in terms of VGs having lost their "charitable missions." For example, there seems to be very little question that many tax-exempt hospitals in the United States tend to have little more voluntary altruism involved in their goals than do for-profit hospitals (Starkweather, 1993; Weisbrod, 1988, pp. 24, 75-76).

There are other theoretical, empirical, and policy implications of the present theory of voluntary altruism and its corresponding definitions that cannot be discussed here due to space limitations.

2

Revising Flat-Earth Maps

The Rest of the Voluntary Nonprofit Sector

This chapter argues that many researchers in the field ignore grassroots associations (GAs) and their associational volunteering as "the rest of the nonprofit sector" (NPS), producing "flat-earth" maps of the voluntary nonprofit sector (VNPS) as a result. For many researchers in the field, a paradigm change regarding the VNPS will be required if they are to accept this thesis. Much nonprofit and voluntary action research is incomplete, distorted, and misleading in systematic ways. Such research ignores GAs as if (a) they did *not exist* or as if (b) they were *not nonprofits* and, hence, not part of the VNPS. By implication, such research also suggests that (c) GAs are *unimportant* even if they do exist and are nonprofits. All three implications are false. I show this for the first two implications in this chapter, and I show in Chapter 9 that the third implication also is false.

I term the research, theory, and discussion in the nonprofit literature that essentially ignores GAs the *paid-staff voluntary group (VG) flat-earth paradigm.* It marks out a flat narrow world of paid-staff VGs as if they all were of the "known nonprofit world." This ignores the rest of the nonprofit world or VNPS, which is analogous to pre-Columbian European cartographers who portrayed Europe as the center and largest part of a flat earth. The fact that GAs, the rest of the VNPS, far outnumber the paid-staff VG flat-earth segment does not seem to

AUTHOR'S NOTE: A reduced version of this chapter was published in *Nonprofit and Voluntary Sector Quarterly* (Smith, 1997d). I benefited greatly from comments by anonymous reviewers of that journal and from the comments of its then editor-in-chief, Carl Milofsky, and its associate editor, John Messer. Burton Weisbrod also made many thoughtful comments and queries that strengthened this chapter a great deal. I am grateful to all of these people for their insightful help.

be known to or matter to those who ignore GAs. And unlike pre-Columbian cartographers, who at least had ignorance and superstition as reasonable excuses, current VNPS flat-earth mapmakers *have had* access to much of the missing but needed data regarding GAs if they wanted it.

I am *not* arguing that volunteer work (labor) has been ignored per se, for program service volunteering has received substantial scholarly attention. Both the paid-staff VG flat-earth VNPS mapmakers and the economists who have been concerned with the informal nonmarket economy have focused on this aspect of volunteering (Herzog and Morgan, 1992; Hodgkinson et al., 1995; Hodgkinson and Weitzman, 1992). However, it seems that the associational volunteering I am concerned with is not adequately tapped by the types of survey questions used. Therefore, all estimates of the value of volunteer time probably are substantial underestimates of the true volume and value of volunteering. Instead of simply asking about volunteering and for whom, one needs to ask about GA memberships and the amount of time given to various GAs, both as a member and as a leader (including committee work).

Many GAs are only semiformal, and most are not formally incorporated as separate entities (Smith, 1992b). Volunteering in GAs is similar to other activities that economists consider part of the informal nonmarket economy such as street peddlers and workers in illegal activities. Volunteer *programs* attached to work organizations such as paid-staff nonprofits, government agencies, and some businesses (e.g., proprietary hospitals) are not GAs, lacking any substantial autonomy.

This relative research inattention by scholars makes GAs and their associational volunteers the main "dark matter" of the VNPS. Many researchers in our field cannot seem to see them—to note their existence, numbers, and impact. The term *dark matter* is an analogy to the similar unobserved dark matter in the astrophysical universe.

Longair (1996) estimates, "Most of the mass of the universe is in some dark form, and its mass exceeds that in the form of visible matter by at least a factor of 10" (p. 145). The data I review in this chapter suggest similarly that the dark matter of the nonprofit universe (the VNPS) exceeds in numbers the commonly observed and counted nonprofits in the United States by nearly a factor of 10. Most scholars in our field notice mainly paid-staff nonprofits, or at most Internal Revenue Service (IRS)-registered nonprofits, and their program service volunteers while ignoring the millions of GAs and more than 100 million associational (GA) volunteers and their time.

Hodgkinson and Weitzman (1996b) and Hodgkinson et al. (1992), in their supposedly definitive and comprehensive *Nonprofit Almanac* (given its title and aims), include no significant data on GAs. The title does *not* say a *Partial Nonprofit Almanac,* a *15% of Nonprofits Almanac,* or a *Flat-Earth Nonprofit*

Almanac, each of which would be more accurate. For all the utility of these volumes in what they *do,* they ultimately fail to provide a VNPS overview map because of what they do *not* do. They focus only on the bright matter of the VNPS, not the dark matter of GAs (although companion volumes on program service volunteering include data on informal volunteering as a secondary type of dark matter [Hodgkinson et al., 1995; Hodgkinson and Weitzman, 1992]). Independent Sector has published similar data volumes roughly biennially since the mid-1980s, except for the teenage volunteering volume (Hodgkinson and Weitzman, 1984; Weitzman, 1983).

Hodgkinson et al. (1992), recognizing this problem to some extent, go so far as to say, "The charitable sector is dominated by a large number of *small* organizations. Other than names and addresses, little is known about 70[%] of *charitable* nonprofit organizations" (p. 185, emphases added). I thank those authors for making that objective statement. Many of these 70% of small nonprofits might be GAs, but I know of no specific data on this point. I assume that they often are GAs from other data given in this chapter.

I believe that it will make sense for scholars to study and for funders to provide grants to study GAs more systematically as an important part of the rest of the VNPS if it can be shown that such GAs and the member benefit sector (or subsector) are reasonably massive. *GAs are very massive, but only in the aggregate,* for the United States and for most other nations, properly studied. Smith and Associates (forthcoming) show that more than 100 contemporary nations have been found to have GAs, when properly studied (Appendix B). Many scholars commit what I term the *fallacy of disaggregation* by failing to see or understand what GAs are, mean, and accomplish *cumulatively.* This logical error leads them to commit related empirical errors of concept and method such as simply ignoring GAs and associational volunteers.

Individual GAs, on the average, certainly are rather small and unimpressive, most with less than 30 members (McPherson, 1983b). So are families and most retail businesses and local governments around the world. Yet, no scholar or societal leader argues that the latter types of groups are ipso facto unimportant and, thus, not worth studying or counting carefully. *This is an absolutely critical point to recognize.* Clearly, too many people, in their passion for bigness and brightness, have been dismissing GAs because of their average diminutive size and their subtle types of broad impact on members and on society that do not leap to the eye. Termites are similarly small and unimpressive organisms individually, but together they can bring down any wooden building, no matter its size.

Let us look at the situation in more detail, considering first the numbers of GAs in the next section of this chapter, then the numbers of people or roles, the time spent or behavior involved, and finally the money and property as indicators of GA magnitudes in the final section.

NUMBERS OF ASSOCIATIONS
AND ALL NONPROFITS

U.S. nonprofits do not *have* to register with the IRS if they have less than $5,000 annual revenues at present (lower income thresholds during earlier time periods) or if they are religious or are affiliates of some larger tax-exempt (state, regional, or national) entities that have tax exemptions. Therefore, those making up the rest of the VNPS—mostly the GAs—are unlikely to register with the IRS at all (even though *some* GAs seem to be so registered). Many GAs with annual revenues in excess of $5,000 are unaware that they are required to register with the IRS. The magnitude of the dark matter of small unknown GAs probably is far greater than what Hodgkinson et al. (1992, p. 185) suggest. They do not mention all the noncharitable IRS-registered nonprofits or the millions of GAs that are mainly unregistered with the IRS and constitute the core dark matter.

Clark (1937, p. 12) noted long ago that statistics on the numbers of small and GA churches or new religions probably were inaccurate undercounts as kept by organizations interested in an overview of U.S. religions. Much more recently, Bowen et al. (1994, chap. 1) conclude that many smaller nonprofits are unlisted with the IRS in the United States or might have dissolved while still on the IRS list. These authors ignore the potentially large numbers of new GAs that might have formed in the meantime, perhaps more than replacing losses of GA numbers through dissolution. GAs tend to have brief life spans, and new GA generations tend to come into existence quickly, thus keeping the genus alive in nearly all societies.

Furthermore, it is extremely important for "round-earth" mapping that some scholars have shown recently that the IRS nonprofit records are very incomplete even for paid-staff nonprofits. Gronbjerg's (1994) article on National Taxonomy of Exempt Entities problems discusses the inadequacy of the IRS nonprofits list as a map of the VNPS in the Chicago metropolitan area. Focusing mainly on paid-staff nonprofits, she compares IRS listings to the composite list from her own census based mainly on overlapping metropolitan and state lists. Some 57% of her final census list of Chicago-area paid-staff VGs were *missing* from the IRS listing of nonprofits. Dale (1993, p. 187) reports on a study of nonprofits in New York City that finds similarly large discrepancies between the IRS listing of nonprofits and independently derived listings from a comparison of local, metropolitan, and state lists.

There are various reasons for these IRS omissions, but most telling to me is Gronbjerg's (1994) statement that non-IRS-listed organizations tend to be "operated by churches and, therefore, not required to file independently; . . . too small to meet the minimum revenue criteria for registering or filing; or they are too new [i.e., young] to have filed the necessary paperwork" (p. 312). The overall result is that her work (see also Gronbjerg, 1989), as well as that of a few other scholars, even calls seriously into question the IRS data regarding paid-staff VGs, all GA omissions aside. If the IRS cannot even list fairly completely the larger "bright" entities in the NPS, namely the paid-staff VGs, then how can it ever hope to be seen as accurate regarding the core dark matter, the mainly unregistered GAs?

This is not a conspiracy; it is merely a result of scholars failing to see the implications of IRS basic purposes that make it more interested in larger organizations with more revenues to keep track of and to tax. Nonprofit listings by the IRS are a very tiny sidelight in the total scope of its activities. It is far more interested in knowing about households or businesses because their revenues or profits tend to be taxable. With VGs, nearly all of which are tax-exempt to one degree or another, the IRS interest is almost "academic" at best. Therefore, no scholar or societal leader should ever trust these figures unless and until the IRS makes major changes in its VG data collection methods. Although paid-staff nonprofit data are perhaps 50% complete, as already noted, we must gather better data on nonprofits by direct sampling of communities and their resident organizations, using methods such as those suggested in Appendix B and by Dale (1993) and Gronbjerg (1989, 1994).

A further implication is that even the paid-staff VG maps that are published by Independent Sector in the *Nonprofit Almanac* (e.g., Hodgkinson and Weitzman, 1996b; Hodgkinson et al., 1992) are seriously misleading, omitting large chunks of the paid-staff nonprofits in those metropolitan areas that have been more carefully studied and probably in most of the nation (which is about three-quarters urban). *These not only are flat-earth maps of the VNPS by lacking GAs, but they also leave out half of the paid-staff VG flatland.* The paid-staff VG maps that exist are, thus, a biased sample even of these larger and more visible VGs, let alone of the whole VNPS. Some scholars (e.g., Bowen et al., 1994, p. 16) have defined *charitable nonprofits* so narrowly that they end up studying only about 10% of the IRS-listed nonprofits or 1% of the total U.S. nonprofits (given IRS undercounting). This is like a flat-earth physical map of one *county* in England 500 years ago being presented as a good overview of the "known world."

How can we fix this mapping problem, creating a round-earth map of the VNPS? In addition to the implications of the research of Dale (1993) and Gronbjerg (1989, 1994), *my community research suggests that IRS listings include at most 10% to 20% of GAs.* I have made four initial estimates of the circa 1990 numbers of GAs in the United States. Each approach is independent of the other, being based on separate computations and data. All point to several million GAs.

Studying eight towns and cities in Massachusetts, I directed the performance of a census of GAs for each one from a variety of sources including fieldwork and using local newspapers as sources. (Appendix B describes that methodology briefly.) The communities varied by sampling in terms of GA prevalence, socioeconomic status (SES), and population size, although all had populations under 100,000. The final census of GAs was about 500% greater than the picture given by the statehouse records of incorporated associations, eliminating non-associations as coder judgments. Thus, only about 17% of the GAs actually found to exist in the eight communities were formally incorporated and in the statehouse nonprofit corporation records. IRS records are unlikely to be more inclusive. Hence, 17% may be taken tentatively as a rough upper limit estimate of GAs present in IRS records.

Now, let us estimate the 70% of "small" VGs in the IRS data to which Hodgkinson et al. (1992, p. 24) refer (quoted earlier). There are 0.70 × 1,024,648 nonprofits circa 1990 = 717,254 nonprofits of the smaller type in IRS nonprofit records. If the latter represents roughly 17% of all smaller nonprofits in the United States, then a little algebra gives us the national estimate of at least *4.2 million* smaller nonprofits, presumably *mostly GAs,* which is **Estimate 1.** To be more certain, we would need data on the percentage of GAs found by local field-work and newspaper coding for many more communities of all sizes around the nation. A study also should be made of IRS-listed VGs, seeking a more accurate estimate of the percentage of GAs rather than merely of "smaller nonprofits."

Paid-staff VGs probably have a much higher level of statehouse incorpora-tion and presence in IRS records, although we have seen that IRS listing is per-haps only 50% complete (Dale, 1993; Gronbjerg, 1989, 1994) as compared to no more than 17% complete for GAs. Overall, the situation is a little bit like looking at the visible stars at night when away from city lights. Visible stars are the ones that are easy to see with the naked eye with normal vision. I once read that there were perhaps 4,000 of them. Yet, in our galaxy alone (out of millions of galax-ies), there are estimated to be more than 100 billion stars based on extrapolation from careful study with telescopes of various types (Ronan, 1991, p. 52). Proper methodology makes a fantastic difference in astronomy in identifying and counting stars. I am not saying that the ratio of error in IRS or statehouse records of nonprofits or even GAs is that bad. But I do argue that such sources are off by a factor of about 5 to 10, and that is bad enough.

In another unpublished study I did circa 1990 of a small suburban Massachu-setts community (Appendix C), about 75% of the nonprofits of all types in the sample, primarily GAs, did *not* have articles of incorporation. Also, 88% of the nonprofits present did not *need* to register with the IRS given low revenues per year, incorporated supralocal affiliates, and/or religious purposes.

If there are 70% of IRS nonprofits that are small according to Hodgkinson et al. (1992, p. 24), then this means that there are 717,254 such nonprofits. If this number is at most 12% of all GAs, then there were about *6.0 million GAs* in the United States circa 1990. This is **Estimate 2.** Clearly, this computation is highly inferential. We need estimates from a large sample of communities regarding the proportion of GAs registered with the IRS. This could be done based on IRS records and local fieldwork. But the present very rough estimate suggests that the actual numbers of GAs are much greater than IRS registrations or state non-profit incorporation records suggest. This points up the systematic fallacy of defining VGs as only incorporated groups, as have Salamon (1992) and some others.

Wuthnow (1994, p. 76) estimates, based on national sample research totally independent of the preceding estimates, that there are nearly *3.0 million small support GAs* in the United States. Although there doubtless are some millions of more formal GAs and paid-staff VGs, this is minimum **Estimate 3,** more than twice the Hodgkinson et al. (1992) and Salamon (1992) IRS-based estimates for *all nonprofits.* These support GAs usually are small and informal, a type of GA rarely found in IRS or statehouse records. They are too often overlooked because of such characteristics that make them dark matter. Crude methodological equivalents of Galileo's early telescope such as IRS records do not show them to be present. If there are nearly 3.0 million of this *one type of GA* out there, then how many more millions of other, probably more formalized GAs also are out there in the nonprofit universe?

With an estimate of the average size of GAs, one can reach another independent estimate of the number of GAs, based on the cumulative number of memberships nationally in such groups and average size of GAs derived from research cited in the next section of this chapter. With an estimate of 50 members per GA (which is high), one derives an estimate of *5.3 million GAs* from 264 million memberships in the nation circa 1990. This **Estimate 4** is about four times the Hodgkinson et al. (1992) estimate of the total number of all nonprofits.

If an average of 30 members per association is used (which is higher than the McPherson, 1983b, adjusted estimate of somewhat less than 30 members), the total GA estimate based on 264 million memberships (see next section) rises to 8.8 million. The 3.0 million support GAs estimated by Wuthnow (1994, p. 76) have an average estimated size of 23.4 members. They probably represent the smaller GAs in a community, so I will not consider the total number of GAs using 23.4 as a size estimate (which would yield a still higher estimate of GA numbers than calculated earlier).

Best Estimate

I take as the best available estimation procedure an extrapolation of the sophisticated "hypernetwork sampling" approach used by McPherson (1982) for five communities of greatly varying populations (McPherson, 1988). He indicates that there is a prevalence of GAs (and relatively few state or national associations lacking local branches) starting at about 30 per 1,000 population in a city of 350,000, with the GA prevalence per 1,000 rising as community size declines down to about 1,000 population. Because the United States is basically an urban country, let us take the lowest estimate of 30 per 1,000 for larger cities (admittedly not the *largest* cities, in the range of 350,000 to 9 million) to compute a national estimate of GAs. This means that our final estimate might be an underestimate of the number of GAs because smaller places tend to have even higher prevalence, according to McPherson's (1982, 1988) data and other studies. (However, lower GA prevalence than in McPherson's city of 350,000 in unmeasured larger cities might balance out any such underestimation or even overpower the "small places effect.")

Several other estimates of GAs per 1,000 population from community studies are lower than 30 per 1,000 for the United States and other countries. These studies are mostly for cities with populations of more than 50,000 in several countries, hence probably underestimating GA prevalence because of less thorough fieldwork (Drake, 1972, for Colombia; Kellerhals, 1974, for French-speaking Switzerland; Koldewyn, 1984, for Argentina; Koldewyn, 1986, for Mexico; Lanfant, 1976, for three different places in France; Meister, 1972a, for France and Switzerland; Newton, 1975, for the United Kingdom), and for my own *initial* estimates in eight U.S. communities ranging in size from 14,000 to 86,000 population.

However, when more careful and thorough data collection is done (usually in smaller places), including extensive fieldwork and interviewing to supplement records and newspapers, the result generally seems to be more GAs per 1,000 population; the figures range from 29 per 1,000 to 100 per 1,000 for nine U.S. communities (Babchuk and Edwards, 1965; Laskin and Phillett, 1965; Warner, 1949; Warner and Lunt, 1941). The data from eight Massachusetts communities on GA numbers, when properly extrapolated by estimating undercounted GAs associated with churches in the towns or cities, yield an average of 30 GAs per 1,000 population. Hallenstvedt (1974, p. 215) estimates that there are about 50 associations per 1,000 population in Norway as a whole nation.

An intermediate average of about 20 GAs per 1,000 population was found in several other U.S. communities that were studied with more intensive fieldwork (Bushee, 1945; Devereaux, 1960; Goodchilds and Harding, 1960; Lynd and Lynd, 1929; Warriner and Prather, 1965) as well as in a small Canadian town (Kerri, 1972). In nine Norwegian communities with populations ranging from 1,000 to 8,000, Caulkins (1976) reported intermediate prevalence rates averaging about 23 per 1,000 population. In eight Massachusetts cities and towns with populations ranging from 14,000 to 86,000, I found an estimated 30 GAs per 1,000 population (mainly by extrapolating for each church present in a town an average number of church-related GAs present in churches studied directly). These data, combined with the other data reported earlier in this chapter, suggest that 30 GAs per 1,000 total population is not out of line if adequate methodology was used in a fairly recent data-gathering effort. Some of these were performed before 1960, when actual GA prevalence and participation might have been lower.

With 248,709,873 resident people in the United States as of 1990 (U.S. Bureau of the Census, 1993, p. 8), this produces an estimate of *7.46 million GAs, one type of VG, in the United States in 1990.* This is **Estimate 5,** my current best estimate of total GA numbers for circa 1990 in the United States. Two decades earlier, Smith and Baldwin (1974b, p. 282) produced an identical but essentially independent estimate of 30 GAs per 1,000 population in 1970. It was based on earlier high-quality GA prevalence studies but obviously did not include the later McPherson (1982) results. In this sense, the present 30 GAs per 1,000 population and earlier 30 GAs per 1,000 population estimates are independent.

The number of IRS-registered VGs combined with the local church congregations as used by Hodgkinson et al. (1992; see also Hodgkinson and Weitzman, 1996b) is substantially different from and relatively nonoverlapping with the 7.5 million GAs of Estimate 5. There are two exceptions to the nonoverlap. One is a small proportion of GAs among the roughly 350,000 church congregations (Hodgkinson et al., 1992, p. 25), probably in the range of 2% to 20% (Hodgkinson, Weitzman, and Kirsch, 1989, pp. 6, 8, 32, although the precise data needed on the percentage of church congregations with less than one full-time equivalent (FTE) of paid clergy or other paid employees are not given). Second, to avoid overestimating, I first subtract from the GA total half the 1990 estimate of 717,000 IRS-registered VGs (or 358,500), which Hodgkinson et al. (1992) say are small and unknown, because I believe that many might, in fact, be GAs and already included in Estimate 5. Thus, there is a question regarding what percentage of the smaller IRS nonprofits are GAs as opposed to paid-staff nonprofits, which is a research question that someone should answer by sampling these smaller nonprofits from IRS records and then interviewing representatives of each group.

One can combine the GA estimate and the paid-staff VG estimate to get an overall estimate of the magnitude of the U.S. VNPS circa 1990. Thus, 7,461,000 VGs from my GA Estimate 5 plus the remainder of the VGs (presumably mostly paid-staff VGs) identified by Hodgkinson et al. (1992) (1,375,000 minus 358,000 possible IRS-registered GAs), or 1,016,500 paid-staff nonprofits, equals 8,477,500 or *roughly 8.5 million U.S. nonprofits* in 1990. This is **Estimate 6T** for total nonprofits circa 1990. The small but unknown number of GA church congregations should make little difference in the estimate. Also, every IRS-registered VG over 358,000 that turns out to be a GA should be subtracted from the forgoing total VGs estimate because each one increases the paid-staff nonprofits estimate by 1.

But there is more to do. One also should add to the total VGs estimate some estimate of non-IRS-registered paid-staff VGs, which are indicated to exist in significant numbers by Dale (1993) and Gronbjerg (1989, 1994). Based on their findings, a rough figure of 50% seems appropriate for such IRS-missing paid-staff VGs. Still working roughly, this means that there must be another 1 million or so IRS-missing paid-staff VGs that belong on the IRS list so as to match the estimated 1,016,500 IRS-registered paid-staff VGs. Adding in this set of missing paid-staff VGs gives *a final best total estimate of about 9.5 million VGs in the United States circa 1990.* This is **Estimate 7T.**

Hodgkinson et al. (1992, p. 24) give an estimate of about 1.4 million total VGs circa 1990, counting "active" IRS-registered, tax-exempt VGs plus local church (or equivalent) congregations. This is **Estimate 8T** of total nonprofits. Salamon (1992, p. 13) gives a somewhat lower estimate of 1.1 million for all VGs circa 1989.

Estimates 7T and 8T constitute a round-earth VNPS map and a flat-earth VNPS map, respectively, of the numbers of nonprofits in the United States. These calculations could be done in different ways with different assumptions and would yield somewhat different results. But inclusion of GAs is the key difference between the two types of maps, with attention also given to the substantial (roughly 50%) incompleteness of IRS listings even regarding larger paid-staff nonprofits as well as the far greater incompleteness (missing 90% to 95%) regarding GAs. The VNPS is not nearly so tiny as the scholars noted earlier and others would believe. *Flat-earth VG maps leave out perhaps half of the flatland (paid-staff VGs) in all its brightness and nearly completely ignore the GAs as dark matter, which is most of the rest of the VNPS.*

Let us also estimate how much of the total VNPS in terms of VGs is being ignored by those who put their methodological faith in the IRS records and write their almanacs and flat-earth maps based on them. Roughly, the number of GAs plus the number of missing paid-staff VGs relative to IRS records, as given earlier, is divided by the total number of VGs. The GA figure, then, is simply my numerical Estimate 5 for the total of all GAs or 7.5 million. The IRS-missing paid-staff VGs are about 1.0 million, as given earlier. Together, these make approximately 8.5 million IRS-missing VGs (which is the IRS-missing total, *not* Estimate 6T being repeated). We now divide this 8.5 million IRS-missing VGs by the 9.5 million total of *all* VGs (Estimate 7T) to give 0.89 or 89%.

This estimate treats all GAs as missing from IRS data. Using my estimate of about 360,000 GAs present in the IRS data reduces the estimate of missing VG data in IRS records to 0.86 or 86%—still very large. This approach also treats religious congregations as IRS known when in fact they are only Independent Sector known.

Nearly 90% of the VNPS in the United States circa 1990 in terms of separate voluntary nonprofit groups or organizations are missing from IRS records and correspondingly missing from Hodgkinson et al.'s (1992) Nonprofit Almanac *and Salamon's (1992) book on* America's Nonprofit Sector. This is not a good record of accuracy. Such flat-earth scholarship probably has convinced most scholars in the field that the VNPS is much smaller and much less interesting than it actually is. This is analogous to the pre-Columbian European cartographers whose Eurocentric flat-earth maps also were greatly flawed. Such maps created half a millennium ago and earlier greatly restrained exploration and trade. In the case of VNPS research, the result of flat-earth maps has been less funding for GA research among mainstream scholars in the field and less scholarly interest in GAs because they do not even exist on the widely accepted canonical flat-earth maps.

The GA blindness, like color-blindness, goes beyond national VNPS estimates, also affecting estimates for U.S. states and metropolitan areas. For example, Ben-Ner and Van Hoomissen (1990) have used data from the New York State Department of Labor in their comparative study of the VNPS versus businesses and governments during the period 1981 to 1987. They not only ignore GAs basically but also combine the probably paid-staff membership organizations in their data with for-profits (p. 102). Other state databases have similar problems (Bania, Katona, and Keiser-Ruemmele, 1995).

The Institute for Nonprofit Organization Management (1995) at the University of San Francisco recently published a comprehensive statistical report on nonprofit activity in California. The very carefully done *California Nonprofit Organizations 1995* study found about 120,000 nonprofits, of which approximately 75% (or 90,000) were volunteer nonprofits, presumably mostly GAs with some small percentage of state subregion or state-level VGs. Thus, this attempted census includes *30,000 paid-staff VGs* out of a total of 120,000 VGs. This is a more thorough representation of volunteer nonprofits, I suspect, than are IRS data.

I will extrapolate from these total figures here using a 1990 U.S. census figure for California's population of nearly 30 million in 1990 (Famighetti, 1997). If we take a conservative estimate of only *10 VGs* of all types per 1,000 population, from earlier research reported in this chapter, this leads to a total estimate of approximately 300,000 VGs, Thus, the 90,000 GAs found in this study equals about 30% of all VGs present in the state circa 1990. This is far better than the IRS data, but it also is far from complete.

If a more reasonable figure of *30 GAs* per 1,000 population is used (as discussed earlier in this chapter), then this yields an estimate of 900,000 GAs present circa 1990. When this large figure is added to the number of paid-staff VGs found, or about 30,000, we can estimate the total of all VGs as 930,000. If half of paid-staff VGs also are missing from this study, as from the IRS listings, then there were about 960,000 nonprofits of all types in California circa 1990. The study performed in the state found 120,000 total nonprofits (Institute for Nonprofit Organization Management, 1995, p. 3) or only 12.5% of my total estimate of VGs potentially present. This estimation approach portrays the California study as similar in its undercounting to the IRS records.

Salamon's project on the VNPS in various major metropolitan areas produced, because of definitions and subsequent methodological approaches, flat-earth maps lacking very many GAs (e.g., Gronbjerg, Kimmick, and Salamon, 1985, for the Chicago area; Salamon, Altschuler, and Myllyluoma, 1990, for the Baltimore, Maryland, area).

Few maps (if any) trying to portray all nonprofits in other nations are any more accurate (Badelt, 1989; Lynn and Davis-Smith, 1991; McCarthy et al., 1992; Robbins, 1990; Starr, 1991). For example, compare the range of data mainly on GAs in Smith (1974), for many nations around the world, to the data mainly on paid-staff VGs in Salamon and Anheier's (1994) report on a 12-nation attempt to map the VNPS in other nations. *Either* of these two books alone is basically a flat-earth map of the VNPS around the world in addition to being very incomplete in numbers of nations included. The second wave of the Johns Hopkins Comparative Nonprofit Sector Project does better (Salamon, Anheier, and Associates, 1998) but still misses the mark.

To take a more specific example of another nation, work on the VNPS in Great Britain also suffers from flat-earth mapping problems. Paid-staff VGs and program volunteering receive a good deal of attention, but overviews do not do justice to GAs and associational volunteering (Lynn and Davis-Smith, 1991). Klausen and Selle (1996) do better for Scandinavia. Data must be gathered simultaneously and systematically in a variety of countries regarding both paid-staff VGs and GAs so as to have a round-earth map of the VNPS around the globe. This has not been done yet, to my knowledge. Again, flat-earth conceptions hold back relevant research as scholars do not venture into "unknown waters" in search of dark matter islands or continents.

The vast majority of organizations in the VNPS are GAs, not paid-staff VGs. This probably is true in other nations as well as the United States (Fisher, 1993; Smith and Associates, forthcoming). This is exactly the opposite from the VNPS portrayal by paid-staff VG flat-earth maps. My estimates here might turn out to be wrong to some degree when we have better data on key points. But the general trends and comparisons I present probably will hold up, usually being based on the research of several other scholars.

My modest proposal for a round-earth VNPS map should not be shocking. The rough similarity of several different independent estimates of the total numbers of GAs and of nonprofits attests to the probable correctness of my basic intellectual thrust here. Large proportions (90% or more) of GAs are missing from IRS listings, and perhaps half of paid-staff VGs also are missing, leading unwary scholars to believe that is all of the VNPS in the United States circa 1990.

In sum, several relatively independent estimating procedures indicate that there are many millions of GAs in the United States and, hence, many times more GAs than paid-staff VGs in the VNPS. These should be included in VNPS statistical overview maps of the sector, supplanting flat-earth maps now in vogue. Also, it seems clear that IRS nonprofit registration data greatly underestimate, perhaps by 90% or more, the numbers of all nonprofits. This IRS-based perspective diminishes the role of GAs in the VNPS and in U.S. society, distorting and misrepresenting both their apparent numbers and their estimated impact. It is clear that the dark matter of the VNPS is far greater in total number of VGs than is the bright matter.

Coincidentally, the relative magnitudes of light matter to dark matter are about the same estimate as in the astrophysical universe (Longair, 1996, p. 145). But *half* of the bright matter is quite available from the IRS nonprofit computer database. It tends to lure nonprofit researchers because of its ease of access and because researchers believe, erroneously, that it contains roughly the whole VNPS, trusting current flat-earth mapmakers and the IRS as their central data sources. This is unfortunate for our field, especially where IRS data are used for sampling purposes.

PEOPLE AND ROLES

One figure that usually captures people's attention about the American VNPS is that it employs millions of people. I do not dispute this, but I dispute some erroneous interpretations that often are made about that fact. Hodgkinson and Weitzman (1996b, p. 44) indicate that the VNPS employed about 9.8 million paid workers in 1992 and 10.3 million in 1994 including both full-time and part-time workers (but not pure volunteers). Although the authors do not present the data on employment categorized by nonprofit size, it is likely that most of these employees were in medium-sized or larger paid-staff nonprofits. That is how both the VNPS and business sectors are structured (Hodgkinson and Toppe, 1991, p. 407).

Salamon (1992) states, quite incorrectly from my viewpoint, "Most of the activity of the organizations in this [nonprofit] sector is not carried out by volunteers at all but [rather] by paid employees" (p. 5). Part of the problem might be that Salamon or one of his assistants made some erroneous computations. Salamon reports, "The volunteer labor available to [nonprofits] translates into the equivalent of almost *[3] million* full-time employees" (p. 27, emphases added). By contrast, using the next edition of *Giving and Volunteering in the United States* (Hodgkinson and Weitzman 1992, p. 25), we find that formal *program* volunteers nationally are the equivalent of *9 million* full-time employees in 1991. By my computation from data supplied, informal volunteers are the equivalent of another *3 million* full-time employees. Recall that informal volunteers are people volunteering without any group context—on their own, so to speak. This usage of mine is not the same as "informal economy activity" in economics, which includes *both* informal and formal (group-context) volunteering in my terms. The volunteering of informal volunteers still is useful work, irrespective of its lack of organizational auspices. And all this omits the *associational* volunteering to help others through GAs—volunteer activity usually viewed by its participants as participation in GAs but that actually is the equivalent of volunteering in volunteer programs.

More recently, Hodgkinson and Weitzman (1996b, p. 44) indicate that, in 1992, volunteer work was equivalent to about *6 million* full-time paid workers, again referring to formal program volunteers as usual. A few years earlier, they had said *9 million* for 1991. How they can be off by a third from their earlier statistic (Hodgkinson and Weitzman, 1992, pp. 25, 41) on the number of FTEs of paid workers, I do not know. Another arithmetic or typographical error is present, I suppose. (I am sure that some will be present in this book as well.) So, what figures can we trust in these Independent Sector or Salamon summaries regarding the VNPS? This statistic on the number of FTEs of volunteer work done in the nation is a *very key figure* and should have been checked carefully and repeatedly for accuracy. If it is wrong in one place or the other, as it must be, then how far off are *less important* figures that are cited but that were perhaps checked less often?

Because there were only 9.8 million paid employees in the VNPS in 1992, as noted earlier, the 9 million employee equivalents (per Hodgkinson and Weitzman, 1992, p. 41) of formal *program* volunteer work done, even most narrowly defined (formal program volunteers only), are roughly the same as the approximately 10 million annual equivalents of work done in 1992 by paid VNPS employees. Note that the program volunteers here are working in government agencies and even some businesses (e.g., proprietary hospitals, other for-profit health organizations) as well as in paid-staff nonprofits.

Associational volunteering in the nation can be computed only very roughly because recent time diary research is not available on such volunteering for a national sample of adults. The circa 1991 estimate from the next section for total hours of GA volunteer time is 27.6 billion hours per year, much greater than the program volunteer number of hours annually. When this figure is divided by 1,700 hours, the figure for FTEs per year, the result is about *16.2 million FTEs for associational volunteering.* Even without including any formal program volunteer employee equivalents, this figure is much greater than the number of regular full-time and part-time VNPS paid employees (approximately 10 million, as noted earlier).

With a properly ample definition of volunteers, including informal volunteering, youth volunteering, and especially GA or associational volunteering at a minimum, and with proper measurement of participant time, the work done by *paid* employees is very clearly in the minority in the VNPS. Associational volunteer work dominates the VNPS in terms of FTEs of work. Adding informal volunteers and formal program volunteers, the total volunteer work of all types done by adults circa 1991 equaled more than *28 million FTEs,* still omitting youth volunteering for which we lack an estimate of associational volunteering. The forgoing figure was computed by taking 20.5 billion annual hours volunteered from Hodgkinson and Weitzman (1992, p. 41), dividing it by 1,700 hours to get annual FTEs, and adding the result to the earlier 16.2 million result for associational volunteers.

The forgoing result is *strongly* contrary to Salamon's (1992) statement quoted earlier. So, in terms of the sheer hours of work done, it is not the paid staff who do most of the work in the VNPS. Volunteers do most of the work in FTEs (see more summary data and discussion in the next section). And that is a good reason to call the VNPS the *voluntary sector*. There are other reasons as well (see Chapter 1). Scholars will reach a conclusion opposite to mine only by making arithmetic or typographical errors and/or ignoring informal and associational volunteering.

VNPS employees are different, on the average, from employees in the business and government sectors. Steinberg (1990) notes, "The typical [nonprofit] worker earns 33[%] less than the typical [for-profit] worker, although [nonprofit] workers are both more educated and more likely to work in a professional occupation" (p. 159). What are these paid staff in the VNPS getting out of it? I argue that they get "psychic benefits" or "psychic income" (Smith, Reddy, and Baldwin, 1972a). Steinberg (1990) points out that nonprofit workers report more job satisfaction and more variety, autonomy, and flexibility in their jobs. Majone (1984) and Mirvis (1992) also find noneconomic rewards for VG paid workers. Hatch and Mocroft (1979) report, from a review of several studies, that even paid staff in VGs tend to have more commitment than do paid staff in government agencies.

Once upon a time, this psychic income was thought to be based on the "voluntary spirit"—now a term out of favor (but see O'Connell, 1983). The voluntary spirit may be viewed and measured as a quality of *voluntary altruism* (see Piliavin and Charng, 1990, for many measurement examples). It is a special type of attitude complex that leads many nonprofit paid staff to accept less than the going rate in the business sector for doing the equivalent job in the VNPS. This usually makes nonprofit paid staff *stipended volunteers* if the difference between their actual pay and the market value of their work done in the job is significant). This same attitude complex of voluntary altruism also leads to *pure volunteering,* which I define as unstipended volunteering (see Chapter 1).

I do not deny that in many paid-staff VGs there presently is little evidence of this voluntary altruism (e.g., many hospitals and universities). But if the empirical results reported by Steinberg (1990) and noted earlier are broadly reliable, then something like psychic benefits *must* be at work in a fairly widespread way among VNPS employees generally to explain these results. If some paid VNPS employees fail to have significant voluntary altruism, being in apparent VNPS jobs for other reasons *only,* then they really are not part of the VNPS no matter how much other scholars or VNPS leaders want to call them VNPS employees to build up the apparent importance of the VNPS. Most of us in the field already know that counting all or most VNPS employees as truly part of the sector probably is overcounting. Many paid-staff VGs are run mainly like businesses and essentially use tax exemption as what critics term tax avoidance, although they tend only to admit being "business-like" as in "efficient" (Bennett and DiLorenzo, 1989, 1994; Brody, 1996; Gaul and Borowski, 1993).

Two inadequate alternative explanations are as follows. First, paid staff in VGs are of poorer quality (less human capital) than are paid workers of the same type in the business sector. But Steinberg (1990) says that the VNPS paid workers usually are more educated and more likely to be professionals, so this alternative explanation does not seem likely. Second, paid staff in VGs are deluded, muddle-headed, or mildly crazy; hence they work against their best personal economic interests. To my knowledge, there is no evidence of systematically more mental health problems among VG paid employees than among employees in other sectors.

Only the psychic income explanation really makes sense here. It fills the wage "deficit" of VNPS employees in actual money income relative to the business sector, on the average. Weisbrod (1988) comes close to what is needed with his notion of the varying degrees of the "collectiveness index" or orientation of VGs (p. 75), especially paid-staff VGs. High collectiveness means high percentage of gifts and grants among all VG revenues. I would go further and suggest that the degree of significant differential between paid-staff VG wages and the corresponding level of business sector wages also is an economic indicator (vs. possible psychological or sociological indicators) of such an orientation and of the presence of voluntary altruism for specific jobs involved.

Hodgkinson and Weitzman (1992, p. 25) report that there were 94.2 million U.S. (*program*) volunteers in 1991 or 51.1% of the population age 18 years or over. By 1993, Hodgkinson and Weitzman (1996a, pp. 1-30) reported that there were an estimated 89.2 million such volunteers or 47.7% of adults. No indication is given of how many volunteers were program volunteers in paid-staff nonprofits versus associational volunteers in GAs. Figure 1.23 in Hodgkinson and Weitzman (1996a, pp. 1-43) does not settle this question. It shows that many program service volunteers, as measured by Independent Sector, also are GA members, but it does not show how many of these volunteers measured by Independent Sector are mainly associational volunteers versus program service volunteers, as I have defined them. GAs depend on associational volunteers, not program service volunteers as do work organizations. Thus, the GA activity missed in Form 990s by IRS-missing nonprofits probably also is *not* picked up in Independent Sector-sponsored surveys of volunteers.

From reading the instrument used (Hodgkinson and Weitzman, 1992, p. 302), it is clear that the question (Question 6) on volunteering was not properly worded, confounding program and associational volunteering as well as service to fellow members versus service to nonmembers. In the subsequent question

(p. 304, Question 14) dealing with types of organizations volunteered for, we still do not know whether the organization was a work organization or a GA. These distinctions are vital theoretically and must be built into future surveys if they are be attain adequacy. Thus, the Independent Sector study fails to inquire about whether the auspices of most volunteering time done by the respondent (p. 338) is a GA or paid-staff nonprofit and whether it is a member benefit or a nonmember benefit. These all are conflated, to the detriment of understanding.

My best estimate is that the wording of the survey leads respondents to report mainly time spent in program volunteering, omitting much or most associational volunteering. In Hodgkinson and Weitzman (1992, p. 327, Question 89), respondents report membership in GAs separately using a constricted list of types compared to Verba and Nie (1972, pp. 178-79) or Verba, Schlozman, and Brady (1995, pp. 60-61). Time spent in these GA types is not queried. A special methodological study would be needed to determine the percentage of associational volunteering *time* that gets reported when this survey instrument is used. Such a study should include attendance as well as other GA activity.

Related omissions in the otherwise useful *Nonprofit Almanac* (Hodgkinson and Weitzman, 1996b; Hodgkinson et al., 1992) are the failure to view GA members, GA active members (associational volunteers), and GA memberships as important enough to count accurately and report. These also were omitted in earlier similar Independent Sector VNPS mapping volumes. This probably has its roots in the origins and political nature of Independent Sector as an organization (Hall, 1992; Salamon 1993). Yet, the leaders of that organization state their interest in civil society, participatory democracy, and the types of contributions that GAs preeminently make to civil society in every nation where they are significantly present.

Association members, including GA members, provide services to each other (and even nonmembers) that are real and important. Association volunteers receive benefits in return, but so do program volunteers, as Hodgkinson and Weitzman (1992) themselves show in their companion volume. O'Neill (1989, 1994) and Smith (1991, 1993b) argue and demonstrate that member benefit organizations, mostly GAs, are important parts of the VNPS. Here, I argue more specifically that memberships in and members of such GAs are important to survey and count, in conjunction with surveys of program volunteers that Independent Sector has been doing for years. GA volunteers are a major chunk of the dark matter of the VNPS. Let us see how large a chunk.

In one fairly recent national sample survey of adults age 18 years or over (Davis and Smith, 1989, p. 370), *67.3% of adult Americans belonged to one or more voluntary associations when aided recall items were used.* Aided recall involves listing different association types, mostly GAs as noted in the National Opinion Research Center (NORC) classification, and asking for each type if the respondent belongs. Another NORC national survey done in 1990 for Verba et al. (1995 [membership data provided thanks to Kay Schlozman]) found that 71% of U.S. adults were members of associations, broadly defined. These NORC figures omitted church/synagogue membership but included membership in other church-related GAs such as church/synagogue women's groups and couples' clubs. Earlier research without aided recall often found much lower membership levels, as pointed out by D. Smith (1975, p. 250; see also Wright and Hyman, 1958). Baumgartner and Walker (1988) improve somewhat on current aided recall methodology and find a still higher membership percentage, although T. Smith (1990) faults their analysis.

Hodgkinson and Weitzman (1992, p. 327) *did* ask about associational memberships. However, their data are seriously flawed methodologically. Only eight purposive types of associations were asked about to the respondents separately as aided recall. The NORC questions (Verba and Nie, 1972, pp. 178-79; Verba et al., 1995, pp. 60-61) use about twice as many aided recall association types. Only 33.1% of the Hodgkinson and Weitzman (1992) national sample of people age 18 years or over belonged to voluntary associations other than religious organizations (pp. 165, 264). Such a result is so low that it can be due only to faulty methodology—too few aided recall prompts in the question used. In the more recent Hodgkinson and Weitzman (1996a) survey using a somewhat better aided recall item (p. E-206, Question 58), 41.4% belong to nonreligious GAs (pp. 4-92).

No competent national sample survey of association membership in the United States during the past few decades has ever found so low a figure, and perhaps 20 such studies have been done. The General Social Survey of NORC (Davis and Smith, 1989; T. Smith, 1990) has for years been finding figures in the 60% or higher range in separate, independent, replicated U.S. national samples of adults age 18 years or over (see also Auslander and Litwin, 1988; Baumgartner and Walker, 1988; Curtis, Grabb, and Baer, 1992; Palisi and Korn, 1989; Verba and Nie, 1972, p. 176; Verba et al., 1995, p. 80).

It is highly unlikely that *all* these national sample studies of associations by experts are wrong and that Hodgkinson and Weitzman (1992) are the *only* ones who are right, using a clearly limited measurement technique. They need to substantially extend the number of aided recall examples given including self-help GAs in particular (Wuthnow, 1994). Science is based on reliable replication, but the Hodgkinson and Weitzman (1992, 1996a) data on GAs are quite inconsistent with all other studies in the United States during the past few decades using a more appropriate methodology.

The question used (Hodgkinson and Weitzman, 1992, p. 327, Question 89) involved aided recall based on a card shown to the respondents. Unfortunately, this card omitted nine different types of associations usually included in the NORC standard question about voluntary associations (Davis and Smith, 1989). Also, three of the eight aided recall association types actually listed were incomplete relative to the NORC standard question. This methodological inadequacy of the Independent Sector data is especially disheartening because it involves the *only* question in the 1992 Independent Sector research (Hodgkinson and Weitzman, 1992, p. 327) that clearly deals with GAs out of very many total questions asked. The more recent Hodgkinson and Weitzman (1996a, p. E-206, Question 58) item still has only 11 examples and an "other" category. Knowledgeable scholars in the GA studies field have avoided this type of error for major studies beginning roughly three decades ago (Verba and Nie, 1972, p. 345, with data gathered in 1967).

Several studies show GA membership in other modern nations—especially in Scandinavian nations, Switzerland, and Canada—to be roughly as high as or even somewhat higher than data on U.S. adults (Boli, 1992, for Sweden; Curtis, 1971, for Canada; Curtis et al., 1989, for Canada; Curtis et al., 1992, for 15 developed nations; Frizzell and Zureik, 1974, for Canada; Hallenstvedt, 1974, for 3 Scandinavian nations; Pestoff, 1977, for 7 nations not duplicating the preceding studies exactly; Verba et al., 1995, p. 80, for 12 nations; see also Smith, 1973b, for university students in 6 Latin American nations). The Scandinavian nations, in fact, tend to be higher than the United States in percentage of adults who are members of associations (GAs and supralocal associations). There also is very substantial variation in the total percentage of adults who belong to associations among industrial and postindustrial nations, ranging from 26% in Italy to 76% in the United States in one study of 12 such nations (described in Verba et al., 1995, p. 80; see also Almond and Verba, 1963). This indicates that the level of modernization or industrialization is far from the only relevant factor here (Smith, 1973c).

Taking a 1991 estimate of 184,400,000 Americans age 18 years or over (Hodgkinson et al., 1992, p. 1), the figure of 67.3% of the adult population who are members of one or more associations (Davis and Smith, 1989, p. 370) indicates that in 1990 there were about *124 million members of one or more voluntary associations, the vast majority GA members,* rather larger than the comparable number of program volunteers. Of course, some of these memberships are on paper only, as the members merely send their dues or contributions by mail. The meaning of the term *member* here is that both the individual and the GA consider that person to be an official member. Usually, the member must pay his or her annual dues to the GA to be an official member for a given year. Most GAs have formal membership lists, but a great many do not, being more informal (Smith, 1992b).

Researchers often fail to ask the additional question about whether the respondent is "active" in one or more associations. When this question was asked, Verba and Nie (1972, p. 176) found that about 40% of their national sample of U.S. adults were active members (associational volunteers) by self-report. Grabb and Curtis (1992), doing secondary analysis with data from 1981 to 1983, found 53% of the U.S. national adult sample to be active in unpaid volunteer work for some voluntary association (i.e., they replied positively when asked whether they were "active members"). If member attendance at meetings also were included, then this figure would be higher.

Using this latter, more recent (but not recent enough) figure of 53% for member activity levels and multiplying it by the 1991 U.S. adult population figure given earlier yields an estimate of *about 98 million active members of U.S. associations, mostly GAs,* circa 1990. This figure is large and meaningful. Sheer membership, without other activity, generally indicates individual support for a GA, both financial and attitudinal. Active membership indicates still greater support and the contribution of time to the GA, whether as an association volunteer or as a "mere" participant. If youth members of GAs were added to the mix, then the forgoing figure would be further enlarged, perhaps by 10% to 20% or more.

Memberships (vs. individual members) are even more frequent than the forgoing suggests. Some people have multiple memberships in associations, and so far I have considered only a single membership per person. Verba and Nie (1972, p. 176), using a national sample of U.S. adults, found that 39% belonged to more than one association. Palisi and Korn (1989, p. 182) found an average of *1.43 association (mainly GA) memberships per capita* for *seven* U.S. national samples from the 1970s and early 1980s. Memberships were instances in which the respondent claimed to be an official member of a given type of GA. These GA-type memberships, if anything, underestimate the number of memberships of a person: some people might belong to two or more GAs of the *same type* category. Auslander and Litwin (1988) found a close 1.35 memberships per capita in which a national adult sample participated. Grabb and Curtis (1992) found a very close 1.45 memberships per capita in their national adult sample.

Extrapolating for the U.S. adult population age 18 years or over (Hodgkinson and Weitzman, 1992, p. 1) using the 1.43 average memberships figure yields an estimate of *about 264 million association memberships for U.S. adults.* This is a bit more than one membership for every person in the nation (significantly more if youth memberships were included). Smith and Baldwin (1974b, p. 279) estimated from various other data that there were 222 million association memberships in 1971. About half of these were polymorphic GA memberships as parts of national associations, and half were purely local and unique (monomorphic) associations. That earlier estimate is close to the more recent one given earlier from other data when one allows for population growth during the two decades intervening, being based on the same number of estimated associations per 1,000 population.

Church memberships sometimes are GA memberships if the churches are GAs by my definition—which many are, given the large inputs of volunteer time in many churches. Wuthnow (1990, p. 4) reports that 65% to 71% of adults belong to churches or synagogues in the United States, according to various surveys (see also Blau, Land, and Redding, 1992). A small proportion of these belonging to GA churches, thus, represents a lot of people numerically.

This is all dark matter of the VNPS, not regularly reported and largely unconsidered by most VNPS leaders and scholars. The magnitudes of GA activity involved simply cannot be dismissed out of hand. They dwarf many paid-staff VG statistics. The data needed to make these estimates nationally have been available for years and even decades in most cases, but making a round-earth map of the VNPS has not been a priority. These hundreds of millions of association memberships and their corresponding associational volunteer activity are viewed by many scholars and leaders of the VNPS as unimportant for describing or understanding the VNPS and the American people. If these types of GA data had been important, then they would have found their way onto major VNPS maps by now. They have not. Only program "volunteerships" and paid employees in the VNPS seem to matter for flat-earth maps and cartographers.

TIME AND BEHAVIOR

Time spent is hard to measure in studying people's behavior. People can tell the researcher what they think, but remembering time put into different activities can result in much distortion (Robinson, 1985). *Time diaries* kept by willing respondents over days and weeks seem to be the best approach (Juster, 1985; Robinson, 1985), although they too have their problems. Unfortunately, and presumably for reasons of practical ease and lower cost, Hodgkinson and Weitzman (1992, p. 302) use as their approach the less reliable method of *simple recall* of hours spent during the past week on volunteering by respondents. This would not be so problematic if they had supplemented their research with a substudy comparing such recall to time diary data for the same week for a representative subsample, *not* allowing the respondents to see their time diaries in making their recall estimates. One hopes that someone will do this important methodological study soon.

For GAs, Hodgkinson and Weitzman (1992, 1996a) do not even inquire about the number of hours spent in each type of GA, although in 1996 they inquire about participation more generally (p. E-206, Question 59: from *every week or nearly every week* to *not at all*). This assumes that their question about volunteer time (1996a, p. E-194, Question 11) picks up on all associational volunteer time in GAs, which I maintain it does not.

Apparently unaware of their methodological problems, Hodgkinson and Weitzman (1992, p. 25; 1996b, p. 69) report that volunteers gave an average of 4.2 hours per week in 1991 and the same in 1993 including *informal* volunteering. This was about 2.1 hours per person for the total adult population in 1991 (volunteers and nonvolunteers). This totaled *20.5 billion mostly program volunteer hours* for U.S. adults in 1991 and 19.5 billion hours in 1993 (Hodgkinson and Weitzman, 1992, p. 25; 1996b, p. 69).

Verba et al. (1995) collected similar time data in a related way, using interviews with a representative random sample of U.S. adults but asking about time spent per week in *charity* participation. They found an average of 1.7 hours per week specifically spent on charity activities among all respondents in their national sample (p. 78). Another 0.9 hours were spent on church participation (p. 78), summing to 2.6 hours per week (not counting political campaign participation, which is more episodic but averages 0.6 hours per week). This figure is 24% larger than the 2.1 hours per capita for program and informal volunteering found by Hodgkinson and Weitzman (1992, p. 25).

For all its methodological validity flaws, survey interview data on time use during the past week can be reasonably *reliable,* even if not necessarily valid. If one has a narrow flat-earth view of VGs and volunteering, then one inevitably misses a lot of what really is out there in terms of volunteer time as in other measurements relevant to GAs. Both of the previously cited data sources (Hodgkinson and Weitzman, 1992; Verba et al., 1995) are incomplete by themselves, and their degree of overlap is unknown. Both omit much GA time. Figure 1.23 in Hodgkinson and Weitzman (1996a, pp. 1-43) shows that, even with inadequate methodology, not all GA members are volunteers and vice versa.

Data from national time diary research during 1975-76 (Hill, 1985, pp. 155, 172) suggest that U.S. adults spend about 2.88 hours per week in "organizational activity" (association [mostly GA] participation). Other estimates from these data when aggregated in slightly different ways are 2.96 hours per week (Dow and Juster, 1985, p. 404) and 3.04 hours per week (Hill, 1985, p. 148 [my average of data given for males and females separately]). In an earlier *urban* national sample also collected by time diaries during 1965-66, Robinson (1977, pp. 13-14) found associational activity to use about 2.35 hours per week, mostly in so-called "nonphilanthropic" activities that benefit *only* other GA members or one's family. This rough similarity of the two studies gives us some reasonable confidence in the reliability of the associational time estimates.

Note that these time diary independent estimates of associational volunteer time are little larger than the interview-derived 2.6 hours per week estimate cited earlier. The greater magnitude of time diary results is quite modest and might be accounted for by the narrowness of the Verba et al. (1995) framing of their interview questions in terms of just charity and church.

Some of the forgoing associational volunteering time *might* overlap with the type of program volunteering counted in the earlier figures I have noted. Let us see. Robinson (1985, p. 57) has indicated that the vast majority of organizational (associational) time is *not* direct helping of others (only 0.1 hour per week is the latter) such as that on which Hodgkinson et al. (1992) focus. Thus, the separation of program volunteer time, as usually measured (Hodgkinson and Weitzman, 1992), and association volunteer time using time diaries (Hill, 1985) seems to be fairly complete and nonduplicatory in these data. The two types of volunteer time, thus, could properly be added to find the approximate total amount of formal volunteer time. *Formal volunteer time* may be defined as time spent by an individual doing volunteer activity, participation, or work in some group, organizational, or program context rather than without any group context (i.e., informal volunteer time). This time can be aggregated over any reasonable time period and is most accurately measured by time diaries kept by willing respondents over some short time period such as a week.

When the estimated yearly total for all associational volunteer activity in 1976 is applied to a 1991 adult population estimate, the resulting estimate is *27.6 billion hours of total associational volunteer time* or 181% of the formal *program* volunteer time. Using 1,700 hours per year as an FTE figure (Hodgkinson et al., 1992, p. 41), this amounts to about 16.2 million FTEs of total *associational* volunteer work circa 1990. Omitting religious practice (church/synagogue attendance), even though it clearly *does* belong here, associational volunteer activity amounts to 1.76 hours per week for the total population (Hill, 1985, p. 172). This aggregates to 16.9 billion hours of nonchurch *associational* volunteer time per year circa 1990, about 10% larger than the 15.3 billion hours per year Hodgkinson et al. (1992) estimate for formal *program* volunteer work. These 16.9 billion hours of nonchurch associational volunteer time amount to 9.9 million nonchurch associational volunteer FTEs circa 1990 in the United States, again about 10% larger than formal program volunteer FTEs.

For present purposes, however, it is sufficient to know that the cumulative total of associational volunteer time (even omitting church attendance time) is roughly similar in magnitude to formal program volunteer time estimated and cumulated over the year 1991. Associational volunteer time is a major chunk of dark matter for the VNPS. It needs better regular measurement by time diary methods, and it also needs to be carefully disentangled from informal and program volunteering.

The issue of church attendance as volunteer activity also needs to be addressed (Blau et al., 1992). I argue that it is volunteer work or volunteer time because one must perform in various ways while attending services, and one's simply being at church involves both opportunity costs and travel costs. Hodgkinson and Weitzman (1996a, pp. 1-43) found that 70.9% of their sample were members of a religious organization, including churches, and 77.0% attended services (pp. 4-93). Ignoring this is subscribing to the secularist flat-earth VNPS paradigm.

MONEY AND PROPERTY

Paid-staff nonprofits shine in terms of economics, as every reader knows—employees, property, income, equity, salaries, and so on. But economics is not what the VNPS really is all about. *Voluntary altruism* explains the common features of VGs. Voluntary altruism ultimately is why VGs are distinctive and why they are given tax exemption of one type or another (see Chapter 1). Of course, the voluntary altruism of groups gets interpreted in a given nation in terms of its existing tax laws, which tend to have various specific factors as tests for tax exemption of the groups (Weisbrod, 1992). This voluntary altruism is manifested in volunteer work, energy, and creativity within a VG or volunteer service program in another type of work organization.

The numbers corresponding to economic measures (Herzog and Morgan, 1992) here fail to capture the attitudinal-emotional dimension of that voluntarism very well (Brown, 1999). As noted in Chapter 1, voluntary altruism can be present in a VG even if its members have significant or substantial egoistic or selfish motivations in addition to some significant altruistic concerns for their fellow members or nonmember beneficiaries of the group. In a recent study of the value of volunteer activity, Brown (1999) concludes, "The standard estimate [of the value of volunteer time] overstates the value of volunteering to the recipients of volunteer-assisted services but understates the overall value of volunteering when the gains accruing to volunteers themselves are included" (p. 3). This was based on program service volunteering and is all the more true for associational volunteering.

The VNPS, in my view, is not mainly about money and property. It is mainly about people's time and their attitudes, voluntary spirit, emotions, ideologies, purposes, values, and even dreams (consider the dedication of Martin Luther King, Jr. and his famous speech "I Have a Dream!"). *On scales of revenue, wage and salary expense, total budget, property, and equity or net worth, the whole VNPS is small compared to the other sectors, especially the business sector* (Hodgkinson et al., 1992, pp. 27, 31, 195). And there is much financial stratification *within* the VNPS as well. Hodgkinson and Toppe (1991) state, "Not only is the independent sector primarily composed of small institutions, but it is characterized also by a small percentage of large institutions that command the bulk of the assets in the sector" (p. 407). They further specify that 4% of the 501(c)(3) organizations, with assets and expenditures of $1 million or more, have 86% of the assets of the sector (p. 407).

Based on a sample of "4,730 [IRS] nonprofits with gross receipts in excess of $25,000" for the 1983 tax year (Tuckman and Chang, 1991, p. 454), the mean revenue figure was about $34 million and the mean equity (assets minus liabilities) was about $30 million (p. 457). Even allowing for the skewing effects of very large and mainly nonmember benefit paid-staff VGs, these data give a picture of IRS-registered larger and usually nonmember benefit VGs ($25,000 or more in revenues) as being very well off indeed. Rudney (1987) found, from similar IRS data earlier, that mainly *member* benefit paid-staff VGs in 1982 constituted only 15% of the earnings of the external benefit (nonmember benefit) paid-staff VGs to which they were compared. This works out to about $10.8 billion in total member benefit paid-staff VG revenues for 1982. So-called "public" or nonmember benefit paid-staff VGs clearly dominate among the larger VGs of the VNPS in terms of most, but not all, economic measures. Member benefit paid-staff VGs exist only in relatively small numbers among the larger paid-staff VGs registered with the IRS, and they usually have weaker finances. Recall, however, that the IRS ignores perhaps 90% of VGs, mostly GAs.

Having seen some evidence on the "establishment nonprofits," what of the GAs? They do not generally file Form 990 tax returns with the IRS because they often are polymorphic affiliates of national associations, poor, or religious and do not have to register or file, as noted earlier. Therefore, standard national or even state economic data on GAs are lacking. They generally tend to have no employees (at most one or two, usually for far fewer than 40 hours a week, by definition), small annual budgets (under $25,000 per year, usually way under), and essentially no property (near zero equity). They tend to meet in members' homes (Chan and Rammohan, 1999).

There are some exceptions, such as veterans' GAs, historical societies, and some fraternal lodges, that often own their own buildings. Paid-staff VGs usually own or rent buildings or space in them. Most GAs do not, renting meeting space only for meeting times at most (not *continuously* by the month or year). GAs most often meet in members' homes or in the buildings of other organizations such as churches and synagogues (Hodgkinson et al., 1989, p. 97), hospitals, schools, colleges and universities, libraries, and bookstores (based on my research in several Massachusetts communities [Appendixes B and C]), either gratis or paying a small use fee. These other organizations who own their own halls or buildings often subsidize GAs by providing meeting space at low or no cost. The imputed value of such subsidization nationally is unknown and should be investigated on a sampling basis.

GAs of some types receive donated goods and services locally, again of unknown cumulative amounts. GAs also receive money donations, some of which is counted in the annual national figures on giving and philanthropy. Most financial aspects of GAs are uncounted on a national or even a lower territorial unit basis; therefore, these are dark matter. I found the annual revenues of 51 GAs (those having complete data out of 59 studied) in one suburb to average $7,805 (median = $2,000). (Chan and Rammohan, 1999, find similar results for 45 GAs in a California county.) Extrapolating that rather flimsy but available mean figure (lacking any other) for 7.5 million associations yields an estimated total of $58.5 billion in GA annual revenues. (Traunstein and Steinman, 1973, find that about 73% of their sample of 48 self-help GAs from one medium-sized midwestern city had annual budgets of less than $5,000.) Better data on many communities' GAs would be nice here, particularly representative national sample data on revenues and similar financial measures for GAs.

This summary figure is quite substantial, even when compared to the $194 billion in 1990 for half the paid-staff VG part of the VNPS found in IRS records (Hodgkinson et al., 1992, p. 27, excluding their imputed values for volunteering). My key point is that, although GAs have small budgets, revenues, and expenditures annually, there are so many millions of them that GAs are economically quite significant cumulatively. It is like the ants and the termites again; they seem small individually but constitute a significant part of the total animal mass on the planet—far more than the combined biomass for the elephants and rhinoceroses. GA funds are raised mainly from dues-paying members, from member donations, and from occasional fund-raising events open to the public (e.g., plant sales, craft fairs, raffles, special meals).

However, *the real "assets" of GAs really are people, specifically members, and more specifically active volunteer members and leaders.* These were counted earlier under the category of "people." But how can one put an accurate monetary value on a really effective, charismatic, volunteer leader of a GA? An economist could do so, I am sure, but probably would be missing my point. The monetization of the "people assets" (in economic terms, meaning annual wage value, imputed value of volunteer work, human capital, etc.) of the GAs in our VNPS, or in any VNPS, is insufficient for understanding GAs. We need far more information to understand how GAs can generate deep member commitment in ways that businesses and government agencies usually cannot. For example, one key question is, what can a given leader accomplish? How can he or she galvanize members into action and nonmembers into becoming activists? Imputing a dollar value to such activity does not really help to explain it, and such imputation is not even valid unless it captures the impact of the leader and his or her activities, not just the monetary value of time spent.

What are Martin Luther King, Jr., Joan of Arc, Samuel Adams, Susan B. Anthony, and Gandhi "worth" monetarily? Alternatively, how much is what they accomplished as association and movement leaders worth? Does it depend on their economic net worth, their pay for the work done, the imputed value of their volunteer time, or their human capital? Or, does it really depend on their total value to humankind, based on something like "psychosocial leadership capital" or skills (human capital) but going far beyond this economic approach? Psychosocial leadership capital could be defined as their ability to generate commitment and activity from many others to bring to fruition the leaders' and followers' own most deeply held beliefs and values through some collectivities or groups. This is one of the biggest and most crucial gaps in nonprofit research—accurately assessing the "value added" in a broad sense of GA and social movement leaders.

A major contribution of economists to the study of volunteering has been the invention and refinement of quantitative ways in which to impute economic value to volunteer work. I believe that this research line was begun by Wolozin

(1975). He assigned a dollar value per hour to national data on volunteering, based on a recent average wage in the service sector of the economy given that most volunteer work is service work of some type. This seems more reasonable for average volunteers than for leaders.

Various other methods of imputing value to volunteering have been used, with the first two discussed here having been considered and rejected by Wolozin (1975) because of their flaws. Herzog and Morgan (1992) present three imputation methods: *opportunity cost* (what the volunteer could earn at his or her normal wage rate during the hours volunteered), *market price* (the current economic or market value of the precise services the volunteer is performing), and *value added* (the economic value of what the volunteer's work adds to a situation over and above what already was there before the volunteer did his or her volunteer work). I prefer the third imputation method because it potentially can deal best with the value of leaders if measured in a broad sense. Brown (1999) has made additional refinements recently.

Hodgkinson et al. (1992) impute value to volunteer time by counting all volunteer activity without trying to eliminate "nonwork" volunteering, an approach that I think is appropriate. The basis for the imputation was the "average hourly wage for nonagricultural workers" in the same year, increased "by 12[%] to estimate fringe benefits" (p. 71). There are other methods as well including use of minimum wage imputation, which greatly diminishes the actual societal value of volunteers. It imputes the lowest hypothetical volunteer wage rate of any method of imputation mentioned.

Using the nonagricultural wages imputation noted previously, Hodgkinson et al. (1992, p. 71) and Hodgkinson and Weitzman (1996b, p. 69) estimate that the imputed economic value of U.S. *program* volunteering in 1989 is $170 billion and in 1993 is $182 billion, omitting informal volunteering and associational volunteering in GAs. Brown (1999, p. 14) estimates a minimum of $203 billion in 1996. Because narrowly defined (nonreligious) associational volunteering is roughly equivalent in total hours to program volunteering, one may take $170 billion in 1989 as a rough estimate of the imputed value of *associational* volunteer time nationally. (See the prior section of this chapter. Using the precise estimate given earlier, associational volunteering is about 10% greater than program volunteering in hours contributed nationally, omitting religious practice. Hence, the $170 billion estimate should be raised to $187 billion, technically speaking. Rough parity is fine with me as an estimate now.) Herzog and Morgan (1992) also show that formal volunteer work (but also informal volunteering) by women and older Americans actually is very valuable even in economic terms. Such volunteer work produces valuable goods and services that can be given a reasonable imputed value. The same productive value of volunteer work is, of course, also true for younger and male volunteers in formal volunteer programs and in GAs nationally.

CONCLUSION

GAs and their activity are massive in their own right, dwarfing by some measures the paid-staff VGs of the VNPS—cumulative number of VGs, cumulative number of individual official GA members, cumulative number of official GA memberships, cumulative number of active GA volunteers (i.e., active members or analytical members), and cumulative number of FTEs of GA volunteer workers per year.

These data on the massiveness of the GAs and associational volunteering in the United States show that the dark matter of the VNPS is very large indeed by several criteria if one starts with the paid-staff VG flat-earth paradigm and then expands to omitted types of data. Few might be aware of this because such national, data-based, round-earth VNPS overview estimates for the VNPS in the United States go systematically unconstructed and unreported in most, but not all (Hall, 1992; Lohmann, 1992; O'Neill, 1989; Van Til, 1988), major research efforts on the VNPS.

We have, therefore, incomplete and inadequate information on nearly every research question that has ever been examined about the VNPS *as a whole* or about VGs generally, mainly because of ignoring GAs and their associational volunteers. This incompleteness also is true about paid-staff VGs alone if samples were based on IRS lists, which seem to omit about half of the existing, active paid-staff VGs, at least in urban areas, which comprise three-quarters of the U.S. population.

We *have* collectively been afraid to sail off the edge of the flat-earth VNPS, comprised of paid-staff VGs portrayed repeatedly as "all the known VNPS world" in widely respected and supposedly accurate but actually quite miserable VNPS maps. As a result, we have information mainly on the bright matter or "visible stars" of the VNPS but not enough information on the smaller and less obvious stars, planets, moons, and comets, let alone the fine-grained dark matter. *About 85% of the VGs in the United States that ought to be mapped are essentially missing from major current flat-earth VNPS maps.* Thus, the commonly accepted VNPS maps are totally inadequate to guide anyone beyond their cozy little patch of obvious paid-staff VG territory. They might be fairly reasonable guides to one's own block, but they will not guide one to other neighborhoods or parts of the VNPS world.

All in all, I think that some major university social research center, such as the Survey Research Center at the University of Michigan or the NORC at the University of Chicago (or various competing university survey research centers elsewhere), should be given the job of providing regularly updated round-earth maps of the VNPS. Such centers can be trusted to do competent jobs of data collection, as they nearly always have done in the past, and they tend to have access to one or more academics who know something about GAs. They also are much less likely than Independent Sector to have ideological axes to grind that lead to inadequate data collection, analysis, interpretation, and reporting.

A Programmatic Research Agenda for Better VNPS Maps

Whoever does the research and analysis, they need to take Hannan and Freeman's (1989) "population ecology of organizations" approach or Milofsky's (1987) "market approach," including GAs through proper methodology in the population of VGs studied. We cannot know the whole of the VNPS if we refuse to study it openly and thoroughly, as most do, even on a sampling basis (McPherson, 1988, p. 52).

Beginning with such a round-earth view of the VNPS, including GAs and informal volunteering at the least (preferably also youths and transnational volunteering and their GAs), researchers need to do the following:

1. Create a proper sampling frame for organizations and groups of the VNPS in a representative sample of localities in the United States (including Alaska and Hawaii and perhaps the nonstate territories as well). To accomplish this, Dale (1993), Gronbjerg (1989, 1994), and Smith (Appendix B) should be consulted.

2. Sample randomly nonprofits from all IRS tax-exempt categories as well as non-profits from random localities selected as part of Requirement 1. Adjust sampling ratios to try to include roughly equal numbers of paid-staff nonprofits and GAs, based on nonprofit names.

3. Do very brief screening interviews or mail questionnaires with random nonprofits to further identify GAs and paid-staff nonprofits. Paid-staff nonprofits generally will be reachable by telephone, but most GAs will not be initially. A letter or post-card to GA leaders generally will yield the phone number(s) of a current leader in each GA willing to be interviewed. Maintain the GA versus paid-staff nonprofit balance of nonprofits in the sample, later extrapolating proportionately.

4. Use telephone interviews, or mail questionnaires if necessary, to obtain structure and process data about sampled nonprofits, attempting to have nearly identical questions for both GAs and paid-staff nonprofits so far as is feasible. Data gathering independently from two or even three different leaders in each nonprofit will yield greater validity. Seek nonprofit published documents and unpublished records, if available, to bolster key estimates.

5. Determine whether analytical members (Smith, 1972c) are paid, partially paid (stipended volunteers), or pure volunteers and in what numbers. Get data from all types of nonprofit affiliates, not just from official members and official employees.

6. Find out what high-probability remuneration or other exchange "items" analytical members (including paid employees) receive for their "work," which includes

"mere attendance" at organizational events and meetings. (Having co-members present is a service to oneself, as one's presence is a service to the co-members. Effort certainly is involved in getting there at the right time and considering opportunity costs.) Determine whether official members of GAs are simply people who show up or are on a preexisting formal membership list.

7. Ask a small subsample of nonprofit analytical members about attitudes regarding the organization and the work, paid or volunteer, perhaps using mail-back questionnaires. Cover other elements of individual voluntary altruism versus other influences (Smith, 1994a) with a subsample of individual respondents.

8. Do the same for the whole organization, examining documents, files, and interview reports regarding purposes, ideology, structure, and so on (see Part II). Obtain recent organization budgets, annual accounting or balance sheets, and so on, if available.

9. Include a national representative sample of adults (and perhaps a subsample of youths ages 12-17 years) who are asked about their GA activities and influences on participation. Also ask about program and informal volunteering, using Independent Sector questions to some extent to check their methodologies. Aided recall for both GA and program volunteering is necessary. Inquiry should detail membership; volunteer activity or active membership; and leadership on committees, in elected or appointed offices, and on the boards of directors for the two or three GAs or volunteer programs in which the respondents are most active. Total GA memberships and program volunteerships should be noted.

10. Induce random subsamples of the national individual sample to keep time diaries for a week or month at different times of the year for different subsamples. Ask respondents to use "VW" as a symbol for volunteer work in their time diaries when it is occurring (work for a GA is volunteering, as is informal helping of nonfamily members).

11. Include a small subsample of businesses and government agencies, preferably from the localities being studied to find VGs. Ask their leaders and a subsample of analytical members (in this case, mainly employees but also including program volunteers affiliated with these work organizations [Smith, 1972c]) the same types of questions asked nonprofit leaders and members, obtaining relevant documents.

12. Analyze the data to create (a) by extrapolation, as accurate as possible, a round-earth VNPS map for the United States dealing with the issues and types of indicators in the present chapter; (b) a rigorous comparison of the results with prior flat-earth VNPS maps and the present chapter's attempt at a round-earth map; (c) a comprehensive view of both volunteering and paid work comparing the motivations for each; and (d) a comprehensive view of VGs, their structure, and their processes, comparing GAs with paid-staff VGs (and VGs generally) to businesses and government agencies. Eventually, data need to be collected for a similar comparison of VGs with households/families.

13. Examine the data for results by community or other locality and by larger territorial units if the sampling permits including the entire VNPS. Also, examine the
data by VG purposive and analytical types (Smith, 1996) and by other important
variables such as incorporated versus unincorporated VGs as self-reported and in
state records, IRS-registered versus nonregistered VGs as self-reported and in
IRS records, Form 990 filers versus not Form 990 filers among IRS-registered
VGs, high SES versus other status VGs, and male-dominated versus non-male-
dominated VGs. This will permit drawing accurate national conclusions about the
nature of the IRS list of VGs in relation to the rest of the VNPS—the other 90% of
nonprofits in the United States.

I argue that GAs, which are mainly the self-production or member benefit
segment of the VNPS (Perrow, 1970; Smith, 1991), are as massive in their own
way and certainly as important as the more established paid-staff VG nonmember service or so-called "public service" segment of the VNPS (Smith, 1997a).
This is true, even though the latter paid-staff VG segment includes most of the
larger VGs and also most paid employees, revenues, and equity of the sector.
Too many nonprofit researchers, in my view, are attracted to this superficial
"bigness" or "brightness" of paid-staff VGs in the VNPS. In so doing, they
ignore the cumulative size and impact of GAs as the dark matter. They ignore the
termites and go for the elephants—the "glamour nonprofits," one might say.
This approach is fine for scholarly tourists but hardly suits the emergent field of
nonprofit and voluntary action research. The strength of GAs lies in their people, their cumulative numbers, their volunteer activities, and especially their
commitment and values as associational volunteers and GAs. Their overall
impact is very large and important, as I show in Smith (1997a) and in Chapter 9.

As for the issue of flat-earth maps, I simply quote Salamon (1993) and suggest that the interested reader contemplate it in the context of data and extrapola-
tions reviewed in this chapter: "There remains reason for concern on the part of
the research community in this field that so much of the basic data gathering on
this sector is being concentrated in an organization [Independent Sector] that
has such a clear stake in portraying a positive public image about the sector"
(p. 166).

Salamon (1993) goes on to state, however, that the *Nonprofit Almanac* is an
"extremely valuable addition to the source materials on the nonprofit sector in
the United States" (p. 171). I concur with both statements, which are not mutually contradictory. Science proceeds by successive approximations to the truth,
and not necessarily in a linear manner. I am attempting to move us a bit further
toward the truth about GAs in the United States and elsewhere, and I cannot do
so without an occasional critique of the published works of my predecessors
in research and even (rarely) their possible motivations. Furthermore, I feel
that it is unfortunate, and perhaps even unfair, that very able and well-meaning

scholars have used IRS or state data on nonprofits for their research, believing them to be reasonably accurate. This assumption probably was reasonable at the time. When in fact this turns out to be false now given additional methodological research, these scholars will be, to some extent, tarred by the brush I wield in this chapter, and I regret this.

Part II

THE DISTINCTIVE NATURE OF GRASSROOTS ASSOCIATIONS

Introduction

Adherents to the paid-staff nonprofit flat-earth paradigm usually ignore the internal structures and processes of grassroots associations (GAs) by omitting GAs generally as a special type of nonprofit. Alternatively, such scholars and practitioners sometimes implicitly assume that the internal structures and processes of GAs are roughly similar to the structures and processes of paid-staff voluntary groups (VGs) without empirical data to support this. Or, the adherents to this flat-earth VNPS paradigm just ignore the internal structures and processes of GAs because they believe that such phenomena are too informal to stand up to careful research scrutiny.

My round-earth VNPS paradigm, by contrast, suggests examining in depth how GA structures and processes can be similar to or different from paid-staff VG structures and processes. So far, I have found no such ideal studies with *internal* comparisons of broad samples of paid-staff VGs and GAs for the same studies and territories, using basically identical data-gathering approaches such as interviews and questionnaires. From studies of GAs only, as intensively reviewed in this part the book, *significant differences from paid-staff VG overview results seem to occur for many aspects of GAs.*

I infer such differences by comparing the literature reviewed here to the synthesized conclusions of major documents of the paid-staff VG literature, presenting the results in tables in the various chapters (except Chapter 8). Documents of the paid-staff VG literature that I have consulted in drawing my conclusions include the following (listing mainly books, although hundreds of articles in the major journals also have been perused): Anheier and Seibel

(1990); Berry (1997); Billis (1993a); Borst and Montana (1977); Bowen et al. (1994); Brilliant (1990); Brody (1996); Bruce (1994); Butler and Wilson (1990); Carver (1997); Connors (1988); Conrad and Glenn (1983); Coston (1998); DiMaggio and Anheier (1990); Drucker (1990); Estey (1981); Feld, Jordan, and Hurwitz (1994); Fisher (1993, 1998); Gamson (1990); Gidron, Kramer, and Salamon (1992); Gittell (1980); Gronbjerg (1993); Hall (1990); Hammack and Young (1993); Handy (1988); Hansmann (1980); Harris (1998b); Herman and Associates (1994); Herman and Heimovics (1991); Herman and Van Til (1989); Hodgkinson, Weitzman, and Kirsch (1989); Hodgkinson et al. (1992); Houle (1989); Howe (1997); Hrebenar (1997); James (1989); Johnstone (1992); Knauft, Berger, and Gray (1991); Knoke (1986, 1990b); Knoke and Prensky (1984); Kramer (1984); Kramer et al. (1993); Leat (1993); LeGrand and Robinson (1986); Lipset, Trow, and Coleman (1956); Lohmann (1992); MacKeith (1993); Mason (1984, 1996); McCarthy et al. (1992); Moyer (1984); O'Neill and Young (1988); Oster (1995); Poulton (1988); Powell (1987); Rekart (1993); Rose-Ackerman (1986); Salamon (1992); Salamon and Anheier (1994); Sills (1957); Smith and Freedman (1972); Smith and Van Til (1983); Smith and Lipsky (1993); Stanton (1970); Van Til (1988); Weisbrod (1988); Wolch (1990); Wood (1981); Yamazaki and Miyamoto (1988); Young (1983); Young et al. (1993); and Zald (1970).

In distinguishing empirically between GAs and paid-staff VGs, my suggested rule-of-thumb cutting point is 1 full-time equivalent (FTE = 1,700 work hours in a 12-month period, according to Hodgkinson et al., 1992, p. 71) of paid staff or more for a nonprofit to be a paid-staff VG, especially when concentrated in a single individual. The more refined criterion is for a volunteer VG to have 50% or more of its "work" (activity) hours performed in a given year by volunteers, whereas a paid-staff VG (including GAs and supralocal volunteer groups) has less than 50% of its work hours performed in a given year by paid staff.

Paid-staff VGs have some of the same general characteristics of nonprofits as do GAs. They are significantly autonomous groups that are "nonprofit in nature," meaning that they manifest by definition some significant degree of voluntary altruism but not as much as GAs and other volunteer groups (see Chapter 1). However, some paid-staff pseudo-nonprofits in developed nations have eliminated most or all of the voluntary altruism and operate more or less as businesses disguised as nonprofits (Bennett and DiLorenzo, 1989, 1994; Brody, 1996; Gaul and Borowski, 1993; Starkweather, 1993). Mason (1984) argues that paid-staff VGs and GAs generally have some common structural and operational features. Seeing both as types of VGs, I agree on most of the points he makes. My view of such similarities and differences is presented in the tables in the various chapters in this part of the book.

Paid-staff nonprofits are the "bright matter" of the nonprofit sector, generally obvious to one and all. They tend to be much larger in financial equity and revenues, as shown in the prior chapter, and also, by definition, larger in paid staff FTEs than GAs. They are much more likely to appear in their state non-profit corporation listings and in IRS tax-exempt listings (see Chapter 2). They have a variety of types of impact on society and, in many cases, on their clients (e.g., schools/colleges, hospitals, social service agencies). The appropriate comparative studies of GAs and paid staff VGs have not yet been done, so it is unclear how much relative impact the two types of VGs have, on average, especially per capita of target individuals per year and per dollar of revenue or per hour of "work" time per year.

Some common examples of paid staff VGs would include larger foundations, nonprofit schools and universities, nonprofit hospitals, nonprofit research institutes, major nonprofit orchestras and museums, and nonprofit social agencies. Some scholars use the term *voluntary agencies* at times to refer to *all* paid staff VGs, but the former term applies mainly to a personal social service-providing subset of paid-staff VGs such as nonprofit health or social welfare agencies. The term *social agencies* does not properly apply to other paid-staff VGs.

In the next seven chapters, I review research and theory on seven major aspects of GAs in contrast to work organizations, particularly paid-staff VGs:

- Chapter 3: Formational characteristics are the result of decisions made in the formation process of a new GA.

- Chapter 4: Internal guidance systems are ideologies and incentive systems.

- Chapter 5: Internal structures are norms that determine the ways in which GAs are set up.

- Chapter 6: Internal processes include miscellaneous operational features such as GA activity timing, action repertoires, socialization and training, and becoming deviant.

- Chapter 7: "Leadership" concerns the usual types of GA leaders, modes of entry into these roles, and leader education and training, whereas GA "environments" refer to how GA structures and operations are affected by the external environment of the GA.

- Chapter 8: Life-cycle changes are ways in which GAs change over their life cycles.

- Chapter 9: Impact deals with how GAs affect members or the GA environment, whereas effectiveness factors are the means used to achieve such impact.

3

Formational Characteristics

In this chapter, I review the generally thin literature on what I call "formational characteristics" and give my own theoretical perspective on each choice. These choices relate to aspects of a grassroots association (GA) that I hypothesize need to be decided initially by the founders or soon after formation so as to pursue the process of GA formation/launching successfully. They are not necessarily the result of conscious choices, but they occur by default nonetheless if a group is to be formed as or is to become a GA.

I take as a given here that there is at least one founder—one leader who is interested in forming some type of group for whatever reasons. Rock (1988) argues correctly that an organization comes about because of at least one person with an idea who must then convince others to act as if the group exists (Smith, 1967). The precise form of the leadership structure is not assumed here but rather is part of formational choices in what follows (e.g., degree of internal autonomy, democracy, and operating style).

THE BASIC GA FOUNDER CHOICES

A number of features of GAs tend to be determined initially by the founders because certain decisions about structure and process are so basic that they need to be made before any set of people can really begin to function as a group (Smith, 1967). These decisions are studied very rarely, both because they are difficult to identify and study and because most scholars take them for granted.

But each decision usually is the result of some consideration of alternative options rather than being forced on the GA founders. We need *much* more knowledge about the GA formation and GA dissolution processes.

Nearly all GA research focuses on the middle period of routine GA operation. Such research ignores the beginnings and endings that are nonroutine disjunctive events of great importance in GA and other voluntary group (VG) life cycles. Ignoring GA births and deaths is analogous to physiologists hypothetically studying humans only from 1 year of age to, say, 1 year prior to death. Such an approach is very incomplete, even though the majority of an individual's life or a GA's span in years would be covered.

Choice of the Nonprofit Sector for the New Group

Even where GA formation has been studied directly, we usually do not have research knowledge regarding how the founders chose the general nonprofit form as contrasted with the government, business, or even household form of organization. In theory, one could create a commune, as a household form of organization, to accomplish nearly any goal that VGs accomplish (Zablocki, 1981). Alternatively, one could attempt to create a government agency (e.g., a town committee in a small town) or a business to accomplish certain goals that are the focus of GAs or other VGs.

A few researchers have examined the general question of the origins of organizational form or sector linkage. Ben-Ner and Van Hoomissen (1991) present a neat, simple, but general theory that assumes that attempts first will be made to meet demand through for-profit firm formation (p. 524). If that fails to meet demand (i.e., market failure), then either a lobby group will attempt to get government financing and form a government agency or a "self-provision coalition" will attempt to form a VG. Either lobbying failure or government agency failure to meet unsatisfied demand will lead to more of the same and to attempts to form VGs to meet that unsatisfied demand. VGs also can fail to meet demand once formed, leading either to more lobbying and government agency formation or to more VG formation attempts. This analysis focuses on paid-staff VGs seeking public or club goods, not GAs.

Weisbrod (1988) was one of the first to point to government failure to meet demand as a source of VGs. Hansmann (1980) argued that VGs arose from a lack of trust in other types of organizations. LeGorreta and Young (1986), using a case study approach, found support for both of the forgoing approaches to sector choice in their analysis of why three for-profit firms and two government agencies became paid-staff VGs. Salamon (1987) argued that VGs could arise from failure to meet demand in the government, market, or nonprofit sector. A few others also have made contributions bearing on this sector choice issue for paid-staff VGs (e.g., Bielefeld and Corbin, 1996; Billis and Glennerster, 1994).

One study bearing on this general issue of nonprofit form choice specifically for GAs is that of Perlstadt (1975), who studied volunteer ambulance corps in Michigan in comparison with nonvolunteer ambulance services. This type of GA is particularly apt here because the ambulance services could, in principle, be done by groups in any of the other sectors. Perlstadt found that in smaller towns (less than 1,000 population), ambulance corps tended to be government supported, whereas in larger towns, volunteer GA corps predominated. In cities, government and business ambulance services predominated. However, it is not clear whether these results come from an initial decision or a later one and whether they were conscious decisions or not.

One might conjecture that group founders have mental images of the different possible group sectoral forms that affect their choices of such group forms. Founders also might have personal attitudes or values that lead to selection of certain sectoral or subsectoral forms (cf. Etzioni, 1961). Or, some people might have a repulsion from a given group form such as "work organizations" or governments (cf. Knoke and Prensky, 1984). Within the voluntary nonprofit sector (VNPS), founders might feel attracted to or repelled by either the paid-staff VG form (Drucker, 1990) or the GA form (see other chapters in Part II). Such personal preferences of the founders might be significantly influenced by societal attitudes around them. For example, Sidjanski (1974) reports that the Swiss generally support the voluntary association form but are strongly opposed to the use of protest, let alone violence, by any group. Such public attitudes would cause most Swiss GA founders to avoid formation of protest groups, let alone violent protest groups, and this seems to be the case.

Thus, my most basic explanation for founder choice of the VNPS as a social or sector location is that the VNPS best reflects public attitudes about where voluntary altruism should be expressed in group form in modern society. Group founders reflect these public attitudes. Nonprofit founders tend to want to associate with like-minded others to pursue voluntary altruism. I argue that the VNPS is the societal niche of nonprofits, not just by definition but also empirically in terms of founder motivations.

Two other interesting ideas in the literature bear on the present issue. Hardin (1977) raises the question of the "carrying capacity of the environment" regarding altruism and altruistic behavior versus egotism. He suggests that only a relatively small amount of "pure altruism" is likely. I have argued the same point (Smith, 1981; see also Chapter 1). If this limitation on altruism is true, then VGs generally, being based on significant voluntary altruism and perhaps some pure altruism (see Chapter 1), would tend to be a minority of all groups, as seems to be the case in all societies studied. Economic, family/household, and governmental needs tend to be more pressing in societies on the whole than do voluntary altruism needs and groups. There might, of course, be other reasons for VGs always being a minority of groups in a society, but the point is intriguing.

Another interesting point is suggested by the findings of Bryman, Gillingswater, and McGuinness (1992), who describe how community transport nonprofits for the disabled tend to become more complex and professionalized over time, attempting to adapt to their environments by adopting private sector practices (see also extensive formalization references in Chapter 8). Such changes of a VG from GA to paid-staff based over the life cycle suggest that sector choices for a group or an organization are not necessarily permanent and can be altered, either with or without making appropriate changes in sector labels and tax statuses of the entities involved (Bennett and DiLorenzo, 1994; Starkweather, 1993). The case studies of LeGoretta and Young (1986) also show directly that group sector choices, even with appropriate legal labels, are not necessarily permanent, so that businesses and government agencies can become VGs. Presumably, the reverse also could occur.

There needs to be more direct inquiry into group founder motivations for choosing one sector or another as a social location for the group in relation to current public attitudes and stereotypes of different group types and their appropriate structures and activities. The role of informal relations with significant others and with reference groups in founders' initial decisions has not been investigated, to my knowledge. The process of making initial formational decisions should be studied as a process over time rather than assuming that it occurs at just one brief point or period in time.

Choice of Member Benefit Versus Nonmember Benefit Goals

Perrow (1961) made an important distinction between official goals and operative goals in organizations. The operative goals are the ones that the organization structure and operations tend to seek in actuality, whatever the organization *says* about its "official" goals. I am concerned here with operative goals of groups, not mainly official goals. Groups, including GAs, can have operative goals that are either nonmember benefit oriented *or* member benefit oriented *or both* (Smith, 1991). Both approaches are important to the total society and the VNPS.

I hypothesize that once group founders have chosen the VNPS, the next most central question is whether to choose mainly member benefit or nonmember benefit goals or a significant mix of the two. Nonmember benefit goals are more likely to be chosen where the founders have either a traditional nonmember service orientation or a focus on sociopolitical issues relating to the common good (i.e., public goods) as they see it. Member benefit goals are more likely to be chosen where the founders wish to emphasize close interpersonal interaction in the pursuit of such other specific goals—self-help in health, religion, sociability, aesthetics, hobbies, self-helping economic system support, and so on. Member benefit goals, thus, tend to be chosen to promote a means primarily and then a specific end secondarily. Most GAs have member benefit goals, whereas most paid-staff VGs have nonmember benefit goals.

In a stratified sample of GAs in a single suburb (Appendix C), I found that informal or semiformal GAs constituted 36% of 59 GAs studied (Smith, 1992b). Wuthnow's (1994, p. 47) recent national sample survey of U.S. adults regarding small mutual support GAs reports similar results; he finds that about 40% of U.S. adults say that they belong to some type of small support GA. He also notes, "Smaller groups have an enormous advantage in adapting to a more fluid social environment. They require virtually no resources other than the time their members devote to them each week, so they can start with relative ease and disband just as easily" (p. 23).

In most cases, the founders of a member benefit group are unlikely to believe that they can make a profit and, hence, be a viable business operating the group. Given significant voluntary altruism, the founders are unlikely to want to make a profit even if it occurs to them and if they think they could. A few for-profits that are directly imitating GAs, such as Weight Watchers, are rare exceptions.

Member benefit group founders also are unlikely to believe that they can form a government or become a government agency given their goals. Governments focus on providing public goods to all the official residents/citizens of a given territory, whereas member benefit groups tend to be much more selective in their memberships. Unlike governments, member benefit groups rarely have a monopoly on the legitimate use of force in their territories and have no interest in gaining such a monopoly given significant voluntary altruism.

Nor does forming some new type of communal household occur to very many member benefit group founders because they usually do not want to radically change their present household living arrangements, usually in conventional marriages and families (but see Carden, 1969, for an example of the Oneida Community as an exception during the mid-1800s; see also Kanter, 1972, and Zablocki, 1981, on communes more generally).

These types of considerations usually leave VGs and the VNPS by default as the group type and sector of choice for most *member* benefit groups. Only if founders and potential members would be willing to live together in the same group household does a commune or "voluntary community" become feasible to accomplish such founder goals. Even if the group founders have nonmember benefit goals, the choice to become a GA is greatly facilitated by the low cost and social simplicity of forming a GA versus forming a commune or a work organization. Forming the latter involves, respectively, much more personal dislocation of founders' or members' prior personal lives or much greater initial investments of money in the formation of the group to pay legal fees for incorporation and tax exemption; to pay full-time staff; to rent or buy a headquarters office; and to pay for furniture, supplies, utilities, and so on.

The more general explanation of institutional isomorphism discussed by DiMaggio and Powell (1983) for organizations probably also plays a role. Founders of GAs tend to follow in the footsteps of sector choice and group structure choice of other founders of member benefit groups and small nonmember benefit groups, founding GAs rather than communes, government agencies, for-profit businesses, or even paid-staff VGs. The barriers to forming a paid-staff VG include the need for substantial resources to be able to do so, as just noted. Also, paid-staff VGs tend to be nonmember benefit organizations rather than member benefit groups and, hence, do not seem to fit the needs of most GA founders.

In sum, I hypothesize that group founders tend to form GAs partly because they have numerous other GAs as models in the same and other places that focus on member benefit goals. GAs seem to be the "right" type of group form for receiving member benefits in the company of nonrelatives (i.e., outside the family/household) given general public attitudes in modern societies. They require very little money or change in lifestyles to form, unlike all the usual alternative forms of groups in modern society including communes. The ease of forming GAs is shown partly by their great frequency in the United States and elsewhere, now and in earlier times (Smith, 1997c; see also Chapter 2).

Founders of GAs tend to be motivated basically by voluntary altruism in addition to the forgoing organizational considerations. Group founders tend to form GAs because such a group form fits best with their voluntary altruism values on a low economic scale, where forming a paid-staff VG combines similar voluntary altruism values with a much higher economic investment initially. GA formation also is more likely than paid-staff VG formation when the founders have member benefit goals for the group. If a paid-staff VG has member benefit goals, then it is likely to have grown larger and more successful from a GA base so as to be able to afford a paid staff and full-time office.

Some GA founders are different from the preceding "standard model." Instead of member benefit goals, some founders of GAs have *nonmember benefit goals* such as local ambulance squad founders, founders of environmental or political influence GAs, and founders of volunteer-run Salvation Army units. In these instances, most of the standard model explanations given previously still apply. There still are difficulties of locating a new nonmember benefit group based on voluntary altruism in the other sectors. If the group is to be a polymorphic branch of a larger national VG, then the location in the VNPS is automatic. The limiting requirement for substantial funding if the founders choose the paid-staff VG or any other work organization form also is crucial. The institutional isomorphism, voluntary altruism, and common interest associational structure preference explanations also continue to be important for nonmember benefit GA founders. There seem to be no research data on these hypotheses.

Choice of Group Style and Subculture

Closely related to the choice of group sector is the choice of group style of operation and its associated subculture. Any group, GA or otherwise, can be operated in various ways. A group needs to establish a consistent way of operating, whatever its purposive type and whether it is a member benefit or nonmember benefit group. Frequent changes of style of operation are likely to be dissatisfying to members and lead to group dissolution. And even if a group has a consistent style of operation and subculture (just as a successful business tends to have one [Ouchi and Wilkins, 1985]), these might be dissatisfying to most members, again leading to group dissolution. I could find no study of such GA situations. This is partly because dissatisfying GAs tend to dissolve fairly quickly; hence, they are especially difficult to find and study. Also, no researcher has yet had sufficient interest to overcome these practical difficulties.

By definition, GA founders must choose to form a group, which means that they need to find other people who will agree to pursue a common goal with each other, to communicate with each other, and to have a sense of collective identity with each other (Smith, 1967). The process of doing this in the formation of a GA is not at all well understood empirically. Founders of a semiformal or formal GA also need to choose some name for their group at an early point, even if the name is fairly general (e.g., "the men's group" is the name of a social support group of men in a Maine town who meet regularly in each others' homes to discuss issues of interest). Membership boundaries and leadership structure might remain vague unless and until a GA becomes a formal GA rather than a semiformal or informal one (Smith, 1972c, 1992b).

In general, GAs tend to be short-lived *even if successful,* with some dissolving quickly, some lasting 5 to 10 years and then dying, and others lasting longer (especially if they are polymorphic, which means they have national or regional headquarters as sponsorship and support). A small but as yet not precisely known proportion of GAs at some time are transformed into paid-staff nonprofits (and, very rarely, into government agencies or even businesses). Sometimes, GA forms might be chosen initially because the founders anticipate only a *short-term need* for their groups, as seems to be true partly in Harambee selfhelp socioeconomic development projects in Kenya (Orora and Spiegel, 1981) and in GAs protesting the siting of a waste facility in their neighborhood (Freudenberg and Steinsapir, 1991). Founder expectation of only short-term life for a GA is likely to be one influence in choosing informal group style.

There are various statements of organizational styles and subcultures in the research literature on organizations more generally, not necessarily describing GAs only or mainly (Ouchi and Wilkins, 1985). Rothschild-Whitt (1979) presents an interesting picture of what she calls the "collectivist organization," in which collective or social values such as voluntary altruism predominate over the utilitarian and coercive values that are more important in the business and government sectors, respectively. In my terms, group founders with more voluntary altruism tend to form GAs as collectivist groups because paid-staff VGs tend to be more bureaucratic work organizations. Collectivist GAs are informal and democratic in operation.

Kanter and Zurcher (1973) make a statement on the importance of valuing small size in groups and "alternative institutions," which certainly fits GAs generally. These authors argue that small size permits greater interpersonal contact and more fulfilling human interaction among participants, more pervasive participation, and more power sharing (less inequality). GA founders probably form GAs in part because they value small size so as to preserve more human and direct, rather than impersonal and mediated, interactions as well as more internal democracy. In valuing small group size, GA founders also are valuing informal group operational style and less organizational complexity. These can be added to the previously noted factors in sector choices and group style choices by GA founders.

Small size and a looser, more personal and informal style of operation also are compatible with holistic service provision in nonmember service GAs, according to Kanter and Zurcher (1973), not just in member service/benefit groups. Others also have written about such alternative service nonprofits, which sometimes are GAs and sometimes are paid-staff VGs. Gummer (1988), for example, describes hospices as alternative agencies with the characteristics of holistic service provision, power sharing with participants, and small size. The author notes that "small size by itself does not deter the growth of bureaucratic practices" (p. 40), but it can *permit* a group to avoid bureaucracy if other factors are present, whereas large organizations inevitably are bureaucratic. Miller and Phillip (1983) also describe the alternative service agency but do so more broadly, citing various VG examples.

Social-emotional support GAs, especially self-help GAs, seem to be more likely to be formed by founders looking for an informal atmosphere in their groups and informal operations (Lavoie, Borkman, and Gidron, 1994; Powell, 1994; Wuthnow, 1994). Steinman and Traunstein (1976) conclude from their study of 67 self-help GAs that such groups try to maintain solidarity and autonomy while avoiding the usual staff-centeredness, bureaucratization, and hierarchy of standard, paid-staff VG, human service agencies. Stanton (1970) gives an excellent illustration of the frequent goal displacement in supposedly nonmember benefit paid-staff VGs, where the needs of the staff bureaucracy overcome the needs of the clients. Part of this difference between informal and more complex organizations seems to result from local versus national scope of the organizations, with GAs affiliated with national organizations tending to be more complex and formalized (Scott, 1991).

The concept of group style can be treated idiographically, seeing qualitative uniqueness of GA style. Or, one can seek quantitative measures of this concept, suitable for survey research. One such quantitative dimension is informality versus formality/complexity. This has been operationalized by many researchers specifically for VGs, sometimes for GAs (Chapin and Tsouderos, 1956; Goodchilds and Harding, 1960; Muehlbauer and Dodder, 1983; Seeley, Junker, and Jones, 1957; Traunstein and Steinman, 1973). More informal GAs are more fluid and lower in structure and usually are smaller in membership (Smith, 1992b). They are quite different from more complex GAs, let alone more complex *paid-staff* VGs (Connors, 1988; Gamson, 1990; Knoke, 1990b).

Riger (1983) notes that low GA complexity can be a result of value systems held by group members. I add here that such a value system in the minds of GA founders is especially important for the subsequent complexity of the GA. The more that *solidarity and financial independence are valued* (no external grants or sponsors), the more likely the GA is to start out and remain informal even if it grows in membership size (Riger, 1983). Valuing efficiency and remunerative rewards, by contrast, tends to result in more complexity and hierarchy, and hence less internal democracy, within a GA. All of the forgoing aspects of informality can vary *within* the context of *formal* GAs—groups with proper names, clear group boundaries, and clear leadership structures (Smith, 1972c). GAs can be informal but still researchable and important, in my view (Smith, 1992b; see also Chapter 1).

Founder choice of the usually informal GA style of operation can be one important way of escaping the "iron cage" of rationalized bureaucratic organizations in contemporary societies that disturbed Weber (1952, p. 182), although he analyzed such bureaucracy so well. Elaborating on Weber specifically for associations, Alexander (1987) argues that the only two basic principles for human interaction are sociolegal compulsion (laws and regulations) and shared commitment that is freely given (voluntary altruism, in my terms). GAs especially represent shared commitment, although paid-staff VGs also represent this principle to a significant degree. For example, quasi-volunteers are hired into sociolegally based work organizations but receive psychic benefits as part of their shared commitment to voluntary altruism and to the related paid-staff VG purposes (see Chapter 1). Paid-staff VGs might tend to be less complex than businesses or governments, but GAs tend to be the least complex and most informal of organizations, sometimes being informal or semiformal groups (Smith, 1992b).

Choice of Relatively Higher Versus Lower Autonomy

Degree of autonomy from external groups and organizations is an initial decision of importance during formation, but this decision can be changed subsequently in some cases (especially by new funding patterns). Autonomy is a dimension that runs from total GA autonomy, as in the case of a unique GA not controlled by or affiliated vertically or horizontally with any other groups anywhere, to total control or domination by some other group or organization, as in the case of a local branch of a national association in which the GA must refer to higher authorities for every significant decision. When a group has no significant autonomy at all, it is not independent but rather part of the group or organization that controls it. Group autonomy also may be seen in terms of independence from major funding received from an external organization or patron and consequent control by this funder such as some government agency or foundation (Horch, 1994; Saltman, 1973).

The present choice dimension emphasizes the power or independence of the GA relative to other external groups or organizations, whether horizontally or vertically. A GA can have or lack autonomy whatever its structural linkage status with another group. Some essentially nominal (i.e., on paper only), external structural linkages leave a GA with very great autonomy, whereas other linkages bind a GA very tightly and leave it little autonomy. Also, a monomorphic (unlinked to a national association) GA can be very tightly bound to and dominated by (a) another group linked horizontally that sponsors it (e.g., church, school, hospital) or by (b) an external funding source to which it has *no* formal linkage, such as a GA dominated by a foundation, a government agency, or a patron as an external funding agency (Horch, 1994; Saltman, 1973).

There is a trade-off between resources and independence of decision making in the founder choice of autonomy level. Founders who try to form a GA that is completely autonomous will tend to have little or no access to the resources of other groups, either locally or supralocally. GA founders who accept sponsorship by some other local organization (e.g., church, school, hospital, foundation) will gain some resource access, if only free meeting space and some local visibility, but will give up some autonomy in decisions and will have to accept some limitations in the GA's activities relative to the policies of its sponsor. Accepting affiliation with a national association (as what I term a polymorphic GA) will bring varying degrees of resource access and limitations on decision making, depending on the policies of the national association. In the extreme case, such a national affiliation might leave the local volunteer group with no significant autonomy at all. I created this typology to refer to whether a group is a unique entity, at whatever territorial level (i.e., monomorphic), or very similar in *form* to one or more other groups as part of some larger whole such as a regional or national association (*poly* = many, *morph* = form) (Smith, 1994b).

A typical *monomorphic GA* would be a unique GA that is not vertically affiliated with any other group or organization at a supralocal level, such as a unique self-help health GA that is concerned with people who have many debilitating allergies, a unique food cooperative GA, or a unique citizen militia GA (see also

DeGrazia, 1957). A typical *polymorphic GA* would be a GA that is like many other GAs as part of a larger state, national, or international nonprofit association such as a local GA branch of the Business and Professional Women's Club nationally, the Ku Klux Klan (with various national organizations in existence), the Freemasons in a U.S. state, or Alcoholics Anonymous internationally.

Scholars who have analyzed national associations with polymorphic GAs attached (vs. without GAs) to a national headquarters generally have remarked on the utility of such GAs, even though the closeness to and amount of control by the national and local associations varied (Seeley et al., 1957; Sills, 1957; Young, Bania, and Bailey, 1996; Zald, 1970). Oster (1992) and Young (1989) have referred to some polymorphic local VGs affiliated with a corresponding supralocal association as "franchise" VGs. A national association typically licenses use of its name, trademark, and logo and also provides some technical assistance in exchange for (a) an annual fee that usually is tied to the membership or revenues of the polymorphic GA and (b) following some nationally set standards of operation. The value of an "established" GA name to a new GA presumably is substantial in attracting new members, although no comparative study has been done to test this hypothesis. The concentration of national headquarters of associations in New York City, Washington, D.C., and Chicago, disproportionately to their populations, is one indicator of the concentration of interorganizational power among national associations (Knoke, 1990b; Smith, 1992a).

GA founders are likely to form a polymorphic GA, I hypothesize, when they have a positive image of some relevant national association and are not fearful about autonomy issues. The positive image involved often results from positive personal experiences of the founders with one or more polymorphic GAs of the national association in the past elsewhere. GA founders are more likely to form a monomorphic GA when they have a stronger "entrepreneurial spirit" and active-effective character (Smith, 1994a) and are more concerned about autonomy issues. GA founders are likely to accept a local sponsor when they are embedded in or have much trust in that sponsor and do not see autonomy as a major issue.

Choice of Appropriate Local Territorial Scope

VGs can vary greatly in initial founder choices regarding territorial scope of operation. The dimension here runs from groups representing a specific local apartment or condominium building to those representing a block, a neighborhood, a community, a multicommunity area, a metropolitan area, a county, two adjacent counties, a larger region of a state, a state, a regional (multistate) base of operation, a national (operating in all four major regions and in 10 or more states) base of operation, a binational (operating in two nations) base of operation, or an international (operating in three or more nations) base of operation.

If the volunteer group formed is to be a GA, then modest local scope must be chosen—no greater than a metropolitan area or two adjacent counties, by my definition. Paid-staff VG founders, by contrast, can choose any territorial scope they wish as part of their VG formation, as can supralocal volunteer group founders. Whether the founders and charter members of a paid-staff VG can create an organization that will be able to meet its intended territorial scope adequately is another question. Grandiose goals for a paid-staff VG might lead to its early demise, whereas some GAs with a very narrow local focus (e.g., a block, an apartment building) might succeed because of this very important "localness."

Founders' initial decision about GA territorial scope can be changed subsequently. In theoretical terms, the "appropriate" territorial scope is one that permits optimal goal attainment by the volunteer group. If a new GA's founders want to affect world peace, then it might be well to have as a scope an entire metropolitan area, where the relative smallness of the proportion of people sharing this interest would have less of a negative effect on GA size. If the purpose of a new volunteer group is to make a particular neighborhood safe for children, then a neighborhood scope GA probably would be most appropriate.

Long ago, Elkin (1978) suggested that much more attention must be paid to the issue of how associations differ in their structures and operations at different territorial levels. Very little comparative research on different territorial levels of associations has been done during the subsequent two decades. When such research is done, it will be useful to compare voluntary associations with similar analytical characteristics and goals across levels of territorial scope. I hypothesize that more localized associations will tend to have greater amounts of face-to-face interaction among members and, thus, will tend to develop greater internal cohesion, other things being equal.

Local volunteer associations with significant autonomy are GAs by definition (see Chapter 1) and are the most prevalent of VGs by far. Milofsky (1988a) notes various special characteristics of local VGs including the fact that their funding arenas or sources of funds (Milofsky and Romo, 1988) tend to differ from higher territorial scope VGs; GAs depend more on internal fund-raising, dues, and contributions, whereas higher territorial scope associations and paid-staff VGs depend more on fees for services (e.g., hospital charges, college tuitions), government contracts, and foundation and corporate grants.

National scope voluntary associations tend to be paid-staff nonprofits, larger in membership and employees, richer in revenues and equity, older, and with headquarters located more often in New York City or Washington, D.C. (Smith, 1992a; cf. local data in Smith, 1992b; see also Knoke, 1990b). Associations of the intervening levels of territoriality (multicounty, state, or regional multistate) are less frequent and little studied. Binational and international associations also are comparatively understudied relative to GAs and national associations, let alone relative to paid-staff nonprofits (but see Feld, Jordan, and Hurwitz, 1994).

Choice of Greater Internal Democracy
(vs. Oligarchy or Elitism)

This is another of those formational decisions that can be changed subsequently, in part because of later desired changes in GA structure and/or in part from changing GA processes. Small membership associations, like mutual aid and social support GAs that are volunteer run and informal, usually are the most democratic in their decision making (Smith, 1992b, 1994b). Larger, more formalized, well-established GAs tend to be less internally democratic and more elitist and oligarchical. Even more elitist and oligarchical are the very large and bureaucratic paid-staff VGs such as Stanford University, the Ford Foundation, and Massachusetts General Hospital (Powell, 1987).

Internal democracy is a founder choice that tends to be associated with the choice of becoming a GA rather than a work organization of any type. Indeed, personal philosophical preferences of group founders for internal democracy often can lead to choice of the GA form in the first place. Those governments that operate as a direct democracy are small and use their citizens as part-time volunteer participants in government decision making, as in New England town meetings. Such a direct democracy is a rarity in modern society, where democracy tends to be representative (if present). When GA founders choose oligarchy initially, the result often is early GA demise when other members become dissatisfied at their exclusion from participation in leadership and decision making (Hamilton, 1980).

Choice of Membership Eligibility Criteria

GA founders need to decide on what types of people or which specific people are desired as members of a new GA. In work organizations, bureaucratic and efficiency considerations tend to dictate performance criteria regarding who might be wanted or needed as analytical members—regular service-providing affiliates of the group (Smith, 1972c). Implicit, informal sociodemographic eligibility criteria such as gender and race/ethnicity are seen as evidence of discrimination in the view of the community and larger society. In GAs, by contrast, formal sociodemographic eligibility criteria can range from very narrow to very wide, as can informal ones. The trade-off for GA founders in this decision on formal eligibility criteria is between creating a greater sense of peer community in the GA by means of restrictive criteria and narrowing down too much the number of potential members in a locality and, thus, dampening GA growth potential there.

Formal sociodemographic eligibility criteria usually are written into the constitution, charter, or bylaws of a GA. Little quantitative study has been done of variations in such criteria, to my knowledge. From my own research on GAs in an eastern suburb (Appendix C), I found that formal eligibility criteria by GAs were relatively infrequent. If present, the most common criteria were some combination of gender, age, and place of residence. Performance criteria for membership eligibility rarely are formalized in GAs.

Far more important for GAs are informal eligibility criteria, which I defined imprecisely in my dissertation (Smith, 1964) as the informal tendencies for certain types of people to be members of given GAs. When eligibility requirements are informal, they are evidenced in shared understandings among established members about the types of persons who *should* be members of a given GA. These understandings are communicated to would-be or actual newcomers to the GA and have real effects on who joins formally or continues to participate (Smith, 1964).

These informal eligibility or attraction criteria for a given GA may be defined more precisely as the average composition of a GA and its dispersion in terms of a variety of sociodemographic and other key personal dimensions. McPherson and his colleagues refer to this as the "niche" or "niche position" of the GA in the local community of GAs (McPherson, 1983a; McPherson, Popielarz, and Drobnic, 1992; McPherson and Ranger-Moore, 1991; McPherson and Rotolo, 1996; Popielarz and McPherson, 1995).

Niches can result in part from founder choices both regarding formal eligibility criteria and regarding which persons to get involved at the beginning in the GA because membership maintenance and subsequent recruitment tend to take place in terms of relatively homogeneous social network ties from initial members (McPherson et al., 1992). Founder choice of a niche with higher competition from other existing GAs will make it harder for that new GA to grow and be successful in its community of GAs because the competing GAs will tend to draw away its actual or potential members (Popielarz and McPherson, 1995).

In semiformal GAs, *member* usually means anyone who participates, or participates regularly, with no formal and complete list of members being kept (D. Smith, 1992b). Typically in such GAs, no one must approve new members for them to join and be accepted (p. 261). I found this in sports booster parent GAs connected with high school sports teams, in 12-step "Anonymous" groups including Alcoholics Anonymous, and in various other types of GAs (Smith, 1992b; see also Appendix C). Fisher (1993, p. 37) mentions loose eligibility criteria for neighborhood groups (*juntas de vecinos*) among the poor in Latin American nations. Goodchilds and Harding (1960) mention similar fairly open eligibility criteria in their study of GAs in a still smaller town, where all GAs seemed to be informal to some degree.

The goals or purposes of the GA can strongly influence founder choices of eligibility requirements. For example, founders of environmental and other advocacy GAs tend to want as many members as possible so as to maximize public, conventional political pressure favoring the environment and ecology

(Yanitskiy, 1992). By contrast, founders of self-help GAs usually keep in mind the basic fact that they tend to work best when small and composed more narrowly of other peer members who share their specific personal problems or stigmas (Powell, 1994; Sagarin, 1969). Relatives or friends of stigmatized people also sometimes are welcomed into self-help GAs but often participate in associated groups that meet separately such as Al-Anon as a family affiliate of Alcoholics Anonymous (Rudy, 1986).

Choice of Diffuseness Versus Specificity of GA Goals and of Specific Goals

GA founders have to choose one or more goals for their new GAs, even given all of the forgoing choices have been made. GAs are groups, and a group must, by my definition, have one or more goals (Smith, 1967). Choice of member benefit or nonmember benefit goals as a type of goal, for example, does not specify which subtype of goal or what mix of specific goals will be sought within either category. The founders also must take a stand, if only implicitly, on the broad question of goal specificity versus diffuseness.

Smith (1997c) indicates that much earlier in human history, GAs tended to have a multiplicity of goals and purposes and, hence, more general goal diffuseness such as guilds for nearly two millennia (Hartson, 1911; Lambert, 1891; see also Scott, 1991, for women's GAs in American history). GAs throughout history have tended to become, as a form of group, more specialized in their goals. GAs can and still do tend to have any of a broad variety of goals or purposes and tend to be successful in their own terms (Verba, Schlozman, and Brady, 1995, pp. 60-61; see also Chapter 9). At a minimum or as a default option, this goal will tend to be mutual sociability and social support among the members. From this base, GAs can take on additional goals if they wish and if they survive long enough based on the mutual support they generate.

There are few goals that cannot be sought and even achieved in a group of the GA form, which gives this latter group form great flexibility. However, among the few goals that are difficult for a group to achieve in GA form are making a lot of money and collecting taxes. The latter really is a subtype of the goal of making a lot of money, but it is one that only governments can follow successfully in the long term by coercion.

GAs usually cannot make a lot of money because of two factors. First, their motivational base in voluntary altruism is contrary to such activity. Second, their economic scale generally is quite low (not much money is involved). On the first factor, GAs and associational volunteer activity in them are leisure time activity, although at times they are serious leisure activity (Stebbins, 1996). Therefore, participants generally do not want to get too involved in economic production that would yield a lot of money. On the second factor, most forms of extensive production of "private goods" rather than services are difficult for GAs to accomplish because they require so much expenditure on capital equipment, participant production time, workspace, tools and equipment, licensing, technological knowledge, and so on. Extensive production of private services by associational volunteers is easier to accomplish, but even here the economic scale is low.

GAs can accomplish most governmental or political goals other than taxation on a small scale in their communities and on a large scale when linked into a national network of GAs (usually with some national headquarters and paid staff). Thus, in certain circumstances, GAs can seek and accomplish war, peace, revolution, guerrilla action, underground resistance, local policing, local fire protection, environmental protection or cleanup, disaster helping, aid and technical assistance to developing countries, public education, and other "public services" as well as the production of some "public goods" such as roads and bridges, riverside levees, and forest and animal preservation.

Nearly all household/family sector goals can be sought and achieved in GAs that begin to overlap in function with households as GA-household hybrids, specifically communes (Kanter, 1972; Zablocki, 1981).

There are trade-offs in the founder choice of one or two specific goals versus many diffuse goals for a new GA. Keeping the goal(s) more specific and singular sometimes permits better goal attainment through more group concentration of energies (see, e.g., Gamson, 1990, for national social movements). On the other hand, Simpson and Gulley (1962) found that diffuseness of organizational goals leads to more membership involvement and internal communication, as usually is sought in GAs.

Choice of How Conventional Versus Deviant to Be in Goals and Means

Nonprofits can be either nondeviant (essentially conforming), partly deviant in a minor way, or fundamentally deviant at any point or for any period of time. This analytical dimension refers to how a GA's goals and activities deviate, if at all, from societal norms and values (Smith, 1995c, forthcoming a). GA founders must choose, at least implicitly, how conventional or deviant the new GA is to be.

Nondeviant GAs. These are conventional GAs in which both the leaders and members are essentially following the societal norms of the society in which the GAs are embedded in terms of both goals and means to achieve them. Such GAs represent by far the majority of GAs in most societies and are viewed by both nonmembers and members as socially acceptable and nonthreatening. Some examples are a Salvation Army local GA chapter, a Unitarian Church Fellowship GA, and a local Parent-Teacher Association.

Partly deviant GAs. These usually are conventional GAs in which some minority of members or one or more of the leaders are temporarily deviant from the relevant societal norms regarding group goals or means or both. Such minor deviance apparently has not been studied in GAs but should be. Minor GA deviance tends to be relatively brief in time once discovered, and when it ends, the GA tends to be able to continue in existence as a conventional GA for a period of at least another five years (an arbitrary longer period) after the minor deviance is discovered and dealt with. Partly deviant GAs usually tend to have a harder time gaining resources—both material resources and participants. A test case of this among paid-staff VGs is the Aramony scandal at the United Way of America (Glaser, 1994). Donations to local United Way chapters fell off significantly around the United States for a few years immediately after the highly publicized scandal, relative to projected organizational and funding growth. This probably occurred because of the widely known crimes and deviance by Aramony and his associates at the national level negatively affecting the image of local United Way chapters as mainly paid-staff VGs.

Fundamentally deviant GAs. These tend to begin their existence as such, with societally deviant goals and/or means, rather than converting from nondeviant or partly deviant GAs. Some examples are witches' covens, underground militia GAs, nudist GAs, cults, and delinquent gangs. Many or most members of partly deviant GAs tend to be oblivious of the existence of such deviance while it is taking place. However, the people who join a fundamentally deviant GA usually know in advance that they are doing so and nearly always know of such deviance once they become members. However, the severity of the GA deviance often is covered up from potential members and even from newcomers for an informal probationary period, until the GA has been able to screen them for GA loyalty and willingness to accept the GA in spite of or because of its fundamental deviance.

The principal founder choice here is between the first and third situations (nondeviant GAs and fundamentally deviant GAs) given that the second situation (partly deviant GAs) tends to occur later on, once a GA has been established as conventional. If GA founders choose to form a fundamentally deviant GA, then they are choosing to keep voluntary altruism rather strictly among the GA members, with possible or probable harm to the general welfare of nonmembers, at least in the view of the latter. This is likely to occur when the founders have powerful positive attitudes toward the deviant goals or means involved, as contrasted with attitudes toward more conventional alternative goals or means.

Such attitudes might spring from desire for special entertainment, from fear, from lust, or from a variety of other emotions that are not spoken to sufficiently well by conventional groups. The default choice is to form a conventional GA, and most founders take this option to avoid the probable hassles of public opprobrium and social control agency counteractivity.

Related to the present founder choice historically is whether the GA was oriented toward benefits for insiders or outsiders in society—the establishment/elite versus the poorer and less powerful (Smith and Associates, forthcoming). Before 1800, I argue, nearly all GAs tended to be founded by and for insiders in society, whether member benefit or nonmember benefit GAs. But since 1800 or so, and somewhat during earlier times, some GAs have been founded by and for outsiders to help them make status progress, improving their categorical status opportunities and life chances. On occasion, and mainly during the past 200 years, insiders have founded and operated some GAs for outsiders as beneficiaries, especially for slaves, depreciated racial/ethnic minorities, the body/mind limited, the poor, and children (Scott, 1991; Skocpol, 1992).

CONCLUSION

Without my being able to make explicit intrastudy empirical comparisons, the reader now should be aware of how greatly GAs, as described and discussed in this chapter, differ from paid-staff VGs and other work organizations with which the reader is familiar. Founders of GAs must make a series of specific choices regarding formational characteristics that have different outcomes from similar choices that paid-staff VG founders must make. It is all the more true that there are important differences in GA founder decision outcomes relative to the decision outcomes of founders of businesses, government agencies, and households/families.

GAs as significantly autonomous local volunteer-run associations are simply very different from paid-staff-based VGs (Smith and Shen, 1996; Smith, 1994b; see also other chapters in Part II). That is one central reason why I am writing this book to complement paid-staff VG overviews (Bowen et al., 1994; Carver, 1997; Connors, 1988; Drucker, 1990; Handy, 1988; Herman and Associates, 1994; Hodgkinson et al., 1992; Houle, 1989; MacKeith, 1993; O'Neill, 1989; Poulton, 1988; Powell, 1987; Salamon, 1992).

Differences and similarities in the outcomes of founder choices between GAs and paid-staff VGs are shown in summary form in Table 3.1. These are ideal types based on this chapter and the research literature on paid-staff VGs just referred to cursorily. Both types of groups choose the VNPS as a sector of location because of the voluntary altruism of their founders. GA founders are much more likely to choose member benefit goals than are paid-staff VG founders, who tend to choose nonmember benefit goals. GA founders tend to choose an

TABLE 3.1 Comparison of Average Outcomes of Founder Choices for Grassroots Associations Versus Paid-Staff Voluntary Groups

Grassroots Associations	*Paid-Staff Voluntary Groups*
Voluntary nonprofit sector location	Voluntary nonprofit sector location
Mostly member benefit	Mostly nonmember benefit
Mostly informal group style	Mostly formal group style
Mostly high autonomy	Mostly high autonomy
Moderate local scope	Moderate local scope
High internal democracy	Low internal democracy
Some sociodemographic membership criteria	Some paid-staff performance criteria
More diffuse goals	Fewer and more specific goals
Conventional goals and means	Conventional goals and means

informal style of group operation, whereas paid-staff VG founders tend to choose a more formal style of operation.

Both types of VG founders tend to seek high autonomy from external groups, even ones with which they are affiliated or that sponsor them. Both types of VG founders tend to choose moderate local territorial scope. GA founders tend to choose greater internal democracy than do paid-staff VG founders. GA founders are more likely to set formal sociodemographic membership criteria such as age, gender, and/or residential location than are paid-staff VG founders for their paid and volunteer staff. The latter founders might set performance criteria for paid staff. GA founders tend to set more diffuse goals than do paid-staff VG founders, with social support and sociability being more important to the former. Both GA and paid-staff VG founders tend to choose conventional goals and means, rather than deviant ones, for their new VGs. All of these differences in initial VG choices by founders tend to persist over time, continuing to differentiate GAs and paid-staff VGs in ways discussed in other chapters in Part II.

4

Internal Guidance Systems

By definition (Smith, 1967), all groups must guide their members to some extent regarding appropriate and acceptable thoughts (ideology), motives (desires), feelings (emotions), and actions (behaviors). The presence of a group goal and group style norms, among other factors, sees to this. The very existence of a group is a type of "fictive reality" in the heads of its members as individual humans—a type of mental computer program for the set of individual members to act, think, feel, and strive differently from nonmembers because they are group members. For example, as a member of the Boy Scouts while a youth, I was supposed to be somewhat more moral in my actions as well as more knowledgeable about "camp craft" than most of my nonmember male friends in elementary school.

The guidance system of a group has two main parts: the ideology and the incentive system. The ideology spells out the goals and the reasons for them. The incentive system is the set of rewards and punishments for members that is manipulated by the group so as to attain group goals by accepted group means. The actions that are most right for members to do are those that are most rewarded by the incentive system of the grassroots association (GA). Those that are most wrong for members to do are the ones most punished by the incentive system of the GA. The incentive system of a GA may or may not correspond to the moral and legal codes of the larger society, depending on whether it is a deviant or conventional GA.

MODERATE AMOUNTS OF IDEOLOGY

Most research attention regarding guidance systems has been given to the ideologies of GAs and supralocal associations. Group ideology can be defined roughly as values and beliefs that support the goals, existence, virtues, structure, and activities of a given set of people such as a local rod and gun club or a local high school alumni club. In brief, ideologies justify and legitimate sets of people, especially collectivities, which are sets of people with some significant density of an intercommunication network and some sense of collective self-identity. Stallings (1973), studying an environmental GA, makes the interesting point that GA ideology tends to be stronger and more consistent in the minds of *core* members (leaders and active members) than in the minds of more peripheral members (nonleaders and less active or inactive members). Sabatier and McLaughlin (1990) found similarly that GA leaders and members had partly congruent beliefs but that leaders tended to be more extreme in their beliefs.

Most GAs have some ideologies, but usually *not* elaborate ones. For example, few GAs have ideologies that attempt to justify the *GA form* of the groups or their importance in democratic and civil societies. GAs tend to accept their own basic form *without question* and focus their ideologies more on problematic issues regarding goals and activities, where legitimation and consensus are needed.

The limited ideology of a typical GA asserts, implicitly or implicitly, the value of the specific GA and its goals; the value of its leaders and other active members because they are trying to achieve the valued GA goals for the benefit of the other members and sometimes the nonmembers; the importance of GA activities because they help to attain GA goals; the necessity of using GA-approved means to achieve its goals; the duty of members to participate in the GA and to support it financially; the importance of keeping present GA members while seeking additional ones as needed; and the necessity of resisting change in GA goals, structure, and activities unless there are powerful reasons for such change. For the typical polymorphic GA, the ideology also asserts the importance of maintaining the linkage with the national association without losing autonomy or giving it too much economic support (based on GA leader qualitative interviews in one eastern suburb [Appendix C]). In doing this, the ideology creates a social reality for the group's functioning (Berger and Luckmann, 1967).

There are exceptions to the generalization of moderate ideology in GAs. Fraternal lodges, such as the Freemasons, often have extensive ideologies that explain their values (Knight, 1984; Wilson, 1980). Veterans GAs are strong on patriotic ideologies that extol national defense. Social movement and political pressure GAs tend to have extensive political ideologies supporting their sociopolitical thrusts. Youth development GAs, such as the Boy Scouts and 4-H, have extensive ideologies that are part of their attempt to socialize young people into becoming responsible citizens and workers (MacLeod, 1983; Reck, 1951). Many church-related GAs tend to include the ideologies of the churches in which they are embedded—couples clubs, women's groups, Bible study GAs, and so on. Self-help GA ideologies often are extensive (Antze, 1976).

National association ideologies tend to be much more elaborate than GA ideologies, often drawing on earlier ideologies of initially monomorphic GAs that now are polymorphic branches of the national association in one country or another (Gomez, 1987). As a result, more recently formed polymorphic GAs tend to draw on the national association formulations of ideology to a substantial extent as new polymorphic GAs are formed (Brown and Philliber, 1977; Huang and Gould, 1974; Picardie, 1988). For example, new Rotary Clubs are expected to and tend to take on the standard Rotary Club International ideology and maintain such an ideology over time. Polymorphic GAs, thus, tend to have more extensive ideologies than do similar monomorphic GAs.

In the Boy Scouts, for example, local troops as GAs use printed materials such as the *Boy Scout Handbook,* prepared at the national level by the Boy Scouts of America, that outline the prescribed ideology for these GAs. Every Boy Scout in every troop (GA) is persuaded to learn a certain amount of ideology in the form of the "scout oath," "scout laws," and other material (MacLeod, 1983). Magrass (1986) argues that the underlying essence of Boy Scout ideology is to get youths to accept authority and work together, preparing them for work as dependent employees in modern organizational society (Boulding, 1953). However, even this well-developed national association ideology of the Boy Scouts is not extensive when it gets down to what is learned by members of Boy Scout troops as GAs at the local level.

Fiske (1973) sees the Elks, a national association with many polymorphic fraternal GAs, as having an "American ideology" that has emphasized patriotism, sociability, charity, localism, ritualism, and racism (the latter for 105 years). The racist aspect of national policy was officially changed in 1973, although the resulting de facto change at the level of local Elks GAs might not have been great. I lack any specific data on continuing racism in the local Elks GAs, but racist attitudes are unlikely to change quickly in the Elks GAs by national fiat, any more than federal antidiscrimination laws aimed at changing racism, sexism, and other forms of discrimination have quickly changed corresponding prejudices in the general public to a significant extent. It takes many years to socialize racial hatred into people, and it takes a similarly long time for people to change if, indeed, they ever can. Sometimes, only the new generation of youths can have a more balanced, less prejudiced view, and the older racists just have to die out for the average racism in a territory to decline.

GA ideologies can be found far back in the history of GAs. For example, Truant (1979) writes that *compagnonnages,* a workers' mutual aid GA type originating in France pre-1500, had a unique central myth (part of the larger GA ideology) stressing the need for a hierarchy of work skills. The Freemasons of today trace their existence and ideology many centuries back into the past (Knight, 1984), as do most established churches today, often beginning as GAs somewhere (Finke and Stark, 1994). Jolicoeur and Knowles (1978) argue that the ideology in the Freemasons is an example of "civil religion" in the United States, maintaining and propagating the U.S. Constitution and Bill of Rights.

Ideologies tend to be appropriate for the goals of a GA or its larger supralocal association—empowerment ideologies for neighborhood protest GAs (Blum and Ragab, 1985), a self-acceptance ideology for a GA of dwarfs and midgets (Ablon, 1981), a "one cannot help oneself" ideology for habitual alcoholics in Alcoholics Anonymous as peer-helping GAs (Rudy, 1986), a "sunshine is healthful" ideology for nudists (Hartman, Fithian, and Johnson, 1991), an anti-Communist, antigovernment ideology for paramilitary militias (Karl, 1995), and so on.

Some GA or supralocal association ideologies are misleading to nonmembers who might learn about them. Salomon (1986) discusses how the ideology of the U.S. peace sociopolitical movement during the 1960s and 1970s was superficially about having peace, not war. However, the central underlying ideology really was mainly anti-Establishment. Some GA ideologies are dangerous to members because they cover up important realities and the probabilities of reaction by authorities (Tobias and Woodhouse, 1985). This is most common in deviant GAs such as hate groups and contemporary citizen militias (Hamm, 1993; Karl, 1995; Sims, 1997; Zellner, 1995).

Those GAs that seem most deviant to nonmembers tend to develop the most elaborate and powerful ideologies (Smith, 1995c). This includes new religious GAs such as small sects or cults (Breault and King, 1993; Lyons, 1988), social movement GAs (Ferree and Hess, 1995; Unger, 1974), extremist or revolutionary political GAs (George and Wilcox, 1992; Hutchins, 1973; Kimmel, 1990), paramilitary militias (Karl, 1995), coup groups (Farcau, 1994), and many self-help GAs (Ablon, 1981; Rudy, 1986; Sagarin, 1969; Suler, 1984). They do this in part to justify themselves in their own minds as much as to justify themselves to nonmembers. Whenever GAs are significantly out of the ordinary by doing (or seeking to do) "strange things" relative to their surrounding communities, they tend to develop and maintain more explanatory ideologies than if their goals and means were more conventional. Their ideologies attempt to explain to members why their deviance is "good" and "worthwhile" in spite of nonmember criticism or "misunderstanding." These ideologies, in the eyes of GA members, counteract or neutralize societal norms and often social control agency (e.g., police, state troopers, Federal Bureau of Investigation) views indicating that such GAs are neither good nor worthwhile.

Extremist political pressure GAs have to explain in their ideologies why their political approaches are the "correct" ones for everybody because of the political regimes and types of society that will result from supporting their party platforms, candidates, and/or issue stances (George and Wilcox, 1992). But this is much *more* of a pressing issue in the case of social movement GAs, whose prescriptions for change and use of protest to seek change are more radical, by definition, than in conventional political pressure GAs, however extreme their goals (Lofland, 1996). Radical religious GAs, particularly new religions such as sects and cults, have to explain the "truth" of their new and different views of religion, morality, reality, god(s), salvation, and what people should do on earth to deserve happiness here and salvation later (Melton, 1990; Wilson, 1970). Self-help GAs need powerful ideologies to support the radical changes in self-perceptions (identities), feelings, habits, and perceptions of others and the world that usually are necessary if members are to be helped (Suler, 1984; Suler and Bartholomew, 1986).

GAs that mainly conform to societal norms and socially constructed "reality" at present do not need such elaborate ideologies to convince themselves and others that what they are thinking, feeling, wanting, and doing makes sense and is right, good, and just. However, any type of GA tends to develop some moderate amount of ideology, as suggested earlier. There are norms in nearly any GA about what members should believe and why they should believe it.

ADEQUATE INCENTIVES AND SATISFACTION

Clark and Wilson's (1961) classic article on incentives in organizations set the direction of initial GA research on incentives, identifying utilitarian, purposive, and solidary incentives. By definition, GAs always are volunteer membership-based associations, with incentive systems based primarily on voluntary altruism—a normative voluntary compliance structure, to use Etzioni's (1961) terminology. GA incentive systems, thus, contrast greatly with a largely utilitarian remunerative incentive system and mostly paid-staff workers accomplishing tasks in paid-staff voluntary groups (VGs) and other work organizations (Etzioni, 1961). But paid-staff VGs are different from other work organizations in that their incentive systems also depend significantly on voluntary altruism (see Chapter 1).

In simplest terms, GA incentive systems tend to reflect primarily voluntary altruism through a combination of purposive, solidary, and other nonmaterial incentives. Paid-staff VGs tend to involve a primarily material/remunerative incentive system, with voluntary altruism expressed secondarily through purposive and solidary components (Clark and Wilson, 1961; Steinberg, 1990, p. 159). The role of voluntary altruism as a secondary nonmaterial incentive in paid-staff VGs is very important definitionally, unlike its role in businesses and government agencies as other work organizations (see Chapter 1). Overall, GAs tend to be more successful and viable when they have more member incentives

(Chinman and Wandersman, 1999), fewer costs (Prestby et al., 1990), and a higher benefit/cost ratio (Warner and Heffernan, 1967). The relationship of costs to participation, however, is more variable (Chinman and Wandersman, 1999). What is very clear is that more benefits tend to be associated with greater GA participation (p. 59).

Knoke (1988, 1990b) and Knoke and Adams (1987) have explored incentives systematically for national associations, which are mostly paid-staff VGs that are not volunteer staffed at the national level. Among other results, Knoke and Adams (1987) show that the incentive systems used by these associations can be predicted from organizational goals. Knoke (1988) also found that normative (purposive or ideological) and social (sociability or solidary) incentives were more powerful in predicting member internal participation than were material/utilitarian or informational incentives, whereas lobbying incentives were most important for contacting government officials. Because many of these national associations have GAs as local branches, these results probably have applicability to GAs to a substantial extent.

The finding regarding the unimportance of material/utilitarian incentives is contrary to Olson's (1965) theory of collective action. But Kilbane and Beck (1990), studying one national professional association (optometrists), found more "free riders" in larger groups and found that selective incentives for membership and participation are important, both confirming Olson's (1965) theory.

Without any quantitative confirmatory evidence but based on reading a good deal of GA literature (including descriptions of deviant GAs) and on participant observation in some GAs, I offer the following list of incentive types that can be important in GAs. Types A, B, and F were suggested by Clark and Wilson (1961); Types D and H were suggested by Knoke (1988); and Type E was suggested by Widmer (1985). I am suggesting the other incentive types for *my* first time in print here, although others also might have suggested one or another of them earlier elsewhere. I present them roughly in descending hypothetical order of frequency of occurrence as positive factors in membership or participation in GAs—mainly a qualitative judgment on my part. However, a recent literature review by Chinman and Wandersman (1999, p. 59) concludes that the first two factors noted in the following are most important for participation in GAs.

Type A: Sociability Incentives

These solidary or social incentives are GA rewards that provide member satisfaction from the sociable presence of, and interaction with, other GA members participating in a given GA at various GA meetings and other GA activities (Clark and Wilson, 1961; Knoke, 1988). Such interactions lead to longer term acquaintanceship and friendship relationships among GA members such that certain other GA members become "close people" and part of one's general social support network in life (Fischer, 1982; Vaux, 1988). When these incentives really are powerful in a given GA, most members will have at least some of their close friends among the membership—sometimes most or all of them (Fischer, 1982). At high levels of sociability incentives, the GA will be a major social support group in the lives of its members, and this can have life-extending results, whether in self-help GAs or in GAs more generally (Maton, 1988; Wuthnow, 1994, p. 53; see also Chapter 9). These are the "signature" incentives of GAs, present in all GAs to some extent and whose intensity particularly distinguishes GAs from work organizations and from supralocal groups (Auslander and Litwin, 1988).

Even highly instrumental GAs as associations with external benefit goals tend to have strong primary groups with sociability rewards for members' interpersonal activity while pursuing these external benefit goals (Ross, 1977). When some volunteers in a mostly volunteer organization lack such sociability and status rewards while other volunteers have sociability rewards, the former tend to feel deprived (Stephenson, 1973). Sociability incentives are utterly basic to most GAs, along with purposive ones. Sociability incentives usually are necessary for the formation of a GA. But if a type of GA or specific GA is dying, then mere sociability incentives and benefits *alone* usually will not tend to keep it alive because they can be obtained in informal relationships or in other GAs (see Picardie, 1988, and Schmidt and Babchuk, 1972, regarding fraternal lodges in the United States).

Type B: Purposive Incentives

These are normative or ideological rewards that virtually all GAs provide to members for working toward or helping to achieve their GA goals (Clark and Wilson, 1961; Knoke, 1988). Receiving such rewards, active participants are gaining satisfaction from sharing in the GA's ideology about what these goals should be and how they should be properly achieved (Knoke, 1990b). In two national association studies (King and Walker, 1992, p. 407; Knoke, 1990b, p. 119), purposive incentives seem the most powerful overall of those incentive types measured. Hirsch (1986) shows that political (purposive) solidarity is important in social movement groups. Cook (1984) shows that in national public interest groups without GA local branches, members tend to get neither sociability nor material incentives but rather purposive incentives. For this reason, sociopolitical movements are likely to attract and hold more members and to have more potential impact if they use a network of GAs to engender grassroots commitment via sociability as well as purposive and other incentives.

King and Walker (1992) argue that this category of incentives "verges on tautology" (p. 397) because it posits that some people join a group simply to advance the collective good that is the group's goal. Thus, they define purposive incentives in their empirical study more narrowly than I prefer—operational-ized as group advocacy and participation in public affairs (p. 405). I think that it makes sense to talk about certain people having attitudes, however formed, that lead them to derive satisfaction from working for the goals of a given GA rather than for other GAs with different goals. And the goals of the GAs involved do not have to be collective goods in the technical economic sense; they can be member benefit club goods instead (Cornes and Sandler, 1989).

Purposive and sociability incentives in GAs usually manifest voluntary altruism. The types of goals involved in GAs with such incentives usually fit under one or more of the seven categories of social values that help to define vol-untary altruism, as stated in Chapter 1. This happens mainly by definition in the strictest sense because GAs are defined as having voluntary altruism as their pri-mary value base. However, a GA could have one or more secondary goals that were not based on voluntary altruism, and these could be served by correspond-ing purposive and solidary incentives.

Purposive and sociability incentives are the most widespread incentive types in GAs, but they might readily coexist with additional incentive types. Few of the following incentive types have been examined extensively as such in GAs, to my knowledge, beyond material incentives in certain types of GAs such as fraternal lodges, unions, consumer cooperatives, rotating credit associations, and friendly societies. Most of the research reviewed in Chapter 9 on the internal member impact of GAs can be seen as related to the present matter of incentives. The difference between the two is that in Chapter 9 research is reviewed regard-ing what in fact GAs tend to do to their members in different categories of impact, whereas here the focus is on what GAs attempt to do and how that relates to attracting and retaining members.

Type C: Service Incentives

Most GAs have at least moderate service incentives. There are two potential types of service incentives of GAs for their members. The traditional nonmem-ber type of service incentive focuses on how GAs serve nonmembers. The emphasis is put on providing altruistic satisfaction to traditional volunteer mem-bers from direct helping of the clients through external service GAs such as paramedic GAs, civic service clubs, and volunteer Salvation Army GAs (which in larger communities are paid-staff VGs). This is a relatively rare type of GA incentive because so many GAs tend to have internal member service goals rather than nonmember benefit goals. However, it is very common in volunteer service programs and among their program volunteers (Hodgkinson and Weitzman, 1992, pp. 224, 226).

The other type of service incentive focuses on GAs as member service or member benefit groups, with member satisfaction coming from how the GA members provide services, broadly conceived, to each other—helping each other. As distinguished from sociability, these co-member services might include encouragement when depressed, help in celebrations, help in emotional crises, help in making major decisions, and help when sick (Wuthnow, 1994, p. 170) as well as emergency loans, emergency transportation, emergency babysitting or other child care, and other services. There is this type of co-member helping, mutual benefit, member benefit aspect of nearly all GAs as an accompaniment of sociability and social relationships established, even if GAs also have some nonmember benefit goals. All social support and self-help GAs are particularly dependent on this second type of service incentive as members get help from each other (Katz, 1993; Powell, 1994; Wuthnow, 1994, pp. 139-40, 170, 320). Service incentives can be seen as a subtype of purposive incentives that are worth distinguishing if one also is at the level of detail of separating out informational and lobbying incentives, which usually also are subtypes of purposive incentives.

Both types of service incentives provide satisfaction from expressing voluntary altruism, either to nonmembers or members of a GA or other VG.

Type D: Informational Incentives

These are GA participation rewards from learning new information and knowledge while participating in GAs (Knoke, 1988, 1990b). They also can be termed *educational incentives* or *knowledge incentives*. Nearly all types of GAs involve some moderate informational incentives, which can be seen as secondary purposive incentives in some types of GAs (e.g., ethnic/nationality GAs, hobby or sports clubs) and as primary purposive incentives in some other types of GAs (e.g., youth development GAs, book discussion GAs). Prospective GA members also might receive informational incentives as part of why they decide to join. For example, members of a self-help GA of lay "lawyers" in Britain who fight their own cases "against lawyers and the system" are promised and provided with much information about the law and the legal system (Moore, 1978). From the standpoint of the individual, one problem with this type of incentive is that the individual member might reach a point where little new information is being learned, depending on the type of GA. In this sense, sociability and purposive incentives can be more lasting for a GA, continuing to satisfy participants indefinitely.

Type E: Developmental Incentives

These are GA rewards from self-actualization (Maslow, 1954) and personal growth that come from experiences in a GA volunteer role (Knowles, 1973). Wuthnow (1994) found that the most common reason given for joining small social support groups in the United States, including self-help GAs, was "the desire to grow as a person" (p. 84). He also found that participants in such groups cited a number of aspects of self-development as consequences of participation (p. 320). Widmer (1985) found that volunteer board members in paid-staff non-profits recognized and valued this type of incentive. But board volunteers and associational volunteers in GAs generally probably value personal development as well (as do service program volunteers [Hodgkinson and Weitzman, 1992, pp. 225, 245]).

It is possible for GA members to receive satisfaction from this type of incentive without consciously recognizing personal growth as the source. This incentive can be particularly difficult to measure accurately, with underestimates of its importance being common. One might measure this incentive in part by questions that first get at how the respondent perceives that other GA members are stimulated to grow on a few personal and social dimensions before turning to the respondent's own possible growth in similar or related ways.

Type F: Utilitarian Incentives

These rewards are economic returns of some type to GA members. Such incentives also can be labeled material, remunerative, occupational, professional, or economic incentives. Knoke (1990b, p. 115) operationalized utilitarian incentives as group travel plans, group insurance plans, group purchasing plans, and certification/licensing programs. By contrast, he operationalized occupational incentives as "providing professional or business contact opportunities" and "running seminars, conferences, and workshops" (p. 115). King and Walker (1992, p. 405) make a similar distinction with different labels. They refer to trips, tours, insurance, and discounts on consumer goods as "personal material benefits," and they refer to conferences, professional contacts, and training as "professional benefits." In these two national association studies (King and Walker, 1992, p. 407; Knoke, 1990b, p. 119), utilitarian incentives broadly conceived are important, particularly occupational or professional incentives, not the minor material benefits.

Utilitarian incentives seldom are important for GAs, by contrast, but they have some relevance in a small way for many GA types (Clark and Wilson, 1961; Olson, 1965). However, utilitarian incentives are more important to specific economic system support GAs such as some local unions; farmers GAs; local professional GAs; and local businesspeople's groups such as Chambers of Commerce, Business and Professional Women's Clubs, and rotating credit GAs; and similar "friendly societies" in developing nations (Estey, 1981; Fisher, 1993; Fletcher, 1985; Hirsch and Addison, 1986; Krause, 1996; Yamazaki and Miyamoto, 1988; see also Chapter 9). One must distinguish carefully between the economic system support *goals* of such economic GAs and the type of utilitarian *incentives* for participation in these or any other types of GAs now being discussed. The former involve shared outcomes and voluntary altruism within the GAs, whereas the latter involve private goods and services for the individual members of the GAs.

Civic service clubs, such as the Rotary Club and Lions Club, as local GAs are based in part on material incentives for some of their members (Charles, 1993). Some local businesspeople and professionals in town get to know and like each other, stimulating each other's economic activities as a perhaps tertiary aspect of these GAs' activities (after sociability and service). Some fraternal lodges have long had material incentives for membership, particularly life and other insurance. Even guilds, found in many societies back to ancient times (Smith, 1997c), usually had material incentives in the form of funeral and burial payments to spouses of members who died.

In spite of there being some types of GAs with substantial utilitarian incentives, most GAs involve little concern for material incentives for most members; rather, they manifest mainly voluntary altruism of some type in sociability or purposive incentives (Cook, 1984). Most GA members do not join or participate in GAs based on utilitarian incentives, and if newcomers do join GAs for utilitarian incentives, then such incentives do not tend to foster active participation, according to Knoke's (1990b) study of national associations, contrary to Olson (1965). King and Walker (1992), also studying national associations (interest groups located in Washington, D.C.), further challenge Olson's (1965) theory that selective material incentives are necessary to attract and retain members in large associations. Retail businesspersons and local professionals seeking to develop business in all types of GAs might be the main exceptions as individuals, but they tend to be a minority of GA members in most communities.

A variety of other types of incentives are less frequent in GAs but have been observed to occur in qualitative studies of one or another type of GA or samples of GAs (e.g., my study of one eastern suburb [Appendix C]). A few examples follow.

Type G: Charismatic Incentives

These are the provided by being led by and participating with charismatic leaders in GAs. Such leaders may be defined as persons with particularly dynamic, "magnetic," or otherwise attractive and influential personalities. Breault and King (1993) describe an extreme case of this in a well-known recent U.S. commune led by David Koresh. Although the attractiveness of charismatic *national* social movement leaders such as Gandhi and Martin Luther King, Jr. have been studied, there seems to be little or no research on charismatic *GA* leaders specifically (although these two and many other national movement leaders often started in GAs in their home localities). For most GA types and specific

GAs, this incentive does not arise regularly. Nevertheless, qualitative results from my research in one eastern suburb (Appendix C) show that some charismatic, or at least especially "dynamic," leaders attracted members and stimulated participation, impact, and effectiveness in various types of GAs. I argue that such GA charismatic leaders, and probably national ones, tend to be more extreme on most of the same dimensions of the active-effective character model that predict higher member participation in general (Smith, 1994a).

Type H: Lobbying Incentives

This type of incentive, also suggested by Knoke (1990b), focuses on how GAs' attempts to have external political influence on the public or government decision makers and administrators can be satisfying to GA members. For members of polymorphic GAs, such satisfaction extends to the political influence accomplishments of the supralocal, and often national, association. This type of incentive can be seen as part of purposive incentives. Indeed, lobbying incentives are essentially what King and Walker (1992) are talking about when they define purposive incentives in a narrow sense as advocacy and "representation before government" (p. 407). Lobbying incentives probably are more usefully distinguished for national associations than for GAs. They tend to be weak in most GAs, although many GAs get involved in political influence activities from time to time (Verba, Schlozman, and Brady, 1995, p. 63), and some focus centrally on such activities (see Chapter 9).

Type I: Prestige Incentives

As rewards, prestige incentives refer to the esteem received by members and leaders of certain GAs (e.g., Rotary Club, Junior League) from other members and from nonmembers, particularly nonmember friends and acquaintances who have reason to know about people's memberships in prestigious GAs. At the other end of the prestige incentive scale is GA stigma as a punishment. Members of deviant and stigmatized GAs, such as Ku Klux Klan GAs and witches' covens, tend to conceal their memberships and participation in such GAs from casual acquaintances and conventional people in their communities because of low esteem or social/verbal "punishment" they might receive if their affiliations were known. Co-members know about these affiliations, of course, but most members of stigmatized GAs reveal such memberships only to very close family members and close friends. This is one of the fundamental bases for the "Anonymous" format, "12-step" self-help GAs. Prestige incentives for GA membership and participation have not been studied, to my knowledge. Most GAs, in the middle range on the prestige-stigma dimension, probably offer few prestige incentives.

SECONDARY IMPORTANCE OF
GA INCENTIVES AND ROLES

In spite of all of these possible types of participation incentives, GAs still usually are of secondary importance in the lives of *most* of their members and leaders (Sills, 1968; Warner, 1972), but not always. Paid-staff nonprofits, thus, usually are more central to their paid-staff members than GAs are to their volunteer members, as is generally true of all full-time paid workers and their work organizations, whatever the sector. Paid work roles simply are more important to most people than their leisure roles in GAs. However, if the individuals in question are not in the labor force (e.g., homemakers, retired), then GA roles can have high importance.

Volunteer service program incentives in work organizations, such as those for hospital volunteers, school volunteers, and library volunteers, similarly have more secondary importance in volunteers' lives, as with GA volunteer members and participants. I know of no data comparing associational and program volunteer levels of role commitment. It also is an interesting question for future research to discover precisely how *some* GAs, such as sect or cult GAs and social movement GAs, can use incentives to generate so much importance to and commitment by their members compared to that generated by other GAs.

CONCLUSION

GAs tend to be moderately developed in their ideologies because of the need to explain to members their voluntary altruism in the form of associational volunteering within the GAs. Associational volunteering is leisure activity for its participants, albeit often "serious leisure" (Stebbins, 1996). GA ideologies explain why it is worthwhile for members to spend their leisure time in given GA pursuits rather than in other leisure activities, whether other GAs, service program volunteering, or other active or more passive leisure.

With remuneration of one type or another as the main incentive for paid employees in work organizations, these organizations generally have less need to develop ideologies to convince their employees to be motivated to work beyond providing remuneration. Paid employees, especially in the more common smaller businesses, work at their jobs primarily to earn money to support themselves and their families/households, although they often have secondary motivations as well (e.g., personal development and expression, service to others). Small business owners are in the same position. Employees and managers/owners in businesses usually need their jobs (or some jobs) and do not have to be as convinced of the value of work organizations that provide them with their livelihoods or profits for owners. Large businesses and franchise businesses sometimes attempt to develop ideologies and subcultures to give themselves a competitive edge in the marketplace (Ouchi and Wilkins, 1985).

Paid-staff VGs are exceptions to the general picture for work organizations because, like GAs, they too involve voluntary altruism. Insofar as voluntary altruism is present in paid-staff VGs (and, by definition, they must have a significant amount), this needs to be nurtured and maintained by organizational ideologies that portray the VGs as worth contributing to as quasi-volunteer employees or program service volunteers. However, paid-staff VG managers often are more convinced by a business management ideology than by a genuine voluntary altruism VG ideology for their organizations (Hall, 1990).

In deviant GAs (or deviant paid-staff VGs), the need for ideology is especially strong because the GAs need to convince their potential and actual members and, to the extent possible, the larger society that what they are doing is worthwhile in spite of conventional norms and views of their goals and activities. Deviance from societal norms and values is present, by definition, in such GAs in either goals or means to achieve them or both, and some stigma from conventional society as nonmembers results. Ideology in deviant GAs attempts to counter or neutralize the perception of deviance by substituting alternative values in terms of which the deviant goals or means seem positive or even "normal." For example, witches' covens might emphasize themselves as representing an ancient polytheistic religion and seek the freedom of religion granted other religions.

Table 4.1 presents a broad comparison of GAs and paid-staff VGs in terms of ideology and incentives. Because volunteers mainly accomplish the work done in GAs and paid-staff mainly accomplish the work done in paid-staff VGs, by my definition, the comparison in the table is between volunteers in GAs and paid-staff in paid-staff VGs. GAs are stronger in voluntary altruism than are paid-staff GAs because they function, by definition, with little or no dependence on utilitarian incentives. Paid-staff VGs, by contrast, provide strong utilitarian incentives in the form of paid jobs to employees. Paid-staff VGs are one form of work organization and share many work organization characteristics.

The voluntary altruism that is the motivational base for GAs is nurtured through their strong sociability, purposive, and service incentives. Sociability incentives are particularly strong and central in GAs. The GA service incentives involved often are co-member service incentives rather than nonmember service incentives. The voluntary altruism that is significantly present in paid-staff VGs, by definition, is nurtured through more moderate sociability, purposive, and service incentives, especially the latter two types. The service incentives in paid-staff VGs are more likely to be nonmember service incentives than co-member service incentives.

Both GAs and paid-staff VGs provide egoistic rewards in the form of informational and self-developmental incentives. Charismatic, lobbying, prestige,

TABLE 4.1 Comparison of Ideologies and Incentives in Grassroots Associations and Paid-Staff Voluntary Groups

Grassroots Associations	*Paid-Staff Voluntary Groups*
Moderate ideology if conventional	Moderate ideology if conventional
Strong ideology if deviant	Strong ideology if deviant
Strong sociability incentives for members	Moderate sociability incentives for employees
Strong purposive incentives for members	Moderate purposive incentives for employees
Strong service incentives for members	Moderate service incentives for employees
Moderate informational incentives for members	Moderate informational incentives for employees
Moderate developmental incentives for members	Moderate developmental incentives for employees
Weak utilitarian incentives for members	Strong utilitarian incentives for employees
Other grassroots association incentives sometimes strong for members	Other grassroots association incentives rarely strong for employees
Other work organization incentives rarely strong for members	Other work organization incentives strong for employees

environmental, ethnic identity, health, sexual, and coercive incentives also sometimes are strong for particular GAs but rarely for paid-staff VGs. On the other hand, work organizations tend to have their own distinctive organizational incentives that are different from GA incentives (e.g., working conditions, level of pay, opportunities for promotion, fringe benefits). These would apply to employees in paid-staff VGs but not to volunteer GA members.

5

Internal Structure

This chapter continues discussing research regarding the special and distinctive nature of grassroots associations (GAs) relative to work organizations, especially paid-staff voluntary groups (VGs). As in the prior chapters, it is based on GA research rather than on much-needed but missing comparative research that samples both GAs and other types of groups such as work organizations and households/families in the same study using nearly identical research methods. This chapter focuses on GA "internal structure," which involves the ways in which GAs are set up in lasting ways. Some of these aspects of structure are specified in legal documents such as GA constitutions or bylaws and letters of understanding from taxation agencies or national associations. Other aspects are strongly embedded in the norms of what the groups are in terms of goals and means of achieving them.

INTERNAL STRUCTURE

1. Basic GA Analytical Dimensions

Some aspects of internal structure of GAs are definitional and were discussed in Chapter 1.

a. Small Locality Base

GAs have a scope no larger than a metropolitan area or two adjacent counties. I could find no research that compares GAs of different degrees of extensiveness of locality base, seeking differences and similarities. Based on Zipf's (1949) law of least effort, one would expect greater member participation at meetings and other events for GAs with smaller territorial scope, other things being equal.

b. Mainly Volunteer Work

GAs usually have one full-time equivalent (FTE = 1,700 hours per year) of paid-staff work at a maximum and often much less. The vast majority of GAs seem to have no paid staff at all, especially the more informal or semiformal ones (Smith, 1992b). Those GAs that have some paid staff, by definition, have only small amounts of staff in terms of FTEs. They tend to use that paid work time either for landscaping/janitorial duties (in the case of GAs with their own buildings) or for clerical/office/accounting activities (in most other cases) (based on qualitative interviews in one eastern suburb [Appendix C]).

c. Autonomous

GAs have autonomy from other groups and organizations to a significant degree. My previously unreported research regarding GA autonomy in one small eastern suburb (Appendix C) shows that 89% of local volunteer groups studied (Smith, 1993b, p. 64) consider themselves to have moderate or complete autonomy. This is true even if they are polymorphic groups and, thus, formal affiliates of some larger associations. It is possible that GAs perceive themselves as having more autonomy from their national headquarters than the latter perceive their affiliates as having. In a study of the latter national associations, Young, Bania, and Bailey (1996) found that 74% of national association affiliates were perceived as having full (49%) or shared (27%) autonomy. If there is no significant autonomy of the local affiliate, then by my definition, it is an integral part of the larger dominating VG and not really a GA (Salamon, 1992; see also Chapter 1). But the percentage of local volunteer groups that are polymorphic and that, nonetheless, see themselves as significantly autonomous is striking.

Greater GA autonomy tends to make for greater membership and leadership participation, other things being equal, but it also involves greater risk of failure. Less autonomous GAs probably take longer to react to local crises, opportunities, and challenges in general, having to wait for decisions to be made by higher VG authorities and to come down the line (some national associations have regional, state, and/or district-level bureaucracies). The trend toward increasing dependence of larger paid-staff VGs on government funding raises major questions about the structural autonomy and independence of these organizations in the voluntary nonprofit sector (VNPS) (Saidel, 1989).

In the case of dictatorships and authoritarian regimes, any surviving nonprofits tend to suffer from having little or no autonomy (Allen, 1984; Bauer, 1990; Swanson, 1974; Zhou, 1993). When dictatorships end, there usually are resurgences of activity by GAs and other VGs (McCarthy et al., 1992; Smith, 1997c; Starr, 1991; see also Part III). We take this latter type of GA autonomy so much for granted in modern Western democracies that most of us forget its fundamental theoretical and historical importance as well as its variability over time. Not long ago in historical terms, most European nations were divine right monarchies or other types of dictatorships that were hostile to most VGs that were not part of the church-state dominance axis.

2. Informal Tax-Exempt Status

Nearly all GAs are tax-exempt, although relatively few have such tax exemption formally in writing from the Internal Revenue Service (IRS) or state taxation agencies. GAs usually do not have to register with the IRS because they are too poor, are religious in nature, or are polymorphic affiliates of some larger tax-exempt VGs (Chan and Rammohan, 1999). But the tax law in the United States still grants them tax exemption, and they rarely try to pay or are asked to pay taxes on their revenues to any government (Simon, 1987). The voluntary altruism of GAs ultimately is responsible for this tax exemption. In addition, their revenues are so small and the groups are so ephemeral that the IRS does not care about them, the IRS has insufficient personnel to deal with them even if it wanted to, and it would not be cost-effective for the IRS to try to get tax revenues from them. Other nations also have tax exemption for VGs including GAs (Weisbrod, 1992).

The current IRS threshold for mandatory registration is $5,000, although most GA leaders probably are unaware of this. The current IRS threshold for mandatory annual reporting of finances on Form 990 is $25,000, and more GA leaders are aware of this, although we lack quantitative data on how many. The IRS periodically raises the threshold amount of revenues for mandatory reporting so as to deal with inflation. I estimate that only 5% to 10% of GAs are directly IRS registered, as discussed in Chapter 2.

3. Tending Toward Informal Organization

There is a continuous dimension of formalization or degree of complexity of organization of GAs (Chapin and Tsouderos, 1956; Gerlach and Hine, 1970; Muehlbauer and Dodder, 1983; Traunstein and Steinman, 1973), and there is a still longer dimension for all groups and organizations taken together. But on the average, GAs are rather informal groups, often not formalized enough to be called organizations (Gartner and Riessman, 1984; Goodchilds and Harding,

1960; Smith, 1972c, 1992b; Steinman and Traunstein, 1976; Wuthnow, 1994). Part of this is simply due to small GA size, on average (McPherson, 1983), and the fact that smaller groups tend to be less complex in organization (Caplow, 1957). Larger groups require more complex administrative structures to run them, on average, other things being equal.

At the opposite pole from complexity is group informality or simplicity. Too many scholars and leaders assume that the more organized or complex a group is, the "better" it is. We are taught this and learn it for ourselves in modern "organizational society" (Boulding, 1953). But it is not necessarily true. Whether more complexity in a group is in fact better depends on one's values and on the group's values. Should our families, households, and neighbor or friendship cliques be more organized so that they can be "better"? A growing number of people are resisting, in various ways, the "iron cage of bureaucracy" that Weber (1952) pointed to long ago (pp. 181-82).

More informal GAs are quite different from more complex GAs (let alone more complex paid-staff VGs), even among GAs as basically small, local, volunteer-run groups. Semiformal GAs may be defined as GAs that have unique proper names and some fairly clear leadership structures but that also have fluid membership boundaries and informal styles of operation (Smith, 1992b). Such GAs tend to have less volunteer support staff such as committees per member or committee members per member, fewer elected officers per member, lower income from membership dues per member, younger age of the group, fewer relationships with other nonprofits, and less autonomy (p. 261; see also Chapin and Tsouderos, 1956). Diffuse goals and external societal pressure also are associated with informal GA organization (Simpson and Gulley, 1962). If larger and more complex organizations such as paid-staff VGs are considered in contrast to GAs, then the forgoing differences between semiformal GAs and other VGs are even more stark.

For GAs specifically, formalization includes the presence of aspects such as an incorporation certificate for a given state, registration with the IRS as a tax-exempt nonprofit, an organizational charter, a constitution and/or bylaws, an annual report, a written annual budget, a board member manual, a committee chair and committee member manual, and a newcomers orientation manual. Such formalization elements vary in their presence among GAs, with only 42% of 48 self-help GAs studied in one city having formal tax-exempt status, 70% having incorporation certificates, and 69% having constitutions (Steinman and Traunstein, 1976; Traunstein and Steinman, 1973).

Although the presence of leaders is common (90%) in the millions of small support GAs in the United States, only 57% have elected officers and 53% have business meetings (Wuthnow, 1994, p. 135)—usually the larger support groups, although they are small in absolute numbers of members (p. 137). Boards of directors were not even mentioned by Wuthnow (1994), nor were they in Wertheim's

(1976) study of food cooperative GAs. However, Traunstein and Steinman (1973) found boards in 85% of self-help GAs in their study of such groups in a mid-sized U.S. city. This seems rather strange, but it seems to indicate substantial complexity in their sample of GAs. The California county sample of GAs by Chan and Rammohan (1999) also finds boards to be widespread but probably sampled more complex and established GAs.

Some community/citizen action GAs also are low in complexity (Boyte, 1980; Milofsky, 1988a). One value cited by leaders of such groups as a reason for resisting complexity was the desire to maintain openness to the larger communities. A simple GA makes it easier for more people to participate directly. Such a GA also makes it easier for poorer people to finance. Other GAs addressing community problems also often are simple in form (DeGrazia, 1957).

In addition to church-related GAs studied by Wuthnow (1994), new religions often are simple in structure (Breault and King, 1993; Gerlach and Hine, 1970, pp. 9-12; Weightman, 1983; Wilson, 1970, pp. 108-9). Clark (1937, p. 224) noted that the small sects in the United States, often beginning as GAs, initially emphasized democracy and simplicity as part of their faith. As they grew in size, however, these sects lost both qualities and became more complex out of pragmatism. Some old sects such as the Amish, however, have been able to preserve their simplicity as GAs over centuries (Nolt, 1992).

Gerlach and Hine (1970) suggest a decentralized and segmented network style of social movement organization that is an alternative to more complex GAs. Stoecker (1993) adds another alternative in his notion of federated front-stage structure for local social movements. This structure is "formed by a single unified constituency creating multiple specialized organizations" (p. 172). The unified constituency is part of a centralized umbrella organization that holds the whole network together while protecting the autonomy of GAs that are part of it.

Austin (1991) studied 60 neighborhood GAs in Oklahoma City, Oklahoma, using number of officer types as a complexity measure. He found more GA complexity where there were a larger GA size, higher neighborhood socioeconomic status, higher percentage of blacks in the neighborhood, lower neighborhood age, and less neighborhood stability. Besides larger GA size, these findings have no neat theoretical explanation and seem inconsistent with each other. Much more research is needed here, using a variety of measures of complexity versus informality of organization of GAs.

Milofsky (1988b, p. 194) discusses GAs as "collectivist" organizations in contrast to bureaucratic organizations more generally. He identifies several important differences between the two types of organizations. Collectivist organizations have their process as a product (vs. an "efficient" good or service), use an informal organizational methodology (vs. a formal one), are more embedded in their context (vs. separate), give indirect returns to members (vs. monetary measured returns), have more permeable boundaries (vs. sharp ones), and have more open decision making (vs. a more centralized hierarchy).

Wuthnow (1994) notes that there is a "relatively high degree of informality [in support groups]—warmth, encouragement, acceptance, and the privilege of talking openly about one's personal problems and interests" (p. 158). But at the same time, there is substantial formal organization—"leaders, goals, and agendas in most groups; lessons to study, business meetings, and elected officers in many others" (p. 158). These two tendencies are in a dynamic tension, each drawing strength from the other (p. 132). Other types of GAs could be described in roughly similar terms. Harrison (1960) argues that the dynamic tension between the need for bureaucratic process and the dislike of centralized authority was basic to the nature of GAs.

Freeman (1975) found that younger feminist social movement GAs were able to maintain their internal democracy and informality because they consciously valued these processes very highly and resisted any tendencies toward formalization, centralization, bureaucracy, or oligarchy as they arose. Keeping their GAs consciously small, informal, and interactive/participative was important in resistance to increasing complexity and decreasing internal democracy. Riger (1983) writes similarly that GA complexity can be a result of value systems held by group members. The more that solidarity and financial independence are valued, the more likely the GA is to remain informal. Valuing efficiency and remunerative rewards, by contrast, tends to result in more complexity and hierarchy within a GA, hence less internal democracy. Steinman and Traunstein (1976) reach similar conclusions for self-help GAs.

Dealing with hospices as small paid-staff VGs, Gummer (1988) suggests that "small size by itself does not deter the growth of bureaucratic practices" (p. 44) but does make such avoidance possible, whereas in large organizations bureaucracy is inevitable. Some of the factors inhibiting bureaucracy in hospices as alternative VGs are a holistic service process, power sharing and participatory decision making, and face-to-face relations based on small size. All of the forgoing aspects of informality can vary *within* the context of *formal* GAs—groups with proper names, clear group boundaries, and clear leadership structures (Smith, 1972c). GAs can be relatively informal but still researchable and important, in my view (Smith, 1992b).

4. More Internal Democracy

Internal democracy refers to structural features such as participative decision making, high turnover in leadership (less oligarchy), and low hierarchy (fewer levels of leadership). It tends to characterize GAs much more than it does paid-staff VGs. Most GA leaders are member-elected officers and board members, usually elected annually or biennially, and there is more turnover of leaders.

Hierarchy is low, usually with only two or three levels of members. By contrast, most nonassociational VGs tend to have self-replacing boards, board-appointed executive directors who are chief executive officers, and other appointed leaders. Generally, paid-staff VGs have less participative decision making, more hierarchy, and more oligarchy than do GAs, like most *work* organizations in general (Corsino, 1985-86; Halliday and Cappell, 1979; Klausen, 1995; Michels, [1911] 1968).

Many people think that democracy is a good and effective way in which to make important decisions. Executives of work organizations, including paid-staff VGs, tend to think otherwise for their own organizations. Such executives usually prefer strong centralization of decision making, hierarchy, and oligarchy (Hall, 1996).

But GAs also face the problem of oligarchy to some degree as they age, grow larger, and/or become more complex and less informal (Burt, 1990; McNamie and Swisher, 1985; Michels, [1911] 1968). Often, a few leaders tend to gather and maintain power over long periods even though elected "democratically" time and again. And former official leaders tend to continue as informal leaders after they have left their formal positions. Although some GAs succumb to oligarchy (Cnaan, 1991; Schmidt, 1973), most GAs still tend to maintain some significant degree of internal democracy, which tends to foster member participation, contributions, and dues paying (Hall, 1995).

GA internal democracy is especially important because GAs, as one broad type of VG, generally are "schools" for politicization that foster citizen participation in a democracy (see Chapter 9). This process is unlike the effects of most paid-staff VGs or other work organizations. It is unclear whether involvement in paid-staff VGs, aside from schools and colleges/universities, has any such positive effect on maintaining participatory democracy and a civil society. Thus, internal democracy is one major foundation of the VNPS more broadly including paid-staff VGs.

GAs are partly successful in resisting oligarchy and maintaining significant internal democracy by means of rules or bylaws insisting on having periodic (usually annual but sometimes biennial) and often contested elections among their memberships for officer posts and boards of directors. This shades into oligarchy if single slates of candidates are repeatedly run for some or all posts (no competition for positions) and/or with little change in who the candidates are from year to year. GAs really eager to codify and maintain democracy usually set leader term limits, such that they cannot succeed themselves in office more than once or hold the same post more than twice.

Lipset, Trow, and Coleman (1956) provide an excellent discussion of the joint problems of internal democracy and how to avoid oligarchy in associations; this is somewhat dated (more than 40 years) but not dimmed in its quality. They cite 22 factors that tend to help create or preserve internal democracy including less bureaucracy in the organization, more homogeneous member interests, more member interest in the organization, more sociability of members with each other, and more opportunities for members to learn political skills in the organization (pp. 465-68). Earlier, the authors had mentioned as important factors both smaller size and greater member participation in the association's political activities (e.g., voting, attending general meetings).

Other researchers studying GAs, not national paid-staff nonprofit associations, confirm some of these points but add many others. DeVall and Harry (1975) argue theoretically that part of the problems of Lipset et al. and many others studying internal democracy is that they study only economic or utilitarian associations. Normative or ideological associations, with more voluntary altruism, are much more likely to encourage member interest in the operations of the associations and a variety of subgroups with different views, thus promoting internal democracy. Knoke and Wood (1981) studied 32 noneconomic GAs and found that communication and participation in decision making increased commitment to and decreased detachment from the GAs, thus having very positive net effects. An earlier study by Tannenbaum (1961) showed that League of Women Voters local GAs had more satisfied members and more reputational impact in their communities if they had more internal democracy. In combination, these latter two studies show that more internal democracy tends to generate both more commitment and more group impact—important positive outcomes for any GA.

Johnson (1990) argues that the "majority rules" type of voting in a GA works toward oligarchy by gradually driving dissenters from the group. The latter need to be kept in the group or else the whole GA will tend to unravel, with each new and important majority vote driving some additional dissenters to leave.

Horch (1988) studied 28 West German GAs of various types, finding that internal democracy was greater where contributions were material resources (but not monetary ones), were transfers into the pool of GA resources (not obligatory contributions), and came more from members (not nonmembers). And McNamie and Swisher (1985) found that internal democracy of associations declines with greater government intervention in community participation. This often results from government grants or contracts to associations, initially GAs. This latter point is related to what I point out elsewhere in the chapter, namely that external funding tends to reduce GA autonomy. Such funding might well also make a particular GA leader seem important to keep in office, leading to greater oligarchy.

5. More Likely to Be Member Benefit Group Than Nonmember Benefit Group

Although *not* a defining characteristic, GAs are very much more likely to be member benefit and member service oriented in goals, on the whole, than nonmember benefit and external service oriented in goals (Chan and Rammohan, 1999; Smith, 1993b). Verba and Nie (1972, p. 42) measure memberships in 16 types of associations. All except professional or academic societies are mainly GAs. Of the 15 grassroots types of groups, only 2 (school service groups and service clubs) clearly are involved in service to nonmembers in addition to member benefit activities, and these are mixed in benefits. This service to nonmembers is only partly true for school service groups such as Parent-Teacher Associations, in which parents also are helping their own children as well as others. Even service clubs such as Lions Club and Kiwanis have a strong member-serving sociability component in addition to their social service component (Charles, 1993). Thus, to one degree or another, there is a member-serving or mutual benefit element in all or nearly all types of GAs (see Verba, Schlozman, and Brady, 1995, p. 63, for similar recent results from a 1989 national sample study).

A higher proportion of paid-staff VGs than of GAs tend to be nonmember benefit in orientation (Billis, 1993a, 1993b; O'Neill, 1989, 1994; Smith, 1991, 1993b; Van Til, 1988, p. 87). Scholars such as DiMaggio and Anheier (1990, p. 138), Salamon (1992, p. 7), Rudney (1987, p. 55), and Hodgkinson et al. (1992, p. 185) tend not to go beyond the admittedly important so-called "charitable" or "philanthropic" nonmember benefit subsector to embrace the rest of the VNPS (Smith, 1991; see also Chapter 2). With all of its potential problems and methodological "messiness," the member benefit subsector must be included in the VNPS if we truly want to deal with the whole VNPS (Smith, 1991). There are two "flat-earth" paradigms at work here (see Chapter 10). One is the paid-staff VG flat-earth VNPS paradigm, which tends to ignore all GAs and other volunteer groups. The other is the traditional nonmember service flat-earth VNPS paradigm, which includes only external service or nonmember benefit VGs in the VNPS.

Harris (1998a) has noted recently that associations are distinctive in having to balance member benefit and nonmember (i.e., public) benefit goals and activities. This is a well-taken point but does not vitiate my more general point here that GAs tend to be member benefit in nature. They often have nonmember benefit goals and activities as part of their service to society, hence my seeing them as partly public serving and not wholly member serving.

During earlier decades, the present dimension was referred to as "expressive versus instrumental" and other terms (Douglas, 1987; Gordon and Babchuk, 1959; Jacoby and Babchuk, 1963; Lundberg, Komarovsky, and McInerny, 1934; Rose, 1954). More recently, this dimension has been called "member benefit versus public benefit" (or "philanthropic" or "public purpose" or "serving the general welfare") (Bowen et al., 1994; Rudney, 1987; Salamon, 1992; Salamon and Abramson, 1982).

I argue that calling the latter part of this dimension "public" is a misnomer (Smith, 1995a). Neither the whole public nor even a representative cross section of it actually is served by such nonmember nonprofits in most cases. Also, member benefit GAs and supralocal associations clearly serve the public and the general welfare in many, often widespread ways discussed in Smith (1997a) and in Chapter 9 (see also Chan and Rammohan, 1999, p. 18). Hence, I term the present version of the nether end of the dimension more neutrally "nonmember" rather than "public," as best reflecting the essence of this pole of the dimension. Such an approach does not make unwarranted assumptions in advance about how much organizations at one or the other end of the dimension contribute to the public interest and the general welfare.

Member benefit nonprofits such as GAs *also* serve the public and the public interest or general welfare cumulatively when aggregated for a territory, again without complete coverage of the public. But there probably is no less coverage of the public by GAs than by paid-staff VGs in the same territory thus aggregated—and perhaps more by GAs. There usually is a need for a middle category to categorize some GAs that have elements of both polar types (Smith, 1993b) such as the Lions Club that involve substantial member benefits as well as nonmember benefits. Blau and Scott's (1962) related typology focusing on "who benefits" adds an alternative third category, so that the public benefit end has two levels: public-in-contact benefit and public-at-large benefit. But even the latter category does not necessarily involve serving all or a cross section of the public in any clear and direct way, nor does the former category.

Member benefit GAs often are very different from the less common nonmember benefit GAs and also from nonmember benefit paid-staff VGs. Comparing just GAs, member benefit GAs differ from nonmember benefit GAs especially in tending to have larger groups; relatively more revenues from dues; relatively less revenues from fees, sales, and grants; more participants per meeting or event; and more meetings or events per year (Smith, 1993b, p. 61). Nonmember benefit nonprofits, whether GAs or paid-staff VGs, are more likely to be noticed by those who attempt to count nonprofits, and their volunteer activity also is more likely to be counted (Hodgkinson et al., 1992; Hodgkinson and Weitzman, 1996b; Smith, 1997a). This is partly because nonmember VGs fit the traditional stereotype of service VGs, as contrasted with, for example, self-help GAs.

Some people believe, incorrectly, that only nonmember benefit nonprofits are providing services or are altruistic. I argue (see Chapter 1) that both nonmember benefit and member benefit GAs can be altruistic and can provide service. Both manifest some voluntary altruism. Only if serving one's fellow members is *defined* out of the service category do member benefit GAs fall out of this category across the board. No one quarrels with economists who include in the service category businesses that provide entertainment, try to restore health, provide education, and so on. But when GAs do these things for their members, somehow "service" gets redefined by some nonprofit scholars as being absent. Lack of payment for the activity does not matter, in my view. If the activity helps other people outside the family, whether members or nonmembers of a GA, then it still is service.

6. More Often Polymorphic Than Monomorphic Groups

This distinction refers to whether a group is a unique entity (i.e., monomorphic), at whatever territorial level, versus being very similar in *form* to one or more other groups as a polymorphic affiliate of some larger whole (*poly* = many, *morph* = form) (Smith, 1994b). Others have referred to this situation, but without a uniquely identifying term for it. A typical *monomorphic GA* would be a unique GA that is not affiliated with any other group or organization such as a self-help health GA concerned with people who have many debilitating allergies, a unique food cooperative GA (Cox, 1994), or a unique citizen militia GA (Karl, 1995). A typical *polymorphic GA* would be a GA that is like many other similar GAs as part of a larger national or international nonprofit association such as a local GA affiliate of the Ku Klux Klan (Sims, 1997), the Freemasons (Knight, 1984), or Alcoholics Anonymous (Rudy, 1986).

Sills (1957, p. 3) makes a further distinction among polymorphic GAs (without using the latter term), differentiating national associations with a more "corporate" structure of less (but still somewhat) autonomous branch chapters and national federations of rather autonomous local groups. The increasing influence of national organizations and events on the local scene, as described well by Vidich and Bensman (1968), surely is a reason for increasing importance of polymorphic GAs, as is modernization generally (see Chapter 10).

There are no national data for all GA types on this issue, but my community data from eight Massachusetts towns and cities in 1967 suggest that about 50% of U.S. GAs are polymorphic, but probably a lower percentage in other nations are polymorphic. Chan and Rammohan (1999, pp. 13, 15) find a similar percentage in a California county sample. In a study of GAs in a suburb of 14,000 people (Appendix C), I found that 53% of the GAs sampled had an affiliation with two or more other organizations, usually a higher level polymorphic affiliation as well as a local-level sponsorship affiliation (as with a church, school, or library). This study also showed that affiliations with other organizations are less frequent among informal or semiformal GAs (Smith, 1992b, p. 261). Babchuk and Edwards (1965) found 27% polymorphic GAs in a sample of GAs from Lincoln, Nebraska. Looking at this from the other end of the polymorphic relationship, Young et al. (1996) found that about 75% of national associations with branches had essentially autonomous affiliates.

My research in one eastern suburb (Smith, 1994b; see also Appendix C) shows that leaders of polymorphic GAs tend to feel that their GAs are rather independent of their higher level affiliates and also are larger in memberships, have more income, have more affiliates besides their central higher level affiliates, are more formalized, are more member benefit oriented, are more active, and are higher in prestige than monomorphic GAs. Kronus (1977) similarly found polymorphic GAs to be larger. Selle and Øymyr (1992) found them to be longer lived. All of this suggests that polymorphic GAs have structural advantages over monomorphic GAs, without necessarily losing their local autonomy. Those who have analyzed national associations with polymorphic GAs attached to national headquarters versus those without GA affiliates generally have remarked on the utility of such affiliates (Oster, 1992; Schafer, 1979; Young, 1989; Young et al., 1996), even though the closeness to and amount of control by the national associations varies among local associations (Seeley, Junker, and Jones, 1957; Sills, 1957; Tannenbaum, 1961; Zald, 1970).

In a study of about 300 local GA affiliates of Mothers Against Drunk Driving, Weed (1989) found that more member support was associated with more central office contacts and more cooperative programming with that office. By contrast, more community organization support of the local affiliate was associated with less central office contact, more policy disagreement, and less program cooperation with the central office. Hunter's (1993) study of polymorphic GAs and their national headquarters federations shows that these linkages are important in connecting the macro and micro orders of society. These linkages often are overlooked by those studying the two orders or levels of society. Young et al. (1996) also discuss the importance of these polymorphic linkages.

There is very little research on this issue in other nations to date. Lanfant (1976, p. 202) found that 58% of GAs in a French province had some link to a "mother organization" or national headquarters in Paris. However, she reports various other types of GA links to other organizations, with most links being reported for GAs to the Catholic Church or to the municipality. In a study of GAs in French-speaking Switzerland, Kellerhals (1974, p. 236) found that the degree of polymorphism, interpreted as a link with a larger institution, was much lower for more recently founded GAs (25% polymorphic if founded after 1946) than for earlier founded GAs (48% polymorphic if founded before 1900). He interprets these findings as evidence of a long-term change from dependency toward autonomy. It could instead be more evidence that polymorphic GAs are more likely to survive.

7. Substantial Sociodemographic Homogeneity

GAs tend to maintain substantial homogeneity in a sociodemographic property space based on variables such as member age, sex, education, race/ethnicity, and marital status (Mayhew et al., 1995; McPherson and Rotolo, 1996). Each GA tends to occupy its own niche in this property space, as represented by a certain mean and standard deviation for GA members on each sociodemographic variable (McPherson, 1983a). For example, the niche of the Rotary Club in a given community (and in most U.S. communities) would be white, college-educated, middle-class, middle-aged married males. GA niches can change over time in predictable ways (McPherson and Ranger-Moore, 1991). Types of GAs also tend to have characteristic niches in a community (McPherson, 1983a, p. 526).

Popielarz and McPherson (1995) show that this GA homogeneity is maintained by a niche edge effect and a niche overlap effect as well as by a tendency to recruit similar (homophilous) new members from within a GA's niche in the community. They note that "ties between co-members in an organization lengthen the memberships of both members" and that "ties between members and nonmembers shorten the duration of the memberships" (p. 702). This produces the niche edge effect that leads to more member turnover for members near the edge of a GA niche than for members near the center of the niche. The result is more GA sociodemographic homogeneity.

Niches change with competitive pressures from other GAs in the community, which results from niche overlap—seeking the same types of members. "Niches facing heightened competitive pressures at the edges contract; niches with less competitive pressure at the edges expand" (McPherson and Rotolo, 1996, p. 186). The niche overlap (competition) effect also contributes to GA homogeneity. When two or more GAs have overlapping niches, member turnover for such members is higher. This accentuates the niche edge effect (Popielarz and McPherson, 1995).

Another way in which to look at GA member composition is to examine dominance by a particular sociodemographic category such as age or gender. Based on a representative sample of adults in Nebraska, McPherson and Smith-Lovin (1982) found that men predominated in larger "core" GAs, which usually were more economically oriented, controlling for individual sociodemographic variables. Women tended to belong to smaller "peripheral" GAs, which were more focused on domestic or community affairs. The result is that men were exposed to far more potential contacts and other resources.

8. Few Economic Resources

GAs tend to operate on a low economic scale, in terms of both financial resources and personnel resources.

a. Financial Resources

Financial resources in the form of annual revenues are low for most GAs compared to those for work organizations, usually being less than $25,000 (see Chapter 2). When GAs begin to have more revenues, they tend to start hiring part-time staff and eventually full-time staff, becoming paid-staff VGs in many cases if revenues continue to increase. Small support GAs tend to have very low revenues, often less than $1,000 per year. In Wuthnow's (1994, p. 135) national study of such groups, only 26% had membership fees. However, donations are regularly collected at meetings of many self-help and other support GAs. In the suburban community that I studied (Appendix C), the average budget of 51 GAs was $7,805 (median = $2,000), and the median amount of equity seemed to be very small, based on qualitative impressions. Some 61% of GAs surveyed in a California county had budgets of less than $10,000 (Chan and Rammohan, 1999, p. 16).

Hunter and Staggenborg (1986) show that, in three cities studied, larger size of city was positively and significantly associated with GA budget size in a causal path model (p. 175). This is consistent with the finding of McPherson (1983b) that GAs tend to have larger memberships in larger places.

GAs usually raise their financial revenues by means of annual assessments (called "dues") or by means of donations at meetings, the latter especially for small support groups and self-help GAs (Smith, 1998a). Additional funds are raised by special events open to the public such as craft fairs, rummage sales, auctions, plant sales, book sales, and pancake breakfasts. Investment income and bequests are rare.

GAs rarely have significant financial assets. Only a small minority own their own buildings, either left to them in bequests or built with member donations. Meeting spaces often are members' homes. The national study of church congregations by Independent Sector (Hodgkinson, Weitzman, and Kirsch, 1989, p. 97) shows that 90% of such congregations provided space for GA meetings of church congregation members and that 60% provided space for meetings of other GAs from the local community at low or no cost. Qualitative evidence indicates that high schools, colleges, and universities provide space for meetings of most GAs of their students at low or no cost.

b. Personnel Resources

Personnel resources in the form of FTEs of people's work time also are low for GAs compared to those for work organizations. The principal personnel of GAs, by definition, are part-time associational volunteers. They tend to put in, on average, no more than a couple of hours per week (see Chapter 2). Paid staff generally are absent, and if present, they usually are part-time and low in FTEs of work time. Some 75% of VGs found in a careful study of California VGs had no employees at all and, hence, were GAs (Institute for Nonprofit Organization Management, 1995, p. 2).

This variable of personnel resources has some complexities of measurement. One can use any or all of the following measurement approaches: number of official members, number of active members, number of employees, administrative component (e.g., leaders, staff, board, committee heads), and number of analytical members (people who regularly provide services to the group) (Smith, 1972c).

There is a presumption in the VNPS, as in business, that "bigger is better." Larger nonprofits are commonly thought to accomplish more. This is unproved, and it certainly depends on whether one standardizes impact per dollar of input or per person of input (Smith 1997a; see also Chapter 9). Larger VGs often process more people and spend more money, but their per capita impact or "bang for the buck" is not necessarily commensurate with their large input or through-put size.

One chastening bit of data here is Gamson's (1990) finding that genuinely successful challenging groups or social movement organizations, which are VGs, over 145 years of American history (1800-1945) were *not* any more likely to be larger (vs. smaller). Size was irrelevant in bringing about social change, but it was important for social acceptance or social visibility (i.e., brightness). In another study of the 90 more formalized (vs. informal) associations in a mid-western county seat, Mulford and Mulford (1980, p. 26) found greater size to be associated with more attendance by members and more cooperation with other groups.

GAs tend to be small in various aspects of personnel resources. Their memberships usually are small, of the order of 20 to 50 people (Lundberg et al., 1934; McPherson, 1983b; Selle and Øymyr, 1992, p. 169). But these small GAs sometimes can grow into the many hundreds of members without losing their volunteer-run status. In the eastern community that I studied (Appendix C), one youth GA had 830 members in a variety of leagues for a popular sport but remained without any paid staff. In this community, the mean size of 54 GAs was 98 members (median = 45 members) in a distribution skewed by several large GAs (Smith, 1992b, p. 263). The results for a California county sample are very similar (Chan and Rammohan, 1999, p. 16). Lundberg et al. (1934) found an average GA size of about 50 members in one town.

Self-help GAs and block GAs tend to be smaller in membership size. Emerick (1989), studying a national sample of mental patient self-help GAs, found a median membership of 33 people (p. 297) and a median budget of $30,000. Traunstein and Steinman (1973, p. 235) characterize their sample of 48 self-help GAs from a medium-sized city as having small memberships, and two-thirds had annual budgets of less than $5,000. Lieberman and Snowden (1994) report that California self-help GAs had a median of 14.5 estimated participants per meeting (p. 44). Prestby and Wandersman (1985) found a mean membership size of 15 in a study of 17 urban block GAs (my computation from their data on pp. 292 and 294).

In a more general sample of GAs estimated by hypernetwork sampling of individuals, McPherson (1983b) found a corrected average size of less than 30 members per GA for the state of Nebraska, again with a distribution skewed by large GAs. He also found that GA size was greater for polymorphic GAs, for GAs in larger places/cities, for more membership stability, for more central locations in interorganizational networks, and for greater linkage to the economy.

The largest and wealthiest of all GAs tend to be some church congregations. They often move toward being paid-staff VGs as they get still larger and wealthier. However, Hodgkinson et al. (1989, p. 32) indicate, from their national sample study of local church congregations, that probably only 2% or so of all U.S. congregations lack any paid clergy and, hence, represent a minimum of GAs (about 7,000 congregations). The data really are not reported properly, to be sure, for there might be other full-time or part-time employees in these cases totaling one FTE (1,700 hours per year). On the other hand, these authors report that 34% of all congregations lack any full-time nonclergy employees (p. 33). And 85% of total staff in religious congregations are volunteers (p. 97). Thus, religious congregations sometimes are GAs, but it is not yet clear in what proportion because the balance of volunteer and paid work in them nationally has not been computed (Hodgkinson et al., 1989; see also Chapter 1). Nor are we clear on the size of GA church congregations nationally once GA congregations have been properly distinguished. The Independent Sector survey data should be reanalyzed to answer these questions, if possible (Hodgkinson et al., 1989).

9. Other Internal Structure

A few other aspects of internal structure require mention here, largely in terms of gaps in research. One gap is the paucity of research on *expressive management* and *expressive structures* (e.g., regular parties, social hours or periods) in GAs and their impacts (but see Mason, 1996, and Smith, 1986a). The emotions and feelings of GA members and participants, as well as task or instrumental accomplishment, need to be considered in research. Often, the latter depends on the former. Nor do we know much about ritual and its emotional effects on GAs generally (but see Smith, 1972d, for research on ritual in college student GAs).

Scholars of work organizations more generally have begun to speak about a subfield of "organizational demography," which applies traditional concerns of population demography to organizations (Stewman, 1988). Such researchers focus on people and job/role turnover rates; labor costs and changes in these rates; innovation and adaptation; opportunity structures; growth, decline, and stability of organizations; and several other aspects of demography that could fruitfully be investigated regarding organizations. However, these business and government work organization researchers take the usual paid-staff work organization flat-earth perspective and seldom seem to mention paid-staff nonprofits, let alone GAs. Some nonprofit researchers have begun to explore a few of these areas of internal structure, and some scholars also have done so for incidence/prevalence/dissolution of GAs (Smith and Associates, forthcoming).

CONCLUSION

The thrust of this chapter is that *GAs are very different from paid-staff VGs in terms of certain aspects of internal structures and processes.* This is shown in Table 5.1, which draws on the general paid-staff VG literature for the second column. This is a presentation of ideal types, based on my review of the literature, and has empirical exceptions for every entry. In terms of group structure, the table shows that although both GAs and paid-staff VGs tend to have small locality bases and substantial autonomy, GAs definitionally depend mainly on volunteer work, whereas paid-staff VGs definitionally depend mainly on paid work. GAs tend to have informal tax exemption, whereas paid-staff VGs tend to have formal IRS and state tax exemption. GAs tend to have informal organization and low complexity, whereas paid-staff VGs tend to be more formal and complex in organization. GAs tend to have more internal democracy of operation, whereas paid-staff VGs tend to have more internal hierarchy and centralization.

Another major structural difference is that GAs tend to have member benefit goals, whereas paid-staff VGs are more likely to have nonmember benefit goals. GAs also are more likely to be polymorphic, whereas paid-staff VGs are more likely to be monomorphic. GAs tend to have substantial sociodemographic homogeneity, each with its own niche in the community, although sometimes overlapping with the niches of other GAs. Paid-staff VGs tend to have less sociodemographic homogeneity, I hypothesize, although comparative data are lacking. GAs clearly have fewer economic resources than do paid-staff VGs in terms of both FTEs of personnel and revenues and assets. Virtually by definition (although the balance of paid and volunteer work hours is key), GAs have fewer paid staff, on average, than do paid-staff VGs. However, the average analytical membership size of GAs might exceed the average analytical membership size of paid-staff VGs (we lack the data to determine this).

The vast majority of general organization research is done on work organizations and does not apply well, if at all, to GAs or even to paid-staff associations anywhere. This was the conclusion of Knoke and Prensky (1984), writing a decade and a half ago, and it still holds true so far as I can determine. Klausen (1995) reiterated this general conclusion more recently.

Researchers on work organizations seem to have learned little from Knoke and Prensky (1984), for research overviews and textbooks in the "organization studies" field still continue to take a paid-staff VG flat-earth approach, which ignores GAs and supralocal volunteer associations, with only minor exceptions. A very popular, but also learned and generally comprehensive, textbook on

TABLE 5.1 Comparison of Structure of Grassroots Associations and Paid-Staff
Voluntary Groups

Grassroots Associations	*Paid-Staff Voluntary Groups*
Small locality base	Small locality base
Substantial autonomy	Substantial autonomy
Mainly volunteer work	Mainly paid work
Mainly informal tax exemption	Mainly formal tax exemption
More informal organization	More complex organization
More internal democracy	More internal hierarchy
More member benefit goals	More nonmember benefit goals
More often polymorphic	More often monomorphic
Substantial sociodemographic homogeneity	Less sociodemographic homogeneity
Few economic resources of money or personnel	More economic resources of money and personnel

(work) organizations by Hall (1996), now in its sixth edition, reads as if no GAs exist. It does not even have the term "associations" (or "clubs") in its subject index, although nonprofit organizations are mentioned on one page and voluntary organizations are mentioned on seven pages of the text, according to the subject index. Paid-staff nonprofits themselves are dealt with on only a couple of pages out of 330 total pages.

The first edition of Hall's text did not even mention nonprofit organizations or voluntary organizations in the index at all, let alone mention associations, clubs, or GAs (Hall, 1972). Nor did most similar earlier overview books pay any significant attention to VGs (under the general labels of either "nonprofit" or "voluntary group"), let alone to GAs (roughly speaking, local voluntary associations) or to supralocal associations (Argyris, 1960; Boulding, 1953; Caplow, 1964; Herzberg, Mausner, and Synderman, 1959; March and Simon, 1958). Even those authors mentioning associations or other nonprofits did so very sparingly, nearly always as an essentially unexplored type of organization that was contrasted, implicitly or explicitly, with the "right type" of organizations to study—work organizations and especially businesses (Barton, 1961; Blau and Scott, 1962; Hage, 1980). Etzioni's (1961) classic book on organizations was the main exception during this earlier period, focusing in depth on how normative voluntary organizations differ from other organizations.

Thus, general (work) organization scholarship also has a flat-earth perspective by neglecting VGs generally as a category, just as paid-staff VG research in turn is analogously limited in ignoring GAs.

6

Internal Processes

This chapter deals with common operations or processes that tend to occur within grassroots organizations (GAs). GA internal processes include miscellaneous stylistic and operational features such as GA activity timing, professionalism, distinctive action repertoires, socialization and training, and horizontal collaboration. The distinction between structure and processes is not always clear-cut, but I have made a primacy judgment for the purpose of locating sections in the present and prior chapters. Both what I am calling *internal structure* and *internal processes* are normatively conditioned by the GA and its members, sometimes with supporting attitudes from the local community (e.g., in the case or deviance or prestige).

INTERNAL PROCESSES

Evening and Weekend Timing of Most Activities

The activities of GAs are scheduled mainly on weekday evenings or on weekends, so that people with paid jobs or businesses can attend them. When weekday daytime activities are scheduled frequently for a GA, the GA tends to have a special type of membership with such time blocks available—homemakers without full-time jobs, retirees, the unemployed, people with part-time jobs, and night or "graveyard" shift workers (who usually work from 4 p.m. to midnight or from midnight to 8 a.m., respectively). Work organization employees work mainly the day shift from about 8 or 9 a.m. to 4 or 5 p.m. on weekdays in the

United States. Such paid employees usually are "off" on weekday evenings and on weekends. Thus, the timing of most GA activities usually is opposite that of work organization activities. This is because the work organization activities are "primary" in priority for most of their workers, whereas GA and program service volunteer activities tend to be "secondary" to most of their volunteers relative to paid work.

Gray (1975) examines this timing effect in a limited way. Controlling for the powerful education and job skill level variables, temporally marginal workers (the shift of workers beginning in the late afternoon) of two manufacturing businesses had demonstrably less participation in GAs than did temporally usual shift workers (day shift such as 9 a.m. to 5 p.m.) from the same two plants. Thus, not only does socially marginal timing of one's main full-time job result in lower GA participation, but the modal timing of GA activities is likely to be on weekday evenings and, to a lesser extent, on weekends, which both shifts of workers in the Gray study had free.

There are a few exceptions to weekday evenings and weekends for GA meetings. The civic service clubs, such as Lions and Soroptimists, tend to meet for lunch on weekdays at the same agreed-on local restaurants monthly and often post road signs on major routes into towns noting this fact. Volunteer firefighters and paramedics do their activities at all times of the day and night through the week.

Intermittent Meetings and Activities

In GAs, there usually are regular membership meetings (monthly is common), regular board meetings (usually monthly or quarterly), other committee meetings as needed for specific projects, and annual membership meetings, not just regular board or executive committee meetings as in paid-staff voluntary groups (VGs) (Katz, 1961, p. 53; Klausen, 1995; Rudy, 1986; Sagarin, 1969; Traunstein and Steinman, 1973; Wertheim, 1976; see also Appendix C). Activity in GAs, thus, has a much more intermittent quality than does activity in paid-staff VGs in which staff work mostly full-time five-day weeks throughout the year (with paid vacation leaves). Some GAs are intermittent in activity over periods of years, with dormancy periods in between. Lindgren (1987) describes a successful advocacy GA of this type.

A few types of GAs meet much more often than the rest, particularly cults, sects, communes, and self-help and other small support GAs (Appel, 1983; Beattie, 1990; Freeman, 1975; Katz and Bender, 1976; Wuthnow, 1994, p. 50). Larger GAs tend to meet less often (Bushee, 1945). Things may or may not be "happening" in a GA during the time period between official membership meetings or other collective events, depending on the activity of leaders and committees. Unlike paid-staff VG participants, the average participant/member of a GA tends to engage in a comparatively low level of activity such as some meeting attendance and payment of dues, amounting to 1 or 2 hours per week (see Chapter 2). McPherson and Smith-Lovin (1982) found that GA members in their representative sample of Nebraska residents spent about 5.6 hours per month in GA meetings. They also found that larger GAs tend to meet less frequently (p. 895).

The intermittent nature of GAs shows up most clearly in some GAs at the low extreme that have only one activity per year such as a dance, an annual meeting, a raffle, a party, or a crafts fair. These often are fund-raising intermediary GAs, which pass their excess revenues along to charitable causes including local schools (but targeted to help with particular facets of the schools that need help in the views of the GAs). At the high extreme are, for example, sports league GAs that have some of their members in activities nearly every day of the week during the season for that sport. In between are the more usual GAs that have weekly, twice-monthly, or monthly (most common) meetings with occasional other activities.

Fortmann (1985) describes how rural GAs in Botswana are seasonal in timing. Rural GAs are most active during the agricultural growing season if the GAs are agriculture related. Some similar seasonality can be observed in high school- or college-related student GAs, which usually are dormant during the summer vacation period in the United States. School service GAs, such as Parent-Teacher Associations and sports booster GAs, tend to have a similar summer hiatus. Indeed, many GAs in the United States tend to be less active during the summer months because of vacations of members and their children.

Political GAs show a cyclical timing with most activity just prior to elections. Youth GAs and church-related GAs also partake in the summer hiatus to some degree. Garden GAs, however, tend to show an opposite seasonal hiatus, especially in higher latitudes, stopping or slowing down markedly because the winter is too severe to grow outdoor plants and to look at members' gardens. Outdoor sports and recreation GAs must be similarly mindful of what is feasible in a given season (e.g., skiing GAs in winter, boating GAs in summer). There also are cultural factors that affect the "proper" timing such as some adults and children playing baseball in GAs during the spring through summer months. GAs for these sports are likely to have participation peaks related to the culturally prescribed proper seasons in which to play certain sports. Recreation GAs concerned with fishing and hunting are affected temporally by when it is legal to fish or hunt specific species or genuses in a given state, with peaks of activity just before and during the official "season" in each case.

But any way in which one considers GAs, they are much more intermittent in activity than are work organizations, which usually employ a 35- or 40-hour weekly paid staff all year long. It is a matter of personal enlightenment to understand that GAs do *not,* for any reason, *need* to become like paid-staff nonprofits or other work organizations in this matter of the timing of activity by participants. There are great virtues in either type of VG—GAs or paid-staff VGs. A prudent approach is to let each do its own thing without interfering with the other subsector any more than minimally.

I have examined the differences between more internally active and less active GAs in my study of one eastern suburb with a stratified random sample of 59 GAs (Appendix C). Statistical analysis showed that more active GAs tended to have more informal and less formal structures (fewer of the usual officers, fewer committees, and less likely to have boards of directors), smaller size, more likelihood of a residency requirement for members, less likelihood of using membership dues for significant revenues, and more likelihood of rating themselves as higher in impact. Interestingly, the more active GAs are *not* older, richer in revenues, more prestigious, or nonmember serving rather than member serving. This all adds up to more activity per capita in small support and self-help GAs of the sort that Wuthnow (1994) and many others have studied.

GAs with high internal activity per capita of analytical members tend to generate higher GA commitment and GA interest in their members (Knoke and Wood, 1981). Simply scheduling or announcing more activities for official members in a low commitment GA will not tend to improve commitment or activity levels in the GA very much. Member motivation and incentives must be approached and changed more directly. Other things being equal, high activity level GAs probably tend to accomplish more per capita than do lower activity level GAs because more volunteer time of members is being applied toward the accomplishment of GA goals and, thus, to higher impact in many cases. Thus, amount of internal activity per capita can be viewed as one simple measure of the "internal organizational health" of a GA. Because commitment is the key resource of GAs, GAs lacking it are unable to generate much activity, on average, and so have little impact, whether their efforts are turned inward or outward (Knoke and Wood, 1981).

Low Professionalism

GAs tend not to be interested or involved in the nonprofit management profession (Rubin, Adamski, and Block, 1989), the volunteer administration "profession" (Fisher and Cole, 1993; Perlmutter, 1982), or complicated GA leadership tactics (Chan and Rammohan, 1999; Flanagan, 1984). Leadership tends to be casual, befitting leisure activity. Self-help GAs are especially antiprofessional and antibureaucratic, many of them formed as a result of dissatisfaction with established health and human services agencies and their professionals (Katz, 1993; Lavoie, Borkman, and Gidron, 1994). GA leaders (and/or some part-time staff) tend not to read relevant journals or books; not to attend relevant training meetings or conferences; not to spend time consciously reviewing and trying to improve GA leadership, structure, and processes; not to create or use leadership manuals for new leaders and committee chairs; and so on.

Walker (1983) argues that strategic management should not be borrowed from business management and applied to VGs because it often is inappropriate. Salipante and Golden-Biddle (1995) similarly argue that VG leaders should not adopt business organizations' externally focused approach to strategic change. These arguments are all the more true for GAs. Klausen (1995) argues specifically for the nonprofessional nature of GAs and their leaders and the inappropriateness of the standard organizational model for understanding them.

There are higher professionalism level GAs, by contrast, with leaders (officers, board members, and others) who tend to do all of the forgoing, but such GAs are less frequent. Some examples are firefighter corps and emergency paramedic squads (Gora and Nemerowicz, 1985; Perkins, 1989). More professional GAs as volunteer-run groups might tend to be more effective on the whole, in part because their leadership takes the task of efficiently achieving GA goals more seriously (i.e., impact and effectiveness concerns). Professionalism in GAs tends to increase as a GA moves toward becoming a paid-staff VG (Perkins and Poole, 1996).

Low External Funding

GAs tend to depend little or not at all on government contracts and foundation or business grants. (A longer version of this section can be found in Smith, 1998a.) This is due partly to the negative attitudes of external funders toward GAs as potential recipients (Hyland, Russell, and Hebb, 1990). GAs also tend not to receive funding from United Ways, which tend to target larger paid-staff VGs for giving (Brilliant, 1990). GAs are more likely to receive funds from alternative, nonmainstream, federated funding campains, if at all from federated funding campaigns. Some examples of such alternative campaigns would include women's funds, environmental funds, public interest funds, neighborhood advocacy funds, Black United Funds, and so on (Wenocur, Cook, and Steketee, 1984). However, alternative funds are small in the amount of money raised compared to the United Ways because of the latter's virtual monopoly on workplace fund-raising (Rose-Ackerman, 1980; Smith, 1977, 1978). GAs with nonmember service goals, in whole or in part, are more likely to seek and obtain external grants or contracts (Chan and Rammohan, 1999).

An exception to the giving of external grants to GAs is the social movement philanthropy practiced by the Haymarket Peoples Fund, as studied by Ostrander (1995), and a few similar foundations in the United States. This foundation democratizes philanthropy by including GA leaders in the grant-making process rather than letting the latter be dominated by upper-status white males, as it usually is. This approach avoids a substantial amount of the usual control of GAs by funding agencies because societal "outsiders" are participating in making the grants. They look at things from a social movement perspective rather than from a status quo perspective (Jenkins and Eckert, 1986; McAdam, 1982; McCarthy, Britt, and Wolfson, 1991). The result is genuine support for social movement GAs and their work with relatively little interference by the foundation. This is one illustration of the resource mobilization perspective on social movements (McCarthy and Zald, 1977).

Most GAs tend to be internally dependent for funds, based on dues and donations and sometimes with small amounts of fees. They also raise money from nonmembers through special fund-raising events such as dances, suppers, auctions, craft fairs, and raffles. Sometimes, a particular fund-raising event is a "trademark event" run only by a given GA in town, according to my study of one eastern suburb (Appendix C)—*the* plant sale, *the* craft fair, *the* pancake breakfast, and so on. The internally dependent GAs tend to be smaller, *all* volunteer-run, younger, less complex, less prestigious groups (Milofsky and Romo, 1988). The rarer, more grant/contract-dependent GAs are toward the high end of the forgoing dimensions. National associations are more like the latter (Knoke, 1990b). Examples of GAs at the two extremes would be a Bible study group (internal funding) versus an ambulance corps GA (external funding, usually by local government).

Thus, the usual *source* of GA funds is important in addition to the *amount* of such funds that a GA has (an aspect of GA size or resources). Source of funds speaks to the issue of how dependent a GA is on other groups and organizations for its normal operations and, therefore, to the amount of influence exerted on the GA by external bodies that might co-opt the GA. Saltman (1973) found that government funding for a small GA distorted the latter's goals. Horch (1994) found a loss of autonomy for 397 German associations receiving government funds, although this was limited somewhat by cultural factors (e.g., government consultation with VGs on legislation) and the perspective of the government agencies involved.

European local governments tend to provide funding support to GAs far more than do U.S. local governments (where U.S. local volunteer firefighters and ambulance corps are major exceptions) (Gora and Nemerowicz, 1985; Perkins, 1989). Van Harberden and Raymakers (1986) found that Dutch government support influenced self-help GAs by encouraging them to fit themselves with government program goals. Similarly, Riiskjaer and Nielsen (1987) found that government money for sports GAs in Denmark threatened their autonomy. In various nations, government subsidies sometimes do not lead to declines in autonomy (Ibsen, 1996), but more often they do (Blum and Ragab, 1985; Fisher, 1993, p. 33; Sharma and Bhatia, 1996, Sharp, 1981). Paid-staff VGs generally risk their autonomy more seriously than do GAs by their greater dependence on external grants and contracting out of government services (Ferris, 1993; Smith and Lipsky, 1993).

Broad But Intermittent Political Involvement

An important reason why GAs have so much impact on creating and maintaining participatory democracy and a civil society is that virtually every type of GA gets involved in political processes *sometimes,* and quite a few GA types have a continuing significant level of politicization. GA members tend to know that taking such political stands on GA-relevant issues is acceptable.

To give an example that most Americans will recognize, consider the National Rifle Association (NRA) in the United States. This highly politicized national recreational association persuades its national membership of the "correct" political view on matters relating to guns (not just rifles). Part of the way in which this politicization occurs is by the national headquarters using its affiliated GAs all over the nation as places for local political discussion on these specific issues. The discussion process in these polymorphic GAs, even if only informal, helps to politicize NRA members but also tends to perform more general political mobilization, getting GA members involved in political issues that concern them.

It is easy to see this political mobilization process in the case of the NRA and its GA branches. Now, consider that there is virtually no type of GA that cares about no political issue, locally or supralocally. Phrased in the positive, all GA types tend to have some significant political involvement on some issues, some of the time, at least in their own communities. Verba and Nie (1972, pp. 178-79) show, with national sample data, that all 15 association types (nearly all GAs) they inquire about are reported by their members to be sometimes involved in community affairs and to be sometimes sites of political discussion. Percentages range from 20% of sports GA members reporting that political *discussion* takes place in the GAs up to 97% of members of political GAs saying the same thing. Reported GA *involvement* in community affairs for each type of GA ranges from 28% to 85% for the same two types of GAs at the bottom and top, respectively. One might expect sports GAs or some other sociability or recreational GA type to be at the bottom generally, but the key point is that the bottom is at least 20% above zero GA political involvement even for the most nonpolitical GA types.

The same types of findings emerge in other Western democracies as well. In a landmark study in Britain, Newton (1975) identifies more than 3,000 GAs in Birmingham, Britain's second largest city. He surveyed these GAs and found that about 30% were politically active at the time. Verba and Nie (1972) gathered and report their data in a different manner, but there is some general comparability with the British data that indicates somewhat lower GA politicization.

Measurement differences could account for some or all of this difference between the two nations in GA political involvement. Among other differences, Verba and Nie (1972) randomly sampled U.S. individual adults, whereas Newton (1975) took a citywide census of GAs and gathered information from some of them. This difference in the sampling lets Newton add the additional point of interest that larger GAs tend to be more politically involved.

Many GA types are *persistently political,* not just officially political GAs such as political party local committees but also school service GAs, civic service clubs, veterans groups, farm organizations, nationality GAs, and professional or academic societies. Members of all these GA types reported 50% or more of the time that their GAs were politically involved on both of the Verba and Nie (1972, p. 178) questions reported earlier.

Low/Moderate External Power

Individually, most GAs tend to be politically weak in their communities. However, local power ranges from weak, small, informal new GAs at the low end (which can accomplish little externally) to GAs such as local branches of national service clubs (e.g., Kiwanis, Lions, Soroptimists), the Junior Chamber of Commerce, the Junior League, and the League of Women Voters (which tend to have substantial power in the community) (Smith, 1967, 1986a; see also Appendix C). The power of GAs to accomplish political goals is discussed and illustrated in Chapter 9. GAs that attempt to develop and wield power locally often are able to do so effectively. On a larger scale, the low-power GAs noted earlier can be contrasted with the most powerful *national* pressure groups such as the American Medical Association, the Chamber of Commerce of the United States, and the NRA (and sometimes their local affiliates).

External power is not the same as, and is more important than, political orientation or degree of politicization of GAs, which varies greatly among and within types of groups (Verba and Nie, 1972, pp. 178-79; Verba, Schlozman, and Brady, 1995, p. 63). Note that some theoretically nonpolitical GAs, such as the local Business and Professional Women's Club and Rotary Club, tend to have a great deal of local community power, in part because they tend to have as members powerful local people from business and the professions. And local Republican or Democratic Committees, which are officially political, can be virtually powerless if they represent only a small minority in their communities (when there is substantial other-party dominance locally).

At whatever territorial level the association represents, a powerful association can get the attention of relevant political decision makers and leaders, successfully getting the group's issues into the policy arena and often accepted. Also, it can successfully block the policy initiatives of others in these same arenas of power, if desired (Rauch, 1994). Powerful GAs attract resources of people and money more easily than do weaker GAs. The former are more likely to bring about sociopolitical change and have other types of external impact. They often generate a good deal of participation and activity.

Smith (1986a, p. 30) found, in a sample of 97 Massachusetts GAs, that those rated more powerful also were rated more effective and active, indicating a halo effect of good reputation. Such powerful GAs were significantly higher in terms of prestige, affiliation with a state or national organization (polymorphic affiliates), active participants, committees and subcommittees, meetings per year, sociability and entertainment activities, decision-making role of the rank-and-file (greater internal democracy), nonmember benefit primary goal, selectivity of membership, and use of the names of the current localities in the official GA names (indicating more community pride). High-power groups tended to have less internal conflict, fewer cliques, and less apathy.

Rated effectiveness also can be seen as a measure of GA power. In a small Boston suburb, Smith and Shen (1996) found that GAs with higher effectiveness reputations tended to have more formalization and be nonmember benefit oriented (vs. member benefit oriented) as well as to have more revenues, more officers, more developed boards of directors, better top staff leadership, and more developed committee structures.

Low/Moderate Prestige

Most GAs have low or moderate prestige in their communities, many of them not being widely known, as in the case of a small Bible reading group of a particular local church or a self-help GA for a particular illness or behavioral condition. There are, of course, some high-prestige/reputation GAs, as in the case of a local Rotary Club or Junior League chapter in a U.S. community (Minnis, 1952; see also Appendix C). A GA can affect its prestige by its member selection processes. If it selects higher status people as members, then the GA tends to have a higher prestige level in the community generally than if it selects lower status people as members. More powerful GAs tend to have higher prestige, other things being equal.

Some GAs are prestige neutral such as many hobby groups. Amateur enthusiasts for this or that hobby come in all social class levels, although hobby GAs that involve the arts or sciences tend to have more prestige (Bishop and Hoggett, 1986; Stebbins, 1979). What is effectively prestigious also varies with socioeconomic status (SES) and social class. In the working class or below, being a member or leader of a union, a sports club, a rod-and-gun club, or a veterans' GA tends to be prestigious among one's same-class friends and acquaintances. In the middle class, being a member or leader of a locally prestigious church (e.g., Congregational, Presbyterian, Episcopalian [Johnstone, 1992, p. 180]) brings prestige benefits among one's same-class friends and acquaintances, as does membership and activity in local professional associations, in civic service clubs such as Rotary and Soroptimists (Charles, 1993), and in certain fraternal GAs such as the Freemasons and Shriners (Clawson, 1989; Schmidt and Babchuk, 1972). In upper-class levels, membership in the local garden club, Junior League, and other highly prestigious GAs can bring high prestige satisfactions to women (Minnis, 1953). Domhoff (1974, 1983) describes elite U.S. clubs, many of which are paid-staff nonprofits—semiresidential social clubs or "country clubs" where members dine and socialize (see also Baltzell, [1958] 1979; Ostrander, 1984; Robinson, 1990). But some upper-class clubs, such as polo and cricket clubs, are GAs. Ostrander (1984) describes similar elite clubs for women to some degree as part of her research on upper-class women.

In any given community, there tends to be a range of prestige of the GAs present, and accordingly, they bring different degrees of prestige satisfaction to their members and leaders from the standpoint of the total community prestige system (Warner and Lunt, 1941; findings from my unpublished eight-town study). However, it is not known whether GA members and participants within a given social class level feel the same degree of subjective prestige satisfaction from their GAs as the members and participants in other GAs feel at other class levels. That is, we do not know whether a veterans' GA member feels as much prestige satisfaction within his circle of acquaintances as a polo club member feels among his. Nor do we know much about intra-GA prestige incentives except that they exist and probably play a role in encouraging leader participation. Leaders of GAs tend to receive more prestige than do average members, and this prestige is one incentive for doing the extra associational volunteer work involved in being good GA leaders.

Young and Larson (1965) found that higher prestige associations in a community tended to be larger, older, and more formalized; tended to originate more interorganizational activities in town, hold programs open to people in town other than members, and affiliate with organizations outside the town (hence polymorphic); had introduced some type of innovation into the town; had leaders who were recent in-movers from elsewhere; placed the same people in leadership jobs repeatedly (oligarchy); and had high-level primary relations and friendship activity within the group. Payne (1954) also found higher prestige GAs to be larger.

Willerman and Swanson (1953), in a study of college sororities, found that greater prestige among these GAs on one campus was associated positively with greater GA age, member SES, and size (hence visibility and social acceptability) of campus fraternities with which the sororities did things as groups. Only greater GA age was present in both studies, suggesting that lengthy survival helps to accumulate GA prestige.

At the very bottom of the prestige continuum, usually, are deviant GAs such as delinquent gangs, nudists, witches' covens, and strange cults (e.g., a local chapter of the Church of Satan) (Adler, 1986; Covey, Menard, and Franzese, 1992; Hartman, Fithian, and Johnson, 1991; Lyons, 1988; Spergel, 1995). Babchuk and Schmidt (1976) argue that greater prestige or public support is accorded to associations that use socially acceptable or conventional *means* to attain their goals. By contrast, associations that seek acceptable *goals* through unacceptable or deviant means, such as the terrorist Angry Brigade in its time (Carr, 1975), often are stigmatized for such means irrespective of their socially acceptable basic goals.

Fundamental Deviance More Likely

Although usually "integrative" in sociological terms and, thus, socially acceptable, a minority of GAs generally are alienated from their larger society, fundamentally deviant, and socially disapproved. Even paid-staff VGs occasionally might engage in deviance (Glaser, 1994), but GAs are more likely to be fundamentally deviant. GAs are more likely to be fundamentally deviant groups than are paid-staff VGs because there usually is little or no risk of losing one's livelihood by volunteer deviance in fundamentally deviant but noncriminal GAs in a functioning democracy with de facto civil liberties including freedom of assembly, free association, and free speech. Individual employee deviance in a fundamentally deviant work organization is more likely to lead to unemployment, fines, or significant incarceration and the resulting long-term stigmatization by mainstream society.

Deviance in a fundamentally deviant GA is deviance in a secondary leisure time role. Deviance in a fundamentally deviant work organization, such as a paid-staff VG, is deviance in a primary, more important work role for employees, managers, owners, and society. It is perceived as more threatening to society by social control agents. Deviance by volunteers in a fundamentally deviant volunteer program of a work organization also is less likely to be tolerated by a work organization of whatever type for the same basic reason: Work organizations are seen as important, and GAs are not, by many in society. Hence, there are few or no fundamentally deviant service volunteer programs, whereas there are some fundamentally deviant GAs in small percentage terms.

Milofsky and Blades (1991) raise the point about paid-staff VG deviance in a milder way, writing about the lack of accountability of health charities: "The health charities are largely insulated from public scrutiny or from effective regulation" (p. 372). Bennett and DiLorenzo (1994) describe a range of deviance and misconduct by health paid-staff nonprofits in the United States. Etzioni and Doty (1976) point out that even seemingly normal paid-staff nonprofits, such as hospitals, can be guilty of abuses that make them seem more like for-profit organizations. Ignoring deviant VGs in the voluntary nonprofit sector

(VNPS) will not make them go away any more than ignoring criminals or the Mafia makes them go away.

There are even more severe problems of deviance from societal norms by some fundamentally deviant GAs than by deviant work organizations (Smith, forthcoming a). Although only a tiny minority of all GAs are involved, nonetheless there are many social movement groups, cults and sects, extremist political groups, racist and other hate groups, witches' covens, delinquent youth gangs, nudist GAs, paramilitary militia GAs, and other types of fundamentally deviant GAs that are disapproved by society generally for deviant goals or activities to achieve them. Most such deviant GAs practice some significant degree of secrecy so as to evade social control agents and agencies in society as well as to fulfill several other functions (Schaefer, 1980).

Every type of social group, structure, and process in society has its "downside" or "dark side." And there *is* a dark side to the VNPS, much as some would like to deny its existence in a misguided effort to pretend that the VNPS and all of its groups are perfect models of decorum and morality (Smith, 1995c, 1995e). The latter people do this either by completely ignoring deviant nonprofits or by *defining* them out of the VNPS. This is more of a "flat-earth" perspective by nonprofit sector scholars and leaders—the "angelic voluntary groups" flat-earth paradigm.

Witches' covens or terrorist GAs cannot readily advertise publicly, being essentially "underground" groups. Deviant GAs probably are more likely to be autonomous, monomorphic, less formalized, younger, more member benefit oriented, less professionalized, smaller, less externally cooperative, less powerful, less prestigious, and more dependent on internal sources of funding (Smith, forthcoming a). However, impact on members can be *very* great, influencing analytical members to engage in very major deviance, as noted in Chapter 1 (Smith, 1995c, forthcoming a).

One major problem with understanding fundamentally deviant GAs is that no studies seem to have sampled representatively different types of deviant *and* nondeviant/socially acceptable GAs. Many case studies of one or a few such GAs are available, and there are books that survey the literature on particular types of fundamentally deviant GAs (Lofland, 1996).

Distinctive Action Norms

The most distinctive action strategies of GAs generally are periodic open membership meetings, periodic board meetings for board members, periodic committee meetings for members of various types of committees, occasional special fund-raising events open to nonmembers, and occasional social events for members and their families. Specific GA types have additional distinctive action strategies. For example, veterans' GAs with their own buildings (e.g., often the American Legion or Veterans of Foreign Wars) usually operate drop-in bars open to members on a daily basis for long hours. Sports clubs have competitions. Hobby groups have shows and sometimes competitions. Some political GAs attempt to influence voters at polling places at election times. Youth development groups often have campouts or other recreational outings. Tenant GAs have rent strikes (Brill, 1971; Lawson, 1983). Recently, major unions have focused on a "corporate strategy" (Perry, 1996).

The tendency of GAs of all types to have distinctive norms about strategies and tactics the groups should use to achieve their purposes rarely has been studied at all. Most emphasis has been on GA goals. The type of research being pointed toward here has been done mainly by social movement researchers, who have studied what strategies and tactics (action repertoires) social movement organizations and whole social movements tend to use over historical time (Gamson, 1990; Hall, 1995; McAdam, 1983; Panet-Raymond, 1987; Piven and Cloward, 1979). Sharp (1973) shows that, for nonviolent protest activities alone, there are more than 200 tactics to consider (see also Carter, 1974).

When all manners of more conventional tactics and strategies are considered, the subfield of research here is seen to be very broad and open. As noted earlier, Babchuk and Schmidt (1976) argue that tactics/means of a GA are far more likely to arouse nonmember opposition than are purposes or ends. Just as Milofsky and Romo (1988) suggest that it is difficult for nonprofits to shift their ways of raising needed funds, one might suggest that it is difficult for GAs to change other normative aspects of their internal processes and structures that affect their members and environments such as major action strategies. In Chapter 8, we see that GAs may change their goals over their life cycles (e.g., deradicalization, goal displacement), but we know little about change in major tactics/means.

Informal Recruitment

GAs usually recruit new members informally by word of mouth. Certain people are more likely to participate in GAs generally than are others in the population. The former include those with higher education and higher occupational prestige who are middle-aged, married, and so on (Smith, 1994a). For a specific GA, newcomers are drawn in because of ties they have to other existing members in that GA and because of sociodemographic similarity to members of the GA (McPherson, Popielarz, and Drobnic, 1992; Smith, 1964). People often are asked specifically by friends or acquaintances to join a given GA (Smith, 1994a). People with general attitudes conducive to participation in a GA as a leisure time activity are more likely to join a GA than to do alternative leisure activities (Mulford and Klonglan, 1972; D. Smith, 1966, 1975, 1994a). Recruitment also occurs informally to specific GAs because of GA public images, prestige/stigma, and perceived incentives. People develop specific attitudes toward particular GAs based on information available about these groups, and various types of positive information and attitudes lead to joining and participation in certain GAs (Mulford and Klonglan, 1972; D. Smith, 1966, 1975, 1994a). There also are territorial conduciveness factors that lead to more GA joining and membership for some people and not others (e.g., living in a higher SES neighborhood [Smith, 1994a]). Paid-staff VGs tend to depend more on formal mass media and employment agency recruitment of new employees.

Informal Socialization But Seldom Formal Training

Paid-staff VGs tend to seek educated and specially trained leaders nowadays as a mark of increasing professionalism in that area of VG activity. Universities and colleges have begun to train (no degree involved but perhaps a certificate of accomplishment) and educate (usually with an M.A. degree for successful completion) paid-staff VG managers in many centers and programs in the United States and elsewhere, particularly Canada and Britain (see Crowder and Hodgkinson, n.d., and two earlier editions). There also now are many books and articles about the functioning of paid-staff VGs that contain accumulated knowledge and ideas by VG practitioners or scholars or both (see the long list of references cited in the introduction to Part II).

In a related development of attempted professionalism, some universities and colleges also have developed courses for training volunteer administrators (Boles, 1985; Brudney and Brown, 1990; Paradis, 1994; Smith and Walker, 1977; Stubblefield and Miles, 1986) and sometimes volunteers themselves (Delworth et al., 1974). And volunteer programs sometimes train their own volunteers briefly (Bodanske, 1972; Broadbridge and Horne, 1996; Brudney, 1990, pp. 107-110; Schondel et al., 1995).

On the other hand, GAs as serious leisure tend to be rather simple to join, to participate in, or even to lead. Newcomers tend to be *informally* socialized, and very few feel the need for any college courses or training to be associational volunteers or leaders. GA members and leaders come to learn and understand the norms and rules of the group particularly through friendships they make with established members in the GA and one or more primary groups (e.g., cliques, sets of friends) established therein (Ross, 1977). More formal educational processes such as training seldom are needed. Longitudinal studies have shown that socialization for future adult GA activity probably takes place among some participating high school students through their high school extracurricular activities such as student clubs/GAs (Hanks, 1981; Hanks and Eckland, 1978).

Hodge and Trieman (1968) have shown that parental GA activity levels had a significant effect on adult GA activity levels of their children, controlling for both the children's SES during early adulthood and their parents' SES. With a colleague, I have shown that parental SES, parental *attitudes* toward GAs, and (to a lesser extent) parental GA activity tend to socialize their children for later adult GA activity (Smith and Baldwin, 1974a). Thus, as would be expected, both the home and the school are sites of significant socialization into adult GA activity. This also might be true of home and school socialization into particular *types* of GAs and perhaps even *specific* GAs, but no one has addressed these research questions yet, to my knowledge.

Religions in general spend a good deal of time not only in socialization of new members but also in formal training through Sunday schools and the equivalent in other religions as well as training sessions for adult converts (Johnstone, 1992, chap. 4). Wuthnow (1994, p. 76) treats Sunday school classes as small support GAs. Other GA types that involve substantial socialization and (sometimes) training include fraternal lodges and women's auxiliaries, fraternities and sororities, and other (mostly sociability) GAs with secret rituals and extensive ideologies (Daraul, 1965; Heckethorne, [1897] 1965; Scott, 1965; Smith, 1972d).

Voluntary Termination of Membership

It is extremely rare for GA members to be formally ejected from membership in their GAs if they pay their dues. Exceptions are some civic service clubs that have attendance requirements so as to remain in good standing. Few GAs have such requirements, so that "on paper only" members are common in most types of formal (vs. semiformal) GAs. GAs attempt to be inclusive of the types of people they want as members and tend to be gentle in pressure to keep them involved. Thus, far more paid-staff VG employees are likely to be "fired" than GA members are to be involuntarily terminated.

Moderate Horizontal Collaboration

The concept here can have various labels, including "cooperation," but it is totally unrelated to the matter of a nonprofit being a consumer or producer cooperative. Many GAs have local collaborative ties with "sponsors" such as schools, colleges, churches, hospitals, and library-based GAs. In my study of one eastern suburb (Appendix C), 53% of sampled GAs had such ties without the presence of hospitals or colleges (which would have resulted in still more such ties). "Isolated" GAs have no ties or collaborative activities with any other local groups, whereas highly collaborative GAs work with other local GAs or with local work organizations to accomplish their goals (Kaplan, 1986).

Such high collaboration can come through bilateral relationships, multilateral collaboration, informal coalitions, or formal federations of groups working on particular issues or projects. For example, a coalition of women's or environmental

GAs that tries to raise funds together is a formal multilateral federation/coalition, whereas two GAs that jointly sponsor a specific public fund-raising event such as a pancake breakfast are a short-term, informal bilateral example of collaboration. The highest level of collaboration leads to merger or acquisition, something that rarely happens to GAs.

Milofsky and Hunter (1994) discuss the origins of GAs and other community organizations. They stress the concept of embeddedness in the community context in a variety of ways. This embeddedness includes horizontal relationships with other groups and organizations in the community in cooperative relationships of the type under consideration at the moment. They also discuss vertical embeddedness relationships of the type that I term *polymorphic*. GAs cannot be understood, they argue, apart from such embeddedness, in terms of both how they arise and how they are sustained. I agree.

Mulford and Mulford (1980, p. 26) found greater collaboration among local associations to be correlated with larger memberships, more meetings, more attendance, more innovations, more previous joint programs, and more present joint programs, but also somewhat more conflict with other groups. GAs, particularly if they are more informal (Smith 1992b, p. 261), tend to be more isolated from and less cooperative with other groups than are many paid-staff VGs. Other than having local sponsors, semiformal GAs are more likely to "do their own thing" by themselves than are more formal GAs or paid-staff nonprofits.

Selle and Øymyr (1992, p. 170) found in Norway that such "introverted" groups were more likely to die out (after shorter lives) during an eight-year period than were more externally oriented groups having more outside contacts. Prestby and Wandersman (1985), in another longitudinal study, found that active block GAs had more links with local block umbrella organizations and with other groups than did inactive block GAs and that the former maintained these links more over time. Weed (1989) found that greater member support for polymorphic GAs led to greater contact with other similar GAs, all affiliates of the same national VG (Mothers Against Drunk Driving).

Collaborative GAs also tend to have more resources and to be more effective in goal attainment because collaborative relationships with other groups/organizations can be viewed as resources in themselves. Indeed, Yuchtman and Seashore (1967), as well as many subsequent work organization researchers following their lead, define organizational effectiveness in terms of the "ability to exploit its environment in the acquisition of scarce and valued resources to sustain its functioning" (p. 393). As one example, Danziger (1983) found that democratic coalitions of GAs had greater impacts on the chief executives of metropolitan counties in the United States in 1975 than did GAs working alone. Furthermore, Sharp (1981) found that coalitions tend to broaden GA goals and cause GAs to adopt both adversarial and cooperative stances with city governments, thus reducing their earlier GA advocacy. Boles (1994) found that inclusion of feminist VGs, including GAs, in broader issue networks, including government leaders, helped to sustain feminism as a social movement.

Henderson and Thomas (1981) discuss some of the advantages of VG federations including increased scope for coordination of activities, development of collective strategies, sharing facilities or resources, stimulation of new projects, and developing new resources. Some risks include neglect of the VGs themselves, less attention by the leaders, differing VG operational styles, need for adequate funding for federation activities, and neglect of alternative forms of cooperation. Most of these apply to GA coalitions or federations as well as to paid-staff VG federations.

The issue of collaboration also relates to competition and conflict among GAs. Rose (1955) initiated research in this area, showing that both competition and conflict affect the internal structures of GAs, causing them to be more cohesive, flexible, complex, and active. More recently, York and Zychlinski (1996) show that competing Israeli VGs in a locality could collaborate in joint forums. Hall and Hall (1996) did a national survey of poor people's VGs in the United States and Puerto Rico, and at both the national and local (GA) levels, competition rather than cooperation was seen as the prevailing external pressure.

Because some aspects of collaboration with other organizations are structural (e.g., membership in a coalition or federation), the present issue could be placed in the category of internal structure discussed earlier.

Younger Age

GAs usually exist for fewer years than do paid-staff VGs. Age ranges from "newborn" GAs struggling to find money, members, and programs at one end to old GAs dating from the 19th century or earlier such as a local Grange GA in a farm community and a fraternal lodge in a small older town. In the United States, there are much older paid-staff VGs such as Harvard University (founded in 1636) and the national headquarters of Phi Beta Kappa (first chapter founded in 1776) with its local chapters being GAs.

Older GAs in most communities might be only 50 to 80 years old or so. These older GAs tend to be sociability GAs (e.g., Elks, Freemasons), service clubs (e.g., Rotary, Lions), or economic support GAs (e.g., Grange or Farm Bureau in rural areas, businesspeople's GAs in urban areas). This results from the fact that GAs usually are short-lived (Selle and Øymyr, 1992; Traunstein and Steinman, 1973) and tend to turn into paid-staff nonprofits if they get much larger and older (see Chapter 8). Over the longer term of decades, Selle and Øymyr (1992) found in a Norwegian province that about two-thirds of GAs died during a 40-year period. Chan and Rammohan (1999) found a median age of 30 years in their sample of more established GAs in a California county.

I am not concerned here with the average age of members or the "age focus" of the GA, which Cutler (1980) has suggested as other bases for GA typology (see also Rose, 1960). However, GA age is closely related to another important dimension, namely "survival." Older groups are higher in survival (life), whereas dead groups are very low in survival and younger live groups are in between (Bowen et al., 1994). Newness generally is a disadvantage among GAs, as with other types of organizations (Hannan and Freeman, 1989).

Greater GA age tends to bring stability to a GA and shows staying power. Age permits the gradual accumulation of people and financial resources (Bowen et al., 1994; Chapin and Tsouderos, 1956), the establishment of cooperative relationships with other groups, the development of a recognizable track record of accomplishment, greater visibility (other things being equal), and so on. Age is related to ease of dissolution of a GA. Younger GAs, with less accumulated resources, are easier to disband. Older GAs, with many more resources, are harder to disband because of the question of who gets these resources (e.g., money, members, property). Thus, members of an older GA are more likely to object to disbanding the GA than are members of a younger group. This occurs both because the members of an older GA tend to care more about their group's accumulated resources but also because they tend to care more for the GA's accumulated prestige and track record of accomplishments. They tend to have more of an emotional attachment to the GA as worth keeping alive somehow.

With survival as a criterion, Selle and Øymyr (1992) show that Norwegian GAs are more likely to survive over an eight-year period if they are older and larger; have fewer women members or leaders; and have middle-aged members, lower internal activities, higher external and public policy influence activities (more contact with local authorities), more subgroups, more affiliations with regional or national organizational networks (more likely polymorphic), and more cooperation with other local GAs. Emerick (1991) found that self-help GAs of mental patients or ex-patients survived longer with interactive support from traditional professions if the GAs were conservative in their affiliations (i.e., if they accepted the existing mental health establishment). Such GAs survived longer with support from social movement people if the groups were radical and anti-mental health establishments in their orientations.

Because they require fewer economic resources and usually operate more informally, GAs are easier to form than are work organizations such as paid-staff VGs, businesses, and governments (Lanfant, 1976). This is the genius of GAs in the United States and elsewhere. If people see a problem in their community or the world, or if they simply have a common interest, then they can immediately start to work on the problem or interest themselves in a GA *now,* as I write—not tomorrow or next year. They require no money to begin with, no grants or contracts, no office space, no paid staff, no legal incorporation, no state or federal tax exemption, and no other trappings of a paid-staff VG or other work organization. Insofar as money is needed, members can make donations, prescribe dues, or hold simple fund-raising events open to nonmembers. Insofar as space is needed for meetings, people can use their homes or space donated by or rented at low cost from local schools, libraries, churches, hospitals, or other work organizations or from other GAs that happen to own buildings (the latter being especially veterans' groups, historical societies, fraternal lodges, and garden clubs).

But ease of formation is accompanied by ease of dissolution. GAs tend to have short lives, on average, and tend to be younger than paid-staff VGs when comparative studies are made (Selle and Øymyr, 1992, p. 152; Smith, 1992b, p. 261). But short average life span does not vitiate their importance. Riots do not last very long, nor do coups d'état (usually only a few hours or days), nor does the sexual conception of human beings. Yet, these events can be extremely important for the local community, the larger society, and the whole human species.

Those few GAs that own their own land and buildings in a community tend to live longer and to be much harder to dissolve, I hypothesize without supporting quantitative data. With a building, GA leaders tend to feel more responsible for its upkeep and, therefore, for keeping the GA going. An obligation to the donor of the GA building or to those who contributed to its building fund also might be felt by the leaders. However, such real estate ownership is not a guarantee of long life. The declining interest and membership in the International Order of Odd Fellows in the United States has not been stopped by the widespread corresponding GAs' ownership of lodge halls built or bought long ago in many communities (Ferguson, 1937). Some remaining local Odd Fellows GAs have shifted their goals and taken to redeveloping office blocks and renting out space in the face of their own excess of useful space and declining membership (based on my personal observations and a discussion with some current Odd Fellow GA leaders in an eastern suburb [Appendix C]).

Other Important Miscellaneous Internal Processes

A number of other internal processes of GAs have received little or no research attention. Zald and Berger (1978), for example, discuss social movements *within* existing organizations such as coups d'état, insurgencies, and mass movements. Some fine-grain qualitative and historical studies would be needed on GAs to ferret out examples of such activities. One example of a coup d'état in a GA comes from my participant observational experience in one youth GA in which a youth leader appointed by adult leaders/advisers was essentially deposed by many GA members in favor of another youth they preferred.

Although the adult advisers tried to resist the massed youths for a few weeks, they eventually gave in to the coup so as to get on with GA activities in comparative peace.

Specific problems that tend to arise with a particular GA type or a specific GA need to be investigated. Selle and Øymyr (1992) found that such reported GA problems in a Norwegian province did not affect GA survival for eight years after initial measurement. Retention is a problem that many GAs have, even those with many members at any given time. Ross (1977) suggests that primary groups developed and maintained in a GA tend to foster member longevity, whereas failure of a newcomer to become integrated into a primary group within the GA fosters his or her exit and, thus, turnover from the standpoint of the GA.

McPherson et al. (1992) show empirically that retention in GAs is significantly related to sharing that membership with more network others—with more other close people and acquaintances. They state that "(1) shared memberships persist longer than unshared ones and [that] (2) the more [others] with whom the membership is shared, the greater the persistence" (p. 164). They also note that ties outside the group decrease the duration of membership and that memberships last longer for older individuals (p. 164).

CONCLUSION

As with the prior three chapters, this chapter shows that GAs are very different in many ways from paid-staff VGs. A summary of these differences is presented in Table 6.1 as ideal types rather than as quantitative summaries. In terms of processes, GAs tend to have evening weekday and weekend timing of activities, whereas paid-staff VGs have more weekday activities on the whole. GA activities also tend to be more intermittent in time, whereas paid-staff VG activities are more continuous. GAs tend to have low professionalism as leisure groups, whereas paid-staff VGs are more professional, befitting work organizations. GAs tend to have little external funding, whereas paid-staff VGs depend much more on such sources. GAs tend to have broad but intermittent political involvement, whereas paid-staff VGs are much more limited in their direct political involvement. The average external power of GAs is low to moderate, as is also true of paid-staff VGs unless they are large. GA prestige is low or moderate, on average, but some GAs have quite high prestige. Paid-staff VG prestige tends to be moderate, but some paid-staff VGs are high in prestige (e.g., colleges, hospitals, museums, symphony orchestras).

GAs are more likely to be fundamentally deviant from societal norms than are paid-staff VGs, although either type of group can be fundamentally deviant. GAs have their own distinctive action norms that are different, for the most part,

TABLE 6.1 Comparison of Processes of Grassroots Associations and Paid-Staff Voluntary Groups

Grassroots Associations	*Paid-Staff Voluntary Groups*
Evening and weekend timing of activities	Weekday timing of activities
Intermittent activities	More continuous activities
Low professionalism	Higher professionalism
Low external funding	Higher external funding
Broad, intermittent political activity	Low, direct political activity
Low external power	Low external power
Low/moderate prestige	Moderate/high prestige
More fundamental deviance	Less fundamental deviance
Distinctive action norms	Distinctive action norms
Informal recruitment	Formal recruitment
Informal socialization of newcomers	More formal training of newcomers
Voluntary termination of membership	Some involuntary termination of employees
Moderate horizontal collaboration	Moderate horizontal collaboration
Younger age	Moderate age

from the distinctive action norms of paid-staff VGs. Where a member meeting would be most typical of a GA, service provision to nonmembers would be most typical for a paid-staff VG as a distinctive action norm. GAs recruit members informally, usually by word of mouth, whereas paid-staff VGs often do formal mass media and employment agency recruitment of employees. GAs tend to give only informal socialization to newcomers, whereas paid-staff VGs often give formal training of some type to newcomers or select newcomers with such training. GAs rarely eject members involuntarily, whereas paid-staff VGs more often fire employees whose performances are deemed unsatisfactory. Both GAs and paid-staff VGs engage in moderate horizontal collaboration in their local communities, although for GAs this collaboration is most likely to be sponsorship by local paid-staff VGs or public schools/colleges. GAs tend to be younger, on average, than paid-staff VGs, and the former tend to have shorter life spans than the latter.

The overall pattern of processes in the two types of groups is strikingly different—a basic point neglected by those who use the paid-staff VG flat-earth paradigm instead of a round-earth paradigm.

7

Leadership and Environments

This chapter deals with leadership in grassroots associations (GAs). Leaders in a GA are seen as one or more individuals who exercise significant control over the principal activities of the GA as a group. There also is a section in the chapter that looks outward from the GA at its environment, asking how the GA relates to that environment.

LEADERSHIP

Leadership probably is more important in GAs than in paid-staff voluntary groups (VGs) because there is less guidance and "social momentum" of other types to keep GAs going (Adler, 1981; Anderson, 1964; Bailey, 1974; Fletcher, 1985; Hamilton, 1980; Lamb, 1975; Landsberger, 1972b). There is a tendency to speak of "leadership" in GAs versus "management" in paid-staff VGs. Leaders of the latter type of organizations apparently wish to associate themselves with the established fields of business management and public administration or with VG management as an emerging field, whether or not they have had any significant training in one of these three fields. Although national associations usually are paid-staff VGs, they are different from most paid-staff VGs in having memberships that ostensibly control the associations (Knoke, 1990b; Nall, 1967; Smith, 1992a). Because of powerful oligarchical tendencies in any large association, however, large and especially national associations tend to operate in many ways like other paid-staff nonprofits in terms of leadership (Drucker, 1990; Herman and Associates, 1994; Knoke, 1990b; Schmidt, 1973).

Knoke and Prensky (1984) make a very useful assessment of the relevance of the usual research on work organizations (mainly businesses and government agencies) to associations at all territorial levels. They conclude that there is no compelling evidence that such research on these different types of organizations will apply meaningfully to associations. This is especially true for the misapplication of such research findings to GAs. Leat (1993) comes to a similar conclusion, comparing for-profit and paid-staff nonprofit organizations in the United Kingdom. She finds that these two organizational types have much in common but also much to learn from each other that presently is different regarding the two types of organizations. She does not consider GA leadership explicitly. Klausen (1995), like Knoke and Prensky (1984), argues that the usual approach of organizational management theory does not fit small associations, especially sports GAs in Denmark. Indeed, he suggests that the attempt to apply such techniques might harm GAs. A special new mix of theory is needed for GAs.

Many scholars have discussed paid-staff VG leadership, based on either their own experiences or research or both (Borst and Montana, 1977; Bruce, 1994; Butler and Wilson, 1990; Carver, 1997; Chrislip and Larson, 1994; Connors, 1988; Conrad and Glenn, 1983; Drucker, 1990; Handy, 1988; Herman and Associates, 1994; Herman and Heimovics, 1991; Herman and Van Til, 1989; Houle, 1989; Howe, 1997; Knauft, Berger, and Gray, 1991; MacKeith, 1993; Middleton, 1987; Moyer, 1984; O'Connell, 1984; O'Neill and Young, 1988; Oster, 1995; Poulton, 1988; Rubin, Adamski, and Block, 1989; Wood, 1981; Young, 1983, 1987; Young et al., 1993).

Based on VG research, I would argue that leadership in GAs tends to be very different from work organization management, especially business and government organization management but also paid-staff VG management. Bush (1992) discusses the maintenance of a "nonprofit spirit" in paid-staff VGs that seem to be losing it. He suggests, among other things, that paid-staff VG leaders should pay more attention to historical voluntary nonprofit sector (VNPS) traditions such as altruism, compassion, and philanthropy; should emphasize cooperation and collaboration more than competition and conflict; and should remain sensitive to the key value of volunteerism. These suggestions could be applied to GA leaders as well.

In studying paid-staff nonprofit management, much attention is focused, not surprisingly, on paid staff, and especially the paid executive director or equivalent, as well as on the board of directors (see long list of reference citations two paragraphs earlier). Hall (1990) finds, from a case study of a museum, that nonprofit and managerial subcultures are in conflict in some, and perhaps many, paid-staff VGs.

General Leadership and Management in Voluntary Groups

I believe that only Mason (1984) has attempted to identify the features of "nonprofit enterprise management" that apply to both paid-staff nonprofits *and* GAs but that make these VNPS groups different from for-profit business organizations. These are quite interesting, although I do not agree completely with all of the points (e.g., Factor 4 in the following list is true for paid-staff VGs but not for GAs generally). Because I think that Mason's book deserves more attention, here I reproduce the list of factors, each of which receives one chapter of attention in Mason's book:

1. The market value of the services of voluntary enterprises cannot be measured as precisely as in business.

2. Their purposes are other than profit seeking.

3. Their principal tool is volunteerism produced by persuasion.

4. The production of resources and the provision of services are two distinct systems.

5. Voluntary enterprises have a special kind of constituency.

6. Money is a means in the voluntary sector, [whereas] in business it is an end.

7. Not-for-profit groups enjoy a special legal status.

8. Voluntary enterprises do not have a profit-and-loss criterion with which to monitor operational effectiveness.

9. Management requires more diplomacy. In business, management has more autonomy [and power].

10. Voluntary enterprises tend to accumulate multiple purposes.

11. Voluntary enterprises have a distinctive social character.

12. The resources available to not-for-profit groups are not as limited [in type] as business resources.

13. The groups can persist even though their consumption of resources consistently exceeds their tangible output.

14. Voluntary enterprises are characteristically more complex than their business counterparts. (pp. 21-22)

A number of other researchers have focused on the same issue, differences between for-profit and VG management, but they usually mean paid-staff VG management without stating this explicitly, taking the customary paid-staff VG "flat-earth" view of so many (Farrow, Valenzi, and Bass, 1980; Leat, 1993; Newman and Wallender, 1978; Unterman and Davis, 1982). Some scholars also suggest similarities between for-profit and VG management (Bailey and Grochau, 1993; Leat, 1993).

This is in part a "chicken and egg" vicious circle. Lack of research on GA leadership leads to its being ignored by scholars and textbook writers summarizing knowledge about VNPS management/leadership, whereas neglect of GA leadership in these sources mistakenly conveys the idea to other scholars that either GAs are unimportant to study regarding leadership or they function similarly to paid-staff VGs in management—both of which are false. Thus, and unfortunately, the paid-staff VG flat-earth view of GA leadership and its nonexistence or unimportance is self-perpetuating. With a "round-earth" view of the VNPS, it is easier to see that GA leadership research is very much (but not totally) neglected.

Walker (1983) makes a strong case that GAs are very different from business in the type of leadership/management required for success. Furthermore, he argues that it is not at all clear whether most GAs can or should be transformed into "managed systems," let alone should use strategic management (which he believes can be harmful for GAs and other VGs, contrary to Wortman, 1981). Many paid-staff VG scholars and leaders would disagree with Walker (1983) for paid-staff VGs, but most GA members and leaders would agree for GAs at least. Planning or using complex management systems for GAs is a bit like putting a large motor on a child's toy boat; it just does not fit or belong there. It does not really help because it is unsuited to the scale of operation and will "sink the boat" if too large and unwieldy.

GA leadership consists mainly of elected officers, board members, and committee chairs operating as volunteers, *not* as appointed paid staff (except for one or a few part-time paid workers in a minority of GAs). By definition, GAs tend to have fewer officers if they are less formal (Smith, 1992b). The committee structure of GAs tends to be more extensive, active, and important per member than in paid-staff nonprofits. Consistent with earlier points, there is no departmental paid-staff structure and much less formalization of leadership generally in GAs, as contrasted with paid-staff VGs (Chapin and Tsouderos, 1956; Smith, 1992b). Informal leaders, often past formal leaders not presently holding official positions, can be quite powerful in GAs, much more so than in work organizations including paid-staff nonprofits. Former GA presidents, for example, often stay in the groups and can wield much influence if they choose.

Volunteer Leaders

As noted earlier, by definition most GA leaders are volunteers, and by and large, their lower participants or followers also are volunteers. As Harris (1998a) noted recently, this limits the amount of management or direction that followers/members will accept with goodwill (see also Pearce, 1993). In paid-staff VGs, employees have less choice about following management directives. Of course, they can evade, complain, or leave, so there still are constraints on what management can order to be done.

Harris (1998a, p. 152) also notes that the presence of paid staff might be disruptive in associations. People know how to treat each other as volunteers, but paid staff in a GA are an unusual occurrence except in churches and synagogues (Hodgkinson, Weitzman, and Kirsch, 1989). Harris (1998a) argues that paid-staff roles might be "unclear or contentious" (p. 152).

I argue further that paid staff in GAs tend to move the groups toward being paid-staff VGs, by definition. Voluntary altruism declines somewhat, and volunteers leave more and more for paid staff to do in GAs. Volunteers also might resent that certain GA participants are being paid for their participation while most are not (case study by me of the Tampa Bay Symphony). Etzioni (1961) argued that this is an unstable situation that usually will be resolved in one direction or the other.

Low GA Leader Professionalism

Rather than having *attached* volunteer programs (as in hospitals or schools), in GAs the groups *are* the equivalent of the volunteer programs. There typically is little attention paid to volunteer management techniques such as selection, orientation, training, motivation, supervision, and retention in GAs, although recruitment gets significant attention, as noted earlier. Paid-staff VGs are not outstanding in the extent to which their volunteer programs attend to such matters either, but they do so more than GAs, on average (Fisher and Cole, 1993). A volunteer administrator in a work organization is far more likely to be a member of the Association for Volunteer Administration, for example, than is a GA leader. And there is no comparable association of GA leaders, to my knowledge. This fact in itself indicates the lesser professionalism and greater amateurism and volunteerism of GAs and their leaders.

Volunteer administration has been going through a process of attempted professionalization for two decades or more (Perlmutter, 1982). However, it actually is more of an occupational or role specialty than a true profession. Only a minority of volunteer administrators even have college degrees, let alone advanced professional degrees of any sort (Brudney and Brown, 1990; Stubblefield and Miles, 1986). Volunteer administration centrally lacks a strong and enduring connection with academia (occasional college courses on volunteer administration notwithstanding [Smith and Walker, 1977]), which all true professions have (e.g., law, medicine, social work, the ministry/priesthood, teaching, engineering, management, public administration). The term *professional,* in terms of advanced education, skill, and knowledge levels, often is confused with the distinction between paid work and volunteer or amateur work. The many paid volunteer administrators in the United States are far more accurately termed *paid staff,* many with some relevant training, rather than *professionals.*

In the same way, with fewer norms of professional aspiration, GAs are far *less* likely to engage in currently accepted nonprofit management practices such as strategic planning, leader and board development, strategic fund-raising, enhanced executive leadership, careful financial management and accounting, and a myriad of other practices promoted for paid-staff nonprofits by the "experts" (Connors, 1988; Herman and Associates, 1994; Herman and Heimovics, 1991; Knauft et al., 1991; Rubin et al., 1989). Christian (1980-81) argues that these skills can be brought into GAs by outside consultants if needed (see also Chutis, 1983).

Nor are GA leaders generally likely to take up nonprofit management as careers except when their GAs grow into paid-staff VGs. If anything, GA leaders might turn to more down-to-earth manuals for GA leadership such as the work by Flanagan (1984) and the type of resources mentioned in her Chapter 24. Speaking of social movement GAs, Kleidman (1994) argues that professionalism can have positive or negative effects on volunteer activism.

All in all, GAs are more likely to "muddle through" with what they can guess or find out by trial and error rather than depend on training, experts, or published materials for their leadership or management assistance (Chan and Rammohan, 1999). Their leaders often are proud to be amateurs rather than professionals at running their groups. Paid-staff nonprofit leaders, quite the contrary, tend to seek out expert advice and publications and even relevant training, wanting to be as professional as they can. Whether the latter "professionalism" succeeds in any significant way is quite unclear, although there is a good deal of credentials provision occurring in college/university centers on nonprofits.

In brief, GA leadership tends to be more informal as serious leisure, whereas paid-staff VG management is much more formal, exacting, and clearly work. When a leader of a GA messes up seriously, he or she usually still keeps the leadership position until the next election, although others might take on responsibility for the tasks involved. When a manager of a paid-staff VG, especially the executive director, messes up seriously, the manager might lose his or her job as a result.

Leadership Entry and the Nature of GA Leaders

Leaders tend to be a small percentage of GA membership; usually, no more than 5% of the members are officers or board members (Austin and Woolever, 1992; Chan and Rammohan, 1999; Scott, 1957). In one sense, entry into leadership roles in GAs is simple; officers and board members usually are elected by the members (by mail or at a general meeting). Committee chairs and committee members tend to be appointed, with the chairs often being appointed by the president or board. When there are many committees and many members on each, appointed leaders probably will constitute most of the leadership superstructure in a GA, depending on its size.

Underlying such election or appointment to leadership roles is the process whereby a member of a GA makes him- or herself known to and respected by other members, especially current leaders. Volunteering to do various needed tasks in a GA seems to be a good entrée into subsequent leadership. Prior leadership positions in other GAs in the same or other places are an important background characteristic that is a route to further leadership in a given GA. Making many social bonds with other members, and especially current or past leaders in the GA, also is important (Fernandez, 1991).

Revenson and Cassel (1991), in studying 45 self-help GA leaders, found that routes to leadership participation include prior professional expertise relevant to GA goals, having been served by the GA and feeling obligated to help the GA as a result, having helped found the given or other GAs (not just the one in question), and being generally active as GA leaders or people who make careers of leadership in the given or other GAs.

Very few studies compare GA leaders to average members of the same groups or even to cross sections of the community populations. Most GA leader studies tend to focus on the leaders by themselves and, thus, lack control groups to permit proper interpretations of the results. For example, Rich (1980) suggests that GA leader motivations included civic duty, devotion to one's neighborhood, friendships, maintenance of property values, role satisfaction, and so on. Elkind (1992) found "anti-nuke" social movement GA leaders to be underemployed, socially marginal, and seeking meaning in their lives. Frohlich (1978) found German GA leadership to be positively associated with more varied activity at work and more positive relationships with colleagues there. Austin and Woolever (1992) found GA board composition to be representative of the local community in Habitat for Humanity GAs. These bits and pieces of research, unguided by a larger theoretical scheme, do not permit much in the way of generalization.

Friedman et al. (1988) compared leaders and members of block or neighborhood GAs in the United States and Israel. They found that although social background variables were weak predictors of this difference in participation levels, attitude variables were much stronger. Most important as attitude predictors of leadership were positive attitudes toward the local area and perception of more opportunity costs. The latter is a realistic recognition that GA leadership requires much time and commitment to the GA and often more direct and indirect financial support as well. Males tended to be leaders in Israel, whereas leaders in the United States tended to be higher in education and occupational prestige than average members.

The forgoing study highlights the two leader characteristics in mainstream GAs that have received the most sociological research attention: socioeconomic status (SES) and gender. GA leaders usually are found to be of higher SES (education and/or income) or at least relatively higher than the average GA members (Elkind, 1992; Friedman et al., 1988; Gros, 1986; Hollingshead, 1975; Trow and Smith, 1983; Wade, 1975). The roots of this finding probably lie in greater skills of the more educated and in the greater ability to afford both opportunity costs and out-of-pocket costs of GA activity if higher in income.

Social movement GA leadership seems to work rather differently. Oliver (1983) found such volunteer activists to be distinguished from average GA members by more availability of discretionary time. Paid activists usually had some adult experience of the 1960s, having turned 18 years old during that decade—involving significantly greater teenage awareness of social movements. Marullo (1988) found that social movement campaign leaders were not distinguished by social background factors but instead were distinguished by past experiences with movement activities and relevant beliefs about the campaigns.

Gender effects on leadership in U.S. GAs seem to have changed little over the past few decades because the basic prestige and power structure of community GAs has changed little. Babchuk, Marsey, and Gordon (1960) studied a large city and found that men were much more prevalent on the boards of civic GAs, especially instrumental (external goal-oriented), large-budget, and highly community-valued GAs—in short, the more dominant GAs. Booth (1972) found more male leaders in instrumental, service, and fraternal GAs, whereas women were more likely to be leaders in expressive (member benefit) GAs such as church-related or recreational GAs. More recently, McPherson and Smith-Lovin (1982, 1986) found that men were more involved in larger core (dominant) GAs and were leaders in them, whereas women were more active in small domestic and community GAs. In sum, men tend to be leaders more in the dominant GA types in the community, whereas women tend to be leaders in largely female GAs that are considered less important because they are less related to occupations and other highly valued activities and outcomes in society generally. In mixed-gender GAs, males are more likely to be leaders (Thompson, 1995). Local GA board members also are more likely to be male (Austin and Woolever, 1992; Trow and Smith, 1983).

Exceptions to male dominance in more powerful GAs are likely to be present more recently, but corresponding recent studies are lacking. There also have long been exceptions in social movement GAs in which women have taken a special interest including, of course, the feminist movement (Ferree and Hess, 1995; Gittell and Shtob, 1980; Scott, 1991).

Psychological Traits

Psychological traits of GA leaders have been little studied. Earlier trait research on leaders in work organizations has shown that leaders tend to be higher in intelligence, masculinity, and dominance (Bryman, 1996, p. 277). My own unreported research on eight towns in Massachusetts found that GA leaders were higher in the active-effective character than were members—higher in intelligence, extraversion, assertiveness (dominance), emotional closeness, ego strength (self-confidence), efficacy (internal control), and other traits (D. Smith, 1975, 1994a; Smith, Macaulay, and Associates, 1980, chap. 19). This line of research, comparing members and leaders, needs to be extended substantially.

Leadership charisma in GAs has been little studied except for biographical studies (Burwell, 1995; Finks, 1984). A laboratory study of groups finds that crises foster the emergence of charismatic leaders (Pillai, 1993). Kay (1994) argues that more attention should be paid to the wisdom, insight, and creativity of VG leaders—aspects more likely to characterize charismatic leaders. Pakulski (1986) found strong charismatic elements in 33 Polish solidarity movement leaders studied. They differed dramatically from more bureaucratic government leaders of Poland during the 1980s. Many other studies of charismatic leadership have been done in the extensive social movement literature (see references in McAdam and Snow, 1997).

There is some research on mobilization by group entrepreneurs, who may be seen as types of charismatic leaders under a different label. For example, Nownes and Neeley (1996) surveyed public interest group founders and did not find patrons to be of major importance. Instead, public interest groups usually formed because aggressive and independent entrepreneurs formed them, often in response to specific events or event series (i.e., disturbances). Entrepreneurs enlist the help of their friends initially, so that the "free rider" problem is not important.

Related to leadership and "entrepreneurship" in groups is the matter of birth order. Sulloway (1996, p. 361) has written a lengthy book in which he argues that, in contrast to later-borns in families, firstborns tend to be more conscientious and extraverted (p. 73) and, hence, more likely to exhibit leadership. Also, later-borns are exposed to life experiences that tend to make them much more likely to back liberal social and religious reforms and radical political revolutions, whereas firstborns are more likely to support the status quo. In Burns's (1978) terms, later-borns are more likely to become transformational (roughly charismatic) leaders as opposed to transactional (roughly bureaucratic) leaders.

The contingency approach to leadership sees leadership as resulting from the interaction of the person and the situation (Bryman, 1996, p. 279). This perspective has not been used in the study of GA leaders, to my knowledge. Existing knowledge from research on work organizations would suggest that GA leaders need to be generally good at dealing with other people because most GA situations have moderate structures. In more semiformal GAs, more task-oriented leaders might be needed to get things done, according to the standard model (p. 279). However, I have my doubts as to whether the standard contingency model applies well to GAs, especially on this latter point.

GA Leader Education and Training

As noted in Chapter 6, there usually is no formal training for members or leaders in GAs except in highly professional GAs such as firefighter corps and paramedic squads (Gora and Nemerowicz, 1985; Perkins, 1989). There are, however, some other exceptions to this generalization. Rare training programs for GA leaders have had some success but also some limitations. Cook, Howell, and Weir (1985) found that a two-year or longer leadership program in rural areas led to more subsequent GA activity in instrumental groups, based on a pre- and posttest. Another report on the same study (Howell, Weir, and Cook, 1987) shows that leadership trainees developed more problem-solving skills, learned new roles, understood public issues better, and became more cooperative with other leaders. Bolton (1991), in still another report on the same study, notes that although trainees learned leadership-relevant information, they did not really increase their capacity for leadership by being better able to *use these new GA skills and information in the community*. This suggests that some emotional and practice elements of training need to be included in addition to information.

Some colleges and universities have experimented with programs to train GA leaders or community activists and have claimed some success (Longdon, Gallacher, and Dickson, 1986; Miller, 1986). Although there also are college-based courses and programs for volunteer administrators (Smith and Walker, 1977), these are not seen as much needed by such administrators themselves (Stubblefield and Miles, 1986). College and university programs for paid-staff VG managers are far more prevalent, especially graduate programs (Crowder and Hodgkinson, n.d.; Wish, 1993).

Leader Activities

In addition to looking at the traits of leaders, which has been done only in a very elementary way for GAs, one can examine what leaders do—how they lead. A few studies have examined GA leader activities without linking up theoretically to standard organization research on leader activities and style (Bryman, 1996). Revenson and Cassel (1991) report that scoliosis GA leaders spend less than 20% of their time in advocacy and provision of help but enjoy these activities most. The rest of their leader activities are not very rewarding. Rich (1980) found that neighborhood GA leaders spend about half of their time on GA maintenance and half on production. The most frequent maintenance activities were providing information to the community and fund-raising, whereas in production regular GA affairs and organization of projects were most common. Klandermans (1989) suggests that social movement GA leaders need to accumulate and then allocate resources, activities that might demand very different skills. Thielen and Poole (1986) usefully provide a list of six GA leader functions or types of activities that could be used to assess either leaders or the content of leader training programs.

GA leaders encounter a variety of special problems on a regular basis. The central one probably is member commitment. Because volunteer effort is central to GAs, commitment to such effort must continually be generated. Knoke and Wood (1981) did an important study of the factors in the generation of commitment in local paid-staff and GA social influence nonprofits. They found that participation and communication by GA members created more GA commitment among members.

High Degree of Consideration

Research on leadership in work organizations suggests that two aspects of leader behavior are central: "consideration" and "initiating structure" (Bryman, 1996, p. 278). The former deals with how the leader treats followers (i.e., subordinates) as people, whereas the latter deals with work supervision. Although we lack quantitative research to demonstrate the fact, it is likely that consideration so defined is far more important for GA leaders than for work organization leaders, even though it is important for the latter as well. The special importance of sociability incentives for GAs and the fact that GA activity is leisure activity make this the case. If GA leaders do not treat their followers and other members well, then the latter will tend to ignore them or leave the GA. Proper leader consideration generates greater member commitment to the GA. Mason (1996) has written at length about the importance of expressive leadership and management, although not specifically for GAs. His general thrust is well taken for GAs as well.

Low Degree of Supervision

Two related problems are supervision (i.e., initiating structure) and sanctioning of associational volunteers once commitment has been generated and applied to a particular task, project, event, or meeting. The idea of supervision of workers, basic to work organizations such as paid-staff VGs, is weak in GAs. Volunteers do not usually like tight supervision because their volunteer work is, after all, leisure time for them—not "work" time, only serious leisure at most. And when someone is not performing properly, it is a GA leadership "art" to correct but at the same time encourage the volunteer. This is a restatement of Harris's (1998a) earlier noted point about the difficulty of managing volunteers. Only as a last resort are volunteers "fired" from assignments. Even then, they very rarely are ejected from GAs for incompetence or nonperformance.

Because most workers in GAs are associational volunteers, when they are given tasks to do in certain instances, supervision by leaders generally is loose.

Most GA members do not have specific tasks but rather are just participating in meetings and need little or no supervision. Those members who are doing special committee or other work, including officers and board members, receive only modest supervision because the entire organization is a leisure time group and is engaged in "serious leisure" at most, not paid work. As a result, things often might not "get done." Tight supervision of volunteer workers is likely to result only from relevant personality traits of leaders, not from GA norms in most cases. An exception is the handling of the GA's funds by the treasurer, but even here, supervision might be casual and auditing of books is not widespread. All of this can be seen as part of the nonprofessionalism of GAs, discussed in Chapters 5 and 6 and earlier in this chapter.

Loose Priority Setting and Decision Making

Priority setting in GAs tends to be loose, as are the basic missions in many cases, especially when compared to paid-staff VGs. Harris (1998a) argues that this results in part from the fact that "setting priorities is constrained by the presence of competing internal interests and factions" (p. 149). This is one of the downside aspects of internal democracy in GAs. Different factions or subgroups can make their influence felt in setting priorities in ways that often lead to conflicting priorities.

Another part of the looseness of priority setting in GAs comes from the GA's needing to balance member needs and goals with longer term group goals (Harris, 1998a, p. 147). In work organizations, the long-term goals of the organization can be given priority more clearly. Employee needs and goals, although important these days (Bruyn, 1977), are more clearly secondary.

Priority setting is loose in GAs in part because it does not need to be tighter. GAs are low in professionalism, as I have argued, and tight priorities are not a major value in most GAs. The informality of GAs contributes to this looseness of priority setting, as does the fact that GAs are only "serious leisure." There is little or no money involved, and there are few or no jobs, unlike the situation in work organizations.

Routine Resource Acquisition

Resource acquisition in GAs is a fairly routine leader function so far as dues or donations are concerned. Leaders set and collect dues or collect donations at meetings. There is leader supervision for special event fund-raising and external grant proposal preparation, if any. Leaders arrange for places to meet. Leaders sometimes lead membership drives, but these are difficult to make successful. Most recruitment is by word of mouth and existing ties to people in the organization (McPherson, Popielarz, and Drobnic, 1992). Leaders of GAs also contribute to membership recruitment by running successful programs that attract people. In paid-staff VGs, marketing is a more developed leadership function (Bruce, 1994).

Leader Succession

Leader succession often is a major practical problem in GAs where the leaders are so important. This has been little studied. Current leaders often play a major role in finding their own replacements and tend to feel obligated to stay in their leadership capacities until they have been able to find others to take their own or other leader positions. This contributes to oligarchy based on apathy, as discussed by Barber (1987). Selecting new leaders through their own social ties results in new leaders of GAs being similar to existing ones. The more prestigious the GAs, the easier it usually is to find leaders for them. And the less actual work involved in the leadership roles, the easier it is to find leaders for them, other things being equal. Leadership elections often take place within a limited field of choices (e.g., small slates of board and officer candidates).

Nonmembers of GAs very rarely are brought in from the outside as leaders, unlike the situation in work organizations. Such an importation of a leader would be viewed as insulting and disruptive by most members except in the extreme circumstance that no one else could be found to do the job. Normally, one has to serve one's time for a few years as a regular member or minor leader in a GA before becoming a major leader.

Mentzer (1993) studied 75 church congregations (probably paid-staff nonprofits) with pastor changes and 75 with no changes as a control group. He found that a new pastor stimulated attendance for a while but not revenues. I doubt that this applies to GAs, but I could find no other relevant study of the effects of new leaders on a GA. *Lack* of GA leader succession can be an even bigger problem, perhaps, because it indicates a very entrenched leader and, thus, oligarchy. Behind-the-scenes arrangement (politicking) of an election to oust the "permanent" leader sometimes can be successful, but it is hard to keep the process secret from an effective entrenched leader. Even if a GA leader does a poor job, removal of a leader is very rare. It is more common for others to let the person's term of office run out and then try to replace him or her. This is consistent with the overall low degree of supervision and low standards of professionalism in GAs.

Leadership Selectivity

Willingness to do the job often is the major qualification for new leaders given that they already are members of the GA. People informally or formally volunteer themselves for leadership roles and are put on the election slate. If they do not get on the slate or are not elected, then they often are appointed to committee leadership positions. In most GAs, the only position for which any special qualifications are felt to be necessary is that of treasurer, for which some bookkeeping experience often is sought. Fund-raising experience, for example, seldom is sought in board members. Nor is administrative experience often sought for any of the officer positions. It is assumed that virtually anyone with the will to do so can do the job satisfactorily. The result often is uneven leadership quality over time and leadership quality problems at any given point in time. The major failing that arises is leaders simply not doing what they are supposed to do or have agreed to do because of a lack of sufficient commitment or time or both.

Leadership Quality Problems

In modern Western societies, we have little concept of the range of problems that can arise with GAs in developing nations (Esman and Uphoff, 1984; Fisher, 1993). Landsberger (1972b) examines a number of these problems analytically. Anderson (1964) provides some concrete examples (e.g., embezzlement, theft), writing about GAs in Hyderabad, a large city in India. There tends to be a good deal of membership apathy and ignorance in these GAs. But poor-quality leadership also plays an important role.

Many GA leaders simply are not sufficiently educated to be good leaders including lower SES people in more modern nations and many people in most developing nations. Anderson (1964) found that many leaders were corrupt, stealing GA funds and faking the records because of their personal poverty and lack of moral scruples. This demoralized their GA memberships and markedly decreased member commitment to the GAs, not surprisingly. Ambiguity of leader roles relative to more familiar traditional roles also was a problem, for the leaders often were personally unfamiliar with GA leader roles and lacked positive role models for them. Finally, voluntary altruism seemed to make good GA leader, but this quality was more rare than in modern, democratic Western nations.

There are stark contrasts among leadership in modern Western paid-staff VGs, leadership in modern Western GAs, and leadership in GAs in developing nations (Chrislip and Larson, 1994; Esman and Uphoff, 1984; Fisher, 1993; Herman and Associates, 1994; see also other chapters in Part II). The central documents of the emerging field of VG management often read like the authors believe that they are relevant to modern Western GAs as well and perhaps to GAs and paid-staff VGs everywhere. This usually implicit assumption is *very* far from the truth and is another example of parochial flat-earth VNPS thinking.

In this case, a developed world flat-earth paradigm is active. This paradigm assumes that GAs and other VGs are roughly the same in other nations, even nations of very different socioeconomic development status (Horowitz, 1972).

This particular flat-earth paradigm is in some ways the opposite of the distinctive nationalist focus flat-earth paradigm, which sees the VG activity in a given nation as essentially unique and very unlike VG activity in other nations. Both are generally incorrect.

GA ENVIRONMENTS AND THEIR RELATIONSHIPS TO GAs

A great deal of attention has been paid during the past 30 years to the nature of work organization environments and their interaction with such organizations, perhaps beginning with the classic article by Yuchtman and Seashore (1967; see also Aldrich, 1979; Pfeffer and Salancik, 1978). Such research indicates that organizations can influence their environments and vice versa (Hall, 1996, chap. 11). Hall (1996, chap. 12) also reviews the literature on interorganizational relations, finding a complex of relationships with much more research needed. Such a conclusion must be raised to some power (squared or the fourth power) to reflect the paucity of GA research on the phenomena included analytically in this section. There is some paid-staff nonprofit research in this area, but even such nonprofit environmental interaction research is very limited.

I deal with issues of GA environment in a number of other places in this book including the following:

Chapter 1: Overall societal niche of GAs

Chapter 2: Map of GAs in relation to paid-staff VGs

Chapter 3: Choice of VNPS, member versus nonmember benefit goals, autonomy level, member eligibility criteria, conventionality versus deviance of group

Chapter 5: Locality base, autonomy, tax exemption, member versus nonmember benefit goals, polymorphic linkage, and overlapping memberships

Chapter 6: External funding, political activity, power, prestige, deviance, recruitment, and horizontal collaboration

Chapter 7: Leadership entry, resource acquisition

Chapter 8: GA age and external relations, GA age and resource attraction modes

Chapter 9: External impact and external factors in effectiveness

Therefore, my primary attention in this brief section is paid to government relationships with GAs in the United States. GAs have very little to do with governments in the United States. Most are not formally registered with taxation agencies and do not receive direct formal tax exemption in documentary form. Most do not receive any funding from governments at any territorial level.

Governments in the United States generally do not interfere with the autonomy of GAs unless the latter are fundamentally deviant and (suspected of being) criminal. Many GAs attempt to influence local governments on issues of interest at one time or another, sometimes successfully (see Chapter 9). The overall success rate of such influence attempts is not clear from research. Most research focuses on a single GA's influence attempts and none on the total set of influence attempts of GAs in a given territory, to my knowledge. Sometimes, GAs collaborate in coalitions with local government agencies focused on particular projects or issues.

Some exceptions to close ties with government would be the following. Volunteer firefighting corps and paramedic squads often are supported in part (e.g., equipment, buildings) by local government money (Gora and Nemerowicz, 1985; Perkins, 1989). Public school-affiliated GAs of students receive some informal support (at a minimum, meeting space) from local governments via the schools that are the GA sponsors. Local GAs might testify before local government committees on issues of interest.

In Europe and elsewhere, GAs tend to have much closer relationships with governments. The corporatism (consultation on legislation) of relationships between national governments and national associations in European nations often is carried through at the local level as well (Boli, 1992; Gjems-Onstad, 1990). This is due partly to the greater dependence of GAs on local government funds in European nations (Boli, 1992; Van Harberden and Raymakers, 1986). In dictatorships, such as China, it is the nature of the governments that makes for close ties between GAs or common interest associations (if without significant autonomy) and the local governments (Mok, 1988; Zhou, 1993).

Relationships with governments are much more important for paid-staff VGs (Gidron, Kramer, and Salamon, 1992; Hall, 1987a; Johnson, Ourvan, and Young, 1995; Smith and Lipsky, 1993). Registration with taxation agencies is formal, and tax exemption is similarly formal. Government funding via contracts or grants is far more common and often is a major part of paid-staff VG funding (Rekart, 1993; Smith and Lipsky, 1993). This results in a significant, and often substantial, loss of autonomy for the VGs. Paid-staff VGs do few direct political influence activities, conscious of legal limitations on such activities if they are to maintain their tax exemptions. National associations or lobbies of particular types of paid-staff VGs, nonetheless, represent their interests generally. Paid-staff VGs often collaborate with local government agencies in coalitions focused on particular projects or issues.

CONCLUSION

There are many differences between GAs and paid-staff VGs in terms of leadership and the environment, as indicated in Table 7.1 (most environmental differences are presented in other chapters). To begin with, leaders seem to be

TABLE 7.1 Comparison of Leadership and Environment in Grassroots Associations and Paid-Staff Voluntary Groups

Grassroots Associations	*Paid-Staff Voluntary Groups*
Leadership essential	Leadership important
Mainly elected	Mainly appointed except board
Volunteer leaders	Paid leaders
Low professionalism	Moderate/high professionalism
Higher status males	Higher status males
High active-effective character	High active-effective character
More charisma	Less charisma
High consideration	Moderate consideration
Low supervision	Moderate/high supervision
Loose priority setting	Tighter priority setting
Routine resource acquisition	Managed marketing
Member succession only	Some nonmember succession
Low leader selectivity	Moderate leader selectivity
More leader quality problems	Less leader quality problems
Few government relations	More government relations

more central to GAs than to paid-staff VGs. Leaders are important in the latter but essential in the former because other forms of structure are low. GA leaders are mainly elected by the membership, whereas paid-staff VG leaders are mainly appointed or elected by the board. GA leaders are mainly or all volunteers, as are their followers. In paid-staff VGs, by definition, leaders are paid staff, as are most of their followers. As discussed in Chapter 6, I reiterate that GAs are low in professionalism compared to paid-staff GAs. In terms of traits, GA leaders tend to be high-status males (or high-status females in women-dominated GAs) and high in the active-effective character, as do leaders of paid-staff VGs. However, there are fewer women-dominated paid-staff VGs than women-dominated GAs. GA leaders are more likely to manifest charisma than are paid-staff VG leaders, who are more likely to be bureaucratic leaders.

The activities of GA leaders give substantially more attention to consideration, or the treatment of other people as people, than do the activities of paid-staff VG leaders, although consideration is important in the latter as well. Supervision of activities by leaders generally is low in GAs, whereas it is moderate or high in paid-staff VGs. This is basically a result of the contrast between leisure and work organizations. Volunteer service programs are hybrids, combining leisure group elements with a work organization context. Therefore, one might expect an intermediate position on this dimension for such programs. Priority setting is looser in GAs than in paid-staff VGs. Resource acquisition in GAs is a fairly routine leader function so far as dues or donations are concerned, but it involves leader supervision for special event fund-raising and external grants, if any. In paid-staff VGs, marketing is a more developed leadership function. Only members become leaders in GAs, whereas nonmembers sometimes are brought in as leaders in paid-staff VGs. The latter would be too disruptive of social relationships in most GAs. GAs are less selective of leaders and, thus, have more problems with leader quality than do paid-staff VGs, which are more selective and can demand more in qualifications and performance for paid jobs. GAs have much less to do with governments in the United States than do paid-staff VGs in a variety of ways including funding and autonomy.

8

Life Cycle Changes

This chapter focuses on the trends in grassroots association (GA) complexity and other GA characteristics over time, the causes of these changes, and alternative approaches that GAs may take to resist organizational complexity change pressures and other life cycle change pressures. Whereas Chapters 4 to 7 were concerned with GA incentive, structure, process, and leadership factors at one stage of development, this chapter focuses on time-series views of such factors.

DEFINITIONS

Complexity is a summary term that I have chosen to capture a wide range of structural and process characteristics of GAs (or any organizations) that deal broadly with the elaboration and rationalization of group structure and process. My own general view here is that *increasing complexity reflects a growing seriousness about how a GA or other organization is organized and uses its resources and opportunities.* Weber's notion of "rationalization" of organizations captures my meaning quite well; leaders and, to varying extents, members are thinking about how to use group resources most *rationally* to achieve group goals. This line of theory and research traces back to Weber (1947, 1952, originally published during the early 1900s), who argued that increasing rationalization of structure and process was characteristic of modern organizations. Weber was particularly struck by increasing bureaucratization in modern organizations relative to earlier, more traditional organizations. He was principally concerned with work organizations, not associations like GAs (but see Weber, 1972).

I define *work organizations* as those organizations in which most or all of the work is done by paid employees (Smith, Reddy, and Baldwin, 1972a). Such organizations include businesses, government agencies, and paid-staff nonprofits; they do not include households or families except in the rare case of communes, in which household members usually also are an organized work unit paid in kind. Work organizations usually are to be contrasted with volunteer groups at different territorial levels such as GAs. If a work group is a formal group, as is usually the case (Smith, 1972c), then it is termed a work *organization*. Informal work groups also exist. Traditional farm families could be termed *informal work groups* but not *work organizations* because of their more informal structure. Paid-staff voluntary groups (VGs), which are more complex than GAs, tend to have far more employees, internal departmentalization, oligarchy, revenues, and equity but less of the informality factors mentioned previously.

Michels ([1911] 1968), another pioneer in the field of organizational study, found what he called an "iron law of oligarchy" in political parties that he studied. This oligarchy reflected a centralization of power in a small number of leaders rather than the presence of organizational democracy with decision-making inputs from all levels of the organization. Some of these parties were GAs, but most were paid-staff nonprofits. His insight has been replicated in many studies of GAs and supracommunity associations. Both the bureaucracy (role specialization or division of labor, multiple levels of hierarchy, limited scope of positional authority, technically competent workers, rules for relatively impersonal work relations, formal work rules or procedures, and variations in worker rewards) identified by Weber and the oligarchy (power centralization in a few top decision makers) identified by Michels are two of several facets of what I am calling organizational complexity or, more broadly, group complexity.

In GAs, degree of *bureaucratization* can be measured by the number of levels of hierarchy present (see Gamson, 1990, and Knoke, 1989, 1990b, for use of this measure in national associations). A GA with several hierarchical levels (e.g., rank-and-file members, committee members, committee chairs, vice presidents, president) is high in bureaucracy, as contrasted with a GA with only two levels (members and an informal leader or chair). Degree of *centralization* (the opposite of internal democracy) can be measured by the "level and variety of participation in strategic decisions by groups relative to the number of groups in the organizations" (Hage, 1980, p. 65). A GA in which all major decisions are made by the president alone is highly centralized, whereas a GA is low in centralization if all important decisions are influenced significantly by all major hierarchical levels of the group, from bottom to top (Tannenbaum, 1961). Frisby (1985) identifies and defines several additional important aspects of complexity that may be applied to GAs as well as to work organizations, where most were first derived. These include formalization (use of formal documents), specialization (specialized responsibilities), professionalism (emphasis on educational qualifications), and impersonality (impersonal work relations).

INCREASING COMPLEXITY IN WORK ORGANIZATIONS, INCLUDING NATIONAL ASSOCIATIONS, WITH AGE

Starting out usually more complex than GAs, work organizations tend to get more and more complex with time. Hall (1996), studying work organizations, suggests that bureaucratization results from an organization being larger (in employees/members), having a history of greater bureaucratization, and having an environment that makes it dependent on only one or a few funding or accreditation sources (which often leads to internal changes toward more rationalization to meet perceived expectations of the powerful external organizations).

Many authors have found a trend toward more complexity over the organizational life cycle in paid-staff nonprofit associations (or GAs that become paid-staff associations) at different levels of territorial scope, particularly in terms of centralization and specialization or internal differentiation (Clark, 1937, p. 19; Ferree and Hess, 1995; Johnstone, 1992, chap. 3 and 5; Kikulis, Slack, and Hinings, 1992; King, 1956; Kleidman, 1994; Lipset, Trow, and Coleman, 1956; McNamee and Swisher, 1985; Michels, [1911] 1968; Nall, 1967; Piven and Cloward, 1979; Scott, 1991; Trojan et al., 1990; Zald, 1970). I probably could list hundreds of similar examples from the formation of all types of regional and national associations and from social movements of all varieties.

The reasons given by researchers for the shift toward more complexity over the paid-staff associational life cycle focus mainly on increasing organizational size (Akers and Campbell, 1970; Caplow, 1957; Ferree and Hess, 1995; Johnstone, 1992, chap. 3) but also include the passage of time as simple organizational age (Ferree and Hess, 1995; Scott, 1991); response to internal organizational demands for more efficiency and democracy (Zald, 1970); mass apathy of the members so that leaders need to do more (Barber, 1987); more external funding possibilities (including insurance and Medicare payments as well as grants and contracts) only if the organization becomes more complex (Abel, 1986; Frisby, 1985; Milofsky and Romo, 1988; Panet-Raymond, 1987; Piven and Cloward, 1979); the search for credibility, acceptability, the appearance of being well run, fiscal responsibility, staying power, and political clout (Frisby, 1985; Gamson, 1990; Knoke, 1990b; Manes, 1990; Milofsky, 1987); the decline of charismatic leadership and growing functional autonomy of leadership bodies (Johnstone, 1992, p. 47); and even the tendency for most work organizations in the surrounding society to become more complex and bureaucratic (DiMaggio and Powell, 1983; Scott, 1991, p. 181). Scott (1991) has a wonderful chapter title that encapsulates, in the broadest way, these various explanations: "As *Organizations* They Could Ask and Gain" (p. 175, emphasis added). Complexity makes a group of people more of an organization and, hence, something to be reckoned with by nonmembers.

With the forgoing in mind, here are some factors that militate *against* greater associational complexity or formalization/bureaucratization with greater age: desire to remain small, informal, and closely interpersonal by engaging mainly in face-to-face contacts (Freeman, 1975; Kanter and Zurcher, 1973; Katz, 1993; Wertheim, 1976), which tends to make for greater internal cohesion and, hence, more task accomplishment if desired (Gerlach and Hine, 1970); desire to maintain independence from external influence or control because of accepting money from nonmembers or nonmember organizations (Freeman, 1975; Riger, 1983); rejection of standard work organization management theories and techniques as not relevant (Knoke and Prensky, 1984; Walker, 1983); more openness to the local community (Boyte, 1980, 1984; Milofsky, 1988a); faith in democracy and simplicity (Clark, 1937); concern for autonomy and solidarity (Steinman and Traunstein, 1976); and fear of being discovered and prosecuted by authorities, especially in deviant nonprofits (Lambert, 1992; Luza, 1989; Manes, 1990; Smith, forthcoming a).

There are many important values of human beings other than efficiency and effectiveness. Some of the worst dictatorships in human history resulted in the killing of many millions of innocent people very efficiently and were quite effective overall in seeking their evil goals (e.g., Hitler, Stalin, Mao) (Rummel, 1994). An alternative goal to efficiency and effectiveness that appeals to many people is being in many caring, friendly, and interpersonal relationships in a group that is small enough to have real internal democracy and poor enough not to be dependent on funds from other organizations that might wield influence.

Harrison (1960) concludes, from a study of Weber, that voluntary groups (meaning GAs especially) are basically antiauthoritarian. He sees such groups as representing a balance between the need for bureaucratic methods and the distrust of central authority. Informed by this alternative perspective on the value of increasing complexity in nonprofits, it is clear that leaders and members of GAs do have a choice about whether or not to increase the complexity of the GAs. There are advantages and disadvantages either way that people need to bear in mind, as suggested earlier. Kleidman (1994) found that greater organizational complexity did not necessarily result in less grassroots member involvement in three American peace campaigns. However, Kraybill and Pellman-Good (1992) point out the dangers of professionalization in community groups.

National associations tend to be larger than GAs because the former usually are older and have a larger territorial population base; hence, they have a larger member and financial resource base on which to draw within their territorial scope (see Knoke, 1990b, Nall, 1967, and Smith, 1992a, for national associations vs.

Wuthnow, 1994, and Chapter 2 for GAs). With larger VG organizational size in membership and/or finances as a basic causal factor, national associations tend to have greater complexity of different types.

Zald and Ash (1966) present an influential theory of social movement organization growth and decline that elaborates this simple relationship. They state the "institutionalization and goal displacement model of organizational transformation," traced back to Weber and Michels, as follows: "As [a movement] organization attains an economic and social base in the society as the original charismatic leadership is replaced, a bureaucratic structure emerges and a general accommodation to the society occurs" (p. 327). Zald and Ash suggest that such organizational transformation is not just a function of time; rather, it is specifically linked to changes in societal support for the group (both sentiments and material resources) that require accommodation or perhaps extremism, more inclusivity and external (societal) change focus, more interorganizational competition for support, and less progress toward goal attainment.

COMPLEXITY AND THE LIFE CYCLE OF GAs

As discussed in Chapter 5, some complexity is found in GAs but less than in national associations, let alone than in business and government organizations or in large paid-staff VGs such as hospitals and universities. This GA complexity tends to increase with time (GA age), other things being equal. King (1956) made an early typological statement of developmental stages in GAs leading to more organizational complexity, with a focus on social movements and their constituent groups. Others have found similar stages for other GA types (Allen et al., 1995; Blair, 1994; Blum and Ragab, 1985; Clark, 1937; Katz, 1961; Katz and Bender, 1976, p. 122; Richan, 1992; Scott, 1991, p. 179; Steinman and Traunstein, 1976; Traunstein, 1984; Trojan et al., 1990; Wertheim, 1976; Wilson, 1970). All of these and many other possible citations indicate greater complexity of one or another type of GA with greater GA age.

Tsouderos (1955; see also Chapin and Tsouderos, 1956) made a classic study of increasing complexity over the associational life cycle for 10 statewide and metropolitan area associations (some GAs). Interestingly, he found that membership increased with time but peaked first, followed later by a peak in the income and still later by a peak in the complexity of the associations. Notably, two measures of complexity (administrative expenditures and number of administrative office workers) and an economic measure of size (organizational property) tended to continue growing even during the period of associational *contraction* in membership.

This suggests that bureaucratization and professionalization are very powerful, even self-perpetuating and self-fulfilling, processes in associations. They go on in the absence of any apparent "objective" need for them by the associations, thus being out of tune with the reality of the associations' needs and the environments they face. This finding also suggests that goal displacement has occurred to some extent, with a focus on sheer associational maintenance becoming more important than the original goals of associations.

It would be useful for GAs and other nonprofits to make a regular, perhaps annual, review of the degree of complexity in their organizations, making sure that ever greater complexity is not running away with itself and with scarce organization resources of people's time and money. In the case of every aspect of complexity, a review committee of the board of directors could ask whether the particular current arrangement is now too complex and resource-consuming or is too simple to have sufficient effects. The whole board could discuss and review the subcommittee's results, making changes as needed. Also, every GA and most other nonprofits could benefit from the following motto: *If more complexity will not clearly improve the total situation of the organization, including both members and the leadership, then do not implement any given proposal requiring more complexity.* Once a GA reaches a new and higher level of complexity, unfortunately, it is difficult to go back to a simpler arrangement.

Studying a stratified sample of 59 GAs in one small suburb of Boston, Smith (1992b, p. 261) found a statistically significant relationship between age and formalization. Older GAs tended to be more formalized in terms of having formal membership lists, availability of formalization documents (e.g., charter, bylaws), seeing both participants and inactive official members as members (vs. the active members only in informal GAs), and volunteered responses by the leaders interviewed that the GAs were "informal."

A related finding of Milofsky (1987) was that community GAs develop bureaucracy in response to fund-raising needs, attempting to present themselves to external funding agencies as responsible and well run and, hence, deserving of support. Bryman, Gillingswater, and McGuineess (1992) report increasing professionalization and use of business practices, with less attention to grassroots concerns for transport for the disabled, in three British voluntary organizations in response to the need for external funding. An alternative type of external resource dependence seems to have fostered professionalization in GA adoption agencies earlier in the 20th century. Paid social workers generated political pressure to have external licensing so that volunteers could be excluded from arranging adoptions (Romanofsky, 1973).

An extreme example of professionalization of GAs is their transformation into paid-staff nonprofits. Timperly and Osbaldeston (1975) describe a continuous process of professionalization over time in a local branch of a management GA in Britain. Levine and Levine (1970) note that this has happened repeatedly in the history of the helping services. Richan (1992) describes a small volunteer social agency that made this transformation to an established social service agency. Scott (1991) found many similar examples for women's GAs in American history. Sports often go through a professionalization process from GAs, to semiprofessional organizations, to professional organizations, as in baseball (McGuire, 1996) or Olympic sports (Whitson and Macintosh, 1989). There are many other current and historical examples for GAs that could be cited.

CAUSES OF COMPLEXITY IN GAs

Weber (1947) argued that bureaucratization was a result of rationalization, with the owners/managers of competitive capitalist firms adopting this approach to maximize efficiency, effectiveness, and profits (DiMaggio and Powell, 1983). Because GAs are in competition with each other for members, money, and other resources, some of the increased complexity of GAs as they age and grow in size might be a result of their leaders perceiving the probable increased efficiency and effectiveness of such complexity and, therefore, making these changes happen to deal with the concomitants of greater GA size.

DiMaggio and Powell (1983) suggest that some additional factors now are at work. Their theoretical argument regarding the growing similarity of form (isomorphism) among organizations can potentially be extended from the usual focus on work organizations to associations including GAs. In particular, these authors see three sources of growing organizational isomorphism that involves high complexity of organization.

Coercive Isomorphism

This refers to common legal environments that require similar annual budget cycles, annual reports, audited financial reporting and accounting, standard operating procedures, and even the development of bureaucracies to satisfy potential outside funders. Milofsky (1987) pointed to this type of process in his study of community organizations. It is fairly clear that receipt of external (non-member) funds puts pressure on a GA to increase its complexity in various ways (Milofsky and Romo, 1988; Saltman, 1973). However, there seems to be little of this coercive isomorphism in GAs (vs. work organizations) because the "legal environment" is very loose and amorphous, not requiring the types of activities that DiMaggio and Powell (1983) mention for organizations in general.

Mimetic Processes

These are situations in which uncertainty encourages imitation of other, established organizations. New organizations tend to model themselves after existing ones that they see as successful. This is especially likely for polymorphic GAs in the process of formation or early growth, as they tend to turn to established GAs of the same types in nearby places for ideas regarding how to organize themselves. The state or national coordinating organizations of polymorphic GAs are likely to present the new polymorphic GAs with "tried and true" ways in which to organize and run their new chapters/branches. New GAs of the monomorphic type also might model themselves after successful local GAs perceived as somehow similar, whether polymorphic or monomorphic.

Normative Pressures

These come mainly from professionalization (really *professionalism* in my terminology given earlier), which controls entry into a profession and molds preentrants and entrants through similar education and professional networks/organizations. "Organizational prestige and resources are key elements in attracting professionals" (DiMaggio and Powell, 1983, p. 154). I do not see this factor as important for explaining GA complexity because, by definition, a GA does not usually have a paid professional executive. Presence of the latter would move the group into the paid-staff nonprofit category in most cases.

DiMaggio and Powell (1983) state many hypotheses regarding when isomorphism is more likely such as when there is more professionalism in a field, fewer visible alternative models, more interaction with government, more dependence on a single (or on several similar) sources of support, greater involvement of organizational managers/leaders in trade or professional associations (professionalism), more reliance on academic credentials in selecting higher staff, more ambiguous organizational goals, and more general dependence on another organization. Very few of these relationships argue for high complexity in GAs because GAs tend to lack nearly all of these factors, on average, unlike paid-staff VGs. Among the forgoing, only ambiguous goals and dependence on another organization suggest that GAs will tend toward higher complexity. Research is needed on these hypotheses.

The factors in the prior paragraph generally predict that most GAs will be low or middling in complexity, with polymorphic GAs generally being higher in complexity than monomorphic GAs. However, polymorphic GAs are quite frequent, making up perhaps half of all GAs. Polymorphic GAs with supralocal parents or coordinating organizations are the GAs most likely to develop increasing complexity and to do so most rapidly with increasing size and time. When GAs are mainly dependent on other VGs in their own communities, this is less likely. GAs associated with churches and educational institutions often are quite informal and low in complexity. GAs associated with schools or colleges tend to be at least moderately complex, on average, but less so than polymorphic GAs with supralocal parent organizations.

Other Factors

Some other factors also tend to lead to higher complexity in some GAs with the passage of time. One is the sheer growth in size of memberships, revenues, and activities. Not all GAs grow with time, but those that do grow significantly in their memberships usually turn to increasing complexity of various types to be able to control what the GAs are doing (Burt, 1990; Traunstein and Steinman, 1973; Wertheim, 1976). Furthermore, with more people and resources, it is feasible to share the work of increased complexity among more people.

Research on GAs, thus, suggests that it is mainly increasing size and not the sheer passage of time that is the chief cause of increasing GA complexity over time, although this type of size increase might be correlated with time. (This probably is true of all types of organizations [Caplow, 1957].) As a GA grows in members, money, and activities, the tasks of leading/managing the GA become more complex and varied. It becomes far more difficult for one or a few individuals to provide all of the leadership and management needed. Increased complexity of the GA permits a broader sharing of leadership tasks such as in multiple vice presidents and multiple committees.

Although many GAs are quite democratic in their decision making, the democratic process often is slow and cumbersome (although use of e-mail can greatly speed this up if all decision makers are on-line). As a GA grows, there often is pressure to shift from direct democracy to representative democracy in the form of elected officers and board members. This centralization of decision making often increases the speed of decision making but also tends to increase oligarchy (Lipset et al., 1956; Michels, [1911] 1968). To many GA members and leaders, such centralization seems to be an improvement given that they seldom are aware of the accompanying tendencies toward oligarchy and centralization. This same type of thinking among some leaders and members tends to eventually lead to professionalization (paid staff, especially a paid executive).

It often is argued at this point in GA development that paid staff will help the GA (which is turning into a paid-staff nonprofit) to get beyond being an intermittent organization that only really "exists" when the members and leaders are meeting together. This type of paid-staff VG management thinking essentially argues that a "real" VG must have a permanent office and paid staff. This argument is invalid and confuses GAs with paid-staff VGs, which are very different forms of VGs (see other chapters in Part II). Very few GAs will ever be able to afford permanent offices and paid full-time executive directors. The vast majority of GAs do not want such paid-staff development (Chan and Rammohan, 1999, p. 19).

Complexity is more likely to develop in GAs that have external goals and seek to provide benefits to nonmembers, possibly including the general public (e.g., environmental health GAs). This outward orientation leads to more GA concern with the control of organizational resources and activities to accomplish external effects. Often, these GAs want to expand and accomplish still more externally, and they see increasing complexity as a means to such ends. Such increased complexity also can make possible external grants or contracts. By contrast, member benefit GAs (e.g., self-help, religious) focus more on solidarity among their members, member satisfaction, member enhancement or improvement, and other internal benefits. In general, instrumental GAs, whose goals focus on affecting nonmembers or society, are more likely to develop complexity (Abel, 1986; Panet-Raymond, 1987). Expressive GAs, whose goals focus on member needs and satisfactions, are less likely to do so (Gordon and Babchuk, 1959). Goal attainment for instrumental GAs is seen as being helped by more complexity, whereas expressive GAs often do not see the need for complexity (Schmidt and Babchuk, 1972; Steinman and Traunstein, 1976; Wertheim, 1976; Wuthnow, 1994).

Ideas about professionalism and professionalization in GAs often are imported by well-meaning GA leaders or members with experience in government, business, or paid-staff VGs (Hall, 1990). Not really understanding how GAs are intrinsically different from paid-staff organizations (work organizations), these "importers" believe that they are helping the GAs when they push for increased complexity including dependency on paid staff (Drucker, 1990). Some leaders or members are particularly impressed by the growing field of nonprofit management and leadership (Herman and Associates, 1994; O'Neill and Young, 1988; Rubin, Adamski, and Block, 1989; Wish, 1993). These "nonprofit experts" in GAs often try to be helpful to their GAs by importing structures and processes from national associations or simply work organizations in spite of the fact that these might not be appropriate (Klausen, 1995; Knoke and Prensky, 1984; Walker, 1983).

These leaders might see this as bringing the GAs more into the "mainstream" of VGs. This often is misguided, however well meaning. GAs are supposed to be small and poor but with much of the "volunteer spirit" or attitude of voluntary altruism (see Chapter 1). In most cases, a permanent office and full-time paid staff would quickly bankrupt the GAs and lead to their deaths. Many millions of GAs in the United States get along fine without such expensive aspects of complexity. I am not arguing against the potential value of all forms of GA complexity, just against a few unnecessary and quite expensive forms.

There seems to be a type of "snowball effect" in regard to GA complexity (Saltman, 1973). Once a certain aspect of complexity is adopted, there often is internal GA pressure to continue down the path of increasing GA complexity, if only for the sake of consistency. Each change toward more complexity can be used by some leaders to justify a further move on the same or another dimension of complexity. It is hard to draw a line and say "enough" to increasing complexity in a GA (or other organization). Also, each increase in complexity can cause a reduction in member commitment and participation, which in turn might require more professionalization and other aspects of complexity (Wertheim, 1976).

Thus, there is a zero-sum game here for GAs in which they cannot have everything. If members do a lot themselves as volunteers, then they tend to be quite committed. But if oligarchy and professionalization (hence complexity) increase significantly, then member volunteer time and commitment tend to decline. *Hypothetical* increased efficiency and possibly greater impact (see Chapter 9) are seen as validating the increased complexity. Often, these hopes are unfulfilled by greater complexity. But even if greater efficiency and impact do result, they might be obtained at the cost of less member commitment, participation, solidarity, and even satisfaction (Steinman and Traunstein, 1976; Wertheim, 1976).

Unfortunately, leaders and members of GAs tend to be unaware of the total "phase shift" that occurs when GAs become paid-staff nonprofits. It might seem like a small matter to them to add a full-time staff person, a full-time rented office, and so on. But this is a grave misperception that has killed off many a promising GA trying to become a paid-staff nonprofit (my qualitative impression from the literature and personal experiences). The deadly part tends to be the financial burden of suddenly being a paid-staff nonprofit, which requires 10 or 20 times as much money and, hence, fund-raising activities by some people in the GA. Even if external grant funding smoothes the financial side of the phase shift, the former GA (now a paid-staff nonprofit) might find itself in a few years without such grant funding and uncertain how to reverse the phase shift successfully. The paid-staff VG form tends to reduce member commitment and volunteer effort substantially, making it quite difficult to return to being a GA based solely on volunteer leadership. Some GAs refuse to become more complex when it is demanded by the volume of activities and members, as seen in the next section.

Complexity should not be viewed as an independent value in itself, contrary to what many organization leaders in all fields believe. It is a tool, an instrument to reach important substantive goals and purposes of an organization. Misused or overused, greater complexity can harm GAs or other organizations by suppressing the human and emotional side of organizations (Mason, 1996) and substituting impersonal instead of personal relations (Schmidt and Babchuk, 1972; Steinman and Traunstein, 1976; Wertheim, 1976) as well as through decision making by a small oligarchy instead of consensus among the membership (Scott, 1991, p. 179; Tannenbaum, 1961; Wertheim, 1976), rule following instead of creativity and innovation, and similar baneful results for GAs.

If size seems to require more GA complexity, then there are alternatives. GAs can be decentralized into independently operating new GAs for smaller territorial units or for different GA subgoals and so on (Wertheim, 1976). The new sub-GAs can be *loosely* federated to preserve the earlier identity if enough members want this. This process generally has worked for small Amish communities as GAs in America for 300 years (Nolt, 1992).

ALTERNATIVES TO
COMPLEXITY IN GAs

My own research on semiformal GAs (Smith, 1992b) examined 59 GAs in a middle-class eastern suburb (Appendix C). About 36% of the sample of GAs were only semiformal in structure and operation as opposed to more clearly formal (as defined in Smith, 1972c). I made additional interviews to explore the logic of such arrangements. The main underlying point made by leaders was that they *liked the informality* and felt that it worked very well and was efficient in spite of some drawbacks. People who came to meetings were called *members.* People who did not come were not members at those meetings, although long-time participants still thought of absent frequent attendees as members. Anyone could reinstate him- or herself by coming to a meeting in the future. The atmosphere was loose and cordial.

Nothing could be considered high in complexity in these semiformal GAs except for the structural aspect of bureaucracy in some groups, each of which had at least one selected leader, sometimes more, and sometimes even a board of directors (but one that listened assiduously to the members). There was no professionalization, no professionalism, no formalization, no standardization, and no career stability of paid staff but often some stability in leadership—oligarchy. Volunteers ran these GAs without any significant pretense of professionalism, doing the best they could, not worrying about professional standards of leadership or nonprofit management or trying to get every little aspect of the operations specifically clear on paper or voted on by the boards, if any. Indeed, the *presence of a board of directors,* taken for granted by those who study work organizations or national associations, is an indicator of complexity (power centralization) among the types of GAs studied.

Returning to my study of one eastern suburb (Appendix C), semiformal GAs differed from regular (more formal) GAs in seeing only active participants as members (100%), in often lacking formal membership lists (43%), in volunteering the information (during leader interviews) that the groups were informal (62%), in seeing informality as a feature of "differentness" of the GAs (67%), and in not having formalization documents available such as bylaws and charters (76%) (all in Smith, 1992b, p. 258). With the exception of the first distinction, which defined the two types of GAs in the study, the other four differences were statistically significant between semiformal and regular GAs at the .05 confidence level or better.

In addition to these elaborations or definitions of the construct of a semiformal GA, semiformal GAs are *more likely* to lack individuals who approve new members, to not use membership cards, to have unusual annual activity patterns, to have fewer volunteer support staff (e.g., officers, board members, committee members) per member, to have less than the usual four elected officers (president, vice president, secretary, and treasurer), to lack extra officers, to have less income from membership dues (thus depending more on contributions or fees), to have fewer relationships with other organizations, and to have less organizational autonomy (Smith, 1992b, p. 261).

Another important finding was that semiformal GAs tended to be significantly younger than regular GAs (Smith, 1992b, p. 261). This suggests that informality or simplicity of form is an early stage of many GAs, but a stage that older GAs often grow out of through increasing complexity. Interestingly, the semiformal GAs were not significantly smaller than the regular ones, contrary to findings about complexity in other studies.

Clearly, a substantial proportion of all GAs might be rather informal or semiformal while still satisfying the criteria of a formal group (Smith, 1972c) but structured and operating in an informal or semiformal way. Wuthnow (1994) has a nice way of putting this, describing what he calls "the small-groups paradox" in millions of small support GAs: "The informality of small groups depends on having formal structure, and the formal structure is tolerated only because of the informality it encourages" (p. 158). There is a continuum here from collectivities, to informal/semiformal groups, to formal groups (organizations), to complex organizations (Smith and Dover, forthcoming).

Other researchers have found similar results. Studying mainly regional or national social movement organizations, but often those with local branches, Gamson (1990, p. 91) found that 55% of the 53 associations under study had rather *informal* structures throughout their periods of challenging the system in search of social change. Gerlach and Hine (1970) argued explicitly that certain informal, network-like organizational structures were more effective for social change groups.

Many women's and feminist GAs dating back to the 19th century were simple in form, lacking resources and legitimation for, as well as interest in, becoming more complex VGs, whether GAs or paid-staff VGs (Blair, 1994; Scott, 1991). Freeman (1975) described GAs of the current women's movement that highly prized their informality and low complexity, strongly resisting efforts by some members to increase the complexity of these GAs. Also studying feminist GAs, Riger (1983) found that the value systems of the groups affected their complexity. Valuing of solidarity and financial independence led to staying intimate, informal, and small. Valuing efficiency and money led to more formalization and hierarchical structure (bureaucratization and complexity). Major conflicts about these values over time sometimes led to the deaths of GAs (see also Wertheim, 1976).

Overall, a certain ideology is needed to stay small and simple in structure. Staggenborg (1989) studied two Chicago feminist groups with very different orientations toward complexity. The more informal and decentralized group encouraged innovation but ultimately died, whereas the more formalized and centralized group stayed alive successfully but at the cost of narrowed strategies and tactics. This is consistent with Gamson's (1990) finding that centralization and bureaucratization combined make for a much greater probability of social movement organization success in achieving new advantages.

Other types of social movement GAs have used simple organization as a defense against the larger society and its social control agencies, not becoming more complex with age. Underground resistance GAs in Nazi-occupied nations during World War II are one example (Ehrlich, 1965; Foot, 1976; Luza, 1989). Radical social movement GAs in the United States during the 20th century constitute a series of other examples. Radical environmental GAs such as local units of Earth First! are quite simple (Manes, 1990; Wolke, 1991). Local GAs of various radical poor people's movements were generally simple (Piven and Cloward, 1979). GAs of various social movements originating in the United States during the 1950s and 1960s favored simple forms as well, at least initially—black power (McAdam, 1982), peace (Chatfield, 1992), civil rights (Blumberg, 1991), and others. Such GA concerns with defense against social control agencies were well founded, as is shown by Blackstock (1976) in his description of the Federal Bureau of Investigation's (FBI) illegal "war" on social movement groups during the 1960s and 1970s and, more recently, by Manes's (1990) description of FBI attacks on Earth First!

Self-help GAs seem especially likely to resist complexity while maintaining intimacy and solidarity. Gartner and Riessman (1984, p. 18) suggest that such GAs often lack formality by choice and design (see also Davidson, 1979; Katz and Bender, 1976, p. 122). Steinman and Traunstein (1976) studied 67 self-help GAs and found support for the hypothesis that such GAs substitute autonomy and solidarity for the bureaucratization and professionalization characteristic of human service paid-staff VGs. These self-help GAs were actively anticomplexity in terms of professionalization, professionalism, formalization, centralization, and so on.

Trojan et al. (1990) present a five-stage model of self-help GA development, with the latter stages involving higher complexity (differentiation and institutionalization). Their findings show that not all such GAs develop up the sequence; some remain small at the stabilization stage (after developing solidarity and orientation). Katz and Bender (1976, p. 122) argue that such GAs show that Michel's ([1911] 1968) iron law of oligarchy is not universally applicable to self-help groups because they are able to resist this tendency consciously as a group goal.

OTHER FACTORS RELATED
TO THE AGE OF GAs

Some of the factors besides complexity that also are related to GA age and life cycle tend to increase fairly regularly with time, whereas other factors or events are more irregular or cyclical. I have selected a small number of such factors for brief review here without attempting to be comprehensive. A special problem in studying GA age in relation to other factors is the tendency for GAs generally to be short-lived, although no national data on GA age seem to be available (Kellerhals, 1974, p. 235; Prestby and Wandersman, 1985; Selle and Øymyr, 1992; Smith, 1992b, p. 263; Wertheim, 1976).

Size

The size of a GA can be measured in many ways (Smith, 1972c). Most common is to count the official members, meaning the number of people that the GA considers officially to be its members. Such a figure can be inflated by a GA wishing to seem larger and more important than it really is. The second most common type of measure of GA size, perhaps, is the amount of its budget, revenues, or expenditures (or sometimes equity) in a given year. Economists prefer these measures. In my view, such economic measures are not very good indicators of GA size given that unpaid volunteer labor is the principal "asset" or type of "revenues" of GAs, to which a dollar value can be imputed if one wishes (see Chapter 2).

A more accurate measure of the internal size of GAs is to count only active (i.e., analytical) members—those contributing some time or services to the group (Smith, 1972c; Verba and Nie, 1972). This reduces or eliminates the puffery of nominal or "on paper only" members and focuses on those people who, for example, actually are giving services and not just money to the group during a given year. And instead of counting just analytical members roughly, one could better count the total of full-time equivalents or simply hours of time contributed by volunteers to a GA during a given year as a size measure. One needs this measure in any attempt to define a GA carefully, comparing paid-staff and volunteer hours.

In terms of both official membership and budget size, there is some evidence that greater GA age is associated with greater size (Trojan et al., 1990; Tsouderos, 1955; Wertheim, 1976). Wertheim (1976) studied 35 food cooperative GAs and found that mean membership increased from 64 to 105 over three years (p. 6), while mean purchases per GA per week increased by 12% over that period (with some GA births and deaths involved [p. 6]). However, the amount of change in size usually is small in absolute terms because GAs by nature tend to be small, on average (see Chapter 2).

Official membership size and budget/revenue size tend to be positively related (Newton, 1975) and reciprocal in influence. More people provide more dues or donations in GAs, which depend relatively little on external sources of income. In turn, more revenues permit GAs to operate more interesting and effective programs and activities, developing greater prestige/power in their communities and, thus, attracting more members. These two measures of size seem to be associated with complexity, with greater size being positively related to greater age and complexity, particularly professionalization (Newton, 1975).

Amount of internal activity is a measure of GA size that has received relatively little attention. It is roughly the volume of participation present in a GA and can be standardized to amount of activity per capita among the membership (either official or analytical). Because of the tendency for increasing membership size with age of GAs, it is probable that there is a gross increase in internal activity with GA age (although I know of no quantitative data to confirm this). However, because larger membership GAs have some tendency for reduced per capita participation because of lowered solidarity and communication, per capita participation sometimes is likely to decline somewhat with age of GA. Also, as GAs grow in membership size and complexity with time, there tend to be more meetings and activities of various types including committee meetings, board meetings, fund-raising activities, and so on in addition to general membership meetings. Thus, GAs become less intermittent, although they remain fundamentally intermittent in activity, lacking full-time paid staff.

Territorial Scope

GAs are local, by definition, but with the passage of time they sometimes increase their ambitions or connections regarding territorial scope. In search of more resources (e.g., people, money) or more influence, GAs might include as members or clients/targets people from wider areas, maintaining their initial bases in given neighborhoods or communities. Such broader resource bases might make the GAs easier to keep alive. This life cycle process is virtually unstudied in GAs, as are several other spatial processes. Also, associations at supralocal levels might try to expand their scope to larger areas. Spencer (1991), for example, discusses a Finnish association that is trying to move from metropolitan and national to international scope. Successful new religions, such as Hare Krishna (Rochford, 1985) recently and Christianity and Islam long ago, have moved from local to national and then to transnational scope over time (Finke and Stark, 1994). All this change of associational scope over time involves some goal succession.

Another aspect of broader GA territorial scope is that a very successful GA might attempt to spin off branches in other communities or neighborhoods. Many national associations began in essentially this way, although few have been studied carefully in this regard. Huang and Gould (1974) analyze the process by which Rotary Clubs spread in the United States from an initial group. United Way (Seeley, Junker, and Jones, 1957) is another documented example. Alcoholics Anonymous also has an identifiable initial GA that spun off similar GAs around the nation and eventually around the world (Rudy, 1986).

Many, and perhaps most, polymorphic GAs and their supralocal parent associations, usually national associations (Knoke, 1990b; Nall, 1967; Smith, 1992a), were formed piecemeal by spreading territorially from an initial GA somewhere. This process has been poorly studied by geographers and other social scientists, to my knowledge (but see Brown and Philliber, 1977, and Huang and Gould, 1974). However, some polymorphic GA networks were started from the top down by national organizations (Sills, 1957). The difference between the spread in scope from one base to a nearby larger base and the spread from one base to other bases is that the former involves broadening the definition of eligible members for a GA in a single location, whereas the latter involves diffusion of some GA idea and form to other locations over time. Both tend to be associated with greater GA age and size.

The fundamental processes of scope expansion among GAs or supralocal associations are not well understood. Geographic models might be applicable, but they fail to explain the intra-association dynamics of such expansion (Huang and Gould, 1974). The one dynamic that is fairly clear is that such expansion by a GA reflects a feeling of associational success among the association's leaders or by its top leader. However, it is not clear what indicators of such success the association leaders use in their projections and decision making for expansion of scope and how realistic such assessments are.

Nor do we know the success rate of such expansion attempts, say, five years later. The role of resource mobilization and other factors in such expansion is unknown but is potentially important. It also is possible that top leader personality is of substantial importance here. Messianic and charismatic leaders probably are more likely to seek such scope expansion sooner and more extensively. There is some evidence that change of territorial venue (association headquarters location), rather than scope expansion, has been attempted to seek more success (Rochford, 1985; Weightman, 1983). This is an associational variant of "the grass is greener on the other side of the fence."

External Relations

A few studies indicate that a GA's cooperation with other, external groups increases with GA age, although the evidence is largely inferential. In their study of Norwegian GAs, Selle and Øymyr (1992) found that more of such coop-eration and relationships with outside groups led to a greater chance of survival (hence more GA age). The logic is clear. External relationships can be seen as resources (Yuchtman and Seashore, 1967). The more such resources a GA has, the more likely it is to survive and get older rather than die, other things being equal. Mulford and Mulford (1980) lend inferential support with their finding from a local sample of GAs that groups with larger membership size tended to have more external relations, more prior external relations (indicating consis-tency in such activities), and more internal activities (e.g., meetings, atten-dance). Because membership size tends to increase with GA age, it might be inferred that external relations also tend to increase with GA age. More direct data would be preferable, of course.

Another piece of inferential data is Smith's (1992b) finding that less complex GAs tend to have fewer external relations. Older GAs tend to be more complex, as we saw earlier in this chapter, so that greater GA age might lead to more exter-nal relations. However, in my study sample (Appendix C), there was no signifi-cant relationship between age and complexity. Again, size, and not age, proba-bly is the real key factor leading to more external relations. The bigger a GA becomes, the more it is a local organizational actor that is taken more seriously by other organizational actors and their leaders and in turn has to take account of other local actors and be taken account of by them. This leads to informal and formal external organizational relations locally.

Power and prestige are relational properties of GAs mainly with regard to nonmembers. Power involves the capacity of a GA to impose its will on indi-viduals or groups. Prestige involves the capacity of a GA to generate feelings of esteem in individuals or groups. Both usually are measured as perceptions by nonmembers and, as such, tend to be confounded in a type of GA halo effect. GAs perceived as powerful also tend to be perceived as prestigious and vice versa (Smith, 1986a). Young and Larson (1965) found higher prestige GAs to be older. Willerman and Swanson (1953) found the prestige of college sororities also to be associated with being older as well as with being larger and having higher socioeconomic status members. Smith (1986a) found, however, that out-standing (high-prestige and high-power) GAs were of about the same age as average-prestige and average-power GAs. Thus, the small amount of evidence is mixed regarding greater age and more prestige and power of GAs, but two studies out of three that are cited support the relationship.

Resource Attraction Modes and Incentives

Although the vast majority of GAs depend on internal sources for funds, older GAs sometimes turn to external funding sources (Milofsky and Romo, 1988). External funding sources mean principally grants and contracts from

foundations, governments, and businesses. When this external funding dependence occurs, GAs tend to lose some autonomy and also become more complex
(Allen et al., 1995; Horch, 1994; Jenkins and Eckert, 1986; Milofsky and Romo,
1988; Saidel, 1989).

In my study of one eastern suburb (Appendix C), I found local GA monopolies on certain fund-raising public events in the town (Smith, 1998a). My qualitative data indicate that such monopolies tend to be more common among older
GAs and, thus, later in their life cycles. Greater GA age gives a GA time to
experiment with different fund-raising events and to figure out, often by trial
and error, what event it might want to have as "its own." This process obviously
is affected by what other special fund-raising events other GAs in town already
have claimed as "their own." I know of no careful study of this process.

Another aspect of resource attraction that tends to change with greater GA
age is the incentive mix (Clark and Wilson, 1961). Most GAs depend mainly on
a mix of sociability, purposive, service, informational, and developmental
incentives to attract members and donations, as do supralocal associations
(Knoke, 1990b; Knoke and Adams, 1987; Knoke and Prensky, 1984; Stephenson, 1973). However, older GAs seem to put somewhat more emphasis on utilitarian (economic) incentives, although still in a minority role in the incentive
mix. Some examples of the latter would include reduced prices for documents,
entry to events, symbolic objects (e.g., T-shirts), insurance, travel, special supplies (e.g., for sports/recreation GAs), food (e.g., as in consumer cooperative
GAs), and so on (Knoke, 1990b, p. 115; Wertheim, 1976). This represents an
attempt to expand incentives for GA members.

Knoke and Wood (1981), in a study of social influence GAs, found virtually
no effect of economic incentives on membership commitment but found substantial effects of purposive incentives. My own study of a broader sample of
GA types in an eastern community (Appendix C) shows some increasing frequency of use of economic incentives by older GAs but does not measure their
impact on commitment or participation. McCarthy and Zald (1977) argue that
material incentives such as career benefits are important to participants in social
movement GAs and paid-staff VGs.

Hirsch (1986) reports that material incentives are more important initially for
individual participants in block clubs and tenant unions but that later sociability
and solidary incentives also become important (p. 384). He presents a model of
social movement organization mobilization that involves the prominence of
different incentive types at succeeding stages of involvement in a group over
time. Union GAs, farmers' GAs, business GAs, and professional GAs, of
course, put much emphasis on economic incentives from their beginnings as
GAs, as do work organizations such as business firms, government agencies,
and paid-staff VGs. Over time, sports GAs might become commercialized to
depend more on material incentives (Mandle and Mandle, 1989).

Goal Succession

The older a GA, the more likely it is to undergo goal succession—changing one or more of its basic GA goals. There are many studies of goal succession in national associations (Michels, [1911] 1968; Schmidt and Babchuk, 1972; Scott, 1991; Sills, 1957, pp. 198-200, 254-64; Zald and Ash, 1966; Zald and Denton, 1983) and local paid-staff VGs (Abel, 1986; Kramer, 1984; Wertheim, 1976; Zald, 1970). But this relationship of age and goal succession has been studied in GAs much less, although the last four studies cited are of groups that initially were GAs.

Scott (1991) studied women's associations historically, finding clear evidence of goal succession with increasing GA age. She also found evidence of goal specialization as a particular type of goal succession in the women's associations, many of them GAs, that she studied. Wertheim's (1976) study of consumer cooperative GAs found decreasing goal emphasis on member participation because of increasing complexity with greater GA age. Richardson (1979) found goal succession and other structure and process changes as a religious group that initially was a GA grew over many years into a national religious association. Finke and Stark (1994) give many examples of American churches that underwent such goal changes, including local churches, that were more often GAs a century or two earlier (see also Clark, 1937).

Saltman (1973) found that, as an open housing (antisegregation) GA got older and accepted external funding from the government, it changed its goals. Instead of continuing to seek its original goal of equal opportunity in housing, the GA responded to the pressure of the government funding agency to focus on meeting the housing needs of the poor. Dissatisfaction by leaders and members of the GA with such goal succession led the GA to turn down further government funding after the second year, and the GA returned to its original goal. Most GAs find it hard to turn back external funding in this way once they became used to it, even in the face of goal succession.

Failure to engage in goal succession as a form of adaptation to changing environment can lead to GA or supralocal association decline. The Women's Christian Temperance Union and the Townsend Movement are examples of national associations that declined over time in part because of their inability to manage successful goal succession (Gusfield, 1963; Messinger, 1955). Some national fraternal associations have been successful in adapting to change through goal succession over time (e.g., Elks, Eagles), whereas others have continued to decline by failing to engage in goal succession—by failure to keep up with changing times (e.g., Odd Fellows, Knights of Pythias), according to Schmidt and Babchuk (1972, pp. 150-51; see also Fiske, 1973). That this divergence of approach should occur within the same GA type shows that leadership perceptions and values are crucial in the ultimate occurrence of goal succession.

The usual motivation for goal succession generally is aspirations of GA leaders for group survival. They often see more complexity, funding by external organizations, and deradicalization as necessities for GA survival. This tends to happen gradually over time rather than all at once. Leaders are trying their best to keep the organization going and tend to make a long series of decisions that eventually produce goal succession, or even goal displacement, with a central focus on GA maintenance rather than on initial GA goals. It is hard for anyone in the GA to criticize such decisions, for the leaders always can say that they are just trying to keep the GA going, thus insulating them from criticism without an analysis like this one. Annual board-level discussions of GA mission and goal succession should be held, in my view, to keep an eye on the trend toward unconscious and nonobvious goal succession. If the GA wants to make a conscious decision to change goals at a certain point in time, then that is much healthier (Sills, 1957). My key point is not that all goal change and goal succession is bad for a GA. Rather, it is that unexamined and gradual goal succession can be dangerous to a GA's mission and general "health" (proper functioning in line with established goals).

Deradicalization

A special form of goal succession that social movement and community GAs, in particular, often undergo is deradicalization when they age. This occurs because of factors such as increasing complexity, the pressures of external funding agencies that they turn to increasingly with time (Milofsky, 1987), the desire to relate to government (Sharp, 1981), and (sometimes) general exhaustion with being "out of step" and, hence, stigmatized by mainstream society. Holmes and Grieco (1991) found that radical community organizations increasingly disguised their founding values and goals so as to get external funding from local and national governments. This led to turnover of personnel committed to initial values.

Community organizing generally has become deradicalized in the United States and Canada since the 1960s (Rosenbloom, 1981), especially during the 1980s and thereafter (Fisher, 1994; Panet-Raymond, 1987, 1989). Neighborhood GAs often have been transformed from advocacy groups into social service agencies maintaining the status quo rather than seeking radical change. Rein (1966) discussed more broadly how social movements tend to turn into more mainstream VGs over time, focusing on the Planned Parenthood Federation of America. Even milder social movement GAs, such as food cooperatives (Cox, 1994), local GAs of Mothers Against Drunk Driving (Katz, 1993, pp. 87, 111), social movement GAs for the homeless (Cress, 1997), and hospices (Abel, 1986), have tended to lose their sociopolitical change ideologies and radicalism over time, giving in to greater complexity and more status quo stances.

Abel (1986) describes the institutionalization of hospices as a social innovation, beginning during the mid-1970s. Although initially somewhat radical, pressing for societal changes of a major sort, hospices quickly settled down to being "professional" and "responsible," seeking and taking insurance and Medicare money for their patients. The volunteer component declined substantially. Kramer (1979) discusses health service nonprofits in the Netherlands that were transformed from mutual aid advocacy organizations to specialized service supplementation activities.

The advent of external funding and professionalization with time are seen by McAdam (1982) as helping to deradicalize and "channel" (influence or subtlely shape) the black radical movement and its GAs in the United States during the 1960s and 1970s. Piven and Cloward (1979) argue similarly for poor people's movements and their GAs and national associations that eventually gained external support. Panet-Raymond (1987) describes a deradicalization process among community GAs in Quebec, apparently going from "radical activism to voluntarism for the state." These GAs wanted government money and a partnership with the government, so they basically dropped their radical and protest activities, focused on economics and not ideology, and developed professional services for their constituencies.

Channeling by the Internal Revenue Service, nonprofit monitoring agencies, the U.S. Postal Service, and other organizations and agencies also deradicalizes large numbers of social movement GAs and, indeed, GAs of all types, pushing them into having more societally acceptable goals and structures (McCarthy, Britt, and Wolfson, 1991; see also Berry, 1997). Jenkins and Eckert (1986) discuss specifically how black insurgency in the United States has been channeled by elite patronage and professional social movement organizations (paid-staff VGs). Emerick (1989) observes deradicalization over time in mental patient self-help GAs (p. 291) as these groups adapt to the larger society and health system. Such deradicalization can reduce the overall effectiveness of more mainstream organizations working for similar goals by reducing the contrast with more mainstream associations of the same purposive type (Haines, 1984).

It is not clear when GAs will become more or less radical, but deradicalization usually seems to be a result of a GA trying to conform to prevailing mainstream GA or paid-staff nonprofit norms so as to obtain, keep, and increase external grant funding from some level of government, a foundation, a corporation, or a funding intermediary nonprofit such as the United Way (Allen et al., 1995; Milofsky and Romo, 1988). These processes work similarly, but more strongly, in paid-staff VGs and national associations because of their greater dependence on external funding agencies (see Kramer, 1979, discussing the situation in the Netherlands).

Sometimes, GAs become *more radical* with time, but this is rare. An example is the study by Ben-Zadok and Kooperman (1988) in which they describe the politicization of a community development GA in Ghana. This happens at the national association level as well (Jenkins, 1977). Rudwick (1972) discusses how the Congress on Racial Equality (CORE) turned from an integrationist national association of blacks and whites into an all-black association concerned with black power and black nationalism. Eventually, it also deradicalized to stay alive. Haines (1984) shows the radicalization of the civil rights movement generally in the United States from 1957 to 1970. The effects of the external environment probably played a major part in this development, with the government and the public gradually becoming more receptive to ideas about social justice over this period. Marullo, Pagnucco, and Smith (1996) found that the U.S. peace movement became more radical in their organizational framing processes in the media from 1988 to 1992.

Goal Displacement

Another special subtype of goal succession is goal displacement. This refers to organizations moving from their initial or later substantive goals to an emphasis on merely maintaining themselves. Among GAs, this is perhaps best exemplified by moving over time from an instrumental to an expressive/solidary goal emphasis. The latter is the GA equivalent of organizational maintenance that would be expressed in other, more bureaucratic ways in paid-staff VGs, businesses, or government agencies. Some types of GAs are particularly prone to goal displacement of this sort including school service GAs (e.g., Parent-Teacher Associations [PTAs]), veterans GAs, youth character development GAs, church-affiliated religious GAs, service clubs, hobby or garden GAs, literary or discussion GAs, and nationality or immigrant GAs. In each case, there usually is an initial instrumental goal other than pure sociability or solidarity.

PTAs, for example, have an instrumental goal of aiding in the education of the parents' and other parents' children by relating to and better understanding the school and its teachers. The usual goal displacement pattern over time is for the goal of sociability to replace the initial instrumental educational goal as primary. Nationality or immigrant GAs tend to have initial instrumental goals of celebrating and preserving a different culture or subculture including its dress, language, foods, documents, history, and other customs (Handlin, 1951; Soysal, 1994). Goal displacement again tends to take place over time, with sheer sociability replacing the cultural celebration and preservation goals as primary. Similar goal displacement over time tends to occur in the direction of sociability for the other GA types mentioned.

Scott (1991) notes gradual goal displacement in women's associations working for suffrage (p. 179). One possible reason for this goal displacement is that the initial purposive incentive of a GA seems to members over time to be more of a vehicle for social relations than important in its own right. Such sociability is self-rewarding, providing important solidary incentives for GA participation. Declining confidence in the effectiveness of the GA in reaching its initial instrumental goal also might play a part, as could essential or partial accomplishment of the initial GA goal.

Increasing complexity leads to goal succession in some GAs over time. This is particularly true when the GA has strong initial participatory values. Greater complexity of the GA over time tends to reduce member participation by increasing centralization, professionalization, professionalism, and other processes. This amounts to a de facto goal change, whether recognized formally by the GA or not. Wertheim's (1976) study of consumer cooperative GAs over time highlights this point. Bryman et al. (1992) make a similar point for community transport organizations for the disabled and needy in the United Kingdom. Romanofsky (1973) discusses this process for GA adoption agencies during the 1920s. However, Kleidman (1994) argues that professionalization can foster or hinder volunteer participation in social movement GAs rather than generally depressing such activity.

Discussing social movement groups, Zald and Ash (1966) suggest, "The more insulated an organization is by exclusive membership requirements and goals aimed at changing individuals, the less susceptible it is to pressures for organizational maintenance or general goal transformation" (p. 332). Such groups tend to be less threatening to society and, hence, less likely to have social control agencies and the general public resist and try to change them. The focus on changing members also lets the group define its own internal reality to a greater extent, paying less attention to societal definitions of what is right to do. Zald and Ash further suggest that goal transformation is related to the interorganizational competition for support. This is a type of "survival of the fittest" statement, with survival based on organizational adaptation to a changing external organizational field and to changing public sentiments relevant to the type of organization. These ideas have relevance to GAs more generally.

Repertoires of Strategies and Tactics

GAs, like other organizations, have their own distinctive strategies for attempting to attain their goals, and these may change with GA age. I have reviewed a number of such changing strategies heretofore—increasing complexity, expanding territorial scope, increasing external relations, developing new resource attraction modes, changing the incentive mix, and conscious goal change (goal succession). The present category of factors changing with the life cycle is noted to suggest that there probably are some other important aspects of distinctive GA strategies and tactics that change over the GA life cycle, although they are little studied. However, my qualitative impression from studying GAs is that they tend to stay with their standard strategies over time rather than making radical changes seeking greater success. In this, they contrast with paid-staff VGs, which tend to be more willing to change in search of greater success in a changing environment (Bielefeld, 1992; McMurtry, Netting, and Kettner, 1991). But the reason for little repertoire change might be little environmental change on the whole. When the environment does change significantly, many GAs change their repertoires (Schmidt and Babchuk, 1972).

Tilly (1978) has done some seminal work in this regard for collective behavior and social movement organizations. He introduced the idea of "repertoires of collective action" to indicate that all groups tend to have repertoires of activities they know, distinctive preferences among the activities in their repertoires, a tendency to choose some forms of action from their repertoires in specific situations, and changes in group action repertoires over time (p. 131). Bearman and Everett (1993) found historical time period changes in the usual protest tactics of national sociopolitical movements active in Washington, D.C., from 1961 to 1983.

Obviously, *all GAs,* not just social movement GAs or national associations, tend to have action repertoires. And there can be repertoires of strategies as well as tactics. I do not know of any research trying to identify the full range of activities in such repertoires for a broad sample of GAs and how they change with GA age.

One piece of research that speaks to this problem, nevertheless, is Lawson's (1983) study of neighborhood GAs in New York City. He specifically writes about one single strategy, the rent strike, and how it was born as a social innovation and then spread, evolving over time so that the strategy changed somewhat. He also writes of the diffusion of this strategy, what types of groups tended to put this activity into their group action repertoires, and variations in the use of other "strategic forms" among neighborhood GAs. Similar research could well be done for all other types of GAs, at least on a local basis as Lawson did. This article and Tilly's related work are new ideas in the GA field, and I hope that researchers will follow up on these ideas.

Survival Rates

Increasing age of a GA leads to increasing chances of survival. There is a liability of "newness" that makes GA death at any subsequent point in time more likely for younger GAs and other organizations than for older ones (Hannan and Freeman, 1977, 1989; Selle and Øymyr, 1992). The literature on this relationship is reviewed in Smith and Associates (forthcoming) under "Decline." Basically, older GAs have more of an opportunity to accumulate and retain resources. These resources include personnel (volunteer time and commitment), revenues and assets, and goodwill (prestige and track record in the community). And such resources help to maintain the GAs and attract still more future resources.

CONCLUSION

The most important conclusion from this chapter is that GAs tend to increase in complexity with size and, to a lesser extent, with age, as do national associations and organizations more generally including paid-staff VGs. I have defined *complexity* in terms of a variety of elements such as bureaucratization, centralization, specialization, formalization, and professionalism. The interrelationships among these variables when properly measured for a broad sample of GAs are unknown.

Many GAs, however, consciously (and sometimes valiantly) resist the tendency to become more complex, unlike most paid-staff VGs. When GAs do resist, it usually is the result of the combined conscious value affirmation of informality and simplicity of structure and processes by their leaderships and memberships. Such GAs seeking to avoid complexity stress autonomy and solidarity over external funding and efficiency. Self-help groups, church-affiliated GAs, and some social movement GAs are particularly likely to take this value stance and resist increasing complexity. They often pay a price in less extensive revenues, lower power/prestige, and less *external* impact. However, their *internal* impact still might be very high, and their internal democracy and member satisfaction tend to be high as well.

A few other aspects of GAs tend to change with increasing GA age, and most of them change in the same way for paid-staff VGs, so I do not present a comparative table here. Size often increases with age, both in numbers of members and in budget/revenues/equity. Numbers and proportion of leaders also tend to increase. Greater GA age and size usually allows the group to attract more financial resources, probably because the GA becomes more well known (i.e., goodwill or successful track record) and/or achieves greater "market penetration" (in the sense of the proportion of local people who are members to the total number of local people who are formally or informally eligible to join the GA). Territorial scope of operations might increase with GA age as groups seem more successful to nonmembers from a broader territory. External relations of GAs increase with greater GA size and age as GAs have more time to establish working relationships with other groups and to see the value of doing so. GAs are more likely to attain higher prestige/power with greater GA size and age. People in the community are more likely to be positively impressed with the activities, track records, leaderships, and other features of older or larger GAs because they are more likely to know about older or larger GAs. New or small GAs often are unknowns in a community, and as such, they are unimpressive to most outsiders. External fund-raising is likely to increase for GAs over time for the reasons already stated: They become better known to outside support agencies and patrons.

Older GAs tend to rely somewhat more on material incentives, seeking to expand the range of incentives they offer members. However, sociability, purposive, service, informational, and developmental incentives usually dominate the incentive systems of most types of GAs (Etzioni, 1961). As part of goal succession, sociability incentives are a usual main fallback in any type of GA.

Goal succession is more likely to occur in older GAs, partly because there is simply more time for these GAs to deviate from or alter their initial goals. But the pressures of external funding agencies on GA goals are more likely for larger and older GAs, which might become significantly dependent on and influenced by such agencies. This is more likely to happen in GAs that are in transition to becoming paid-staff nonprofits. Such external pressures, for example, lead to deradicalization of some social movement GAs. This deradicalization is less likely in paid-staff VGs than in GAs, which are more likely to be radical or fundamentally deviant in the first place. Both GAs and paid-staff VGs can undergo goal displacement, in which sheer maintenance of the groups replaces initial goals. On the other hand, failure to engage in goal succession in a changing GA environment can lead to GA decline and death, as with other types of organizations.

GA distinctive strategies of action tend not to change much with time, aside from the forgoing. Older GAs hold meetings much like younger ones, although procedures for meetings might get more formalized. Fund-raising events in older GAs tend to look much like similar events in younger GAs, although perhaps a bit better run. Overall, older GAs, like younger ones, just tend to "muddle through" in their leisure activities as GA members and leaders. But older GAs are more likely to survive to become older still, for various reasons of accumulated resources.

Research also is much needed to shed light on the following interrelated issues. When in its life cycle of development does a GA shift in its structure and operation toward the paid-staff VG style and leave behind most of the GA style? How incompatible are elements of the two styles in the same nonprofit at the same time? That is, how much middle ground is there between the extremes portrayed in my ideal types of Chapters 4 to 7. Is there a gradual group style transition as more and more paid staff are added, or does the transition happen quickly at some point or phase (turning point or crystallization phase)? If a rapid transition or turning point occurs, at what relative or absolute paid-staff size does it occur? Does this vary according to other VG characteristics such as those discussed in Chapters 3 to 7?

Goal succession, perhaps without goal displacement, seems to be another particularly important factor to understand in more detail. When will goal succession really help a GA grow and survive? Can one predict in advance which particular types of goal succession (additional goal choice) will be most promising and effective? To what extent should prior goals be preserved in a goal succession process for optimal outcomes—for example, to avoid rapid and excessive member turnover as a result of goal changes?

Many other features of GA life cycles that might be studied have not been, and much remains to be done in understanding and confirming the relationships noted essentially as working hypotheses in this chapter. Each of the aspects of structure, process, and leadership in Chapters 4 to 7 could be studied over time in GAs, but not all have been.

9

Impact and Effectiveness

In this chapter, I am concerned with the causal impact of grassroots associations (GAs) internally, or on their members, and externally, or on their environments. I also am concerned with the organizational factors that tend to affect such impact. The extended literature review to support my conclusions here is mainly published elsewhere (Smith, 1997a, 1999a, 1999b). Earlier overviews were given in Smith (1973a) and Smith and Reddy (1973). Although the literature reviewed refers almost wholly to specific GAs or samples of GAs, I am concerned here with the national implications of cumulating such narrower views of impact. Space considerations preclude my providing a methodological discussion of impact evaluation except to say that I take a broad view of demonstration of impact, consistent with the literature (Murray and Tassie, 1994; Steers, 1975), and that there is very little methodological discussion of GA impact evaluation per se (but see Torres, Zey, and McIntosh, 1991).

Many scholars use the terms *impact* and *effectiveness* (or *performance* [Shenhar, Shrum, and Alon, 1994]) synonymously, but I do not. I consistently use the term *impact* here to refer to changes that a GA brings about, whether internally or externally. By contrast, the term *effectiveness* here is used to refer to how GAs accomplish their impact in terms of structure and operation. *Effectiveness* has a connotation that suggests using organizational resources so that the goals of the organization clearly are accomplished. Used in this way, *effectiveness* is similar to, but still different from, *efficiency,* where some outcomes or products are assumed and one investigates how well organizational resources were used to make for optimal achievement of those outcomes.

I undertook my review of GA impact literature with an open mind but realizing that many social scientists argue that GAs have few or no important types of impact. My working hypothesis was that GAs might have such impact if one looks in the right activity purpose areas and if one focuses carefully on local-level volunteer associations (GAs) rather than focusing mainly on national-level associations. At the local level, GA impact is likely to be less difficult to establish because of the smaller scale of associations (GAs) and the less complex or varied set of potential alternative actors that might account for change or lack of change in individuals, in clients, or in local communities.

GA IMPACT

Several expected types of impact tend to be present as a result of GA activity, flowing from the structure and processes common to GAs generally in relation to individuals and their relations to the larger community and society. One way of seeing these different broad types of GA impact is in terms of what sociologists and anthropologists call "the major institutions of society" (Stark, 1994). These institutions are present in every society, even preliterate societies. For each major institution, there usually is a corresponding type of GA impact because these five institutions represent major clusters of behavior and norms in any society.

Corresponding to the institution of the family is the first type of impact, social support/helping/self-expression, as manifested in both fellowship/sociability as member impact and helping/service to others as external impact. Corresponding to the institution of education is stimulation/information as a type of member impact and information provision as an external impact. Corresponding to the institution of the polity/government is sociopolitical activation as a member impact and sociopolitical influence as an external impact. Corresponding to the institution of the economy/business are economic outcomes for members and the larger community/society.

The final one of the five major institutions is religion, where categorization of the general impact of GAs is less clear. Most churches are paid-staff nonprofits, so technically I need not consider them in this book on GAs. There are overviews of the sociology of religion that include some attention to the impact of churches (e.g., Johnstone, 1992). However, some smaller church or other religious congregations are GAs. On the one hand, religious outcomes are perhaps other-worldly, where we have no scientific evidence of outcomes. On the other hand, many religious outcomes in this world, like religious self-identity and the expression of deep joint emotions, might fit best in the stimulation/information category, as elements of self-expression. Other religious outcomes, such as religious beliefs and religious knowledge, seem to fit with information, as another aspect of that category. Religious participation in worship services and integral church maintenance activities (e.g., choir, Sunday school, fund-raising) can be seen as fitting into the sociopolitical activation and influence category because they involve people becoming and being more active in their churches.

The fifth substantive type of impact in my classification scheme, therefore, corresponds to one of the lesser institutions, namely the health institution, which I see as corresponding to happiness and health as GA impact.

The following subsections provide general descriptions of the five major substantive types of GA impact that I theorize are most important for GAs (Smith, 1997a). I have combined some substantive types of impact that could be separated so as to make the total set of impact types more compact and readily grasped by the reader.

Social Support/Helping/Self-Expression

GAs are inherently social and interactional, usually on a face-to-face basis because of their locality base and goals. They *all* tend to generate interpersonal support and informal helping among members as one type of member impact (Auslander and Litwin, 1988; Clary, 1987; Coombs, 1973; Vaux, 1988; Wagner, 1991; Wuthnow, 1998). Fischer (1982), in a study of people from 50 Northern California communities, shows that co-members of GAs constituted at least 6% of people's overall social support networks—about 20% for people in churches and religious GAs and 10% for people only in secular GAs (pp. 41, 111). About half of these GA co-member "friends" had been met through the GAs (p. 356). Moreover, Fischer found that co-members of GAs were more likely than co-workers or neighbors to be "especially close" and to go out socially with the respondents (p. 109).

Some 40% of American adults (Wuthnow, 1994, p. 47) are in small, social support, mutual aid groups that are especially important sources of social support by definition—self-help groups, Bible study groups, Sunday school classes, book and discussion groups, political and current events groups, sports and hobby groups (pp. 76, 170). Wuthnow's (1994, p. 170) national representative sample research on such "support groups" shows that these groups were credited by 82% of members with making them feel as though they were not alone, by 72% with giving encouragement when they were feeling down, and by 43% with helping them through emotional crises, among other types of help. Many researchers have noted the key importance of social support and interaction specifically in self-help GAs (Katz and Bender, 1976; Lavoie, Borkman, and Gidron, 1994; Powell, 1994).

Interpersonal support and friendship constitute major types of impact for GAs whose major goals are sociability (Barker and Gump, 1964; Clawson, 1989; Morgan and Alwyn, 1980), social service (Charles, 1993), youth development (MacLeod, 1983; Reck, 1951), hobbies (Bishop and Hoggett (1986), immigrant relations (Maeyama, 1979; Soysal, 1994), and self-help (Droghe, Arnston, and Norton, 1986; Wuthnow, 1994). Even GA political influence activities can increase social support networks of participants (Cable and Degutis, 1997).

On an aggregate basis, GAs provide some social integration and residential stability within a territory as an external impact, linking the people in a territory together through first-order and higher order membership overlaps (Babchuk and Edwards, 1965; Litwak, 1961; Moller, Mthembu, and Richards, 1994).

In some instances, GAs have nonmember-serving goals and are able to turn internal cohesion into various types of service activities of potential or actual use to target nonmembers (DeGrazia, 1957) such as helping after disasters (Coston, Cooper, and Sundeen, 1993; Drabek, 1986; Stallings and Quarantelli, 1985; Zakour et al., 1991), firefighting (Lozier, 1976; Perkins, 1989; Thompson, 1993), emergency medical services (Gora and Nemerowicz, 1985; Mausner, Benes, and Gabrielson, 1976; Perlstadt and Kozak, 1977), and crime control (Curtis, 1987; Fagan, 1987; Podolofsky and DuBow, 1981) as well as indigenous service for development in developing countries (Clark, 1991; Esman and Uphoff, 1984; Fisher, 1993; Freeman, 1989). Although local religious congregations in the United States probably are mainly paid-staff voluntary groups (VGs), some are GAs and most congregations provide some community social services (Hodgkinson, Weitzman, and Kirsch, 1989; Wineberg, 1992).

Social support often encourages self-expression. Thus, GAs tend to provide an impetus toward and means of self-expression/personal growth (Bender, 1986; Daniels, 1988; Wuthnow, 1998, p. 237; Zipps and Levine, 1984). This is particularly important for societal outsiders in outsider-run GAs (e.g., minorities, women, the handicapped, youths, the poor) (Blair, 1994; Fisher, 1993; Freeman, 1975; Lipset and Wolin, 1965; Matson, 1990; McAdam, 1982). Some GAs permit or encourage deep joint emotional expression, as in sect or cult GAs (Adler, 1986; Johnstone, 1992; Kephart and Zellner, 1994; Lyons, 1988; Zellner, 1995). A nonreligious example would be the GAs of Mothers Against Drunk Driving that channel members' anger and grief aroused by the loss of loved ones in automobile accidents (Marshall and Oleson, 1996). Self-help groups specifically for the bereaved also help with deep joint emotional expression (Schwab, 1995-96). I have argued (Smith, 1972d) that emotionally powerful rituals in sociability GAs, such as college fraternities and sororities, play a central role in developing and maintaining member commitment (Scott, 1965).

Stimulation/Information

In modern society, especially information/service postindustrial societies, all organizations tend to create a social reality for their members (Thompson, 1980). GAs specifically tend to provide both their members and much of the nonmember population cumulatively with various types of stimulation/information/education experiences (Blair, 1994; Fine and Holyfield, 1996; Knoke, 1988; D. Smith, 1990; Whitmore et al., 1988; Wuthnow, 1998, p. 237). Deacon and Golding (1991) performed a broad mail questionnaire survey of voluntary organizations in the Midlands of England. They showed the importance in most types of GAs of providing information to members and others in the current "information society."

Some other types of GAs have a central focus on information. For example, book discussion GAs combine the provision of information with personal growth (Bauman, 1994; Davis, 1961). Local "free" public libraries in the United States were promoted during the late 19th and early 20th centuries by GAs concerned with making information and written experiences available to everyone (Watson, 1994). Youth development GAs (MacLeod, 1983; Reck, 1951), such as the Boy Scouts, the Girl Scouts, and the 4-H, emphasize skill and knowledge development in practical areas. As a narrower example, college political activist GA members tend to have much more political knowledge than do control non-GA members (Lacy, 1971), although this could be due partly to selection effects. Similarly, participation in a community crime control GA leads to more knowledge of neighborhood crime among participants (DuBow and Podolofsky, 1982), and participation in amateur scientific GAs leads to accumulation of related scientific information (Stebbins, 1979).

Lawson (1983) studied social movement GA members who learned new skills and techniques of protest and political action from their GAs such as when and how to conduct a rent strike. Also, immigrant ethnic/nationality GAs can help second-generation immigrants who have returned home, giving them moral and informational support to fit into the society that they lost (Spain) when their parents emigrated (Mancho, 1982). Even fraternal GAs, such as the 19th-century Freemasons in France, convey information to members (Bolle de Bal, 1989).

In addition to emphasizing experiential knowledge as the basis of their healing and supportive effects (Borkman, 1976), self-help GAs usually convey information to participants about their problems of focus, how to deal with them in everyday life, available services, available supportive people/sponsors in the GAs, and how people can think about themselves in new ways (Ablon, 1981; Chesler, 1991, p. 291; Gonyea and Silverstein, 1991). This latter matter of "worldview transformation" (Kennedy and Humphreys, 1994) is the most extensive and encompassing process. The information absorbed is internalized and leads to dealing with everyday life in radically new ways. For example, the Alcoholics Anonymous (AA) member who makes such a transformation not only stops drinking alcohol but also avoids bars and drinkers and has a new philosophy of life (Rudy, 1986). Sects and cults provide similar worldview transformations (Barker, 1984).

One of the most convincing impact studies of self-help group information provision was performed by Azrin, Flores, and Kaplan (1975). Using a pretest-posttest control group design for a job-finding club, they found that the experimental group (and also GA) members had learned information about job hunting that resulted in a job-finding rate that was 35% higher than that of the control group of nonmembers after two months. *All* of the GA members found jobs within three months, whereas 40% of matched nonmember controls did not find jobs by that time. Job contact information from fellow members of the club markedly helped co-members, as did other job-seeking information and skills that were learned.

Sociopolitical Activation and Influence

GAs often politicize their members and generate sociopolitical influence activity directed at nonmembers and external organizations. Members learn democracy directly from participation in GAs, partly because GAs of every type sometimes get involved in public affairs/issues when they are relevant to continued GA existence and/or to specific GA goals (e.g., health, education) (Verba, Schlozman, and Brady, 1995, p. 63). GAs also politicize their members because of internal democratic processes and political discussion (Verba and Nie, 1972, pp. 178-79) that involve learning experiences for many members. The result is that active GA members tend to get more involved in a wide variety of political activities than do less active members or nonmembers (Almond and Verba, 1963, p. 256; Baumgartner and Walker, 1988; Hanks, 1981; Hanks and Eckland, 1978; Knoke, 1982, 1990a; Verba et al., 1995, p. 338; Verba and Nie, 1972).

Some examples of politicization types positively related to GA participation that are found in the literature include voting turnout (Thomson and Knoke, 1980), registration to vote and becoming a political candidate (Hargreaves, 1991), attending a political meeting or signing a petition (Rosenstone and Hansen, 1993, p. 72), creating or reinforcing commitment to advocacy work (Bond and Kelly, 1983; Kalifon, 1991), creating interest in social issues (Wuthnow, 1998, p. 237), and composite political participation measures (Verba et al., 1995, p. 338).

A few important longitudinal studies have been performed confirming the forgoing general politicization effect of GAs. Hanks and Eckland (1978) studied about 2,000 respondents in longitudinal research from 1955 to 1970. They found that high school extracurricular activities, including GA activities, led strongly to adult GA activities, which in turn led to more voting and less alienation. Also important is a national sample longitudinal survey of youths (N = 10,245) studied in 1972, 1973-74, and 1974-75 (Hanks, 1981). Hanks (1981) found that participation in GAs by youths led to more adult political participation of various types as a direct effect. There also were some indirect statistical effects of adolescent GA participation mediated by resulting greater young adult GA activity, which in turn led to more political participation. These effects were stronger for participation in instrumental GAs that were seeking to affect people or groups outside their own GAs.

Leighley (1996) shows that a substantial amount of this political mobilization by associations is unintentional or informal. However, intentional mobilization by GA leaders tends to occur more in political associations and has a significant political mobilization effect on GA members who have lobbying, normative, or occupational incentives. Rogers, Barb, and Bultena (1975) found that the political mobilization effect was stronger in instrumental (external benefit) GAs.

Psychological empowerment represents a type of internal factor viewed as related to political activity as overt behavior, particularly through the exercise of group power (Zimmerman, 1995). GA participation fosters such psychological empowerment (Ahlbrandt, 1984), especially for members higher on self-efficacy (Zimmerman and Rappaport, 1988). This also seems to happen more for GA members who feel greater social intimacy in their GAs and less control by them (Speer and Hughey, 1996). Self-help GAs often result in psychological empowerment (Chesler, Chesney, and Gidron, 1990, p. 257; Kahn and Bender, 1985). In developing nations, psychological empowerment often results from the evangelization and liberation theology in Christian base communities (Catholic GAs of poor people), which in turn leads to different aspects of political and economic development (Anderson and Colombo, 1988; Mehta, 1987). According to Maton and Salem (1995), psychological empowerment results from organizational settings with belief systems that inspire growth; highly accessible group opportunity structures; support systems that provide members with a sense of community; and shared, talented, and committed leadership.

This sociopolitical activation of members also spills over into other GA activities of members such as more giving and volunteering in the same GA but also more GA activity in other groups (Hanks, 1981; Hanks and Eckland, 1978; Morgan, Dye, and Hybels, 1977; Snyder, 1970). This occurs in part because intrinsic satisfaction of GA participation is generalized by individual members. GA activity also can lead to more program service volunteering (Hodgkinson and Weitzman, 1992, p. 227). The spillover effect also can affect other socioculturally approved leisure activities such as friendship, neighboring, print media consumption, and outdoor recreation (Smith, 1994a; Smith, Macaulay, and Associates, 1980, chap. 19).

GAs with either internal or external goals that relate to public issues often have a political impact locally (Berry, Pourtney, and Thomson, 1993, chap. 12; Boyte, 1980, 1984; Fisher, 1994; Larsen, 1992). This can come, for example, through environmental health groups successfully resisting the siting or operation of a hazardous waste incinerator or waste dump in their locality (Freudenberg, 1984; Freudenberg and Steinsapir, 1991; Jacobs, 1992-93; Kraft and Kraut, 1985). Or, GAs can successfully resist broadcasting license renewals and affect television program formats (Longley, Terry, and Krasnow, 1983), among other manifestations of local influence. One GA influenced its city government to establish a short-term care center for the homeless (Wittig and Schmitz, 1996). Another GA affected city land use decisions (Hudson, 1988). There are numerous other examples of GA local political impact.

However, GAs are far from uniformly successful in their local political influence attempts, limited as they are by local and higher level business and government sector elites (Logan and Rabrenovic, 1990; Mills, 1956; Smiley, 1975; Wiewel and Rieser, 1989) as well as by competition or conflict with other GAs (Mulford and Mulford, 1980; Rose, 1955). Many countries put legal limits on political advocacy and campaigning by GAs and other nonprofits (Randon and Perri 6, 1994). GA internal weaknesses also play a role in advocacy failure, as do the type and scope of the problem (Cohen and Ely, 1981).

A different type of failure was the 1960s-70s U.S. government-sponsored program of "maximum feasible participation" by the poor and minorities, in which government funds were used in paid-staff community VGs. This program failed because government control at different territorial levels blocked and channeled genuine, autonomous citizen action (Brokensha, 1974; Gittell, 1980, 1983; Landsberger, 1972a; Moynihan, 1970; Warren, Rose, and Bergunder, 1974). What often began as independent GA citizen advocacy many times became controlled paid-staff VG service delivery and monitoring (Gittell, 1983). Power offered to community organizations with one hand was withdrawn by the other hand. The government-mandated community organizations are very different from free autonomous GAs with political interests in the community.

Paid-staff or volunteer autonomous community VGs, either inspired by or initiated by Saul Alinsky, have had much more success (Alinsky, 1969; Lancourt, 1979; Marquez, 1990; Reitzes and Reitzes, 1984; Robinson and Hanna, 1994), being based more clearly on the practical goals of grassroots people. Feminist autonomous VGs, emphasizing low hierarchy and consensual decision making, also have been more successful (Bradshaw, Soifer, and Gutierrez, 1994; Iannello, 1992). Bradshaw et al. (1994) propose a hybrid model combining the preceding two sometimes successful models, calling for continuing flexibility to adapt to the changing context of organizing and to the dynamics of race and ethnicity. Feminist VGs tend to do better than Alinsky-style VGs in linking utilitarian goals with broader values (Iannello, 1992; Stein, 1986).

GAs have more political impact when they act as parts of local coalitions or alliances (Danziger, 1983; Harris, 1984) and when they are polymorphic (Delgado, 1986; Fisher, 1994, pp. 223-24). National or other supralocal associations (including coalitions and federations) that support GAs and vice versa are particularly important for the accomplishment of basic, long-term structural changes for the disadvantaged and outsiders in a locality (Fisher, 1993; Marquez, 1990; Obinne, 1994; Reitzes and Reitzes, 1984). State-level mediation might help to resolve local conflicts involving GAs (Kraft and Kraut, 1985). When GAs are parts of regional or national social movements (Lofland and Jamison, 1984), they are more likely to help contribute to basic societal changes (Gamson, 1990; see also references in McAdam and Snow, 1997). Gamson (1990, p. 37) found, surprisingly, that such social movements were able to attain new advantages for their "targets of benefits" (intended beneficiaries) about half of the time over 145 years of American history.

Economic Outcomes

Nearly everyone and every GA has some economic concerns. Most GAs tend to have some revenues, however small, and these can cumulate nationally into a large amount of money, as seen in Chapter 2. All GAs involve some imputed economic value of participants' time (Herzog and Morgan, 1992), which similarly cumulates nationally into a large dollar amount (see Chapter 2). All GAs also can increase business or professional job contacts of members, especially males (Granovetter, 1974; McPherson and Smith-Lovin, 1982, 1986). Many GAs can help to provide members with some relevant experience for obtaining jobs to those lacking recent paid job skills, often homemakers returning to the labor force (Mueller, 1975; Zipps and Levine, 1984). Through GAs, people are more productive, if only informally, than otherwise would be the case. Valuable practical services for members and nonmembers are accomplished in the community that can reduce municipal costs and taxes or can increase municipal efficiency (e.g., volunteer firefighting corps: Perkins, 1989; Stinson and Stam, 1976; volunteer town committees: Luloff et al., 1984). Cumulatively, these economic situation improvements help not just GA members but also the economy and society more generally.

GAs and networks of GAs play key roles in sustaining economic development and promoting psychological empowerment in developing nations (Anheier, 1987; Clark, 1991; Esman and Uphoff, 1984; Fisher, 1993; Freeman, 1989). Successful results have been obtained from GA projects in agriculture, producer cooperatives, marketing cooperatives, consumer cooperatives, micro-enterprises, rotating credit availability, irrigation, well digging, housing, road and bridge construction, other construction, health, family planning, education, and other activities related to economic development. GAs that are rotating credit cooperatives are especially important, enabling self-development proj-ects (Cope and Kurtz, 1980; Fisher, 1993). Another common type of GA in developing nations is urban squatter neighborhood GAs in various Latin Ameri-can nations, which have attained new services and other tangible benefits for their neighborhoods (Fisher, 1984). Some GAs in developing nations make a new similar GA easier to form if the initial GA dies, thus increasing local social capital (Fisher, 1993).

In addition, there are specifically economic system support GAs that have a positive effect on both members and nonmembers locally, although most are polymorphous—farmers groups, unions, businesspeople's groups, professional groups, and so on (Abbott, 1988; Browne, 1988; Coleman, 1988; Krause, 1996; Morrison, 1970). For example, unions tend to raise their members' average wages locally compared to nonunionized workers' wages in the same localities and industries (Estey, 1981, p. 134; Hirsch and Addison, 1986, p. 153). Estey (1981, p. 136) found that unions hasten technological change and raise overall firm efficiency (p. 137) while reducing the scope of management (especially personalized) decision making (p. 135).

Happiness and Health

The social support and other positive results (e.g., entertainment) generated by GAs tend, as a by-product, to create more happiness and satisfaction with life and less depression (Bradburn, 1969; Bradburn and Caplovitz, 1965; Cutler, 1981-82; Lin, Dean, and Ensel, 1986; Palisi, 1985) as well as to foster better health, less illness, less mortality (death), and quicker recovery from illness among members (Adler and Matthews, 1994; Moen, Dempster-McClain, and Williams, 1992; Rodin and Salovey, 1989; Vaux, 1988). Social support also lessens distress or strain, the negative impact of stressors and life crises on indi-viduals, and reduces the likelihood of "health-damaging behaviors" as a result of stress (Adler and Matthews, 1994, p. 243; Brown et al., 1992; Rietschlin, 1996; Vaux, 1988). The social support referred to here is broader than, but includes the social support generated by, GAs as in the first impact type given earlier (social support).

Self-help GAs specifically have been shown to have positive effects on the mental health, physical health, and health-related behavior of their participants (Humphreys, 1997; Kurtz, 1990; Lavoie et al., 1994; Maton, 1988; Powell, 1994). Most well studied is the positive, if modest, effect of AA on reducing alcohol abuse and increasing psychological adjustment among participants (Emrick et al., 1993; Makela, 1994). Similarly, other "Anonymous" format or "12-step" self-help GAs have been found to have significant impact on partici-pants at times (Grimso, Helgesen, and Borchgrevink, 1981; Kurtz, 1990). Self-help GAs also can "improve members' knowledge of and coping with their [chronic] illness and promote self-care behavior" (Humphreys, 1997, p. 13). Similar results can be obtained by self-help GAs relating to life crises or transitions such as having a premature infant (Minde et al., 1980), adjusting to divorce (Kunz and Kunz, 1995), and dealing with the death of a spouse (Caserta and Lund, 1993; Lieberman and Videka-Sherman, 1986). Self-help GA participation also has been found to reduce member use of health care resources (e.g., hospitals, professional services [Humphreys, 1997, p. 17]) and to reduce the use of sick days while employed in stressful work (Cullinan, 1992).

Level of involvement in the group is an important factor in these outcomes: "Evaluations suggest that most involved members report greater life satisfaction, shorter hospital stays, less dependence on professionals, raised self-esteem, and improved attitudes. These benefits are intensified if the member involves him[self] or herself heavily in the self-help group and both gives and receives support within the group" (Kurtz, 1990, pp. 110-11).

All of these types of impact rarely are turned toward nonmembers except in attempts at their recruitment, specifically in health-oriented GAs. However, such spillover effects are possible and sometimes happen. In Brazil and Canada, GAs have improved health care (Pedalini, Dallari, and Barber-Madden, 1993; Rousseau, 1993). In Nicaragua, volunteers from GAs who distributed anti-malaria medicines caused a decline in malaria nationwide (Garfield and Vermund, 1986). Another example of such external health impact is advocacy GAs that try to safeguard nursing home residents and help them in various ways, improving nursing homes if feasible (Finlinson, 1995; Williams, 1986). Unions in an Australian community helped improve the health and safety conditions of their workers (Savery and Soutar, 1990). Unions in the United States and elsewhere also have done this (Estey, 1981; Hirsch and Addison, 1986).

Other Outcomes

Sometimes, GAs have other outcomes (Smith, 1973a) such as causing more deviance; increasing tolerance; providing entertainment and the play element in society; making social innovations; providing countervailing definitions of reality and morality; providing "negative feedback" (criticism) of society; providing a sense of mystery, wonder, and the sacred; preserving old ideas, values, and objects; and providing a latent resource for all types of goal attainment in a territory.

When extrapolated to the full range of GAs in the nation's population, these six broad types of GA impact generally are of major importance to a society. In dictatorships or even less authoritarian societies, the impact of GAs, however, is much diminished (Allen, 1984; Bauer, 1990; Belyaeva, 1992; Hegyesi, 1992). Some GAs also affect the achievement of other outcomes on which they focus that may or may not be socially approved. Deviant or socially disapproved outcomes of nonprofits, including GAs, need a great deal more attention (Smith, 1973a, forthcoming a). They too are left off the map by "flat-earth" nonprofit scholars with restrictive views of the nonprofit sector.

GA EFFECTIVENESS

There are specific structure and process elements of GAs common to many GA effectiveness studies for either internal or external impact. I view the following as tentative working hypotheses of a theory of GA effectiveness rather than as very solid empirical or theoretical generalizations (but see the literature reviews in Smith, 1999a, 1999b). Given the initial requirement that a GA has been formed (Smith, 1967), *internal impact* on its members and *external impact* on its clients (i.e., public in contact), community, society, and/or the world (the human species and its biophysical environment) are rather systematically fostered if a GA has the following characteristics:

Better Resource Mobilization for GA
Means/Activities and Ends/Goals

1. Has a successful track record of past accomplishments that must be communicated to potential members as part of recruitment (this makes it difficult for new GAs to have much impact but draws newcomers to successful GAs)

2. Recruits enough active members (i.e., associational volunteers) to permit reasonable accomplishment of operative GA goals using approved GA means, without seeing sheer numbers of analytical members (Smith, 1972c), let alone official members, as the key to external impact

3. Seeks and attains high internal activity/participation levels in key GA activities such as meetings, fund-raising events, and protests (if any)

4. Recruits mainly "peer" members—people with a common problem, interest, experience, and/or background, leading to substantial intragroup homogeneity (i.e., homophily) and a sense of exclusiveness, even with an open recruitment policy

5. Depends mainly on internal funding such as dues and donations and other internal resources, especially during the initial phase of group formation and development, viewing this broadly as mutual aid/self-help rather than using mainly external resources from the beginning or even later on

6. Can accept modest amounts of external resources, especially as technical assistance/expertise, training/education, and small amounts of grant funding that are given with few or no GA obligations to, or GA control by, an external agency or organization

Better GA Ideology and Incentives/Values

7. Develops an effective ideology including values and a world perspective that explain the situation of the members and what the group will do to improve this situation, justifying and legitimating GA means and ends, thus providing more purposive incentives to members

8. Provides more and stronger incentives for member/leader participation, both ego-istic and altruistic incentives including self-actualization/personal growth, pur-posive, solidary/sociability, informational, charismatic, (sometimes) material, and other incentives

9. Generates more overall commitment to the group by members/leaders—to its goals, means, members, leaders, and "track record" (prior achievements)—even though this might lead to less duration of membership (Cress, McPherson, and Rotolo, 1997)

Better GA Maintenance/Internal Control

10. Creates and maintains significant internal democracy, with rotating leadership and participation in decision making on major issues by members from all hierar-chical levels

11. Has high-quality volunteer leaders who are reasonably skilled and responsive to members' needs and are able to help members and the group as a whole attain their goals

12. Involves members in face-to-face interactions in meetings and other group activities

13. Creates high internal cohesion and solidarity among the members, providing some social support to each member

14. Avoids goal displacement in which sheer GA maintenance activities become cen-tral and in which original GA goals and activities are lost sight of, perhaps permanently

15. Persists for one or more years so that its goals can be achieved at least gradually

Better, More Fruitful Relationships and Interactions With the GA's Environment

16. Maintains optimal (usually substantial) autonomy of goals, means, and activities relative to all other, external organizations, groups, and collectivities

17. Has greater vertical integration in the sense of belonging to some supralocal feder-ation, coalition, or regional/national association as a polymorphic (i.e., many [similar] forms) GA, but doing so while accomplishing Point 16

18. Cooperates informally and locally with other groups and organizations more frequently, again still maintaining basic autonomy

Collectively these factors promote attachment of GA members to each other and to GA goals and values. If the basic mission of the GA is focused outward, toward changing its clients, other groups, the community, or wider structures and processes, then such key effectiveness elements as those just mentioned will help the GA use its volunteer resources to have an external impact. If the GA has member impact goals, then such effectiveness elements will help the group have a significant internal impact.

The bases for finding these elements of GA effectiveness in regard to the impact of GAs lie in the structure and operations of GAs generally, particularly the central need that GAs have to attract and retain volunteers with high levels of commitment to the GAs' goals and then to use these personnel resources rationally in GA goal achievement using GA-approved means.

Special Internal Impact Effectiveness Factors

In addition, *internal impact-seeking GAs* tend to have nine factors in common that make them different from external impact-seeking GAs on the whole (few GAs do both well):

- Central focus on internal impact goals and activities, but sometimes some secondary focus on external social change or advocacy goals as well, viewing the external society as "part of the problem"

- Tends to have a member sponsorship system, at least informally, for entry into the GA and/or as a new member

- Each member's tending to have at least one reciprocal social exchange relationship in the GA—essentially a personal friend in the GA or other person who is a "significant other"

- Members tending to feel particularly affirmed and accepted as persons, either before joining or soon after joining the GA

- Members coming to use co-member peers as a significant reference group for themselves in various ways, fostering personal change

- Promotes self-help/mutual aid of younger/short-time members by older/long-time members in learning about the GA ideology and practices and about causing internal impact

- Tends to have a generally informal, nonbureaucratic internal structure and processes, often with only informal leadership processes in the sense that leaders, even in formal elected offices, tend not to have a great deal of arbitrary power over nonleaders and practice participatory/egalitarian leadership

- Practices encapsulation significantly for new members—physical isolation, social isolation, and/or ideological isolation (the latter means that the GA has a powerful ideology that, when internalized, shields members from nonmembers, even when members continue relating to and interacting with nonmembers)

- Needs fewer members to succeed (e.g., small support and self-help GAs)

Special External Impact Effectiveness Factors

The following eight factors seem to be *important as well, especially for external impact:*

- Creates and sustains a greater sense of local community and identification (i.e., "we" feeling) with the local community, which is the level of society on which external goal GAs mainly focus

- Has and maintains an external sociopolitical advocacy and/or service goal (rarely will both be simultaneously possible for a GA to seek successfully)

- Develops and maintains the optimal mix of advocacy versus service external goals for any given stage of GA development in relationship to its external environment

- Develops and maintains the right mix of external and internal goals and activities for any given stage of GA development (before a record of successful achievement has been established, a GA tends to need substantially more attention to internal goals than it does later on)

- Creates and maintains more horizontal integration, cooperating with similar or identical external groups and organizations in the community and elsewhere

- Has more informed and politically skilled leaders who can gain access to decision makers and/or external resources when needed

- Avoids internal divisiveness and factionalism, especially of the intensity that it might (a) split the group into two or more independent subgroups or (b) cause an internal stalemate in which little can be done to seek external impact goals

- Needs more members to succeed than does an internal impact GA, on average

GENERAL EFFECTIVENESS STUDIES

Although organizational characteristics do not necessarily affect the perceived policy impact of a GA (Burt, 1990), there are a few studies of general samples of GAs that have found such organizational effectiveness factors. Smith (1986a) compares leader-reported data on (a) 45 GAs from eight towns rated "outstanding" (high in terms of peer-rated GA power, impact, and level of activity) to data on (b) 52 GAs of a more ordinary sort selected randomly from the Boston metropolitan area. Although there were many characteristics that did *not* differentiate the two groups significantly, certain other factors significantly made such differentiations as organizational effectiveness elements.

High effectiveness GAs tended to have greater prestige ratings of the groups, more estimated average member income and education, and higher average member socioeconomic status. They were part of state or national organizations (polymorphic affiliates). They had more instrumental task-oriented committee and subcommittee meetings; more general meetings per year; more expressive meetings/events for sociability, recreation, entertainment, and sports activities; and less internal conflict. They used membership cards (greater identification with the GAs). They had more rank-and-file members in decision making (decentralized power structure and internal democracy). Their primary goals served the general welfare (sought external benefits and impact). They had town/city names in the group names (reflecting more town pride) and more selectivity in membership including a residency requirement (Smith, 1986a, p. 30).

Smith and Shen (1996) studied 39 GAs from a different sample of all GA types in a small Massachusetts suburb. Their measure of impact was other leaders' peer ratings of the impact of the GAs, omitting GA leader self-reports on their own GAs' impact as potentially biased. GAs with higher reputational effectiveness were better resourced and were at least partially public/nonmember benefit organizations that were more developed in terms of a number of measures, especially formalization and various aspects of governance (e.g., officers, board, committees). These results confirm ideas and/or findings of many researchers writing mainly about effectiveness for *paid-staff* nonprofits (Bradshaw, Murray, and Wolpin, 1992; Connors, 1988; Gamson, 1990; Herman and Heimovics, 1991; Herman, Weaver, and Heimovics, 1991; Knauft, Berger, and Gray, 1991; Widmer, 1991). These results also confirm some of my hypotheses about *GA* effectiveness (Smith 1981, 1992b, 1993b, 1994b).

Abell (1989) develops an interesting economic theory of associational effectiveness generally, taking a "rational choice" approach. He argues that an association's performance (impact) is proportional to the total utility (satisfaction) generated within the association, including both egoistic satisfaction and altruistic satisfaction. This model needs independent testing on a broad sample of GAs, and both internal and external impact and effectiveness should be examined.

Holland's (1988) model of effectiveness for nonprofits in general has some similarity to the earlier suggestions specifically for GA effectiveness. He suggests that the usual model of paid-staff nonprofit effectiveness argues for more impact where a nonprofit is characterized by goal attainment, resource attainment, avoidance of internal conflicts, catering to major supporters, higher quality of leadership, and more ability to deal with effects from the external environment. Only the factor of catering to major supporters does not fit well with GA effectiveness working hypotheses stated so far in this chapter.

A similar study, but one of mainly paid-staff nonprofits, was conducted by Hawkins, Steger, and Trimble (1986), who investigated how 57 United Way-affiliated community organizations adapted to reduced funding. They found that adaptation to such funding changes was better where nonprofits had more professional specialists available (e.g., lawyers, computer specialists), did more of their own fund-raising (vs. total United Way dependence), and used more volunteers. I note these findings here to show that well-done studies of samples of paid-staff nonprofits *might* show effectiveness results quite similar to GA effectiveness results, even though this will not *necessarily* be the case and cannot simply be assumed in the absence of contrary evidence. There are many similar studies of paid-staff nonprofits, usually with small samples, that I will not mention here given my central GA orientation.

The forgoing studies of general GA samples constitute one way in which to get an overview of the elements of effectiveness of GAs. Another way is to review the lists of effectiveness elements by GA type presented elsewhere (Smith, 1999a, 1999b) so as to see whether there are elements in common across many GA types. By examining these and other sources, I have developed the forgoing inductive theory of GA organizational effectiveness factors for either internal or external (or both types of) impact.

CONCLUSION

Table 9.1 presents comparative ideal type results for GAs and paid-staff VGs on the major impact variables of this chapter. The organizational effectiveness factors already are in summary form, so I omit them from the table. GAs tend to produce more felt social support than do paid-staff VGs, owing to their emphasis on sociability goals and activities. Both types of VGs result in high information gain, I hypothesize. But sociopolitical activation is far greater in GAs than in paid-staff VGs, as is political influence, on average. Participants in GAs tend to make many more economic contacts than do participants in paid-staff VGs given the greater sociability emphasis.

GAs are more likely to support the economic system, on average, although national business and professional lobbies play a major role in such support. But the average paid-staff VG is a health, educational, or other human service institution not actively involved in economic system support. GAs are more likely to contribute to the happiness and health of their participants than are paid-staff VGs, although they do so to some extent because of voluntary altruism.

The findings here suggest how local volunteer units of national associations (polymorphic GAs) might best be structured to obtain member impact in accord

TABLE 9.1 Comparison of Impact in Grassroots Associations and Paid-Staff
Voluntary Groups

Grassroots Associations	Paid-Staff Voluntary Groups
High social support felt	Moderate social support felt
High information gained	High information gained
High sociopolitical activation	Low sociopolitical activation
Moderate political influence	Low political influence
Make more economic contacts	Make fewer economic contacts
Support economic system	Less economic system support
Significant happiness felt	Some happiness felt
Significantly better health	Some better health

with national or international mission statements. But the findings also suggest
how structurally autonomous or monomorphic GAs could work toward greater
effectiveness and impact. Many of the generalizations of my inductive theory
also might be applicable to volunteer programs of work organizations (viewing
them as external goal "pseudo-GAs" seeking an external service impact), but I
do not claim that similarity in detail here, leaving that inquiry for some other
scholar to perform.

There surely are *some* overlapping elements of effectiveness among *all* types
of organizations, not just among all nonprofits. Holland (1988) notes that avoidance of internal conflicts and high quality of leadership, for example, are general VG effectiveness elements, and they have surfaced as important for GAs
here as well. The most general problem is that virtually no studies have been
done with adequate samples of both GAs and paid-staff VGs using comparable
sampling and research methodologies to identify types of impact and their corresponding organizational effectiveness factors. Internal analysis of such data
naturally would include determining which organizational factors seem to work
best for internal impact-seeking GAs and which tend to work best for external
impact-seeking GAs. It would be even more useful to sample some businesses
and government agencies to some extent in such a study to permit comparative
analyses, hoping to identify organizational effectiveness factors that "work"
for all types of work organizations versus for GAs and supralocal volunteer
associations.

Part III

THEORETICAL PARADIGMS AND CONCLUSIONS

Introduction

A research-based theory of grassroots associations (GAs) as part of a round-earth voluntary nonprofit sector (VNPS) paradigm has been presented in the forgoing chapters. Chapter summaries present the theory here in reduced form. This theory is based specifically on the research literature cited for this book and qualitative results of my own research. It consists of the empirical conclusions I have reached in each chapter along with theoretical linking statements. Also, this theory draws on many more publications about GAs and nonprofits *not* cited for due to space limitations. I also draw on several decades of personal experiences in studying and participating in such associations and teaching courses related to these associations as well as on my own attempts over the course of my career to make sense of associations, especially GAs.

Most of the empirically testable statements in the present version of my theory are basically working hypotheses and, hence, are tentative generalizations usually based on some prior research, sometimes substantial prior research. Some aspects of my general theory of GAs and the VNPS would not fit into this book given page space limitations. In these cases, I refer at least to those additional former "chapters" as separate, sometimes unpublished, documents. These now at least partially "missing" chapters deal with the world history of GAs and other nonprofits (Smith, 1997c); the impact of GAs (Smith, 1997a); individual volunteer participation (Smith, 1994a, forthcoming c); the prevalence, growth, and death of GAs and other nonprofits (Smith and Associates, 2000); the nature and operations of deviant nonprofits (Smith, 1995c, forthcoming a); researching GAs and other nonprofits as a field of study (Smith, forthcoming b); and defining and interrelating VNPS concepts and terms (Smith and Dover, 2000).

The substance of my round-earth version of the GA part of a VNPS theory exists in parallel at the societal, group, and individual levels of abstraction. Generally, Parts I and III deal with the whole VNPS but most especially with all GAs of the VNPS. Part II deals with GAs as groups or organizations. Smith (1994a, 2000) deals with the level of the individual volunteer as a unit of abstraction. Other related documents also deal with all three levels of abstraction.

One central conclusion of this book is that *GAs, as voluntary groups (VGs), need to be taken into account to a far greater degree than previously has been the case by those still using one or more of the many inadequate flat-earth VNPS paradigms.* My GA part of a round-earth VNPS paradigm seeks comprehensiveness and balance appropriate to the reality of human societies and activities in a socially constructed and interpreted world (Berger and Luckmann, 1967). That is what a round-earth VNPS paradigm will be if we can have it.

I am attempting to present the GA part of a new, better balanced, more comprehensive round-earth paradigm of the VNPS as a substitute for the many narrower, earlier, inadequate, sometimes familiar, and still very powerful flat-earth paradigms as social constructions of the reality of the VNPS and GAs. These are described in Chapter 10.

There is no accepted corresponding and comprehensive theory of paid-staff VGs using a round-earth paradigm. If there were, then such a theory could be added to the contents of the present book and to the rest of the GA portion of an adequate general VNPS theory (in related material published elsewhere separately [Smith, 1997a, 1997c, 2000; Smith and Associates, 2000; Smith and Dover, 2000]) to make a larger synergistic whole.

I view my identification of these many inadequate, narrow, flat-earth VNPS paradigms, as contrasted with my sketch of the outlines of a much-needed, more comprehensive, round-earth VNPS paradigm, to be a set of additional central conclusions of this book (see Chapter 10). I have indicated in this book what the GA part of a round-earth VNPS paradigm would consist of, counteracting many flat-earth views with balance from their opposite or alternative view.

10

Flat-Earth Paradigms and a
Round-Earth Paradigm Outline

After reviewing the mapping metaphor for understanding the research literature on the voluntary nonprofit sector (VNPS), this chapter discusses 19 specific flat-earth VNPS paradigms in use by scholars in the field today. An outline of a more comprehensive round-earth paradigm of the VNPS is then presented.

METAPHORS AND PARADIGMS
FOR UNDERSTANDING THE VNPS

I have chosen the central metaphor of maps and mapmaking in this book and theory because it effectively captures the pitfalls of having an incomplete or distorted view of any intellectual terrain or type of social processes and activities. Van Til (1988) wrote an important earlier book with the apt title *Mapping the Third Sector,* on which I draw in various ways here. When numerous scholars ignore a variety of important phenomena of the VNPS, they are not just being intellectually complacent and narrow in their views; they are actively closing off from themselves, their scholarship, and the practitioners who rely on their scholarship a variety of relevant and important VNPS phenomena that clearly exist and whose existence can prove fruitful both intellectually and pragmatically.

The mapping metaphor I introduced in Chapter 1 is powerful in helping me to draw attention to a wide variety of neglected VNPS phenomena, especially phenomena studied by one set of scholars and ignored by others, and vice versa, without seeking linkages and balance. It is one thing for me to talk or write about the "dark matter" of the VNPS "universe" because few scholars, except for astronomers and astrophysicists, care at all about such matter as ignored phenomena, which are too distant in two senses of the word. It is a quite different thing for me to show that many VNPS scholars in every relevant discipline, interdisciplinary field, and profession are carrying around in their heads quite inadequate and distorted general cognitive maps (paradigms) of the VNPS, its components, and its interrelationships with the other sectors of society.

Such VNPS "flat-earthers," such as members of the Flat-Earth Research Society International (Jaszczak and Sheets, 1997, p. 631, Organization 6394), are not just studying mainly the phenomena of interest to them. That is not the problem here. They *also* are implicitly or explicitly denying the existence or relevance of different but related types of VNPS phenomena. This basic issue is how psychosocial reality is being construed by researchers and theorists in the field of VNPS studies.

In this chapter, I attempt a brief critique of the whole literature on the VNPS, with special reference to grassroots associations (GAs). In a sense, I am attempting here a very superficial "deconstruction" of current VNPS paradigms. I make no claims of adhering to the current traditions of deconstruction as a philosophy and linguistic analysis. Instead, I claim that GAs can be properly understood only in the context of an adequate larger theory of the VNPS that is balanced and properly complex. By identifying different paradigmatic flaws in current VNPS research and theory, I hope to contribute to enhancing both balance and proper complexity.

The VNPS can be understood adequately only with what I call a "round-earth" paradigm or perspective. In this book, I present one version of such a paradigm *as it relates to GAs,* examining GAs and associational volunteers together as one of the many types of data and concepts that are omitted in various flat-earth paradigms of one sort or another. Thus, *this book has at least two separate but overlapping levels of discourse: (a) literature reviews of empirical studies of GA phenomena* (as in Chapters 2-9) *and (b) descriptions of many flat-earth paradigms and elaboration of how a round-earth paradigm regarding GAs and the larger VNPS needs to be structured* (as in Chapters 2 and 10). Theoretical overviews of many flat-earth paradigms are presented in the next section of this chapter.

My new round-earth paradigm is intended to replace many types of flat-earth paradigms in current widespread use by scholars and practitioners/leaders in the VNPS field. Individual scholars or practitioners can manifest one or more of the following flat-earth paradigms simultaneously. However, some adjacent pairs of flat-earth paradigms in what follows represent more or less mutually exclusive alternative perspectives. For example, one can hold either a social movement *or* status quo VNPS flat-earth paradigm as an ideal type, but not primarily *both* as mutually exclusive typological alternatives. Empirically, there probably are VNPS perspectives held by specific individuals that seem to be some type of mixture of both ideal types. Various types of flat-earth paradigms that I have identified so far are described in the next section.

OVERVIEW OF FLAT-EARTH VNPS PARADIGMS

As I have indicated elsewhere (Smith, Macaulay, and Associates, 1980, Parts 1 and 5), I see many problems with social science theory and empirical research. Many of these problems could be put in terms of flat-earth versus round-earth social science paradigms in general, just as I do here for VNPS research more specifically. However, to conserve page space, here I examine only the problems I see specifically with regard to VNPS paradigms. None of us is perfect at being interdisciplinary and international with just the appropriate balance and comprehensiveness. Nevertheless, we all need to do the best we possibly can in reaching for these goals if we are to understand human phenomena, and especially nonprofit phenomena, adequately (Mudimbe, 1996).

There are many types of flat-earth VNPS paradigms that I have identified in writing this book. *Each of these represents a conclusion I have reached regarding the problems with existing theory and research on the VNPS. Each flat-earth VNPS paradigm has in common with the others the fact that some significant phenomena of the VNPS broadly conceived usually are ignored both theoretically and empirically by many VNPS scholars as well as by many practitioners/ leaders using such a paradigm.*

Given the general meaning of *flat-earth VNPS paradigm* in this book, *such narrow perspectives with regard to the VNPS are defined principally by what they tend to ignore or omit.* The contrasting positive or "adequate" social science perspective on VNPS phenomena in every instance is the round-earth paradigm, which is a more inclusive approach. Mention of a publication under a given flat-earth paradigm does not mean that the work is without merit, even strong merit, nor does failure to mention a work here indicate that some particular unmentioned work has merit given my critique. I have been selective. All of the flat-earth paradigms distinguished in what follows are VNPS paradigms, but henceforth I omit the *VNPS*.

The "Nonprofit Sector Is Unimportant" Flat-Earth Paradigm

This approach simply ignores *all* VNPS phenomena, assuming implicitly or explicitly that only the public (government) and private (business) sectors are important and worthy of careful scientific study in modern society. Most people in the labor force in any modern society have long been seen as working for businesses or governments, not for nonprofits. The work of Independent Sector in documenting the magnitudes of paid-staff nonprofits in U.S. society and the numbers of service volunteers in volunteer programs has been a great service to the VNPS in spite of Independent Sector's neglect of GAs and associational volunteers (Hodgkinson and Weitzman, 1992, 1996a, 1996b; Hodgkinson et al., 1992, 1995).

The "ideal type" of the VNPS generally is seen by non-VNPS scholars who ignore the VNPS as too trivial, weak, poor, small, secondary, volunteer based, ephemeral, and tenuous to be able to accomplish anything important in society. To a significant extent, this approach is part of an ideology about society and human activity that depreciates anything but economic activity, narrowly defined in terms of financial assets, annual revenues, market exchange, and paid jobs. More recently, unpaid housework, volunteering, and other "informal" economic activities have been studied by some economists who attribute economic value to these nonmarket activities (Brown, 1999; Herzog and Morgan, 1992; Hodgkinson et al., 1992; Wolozin, 1975). The latter work shows a gradual decline in the power of the "anti-VNPS" flat-earth paradigm during recent decades.

By my definition here, nonprofits of any type rarely are on the intellectual or cognitive maps of anti-VNPS flat-earth scholars, whether economists or other social scientists. Thus, it should come as no surprise to anyone that such scholars seldom seem to notice even paid-staff nonprofits, let alone GAs, in society. A glance at the index of any well-known university economics text would show this to be true (e.g., Samuelson and Nordhaus, 1995).

Ignoring the VNPS is very shortsighted and presents far from a comprehensive view of society and human behavior. There is a need for more breadth in VNPS research involving those who are economists because that social science objectifies and promotes this first flat-earth paradigm on the whole. I suggest that a larger proportion and number of economists should inquire into the whole VNPS. In recommending this, I am not suggesting that economists have completely ignored the VNPS. There already is some excellent general economic research on the VNPS by many scholars (Boulding, 1973; Cornes and Sandler, 1989; Hansmann, 1987; James, 1989; Olson, 1965; Steinberg, 1987, 1990; Tuckman and Chang, 1991; Weisbrod, 1977, 1988). If one includes the subfields of political economy, labor economics, economic pressure groups, agricultural economics, and consumer cooperatives, then the list of VNPS-relevant published economic research becomes much longer.

In addition to Independent Sector statistical overviews, the very extensive existing set of published theoretical and empirical research contributions in mainstream *paid-staff* nonprofit research in the United States refutes in part this first flat-earth paradigm that ignores the general relevance of the VNPS in society and the economy (Billis, 1993a; DiMaggio and Anheier, 1990; Herman and Associates, 1994; Hodgkinson et al., 1992; O'Neill, 1989; Powell, 1987;

Salamon, 1992; Salamon and Anheier, 1994; Salamon, Anheier, and Associates, 1998).

Hall's (1996) review of the organization literature says next to nothing about voluntary groups (VGs), whether paid-staff nonprofits or GAs. The relative inattention paid to the whole VNPS by organizational sociologists, other organization studies scholars, and social science scholars more generally cannot be due to the intrinsic unimportance of nonprofits. Nonprofit groups or organizations are an important analytical type of group in history and at the present time, although many social science scholars seem not to know of this importance (see Smith, 1973a, 1997a, for an overview of this importance focused mainly on the United States; see Smith, 1997c, for an international historical overview).

For example, Hall (1987b, 1992) shows the importance of GAs and paid-staff nonprofits over four centuries of American society, as have Ellis and Noyes (1990) and O'Neill (1989). In a recent article, I (Smith, 1997c) show the existence and importance of GAs over about 25 millennia of human history and especially during the past 10 millennia in which GAs have flourished around the world (Anderson, 1973; Hartson, 1911; Lambert, 1891; Ross, 1976). Chapter 2 of this book gives a round-earth overview of the magnitudes of the United States VNPS, its nonprofits, and volunteers. Partial overviews of the VNPS in other nations are given by various scholars (Anheier and Seibel, 1990; Badelt, 1989; James, 1989; Klausen and Selle, 1996; McCarthy et al., 1992; Pestoff, 1977; Robbins, 1990; Salamon and Anheier, 1994; Salamon et al., 1998; Smith, 1973b, 1973c, 1974; Smith and Elkin, 1981; Smith and Van Til, 1983; Starr, 1991). The VNPS clearly exists and is important all over the world. It has existed for thousands of years.

The "Three-Sector Model of Society" Flat-Earth Paradigm

Before the "discovery" or "invention" (Hall, 1992) of the VNPS concept by Cornuelle (1965), most social scientists viewed society as having two main sectors if they thought about this issue at all. The "original" two sectors of society seen before the mid-1960s were the government sector and the private sector. The latter included *both* businesses and nonprofits, although businesses dominated attention. Terminology was vague about when one was speaking or writing about nonprofits versus businesses. Sometimes, the household sector also was considered by economists or sociologists, but it was placed by economists in the category of consumption rather than in that of production in modern societies.

More recently, during the past three decades, the VNPS has come to be recognized as a "third sector" of society, with business and government as the other two. The term *third sector* often is used by those individuals or groups that despair of ever reaching an acceptable analytical definition of or label for the VNPS (Evers, 1995; Hodgkinson et al., 1992; Levitt, 1973; McCarthy et al.,

1992; Nielsen, 1979; Powell, 1987; Salamon, 1992; Schuppert, 1991; Smith, Reddy, and Baldwin, 1972a; Van Til, 1987; Wagner, 1991; Weisbrod, 1977, 1988; Wilson, 1992).

Knowing their own limitations, proponents of the VNPS have not taken the reverse stance, arguing that the business and government sectors do not exist or that they are unimportant in modern societies like the United States. Calling the VNPS the third sector is historically inaccurate, leaving out the household/ family sector (Ortmeyer and Fortune, 1985), as the original sector of our species, without any good theoretical reason for doing so. There are at least four major sectors of society worth distinguishing, with some good reasons for distinguishing five sectors (noted in Smith, 1991). But regardless of whether four or five need to be distinguished, the number certainly is not three (Ahrne, 1992; Grindheim and Selle, 1990; Leat, 1986; Lohmann, 1992).

The Paid-Staff VG Flat-Earth Paradigm

This view largely ignores volunteer nonprofits of all types including GAs, supralocal volunteer groups, and their associational volunteers. It argues implicitly or explicitly that *mainly* paid work, usually by full-time employees, is very important or worthy of study. Thus, when the VNPS is considered, there is a principal or sole focus on VGs that depend essentially on their paid staff for getting the work of the groups done—paid-staff VGs. Volunteers might be present in service volunteer programs, but these are seen as less important than the paid-staff component of the organizations. Relative to GAs and supralocal volunteer groups, this perspective pays attention mainly to larger, wealthier, and more "visible" paid-staff VGs as well as to people, places, things, structures, processes, and events that concern such paid-staff VGs.

The paid-staff nonprofit flat-earth paradigm reflects a type of elitist or "establishment" view of groups and organizations in human society and the VNPS (Billis, 1993a, 1993b; DiMaggio and Anheier, 1990; Hodgkinson and Weitzman, 1996b; Hodgkinson et al., 1992; Knoke, 1990b; Kramer, 1984; Kramer et al., 1993; Olsen, 1982; Powell, 1987; Salamon, 1992; Salamon and Anheier, 1994; Smith and Lipsky, 1993; Weisbrod, 1977, 1988; Wolch, 1990; Young, 1983).

Work organizations are organizations in which the majority of the work done in and for the organizations is done by paid employees, usually in a full-time primary life role. The three main types of work organizations are business, government, and paid-staff VGs. By contrast, volunteer groups or organizations are VGs in which the majority of the work done in and for the groups is done by volunteers. As a very rough rule of thumb, groups or organizations with one or two full-time equivalents (1,700 hours per year) of employees are, or are getting to be, paid-staff VGs. However, one must gather some empirical data on the amount of time worked for an organization by paid employees versus by volunteers to make a firm and accurate decision about whether the group is a paid-staff organization or a volunteer group or organization.

One may view the latter pair of concepts as two ideal types or, alternatively, as the ends of a continuum ranging from 100% paid employees to 100% unpaid volunteers. We do not know, for lack of relevant research, what proportion of all nonprofits would fit into either ideal type end category. Nor do we know what proportion of a random sample of nonprofits from any territory might fall into some middle category where there is a balance of paid-staff time worked, say between 40% and 60% toward either end of the dimension.

When people studying work organizations generally examine VGs or associations, they tend to assume without solid evidence that associations, including GAs, operate in the same manner as do work organizations (Klausen, 1995; Knoke and Prensky, 1984). Like all the flat-earth paradigms of the VNPS or of human society more generally, this one has powerful blinders on.

As one simple empirical example of the power of this mistaken paradigm, I point to the otherwise excellent recent book by Hall (1996) summarizing what social scientists know about organizations of all types. Of the 301 pages of text, grassroots or supralocal volunteer associations are mentioned on only a few pages and with only a few references given to the extensive literature that undergirds this present book and my inductive theory of GAs. Obviously, to Hall and the many hundreds of others who write in the general scholarly field of "organizations," "organizational behavior," or "organizations studies/science/administration/management," GAs are just "not on the map," as with all the flat-earth paradigms mentioned here.

Such a flat-earth paradigm assumes that only paid-staff VGs matter in scholarship and society if the VNPS is to matter at all in these areas. The paradigm is in widespread but not exclusive use in the main journals (e.g., *Nonprofit and Voluntary Sector Quarterly, Nonprofit Management and Leadership, Voluntas*), in well-known books (e.g., Herman and Associates, 1994; Hodgkinson et al., 1992; Powell, 1987; Rose-Ackerman, 1986; Salamon, 1992; Salamon and Anheier, 1994; Weisbrod, 1977, 1988), in book publishers' series on nonprofits (e.g., Jossey-Bass "Nonprofit Sector Series," John Wiley "Nonprofit Law, Finance, and Management Series"), and in scholarly associations of the nonprofit research field (e.g., Association for Research on Nonprofit Organizations and Voluntary Action [Appendix A]).

There is a tendency among mainstream VNPS scholars, practitioners, and perhaps some members of the general population to be lured or misled by the superficial size or apparent "brightness" of many individual paid-staff nonprofits, mostly with nonmember benefit goals. Such scholars and practitioners tend to assume incorrectly, without adequate empirical data, that paid-staff nonprofits as a category *must* have a greater cumulative impact on society in all areas than do poorer, "puny," more informal, and short-lived GAs that, by definition, operate with volunteer time of their members. Chapter 9 and my recent article on GA impact (Smith, 1997a) challenge that assumption.

This narrow approach also is concerned mainly with *program volunteers* and their "volunteer programs" attached to paid-staff nonprofit and other work organizations as "volunteer departments." The paid-staff VG perspective specifically ignores GA associational volunteers working for substantially autonomous groups with any territorial level of scope including GAs. Chapter 2 details how GAs and their associational volunteers generally are ignored by those using the present flat-earth paradigm.

Whoever does the relevant research and analysis for a new and better round-earth paradigm, including GAs and their volunteers, after my initial attempt here needs to take Hannan and Freeman's (1989) "population ecology of organizations" approach or the Milofsky's (1987) similar "market approach," including GAs through proper methodology in the population of nonprofits studied. We cannot know the whole of the nonprofit sector if we refuse to study it openly and thoroughly (as many scholars do), even on a sampling basis (McPherson, 1988, p. 52).

In my view, this paid-staff VG flat-earth paradigm has been the most destructive and misleading for our mainstream VNPS research and for the VNPS itself in society as a whole. It clearly is the one to work toward changing as a top priority. The paradigm's power for many proponents of a flat-earth VNPS currently is perhaps the main obstacle to having a round-earth perspective of the VNPS *including GAs.* It is powerfully entrenched among most of the nonprofit academic centers at universities in the United States and elsewhere, and it is the most highly regarded among the various flat-earth paradigms by book publishers and journal editors.

In making the preceding unequivocal statement about flat-earth paradigm removal priorities, *I hypothesize that making a clear distinction theoretically and empirically between paid-staff VGs and volunteer VGs, especially GAs, will prove to be of substantial value to our understanding the VNPS and its relation to other sectors of society.* My review of the relevant literature leads me to believe that the power of this theoretical distinction has not been properly appreciated by VNPS scholars in the past. That is why there are very few empirical studies comparing paid-staff VGs to volunteer VGs, especially GAs. How else can this latter fact be explained?

The Volunteer and Membership VG
Flat-Earth Paradigm

This view largely ignores the paid-staff VGs and often the VGs with a major focus on nonmember goals. This narrow perspective is the reverse of the paid-staff

VG flat-earth paradigm. This perspective looks solely or mainly at volunteer-run and volunteer membership groups such as common interest or voluntary associations at different levels of territorial scope in human societies. At higher territorial levels of VG scope, this paradigm includes some paid-staff nonprofit associations (Knoke, 1990b; Nall, 1967; Smith and Freedman, 1972; Smith, 1992a). Whichever is overemphasized, paid-staff VGs (as in the paid-staff VG flat-earth paradigm discussed in the previous subsection) or volunteer and membership VGs here, the result is an incomplete and, hence, distorted perspective on the whole VNPS.

This perspective often is used by some political scientists concerned with political participation, pressure groups, pluralism, and civil society; by some sociologists concerned with voluntary associations; by some anthropologists concerned with sodalities or common interest associations; by some researchers in social work concerned with community organizations and organizing; and by some psychologists concerned with altruism, volunteering, and community organizations.

We could, of course, just separate these two key types of VGs into two distinct sectors, using a five-sector model of society (Smith, 1991). The findings in Part II of this book are consistent with such a decision because GAs as volunteer VGs are very different from paid-staff VGs in many ways. However, both types of VGs share the definitional fact that their analytical members are motivated significantly by voluntary altruism. This fact makes both major types of VGs somewhat distinct from businesses, governments, and households/families.

I suggested earlier that the member benefit versus nonmember benefit subsectors or sectors are the most central analytical difference one can make in the VNPS (Smith, 1993b). After further thought, research, and literature review, as well as the comments of colleagues (especially by Michael O'Neill), I now take the preceding slightly different position. Nearly all member benefit VGs are GAs, and nearly all paid-staff VGs are nonmember benefit VGs. But there also is a large percentage of all Internal Revenue Service (IRS) 501(c)(3) nonmember benefit VGs that are GAs (I estimate 37.5% in Chapter 2).

Volunteer VGs, therefore, are the most common form of nonprofits, greatly exceeding the number of paid-staff VGs in U.S. society circa 1990. Comparative research relevant to determining the effects of either type of VG on other analytical aspects of VGs would be a big help here.

The Status Quo/Establishment Flat-Earth Paradigm

This view ignores social movement VGs, protest, and advocacy volunteering. It focuses only, or nearly exclusively, on those VGs and volunteers that are mainstream, "integrative," and establishment oriented (Bowen et al., 1994;

Brudney, 1990; Gidron, Kramer, and Salamon, 1992; Hammack and Young, 1993; Hodgkinson and Weitzman, 1992, 1996a, 1996b; Hodgkinson et al., 1992; Lohmann, 1992; McCarthy et al., 1992; Powell, 1987; Salamon, 1992). The latter groups are aimed at preserving the status quo as dominated by societal "insiders" or elites/"dominants" (Becker, 1963; Mills, 1956; Smith and Associates, forthcoming). Also, this flat-earth paradigm ignores, to an even greater degree, the more deviant voluntary collective behavior such as riots, rebellions, coups, and revolutions, all of which seek some sociopolitical change by societally disapproved means. It also ignores the fact that many major changes in human history have been caused by social movements—the abolition of slavery, improvement of the situation of women and depreciated minority ethnic/racial categories, emergence of religious freedom in Europe, rise of social security and social welfare arrangements in modern societies, and so on (Blumberg, 1991; Ferree and Hess, 1995; Lambert, 1992; Skocpol, 1992).

Sociopolitical change orientation in the round-earth paradigm should be viewed as a hypothetical dimension on which any VG's goals can be placed analytically and/or empirically (Verba, Schlozman, and Brady, 1995, p. 63; Verba and Nie, 1972, pp. 178-79). But without having a round-earth paradigm that suggests that this dimension should be explored for *any VG,* the necessary empirical data usually will not be gathered for each VG to examine the extent to which this sociopolitical change orientation of VG goals relates to other dimensions of VGs, especially for GAs. For example, change-oriented VGs might be ignored in the sampling as hard to find unless a paradigm is used that requires one to search for and include them. The same logic can be used with regard to protest activities as a means of attaining change-oriented VG goals. VGs can vary greatly in their degrees of use of protest activities (e.g., symbolic protest, direct action, violent protest [Carter, 1974]), and this needs to be studied routinely for broad samples of VGs to have a round-earth view of the VNPS.

The Social Movement/Protest
Flat-Earth Paradigm

This view largely ignores the more mainstream, non-protest-oriented nonprofits including both GAs and paid-staff VGs, unless they are directly part of "the opposition" or are "sponsors" for social movements (Gamson, 1990; Lofland, 1996; see also references in McAdam and Snow, 1997). Thus, this paradigm tends to overemphasize sociopolitical protest in society without sufficient concern for the rest of the VNPS, especially its mainstream interest groups that do not use protest tactics and, hence, are not social movement groups (Smith, 1986b). The latter category includes all types of GAs because any GA can act as an interest group or a pressure group at times when its political interests are at stake locally (Verba et al., 1995, p. 63; Verba and Nie, 1972, pp. 178-79). Many specific social movement/protest GAs and paid-staff VGs also tend to be ignored because the focus of the paradigm is so much on the larger social movement and its organizations at the national or international level (Lofland and Jamison, 1984). "Professional" (paid-staff) social movement organizations are favored for study over GAs.

Mainstream VGs of various types should be better integrated into social movement theory and empirical research. In particular, more attention needs to be paid to informal and semiformal GAs as the grassroots base and, hence, potentially one basic source of strength or weakness of social movements (Lofland and Jamison, 1984; Piven and Cloward, 1979). Mainstream GAs that function as micro-social movements locally and temporarily also need better integration. Many of them used to be social movement VGs or might again use protest under certain circumstances. We do not know enough about the circumstances of change in such strategies and tactics by GAs.

Both mainstream GAs and mainstream paid-staff VGs are important potential sources of resources and collaboration as well as opposition to social movements and their constituent groups and individuals as participants. But beyond ignoring some of these potential microenvironmental relationships, the social movement flat-earth paradigm does not consider well enough how the social movement of interest fits into the larger context of the VNPS. This latter point can be rephrased to say that the present flat-earth perspective often fails to see the VNPS "forest" as an organizational field by focusing too much on certain specific other nonprofits as sources of resources or opposition. In addition to the business, government, and family/household sectors, the whole VNPS also is a context for any informal, social protest, collective activity such as many riots and some rebellions.

The Traditional Nonmember
Service Flat-Earth Paradigm

This view makes two separate but related errors. First, it continues to present and use a long-outmoded view that the only types of nonprofits or volunteers that matter are those that focus on personal, direct, face-to-face social services and welfare activities (Bowen et al., 1994; Bremner, 1960; Brilliant, 1990; Humphreys, 1995). Second, it correlatively continues to view nonmembers of a given nonprofit as the *only* people who can be seen as the "recipients" or "targets of benefits" of such personal social service volunteering (Bowen et al., 1994; Rudney, 1987; Salamon, 1992). (I am grateful to Thomasina Borkman for suggesting this particular flat-earth paradigm that she has to struggle against continually with her special interest in self-help groups.)

In addition, this flat-earth approach tends to mistakenly refer to the nonmembers served as "the public." In no real way are such traditional social service

VGs or their corresponding volunteers helping a genuine cross section or all of the public in any territorial unit of significant size (e.g., larger than a neighborhood of a city or a small town).

The concept of service is defined so narrowly here that it *excludes by definition* self-help and member benefit activities in general. Thus, this flat-earth paradigm eliminates member benefit VGs and self-help/mutual aid volunteers from the VNPS by *definition*. And if mutual aid or self-help groups are, by definition, not part of the VNPS or of the set of VGs therein, then there is little point in considering them to be VGs, let alone to count or try to understand them (or so the erroneous logic goes). This flat-earth approach, thus, would have us ignore millions of mutual support groups that Wuthnow (1994, p. 76) indicates are present in the United States, member benefit VGs that are seen by O'Neill (1994) as an important part of the VNPS and that represent a type of new movement in the VNPS in the United States and elsewhere (Katz, 1993; Lavoie, Borkman, and Gidron, 1994).

This flat-earth view harks back to the "lady bountiful" or noblesse oblige version of nonprofits and volunteering of earlier times (Ellis and Noyes, 1990; Jordan, 1960; Lubove, 1965; Scott, 1991). This obsolete approach defines the VNPS *only* in terms of totally altruistic social service by nonprofit volunteers devoted to helping nonmembers (T. Borkman, personal communication, June 1997; Rudney, 1987; Salamon, 1992).

I have argued that any individual altruism in volunteering has to be relative, based on at least some minimal individual expectations of "psychic benefits" from having been altruistic (Smith, 1981). The current women's movement often has been strongly opposed to the present flat-earth stereotype of women and volunteering (Ferree and Hess, 1995; Gold, 1971, 1979; L. Smith, 1975). Eriksson-Joslyn (1973) argues that more traditional program volunteering draws millions of potential volunteers away from associational volunteering, mostly in GAs, and sometimes keeps volunteers away from volunteering in sociopolitical, change-oriented GAs and supralocal associations with similar goals.

This channeling, managing, and manipulating of volunteer work potentials into service (mostly program) volunteering rather than into associational and sociopolitical change volunteering probably suits the "power elite" or insiders of America understood more broadly (McCarthy, Britt, and Wolfson, 1991; Mills, 1956; Smith and Associates, forthcoming). Panet-Raymond (1987) argues similarly for Canadian GAs.

An older, unpopular, and too narrow way of referring to voluntary altruism in personal social service volunteering and corresponding groups is to speak of the "voluntary spirit" (O'Connell, 1983). But using my broader definition of social service that includes self-help and advocacy GAs, the "revised voluntary spirit" concept can be seen as very similar to voluntary altruism as defined in this book.

The Modern, Member Benefit, Self-Help, and Advocacy Flat-Earth Paradigm

This view tends to ignore traditional nonmember personal social service nonprofits and their corresponding volunteers as if they no longer are of any value (Katz, 1993; Lavoie et al., 1994; Powell, 1994). As the "up-to-date" opposite of the preceding flat-earth paradigm, this view just bends over too far in the opposite direction, relative to the traditional nonmember service flat-earth paradigm discussed in the previous subsection. Self-help GAs and members play a prominent role in one version of this paradigm, but they seldom are called "member benefit service volunteers"; usually, the terms "members" and "leaders" are used instead. The concepts and theory of self-help GAs and their participants seldom are integrated with the related concepts of GAs and their associational volunteers more generally. To have a round-earth view of the VNPS, this integration must take place.

Some other researchers who use this narrow paradigm and are interested mainly in sociopolitical change and protest tend to write only about "activists," "advocates," "protesters," "revolutionaries," and so on, also often omitting the terms and concepts of "volunteer" and "GA" (Kimmel, 1990; Lofland, 1996). Once again, conceptual integration is needed, this time to see the similarities and differences between mainstream GAs and their volunteers, on the one hand, and social movement GAs and their volunteers, on the other (D. Smith, 1975, p. 256). Comparative studies are needed here, sampling both.

In addition to seeing that volunteers, by my definition, are doing these protest activities and that social movement organizations often are GAs, careful inquiry usually will show that advocacy GAs or self-help GAs still use some volunteers doing traditional social services in their own GAs. Even activists are people, after all, and sometimes they have personal social service needs that can be met by other members of a given GA. And there always are minor office tasks that someone must do for the advocacy VG, whether or not such more traditional social service volunteers also march in a protest (Schwartz-Shea and Burrington, 1990). In self-help GAs, the equivalent is participants who take care of refreshments for meetings or get involved in supralocal activities to which the GAs are linked (e.g., district- or national-level activities in Alcoholics Anonymous).

The Angelic VGs Flat-Earth Paradigm

This perspective omits consideration of the negative, deviant, criminal, or dark side of some VGs and other nonprofit phenomena in any nation or time as part of the VNPS. Social movement groups and their volunteers often are categorized here by status quo insiders. However, the present type of flat-earth paradigm reflects the ignoring of a wider scope of nonprofit deviance than merely VGs trying to cause sociopolitical change using protest. Such deviance is defined out of existence by this overly optimistic "Pollyanna" paradigm. Also, the angelic nonprofit flat-earth view is caused partly by the traditional nonmember service flat-earth paradigm discussed earlier, which allows only more altruistic nonprofits or, by implication, nonmember benefit VGs into theoretical or empirical consideration (Bowen et al., 1994; Hodgkinson and Weitzman, 1996b; Hodgkinson et al., 1992; Kramer, 1984; Lohmann, 1992; O'Neill, 1989; Rudney, 1987; Salamon, 1992; Wolch, 1990).

All aspects of human behavior have their dark side, their forms of deviance from societal norms. People are imperfect, and socialization rarely results in 100% compliance with social values and norms for many reasons (Wrong, 1961). There are *fundamentally* deviant groups in all the sectors of society in any type of society, from the agrarian level of complexity up to and including postindustrial/service/information complexity (Lenski, Nolan, and Lenski, 1995; Smith, 1998b).

Jeavons's (1994) discussion of an ethics of "integrity" is a good example of the general angelic nonprofits approach. Although this perspective might apply to *most* paid-staff VGs and even to conventional GAs, it is overly idealistic and, hence, unrealistic and incomplete in its approach insofar as it claims to be applicable to the *whole* VNPS. Minor deviance in or by conventional VGs (e.g., the Aramony scandal at the United Way of America [Glaser, 1994]) must be studied as part of VNPS research. And we also must examine major deviance in or by *fundamentally deviant* nonprofits such as political extremist groups (George and Wilcox, 1992), deviant self-help groups (Sagarin, 1969), outlaw motorcycle gangs (Lavigne, 1994), the Ku Klux Klan (Sims, 1997), witches' covens (Adler, 1986), citizen militias (Karl, 1995), and extremist cults (Reavis, 1995). Similar nonprofits to these, including GAs, can be and have been present in numerous nations.

Deviant nonprofits are a "doubly dark" continent also added into the new round-earth paradigm, forcing mainstream VNPS scholars and leaders to consider and study the dark side of voluntarism. My forthcoming book, *Organizations on the Fringe* (Smith, forthcoming a), analyzes in-depth the similarities and differences among such deviant nonprofits, which sometimes are GAs, that the angelic nonprofits paradigm omits.

The Damned VGs Flat-Earth Paradigm

This view omits the mainstream majority of VGs including GAs. This is a type of "muckraking" perspective that usually overemphasizes, and sometimes even sensationalizes (Kahaner, 1988), the bad aspects of some VGs. The focus of these exposés usually is paid-staff VGs because they are more visible and are competitors with businesses. The paradigm treats VGs (especially paid-staff VGs) as if they were *generally* bad, deviant, corrupt, selfish, and/or worthless, which they are not. Major examples of the present paradigm include Bennett and DiLorenzo (1989, 1994), Brody (1996), and Gaul and Borowski (1993). The damned nonprofits flat-earth approach can be applied to GAs as well as other nonprofits. In general, GAs and other nonprofits are not angelic, but most of them do tend to be valuable for the VNPS and for society at large.

This flat-earth paradigm tends to argue a hard line that the vast majority of VGs are not worthy of their tax exemptions, having little or no value that is different from that of for-profit corporations. Nonprofits are broadly seen as at least covertly seeking, and often getting, profits that are passed on to paid staff in high salaries and fringe benefits without paying taxes on "excess revenues" (Etzioni and Doty, 1976; Starkweather, 1993).

This negative view of nonprofits shows inadequate understanding of the VNPS and nonprofit activity generally. It denies the existence and relevance of voluntary altruism as I have defined this term. Insofar as there is a kernel of truth in this flat-earth paradigm, it lies in the fact that there are *some paid-staff* nonprofits, such as hospitals and universities, that may or may not merit tax exemption at present. This could be true to some extent, from my standpoint in this book, because most or all of the paid staff in such nonprofits are fully remunerated at existing market rates and, thus, are not quasi-volunteers in their organizational settings (see Chapter 1; see also Rose-Ackerman, 1990).

The "Money Is the Key" Flat-Earth Paradigm

This flat-earth paradigm, steeped in the importance of money and property in human society and activities, mistakenly ignores the seven humane social values (see Chapter 1) that specifically define voluntary altruism in individuals or groups and, hence, cause voluntary action. It also ignores the huge amounts of work time and participation contributed to GAs and volunteer programs in this nation and others. Money and material things clearly are important, but they are far from the "end all" and "be all" of human existence. Both the VNPS and the household/family sector demonstrate this fact.

The present flat-earth paradigm tends to assume that more money always is good for VGs, whether they be paid-staff or volunteer VGs (including GAs). The round-earth paradigm here views money as one type of resource for GAs that may or may not benefit group impact in the long run. This more adequate paradigm also argues that GAs are a type of volunteer VG that is particularly susceptible to goal and activity distortion relative to the preexternal grant situation (Horch, 1994; Saltman, 1973). This may or may not be the case for paid-staff nonprofits (Smith and Lipsky, 1993), which nearly always require much more money to sustain themselves and have their intended impact over time.

The Distinctive Nationalist Focus Flat-Earth Paradigm

This perspective takes the view that only nonprofits within one's own country or some smaller territory are important and worthy of careful study. Thus, this view dismisses nomothetic generalizations derived by any of the remaining social sciences. Frequent remarks are made about the supposed uniqueness of the United States in terms of voluntary altruism (i.e., revised volunteer spirit concept), the large and diversified VNPS, the extent of volunteering, the numbers of voluntary associations, and (in some cases) the supposed origins of nonprofits and volunteering (DeTocqueville, [1845] 1945; Ellis and Noyes, 1990; Hall, 1992; Levitt, 1973; O'Neill, 1989; Schlesinger, 1944).

These appeals to distinctive national qualities in a given VNPS might be true, but many studies of GAs in different sociocultural systems indicate that there clearly are some important nomothetic generalizations that can be reasonably made about the VNPS across nations (Davis-Smith, 1993; Salamon and Anheier, 1994; Salamon et al., 1998). And specifically on the matter of high levels of U.S. participation in associations, Hallenstvedt (1974, p. 217) shows that Sweden, Norway, and Finland had higher percentages of association membership than did the United States. Curtis et al. (1989) show the close similarity of U.S. and Canadian GA membership and participation rates.

The Purposive Type Flat-Earth Paradigm

Purposive type classification schemes for VGs focus on categories such as health, education, and environment. The creators and users of these superficial classification schemes for VGs, such as the National Taxonomy of Exempt Entities (NTEE), tend to assume implicitly that purposive classifications are the most important if we are to understand VGs and how they work (Hodgkinson and Toppe, 1991; Salamon and Anheier, 1992b). Such an assumption is unwarranted. What we need is some round-earth research on the major *purposive* classifications now in existence to test their general comparative utility as against the utility of *analytical* classification variables, based on relevant data collected from the same large representative sample of VGs including GAs (Smith, 1996). This never has been done to validate any of the purposive classification schemes for nonprofits, to my knowledge.

What we mainly tend to find in the published literature on VG classification are purposive classifications without any comparison to the utility of analytical classifications for the same VGs. My round-earth VNPS approach argues that it usually is far more important to know where a given VG fits in terms of an analytical or theoretical (synonyms here) classification or dimension, such as being a paid-staff VG versus a volunteer VG, than to simply know that a VG works on health versus educational or other purpose activities.

This hypothesis of my round-earth paradigm is quite testable empirically. One needs a good comprehensive sample of VGs, including GAs, on which both types of classification data are collected. Then, one should analyze these data to see the average correlation of analytical classification variables such as size, wealth, proportion of volunteers as analytical members, and internal democracy (Smith, 1995d; Smith, Seguin, and Collins, 1973) with each other and with purposive type categories as dummy variables (e.g., health purpose vs. not health purpose, environmental purpose vs. not environmental purpose). I predict that there will be a greater utility of the analytical variables in explaining any given dependent variable of interest, purposive or analytical, on average.

The Antihistoricism Flat-Earth Paradigm

One major problem with most social and behavioral science disciplines is that they tend to ignore the histories of phenomena in their fields as essentially irrelevant to understanding recent or current phenomena. Similar phenomena in the past, especially if they involve important differences from recent or current phenomena or if they use different concepts or terms, tend to be viewed as nearly totally irrelevant to our understanding of recent or current phenomena.

This is not an empirical judgment in most cases; rather, it is a prejudiced antihistoricist mind-set. Recent phenomena are seen from the standpoint of the antihistoricist perspective a priori as being intrinsically too different and distant historically, for example, to be worth studying now (Bowen et al., 1994; Esman and Uphoff, 1984; Weisbrod, 1977, 1988; Wuthnow, 1994). The antihistoricism flat-earth paradigm actually distorts history about GAs, just as it has long distorted history about stigmatized categories of people such as women and blacks in America and people of color elsewhere in modern "wealthy white nations" and in the world as a whole. Many paid-staff VGs actually grew out of the increasing formalization, bureaucratization, and professionalization of GAs (see Chapter 8).

Few sociocultural developments in human societies have arisen entirely de novo, without any links to the human past in a given society or to similar developments in other societies. Human cultures maintain the social momentum of earlier versions of a given society (Adler, 1981), just as memory, personality, self-image, and habits tend to maintain some momentum for individual lives. There clearly are *some* totally new ideas as well as new structures and processes that arise in human societies and cultures, especially in the realms of science and technology, as well as in human individual lives. But such conclusions regarding novelty should follow rather than replace historical and anthropological studies of links to the past in the same or other societies.

The recent Gulbenkian Commission report (Mudimbe, 1996), titled *Open the Social Sciences,* correctly concludes that any social science phenomenon requires some significant historical study if we are to properly understand the present versions of such a phenomenon. That is the thrust of the present paradigm critique.

The Developed World Flat-Earth Paradigm

Horowitz (1972) brought to everyone's attention the three worlds of development, with the Third World being the underdeveloped nations. Although there is a large quantity of published work on GAs in underdeveloped or, to use the currently preferred term, developing nations (Clark, 1991; Esman and Uphoff, 1984; Fisher, 1993), mainstream nonprofit scholars generally do their research and write ignoring such information and do not try to integrate work in developed nations with research in less developed nations (Gidron et al., 1992; Hammack and Young, 1993; Lohmann, 1992; Wolch, 1990). The Johns Hopkins Comparative Nonprofit Sector Project is an exception here (Salamon and Anheier, 1994; Salamon et al., 1998). Nonprofit research on developing nations generally tends to be "ghettoized," or kept separate from similar research on developed nations, and vice versa.

Given the fact that most people on earth live in developing nations, there should be much more effort to integrate VG research from such countries with VG research in developed nations. The powerful impact of indigenous GAs on sustained development in developing nations also argues for such integration (Fisher, 1993), as does the importance of developed nations' transnational development assistance and aid VGs for developing nations (Fisher, 1998; Lissner, 1972). We need an understanding of the VNPS worldwide, not just in the developed nations. We also need an understanding that carefully analyzes the similarities and differences in the VNPS in both developed and developing nations and also speaks to the issue of what happens to the VNPS when a developing nation achieves industrialization and other aspects of modernization.

The Formalized Group Flat-Earth Paradigm

This flat-earth paradigm argues or implies that only quite formalized groups, such as organizations, should be studied as part of the VNPS (Bowen et al., 1994; Hodgkinson and Weitzman, 1996b; Hodgkinson et al., 1992; Powell, 1987; Salamon, 1992; Salamon and Anheier, 1992a). Often, such formalization is taken to mean that a VG must have a written constitution and bylaws, a formal written membership/employees list, a board of directors, and elected or appointed officers. This is too narrow a position to take regarding VGs.

As I have shown in a study of an eastern suburb, semiformalized, fluid membership VGs constitute a substantial proportion of all VGs present (Smith, 1992b). These semiformal VGs lack some or all of the forgoing features but still clearly are VGs. The work of Katz (1993), Lavoie et al. (1994), and Wuthnow

(1994) further substantiates my point by showing the importance of less formalized self-help GAs in different nations. The community study by Goodchilds and Harding (1960) suggests that all types of GAs tend to be informal on an absolute scale, as does my own recent study of the eastern suburb (Smith, 1992b).

Some scholars go so far as to define VGs as *only* state-incorporated or *only* IRS-registered groups, essentially discarding less formalized groups such as GAs (Gronbjerg, 1989, p. 65; Gronbjerg, Kimmick, and Salamon, 1985; Salamon, 1992). This is even more restrictive and problematic than the formality criterion discussed in the first paragraph of this subsection. It is, therefore, even more off the mark and less useful, particularly if one wants to include GAs in the VNPS, as I insist on doing. Most GAs are not themselves incorporated, although the polymorphic GAs can claim some degree of incorporation-by-proxy or IRS tax-exemption-by-proxy through an affiliated supralocal organization. And the vast majority of GAs are not directly registered with the IRS, as noted in Chapter 2. Nor can one insist, by definition, that GAs be affiliates of larger regional or national associations, for only about half of GAs are affiliates of any other organizations in the United States, according to my research in eight Massachusetts communities.

Semiformal GAs are readily identifiable by name, just as more formal ones are (Appendix B). Thus, there is no methodological barrier to their inclusion in an adequate VG sample once one gets beyond the present flat-earth paradigm as a theoretical barrier. The key methodological problem with studying semiformal GAs is that their membership boundaries are, by definition, fluid rather than strict (Smith, 1992b). The result is that one has to define membership for such semiformal GAs in terms of those who actually participate during some period of time rather than in terms of people on a list of formal members kept by the GA. Most types of VG research still are possible on such semiformal GAs, and they should not be dismissed out of hand as the present flat-earth paradigm dismisses them.

The Secularist Focus Flat-Earth Paradigm

Local congregations of churches are voluntary associations with membership bases and strong volunteer components (Scherer, 1972). Some are GAs in terms of my definition, although the Independent Sector study (Hodgkinson, Weitzman, and Kirsch, 1989) of U.S. local congregations was not analyzed in such a way that one can tell just how many local congregations are GAs and what their characteristics are in contrast to paid-staff church congregations. Smith (1984) wrote an article titled "Churches Are Generally Ignored in Contemporary Voluntary Action Research" (see also Moberg, 1983). That situation has improved somewhat during the interim, but there still is an overall secularist paradigm present. For example, the widely known handbook by Powell (1987) has no chapter on churches or other religious VGs. Salamon's (1992) overview of the U.S. VNPS similarly lacks such a chapter, although O'Neill's (1989) overview has one. Knoke's (1990b) study of national associations omits churches. Studies based solely on IRS data usually omit churches and most religious GAs because they do not have to register with the IRS.

Signs of increasing attention to church congregations as associations, sometimes GAs, include the national study of such congregations by Independent Sector noted earlier (Hodgkinson et al., 1989), a special supplemental issue of *Nonprofit and Voluntary Sector Quarterly* on religious voluntary action (1997, Volume 26), Gronbjerg and Nelson's (1998) article on small religious nonprofits, and Harris's (1998b) book on the organization of local church/synagogue congregations. If there were more research on the religious impacts of GAs, then I would have included this as a section in Chapter 9 on GA impact. Unfortunately, the literature on the religious impact of churches does not distinguish GA from paid-staff VG churches, with this distinction not being important to religion scholars (Johnstone, 1992). Hopefully, future research on church congregations will assess the extent to which they are GAs versus paid-staff VGs and analyze the results separately for the two categories of congregations given the theoretical and empirical significance of that distinction in this book.

It is important to include churches as associations and as potential GAs in any broad sample seeking GAs. Smaller churches might well fit my criteria for being GAs (e.g., no paid full-time minister or other full-time employee), and there are many of them numerically, according to the national study of church congregations by Hodgkinson et al. (1989). Churches form moral communities, but so do many secular GAs and paid-staff VGs (Coakes and Bishop, 1996). Self-help and social movement GAs are examples of the latter. Churches are important not just because of their religious impact (Johnstone, 1992) but also because of their social services to their local communities (Wineberg, 1992). In rural and small town areas, churches are especially important in being major sources of people's social support networks (Fischer, 1982). Also, the majority of household charitable giving in the United States is to religious institutions, and the plurality of service volunteer program assignments are to such groups (Hodgkinson and Weitzman, 1992, pp. 36, 42, 45). Wuthnow (1994) further makes clear, from his national survey, that small support GAs in churches are frequent and important in their effects. My own study of eight Massachusetts towns shows similar results for churches as a frequent source and location of GAs.

The Sociodemographic Participation Predictors Flat-Earth Paradigm

This flat-earth view uses exclusively or nearly exclusively sociodemographic variables to predict individual volunteer participation (Curtis, Grabb, and Baer,

1992; Palisi and Korn, 1989; Vaillancourt and Payette, 1986). This sociological approach goes back more than 40 years (Wright and Hyman, 1958). Beal (1956) was one of the first to call for additional types of variables in studying individual participation. I took up his challenge in my dissertation research including measures of personality, attitudes, and intelligence (Smith, 1964, 1966).

In D. Smith (1975, 1994a) and Smith, Reddy, and Baldwin (1972b, Part 2), I show with others that many non-sociodemographic variables are important predictors of volunteer participation. In Smith et al. (1980, chap. 18), I describe in detail my interdisciplinary sequential specificity time allocation life-span (ISSTAL) model for organizing the predictors of individual leisure activity such as volunteering. In Smith (forthcoming c), I note that studies using multiple predictor realms beyond the sociodemographic realm tend to explain, on average, twice as much of the variance in individual volunteer participation.

The research setting in which sociodemographic variables are most appropriate as predictors is when one is attempting to predict who will or will not become a member of a given GA. I pointed out in my dissertation (Smith, 1964) that it usually is simple to predict membership in a given GA from knowledge of the sociodemographics of its members as contrasted with the average for the larger population. McPherson and his colleagues have shown this to be true statistically in their extensive research during the past decade (McPherson and Ranger-Moore, 1991; McPherson and Rotolo, 1996). In Popielarz and McPherson (1995) it is shown that GA members who fit a given GA's sociodemographic profile most closely are most likely to stay in the GA, whereas those who fit least well are most likely to leave. This type of sociodemographic analysis is not part of the flat-earth paradigm addressed by the present section. Indeed, I am not suggesting that sociodemographics are unimportant; I am merely suggesting that they are insufficient for fully understanding individual volunteer participation.

The Isolated VG Flat-Earth Paradigm

This widespread view tends to look within VGs to understand them without sufficient attention to their environments—the community and the larger society. The typical work in this genre focuses on paid-staff VG management, with resource attraction as the principal external concern (Billis, 1993a; Bruce, 1994; Carver, 1997; Gronbjerg, 1993; Handy, 1988; Herman and Heimovics, 1991; Houle, 1989; Knauft, Berger, and Gray, 1991; Poulton, 1988). In this paradigm, there is extensive concern with relations to government as an external concern given the importance of government contracts for human services provided by paid-staff VGs in welfare states (Coston, 1998; Gidron et al., 1992; Rekart, 1993; Smith and Lipsky, 1993). There also is some growing concern with how paid-staff VGs relate to the economy more broadly in this paradigm (Hammack and Young, 1993; Rose-Ackerman, 1986; Weisbrod, 1988).

What is lacking, in my view, is sufficient attention to how VGs are embedded in "interorganizational fields" or populations of organizations (Hannan and Freeman, 1977, 1989; Milofsky, 1987; Warren, 1967). Milofsky and Hunter (1994) challenge this flat-earth paradigm in stating, "Nonprofit organizations emerge, and often continue to exist, as subunits of *background communities,* larger social systems like residential communities, interorganizational systems, or network organizations" (p. 1, emphases in original). The present flat-earth paradigm fails to see the forest of organizations of all types in which VGs are embedded as individual trees or background communities. This neglected interorganizational field is both local and supralocal. The result of this isolating view is that insufficient research is done on VG interorganizational collaboration and the influence of the population of organizations on the structure and processes of any given VG.

Another negative outcome is that solid generalizations are difficult to make because sampling of VGs for study tends to be small in numbers and haphazard in nature. Random sampling of populations of VGs rarely is done because researchers using the present paradigm simply fail to think in terms of populations of organizations. And, of course, when random sampling is done, it tends to be done from faulty IRS or state incorporation lists (see Chapter 2). The methods of Appendix B suggest how better sampling frames can be created including GAs in addition to paid-staff VGs.

Other Flat-Earth Nonprofit Paradigms

There must be other flat-earth paradigms that I have overlooked that are strictly related to studying the VNPS rather than being more general foibles or inadequacies of social science generally. Perhaps readers of this book will suggest some.

OUTLINE OF A ROUND-EARTH PARADIGM OF THE VNPS

Each of the prior flat-earth paradigms indicates some major phenomena of the VNPS that are left out by some scholars and practitioners in this field. Therefore, a round-earth paradigm of the VNPS is basically a perspective that does not ignore any of the VNPS phenomena identified in the preceding section.

To begin with, a round-earth paradigm requires a clear and solid conceptual base. Chapter 1 presents brief versions of my definitions of the major concepts of my GA segment of a round-earth VNPS theory. These concepts and definitions should be considered as is printed here, again, as a *brief* conceptual part of my theory. In addition, as noted earlier, there is a much longer document (Smith and Dover, forthcoming), titled *Concepts and Terminology for Nonprofit and*

Voluntary Sector Studies, that gives an ordered sequence of definitions from simple to more complex concepts. That document contains a dictionary of more than 200 VNPS terms. I consider all of this theoretical material to be part of the *expanded* version of my general round-earth VNPS theory of voluntary altruism.

In addition, a round-earth paradigm of the VNPS includes careful attention to and accurate empirical data regarding all of the following (some of which is presented in this book) in a balanced and comprehensive way:

- Viewing the VNPS as important for social science scholarship, VNPS practice, and the whole of society or any other sociopolitical territorial unit

- Viewing the business, government, and nonprofit/voluntary sectors (including GAs) of a nation or other sociopolitical territories as three of the important sectors of society, but also including the household/family sector broadly interpreted as a fourth sector that probably arose first in human history as groups

- Viewing work organizations, including paid-staff VGs, as one important type of organization, one aspect of society, and one focus of social science scholarship, but also including volunteer and membership groups (e.g., GAs) and their volunteers at any territorial level of scope in one's round-earth VNPS paradigm

- Including social movement/protest VGs and activities as important to the VNPS and worthy of study because of their importance in actually changing human society in a long-term way (see, e.g., Gamson, 1990), but also including the much larger set of mainstream VGs and volunteers who are *not* working on sociopolitical change, let alone using protest at all, and a minority of the latter using protest to maintain the status quo or to reverse changes already made by social movements and protest

- Including in the VNPS paradigm modern, member benefit, mutual aid, self-help, and advocacy VGs and activities as well as the more traditional, personal, social service VGs that attempt to help nonmembers, often mistakenly calling themselves "public benefit" groups as if only they were VGs with benefits for the public (in the aggregate, both member benefit and nonmember benefit VGs serve the public)

- Including in the round-earth view the large majority of conventional, nondeviant "angelic" VGs as well as the more deviant, "damned," and potentially or actually stigmatized deviant VGs (the deviant VGs might exhibit only minor and temporary deviance by a minority of their members, or they might manifest a more fundamental deviance throughout the VGs, often from their initial formation)

- Understanding that money is *not* the key to understanding GAs because their principal resource is the commitment of their members and its manifestation in the volunteer activities of such members (the small amount of money needed by a GA usually can be easily raised by charging dues or getting donations from members and holding some modest fund-raising events to which nonmembers are invited, and meeting space usually can be obtained at no or low cost)

- Realizing that VGs have been found all over the world for many millennia (Smith, 1997c) and also have been found, when sought by appropriate methodology (Appendix B), in all or nearly all existing nations and territories inhabited by humans since at least 10,000 years ago (nonetheless, there might be socioculturally unique factors at any territorial level of scope in any nation that explain in part the nature of the VNPS, including GAs, in that area)

- Using a variety of analytical type classifications (Smith, 1995d, 1996; Smith et al., 1973) for VGs as well as one or more purposive type classifications, preferably a revised International Classification of Nonprofit Organizations (ICNPO) (Salamon and Anheier, 1992b; Smith, 1996) rather than the cumbersome NTEE (Hodgkinson and Toppe, 1991)

- Doing some historical study of the phenomena of interest so as to understand something of the context out of which current phenomena have grown (in the same vein, historians might spend more time relating their work to current phenomena to the greatest extent possible)

- Integrating study of developing country phenomena with developed country VNPS phenomena, seeking both similarities and differences

- Studying semiformal and even informal GAs as well as formalized GAs and paid-staff VGs

- Integrating church congregations and other religious VGs and their volunteers into the study of GAs and other VNPS phenomena

- Going beyond sociodemographic predictors in studying individual volunteer participation including factors such as personality traits, attitudes, intelligence, situational characteristics, and environment

- Studying the entire interorganizational field or population of organizations in which given VGs are embedded as well as analyzing the internal structure and processes plus external relations of individual VGs

- Being open to the potential existence of additional flat-earth paradigms that I have ignored here, which will require suitable further attention in a still better round-earth VNPS paradigm than I have sketched here and in the overview of flat-earth paradigms presented in this chapter

RATING MY OWN SUCCESS IN FOLLOWING THE ROUND-EARTH PARADIGM

I believe that this book does pretty well in terms of avoiding many of the flat-earth paradigms. However, it might be said to fall into the volunteer and membership VG paradigm in giving too much attention to volunteer groups.

Nonetheless, I am attempting to redress a balance in so doing. I have not given as much attention as I would have liked to the social movement literature, so that the book might fall into the status quo/establishment paradigm. Due to space considerations, the book does not deal with the history of GAs (Smith, 1997c), possibly falling into the antihistoricism paradigm, and also falls prey to the developed world paradigm. Because it is hard to tell which churches are GAs, and because GA churches tend to be combined with paid-staff churches in research (Johnstone, 1992), the book also is secularist in focus (secularist focus paradigm) as is the literature. There was no room in this book to consider individual volunteer participation (Smith, 1994a, forthcoming c), so that it succumbs to the sociodemographic participation predictors paradigm by default. And the same is true of consideration of populations of GAs and other VGs that I consider elsewhere (Smith and Associates, forthcoming), falling prey to the isolated VG paradigm here.

CONCLUSION

This chapter has discussed in some detail 19 flat-earth paradigms that I see as hampering GA and larger VNPS study in one way or another. Of the first 10 listed, 8 are alternative pairs, representing polar stances that can be taken on a theoretical dimension. In each case, I am pointing to some phenomena that often are left out of consideration but should be included "on the map," to continue my mapping metaphor.

I then gave a brief outline of a round-earth paradigm of the GA part of the VNPS. Much of what I say also applies to the paid-staff VG part of the VNPS. The findings reported in this book fill in empirical and theoretical details not included in the broad sketch of the round-earth paradigm here, as do related publications (Smith, 1994a, 1995c, 1996, 1997a, 1997c, 1997d, 1998b, 1999a, 1999b, forthcoming a, forthcoming b, forthcoming c; Smith and Associates, forthcoming; Smith and Dover, forthcoming).

Balanced high-quality research is hard to do in any field, in GA and VNPS research as much as in any other. It is useful, from time to time, for someone to suggest the pitfalls awaiting the unwary researcher in a given field, attempting to raise the quality level of research in that field.

11

Some Conclusions and Forecasts

The Advent of **Homo Voluntas**

This chapter discusses some broad conclusions of the book regarding the voluntary nonprofit sector (VNPS) and considers the general role of volunteer groups in society. It also examines past and near future trends in voluntary group (VG) prevalence in society and the determinants of such trends worldwide. A major thrust of the chapter is a series of predictions about the expansion of voluntary role choices in the future, leading to *Homo Voluntas,* a new type of person.

LONG HISTORY OF THE VNPS

Contrary to the beliefs of some, and perhaps of many, the VNPS is ancient in origin, going back at least 10,000 years to the neolithic revolution of primitive humans as they changed from roving nomadic bands to more settled villages of larger size (Anderson, 1973; Lenski, Nolan, and Lenski, 1995; Smith, 1997c). The VNPS initially began as grassroots associations (GAs), with paid-staff VGs coming thousands of years later, in major ancient civilizations. Undergoing many internal changes over the centuries, the VNPS also has been found in most agrarian or, where present, industrial societies for hundreds of years more recently. It is not an American or British invention, although each of these nations tends to have a high per capita prevalence of GAs. Scandinavian nations today seem to have the highest per capita prevalence of GAs and supralocal associations.

ONE NONPROFIT SECTOR OR TWO?

A large theoretical and empirical gulf separates paid-staff VGs from GAs and supralocal volunteer groups in terms of how these VGs are formed, supported, structured, operated, and influenced as well as how they "die" or are "killed." I have attempted to demonstrate this in Part II with available data and argumentation including qualitative research of my own. These differences are so great that, in some ways, it would be preferable to declare volunteer nonprofits, mainly GAs, to be a separate fifth sector of society, as I have roughly suggested in the past (Smith, 1991, 1993b). I leave this issue open, but I believe that the identification of GAs and perhaps other member benefit groups as a new sector will happen within a decade or two unless scholars and leaders of paid-staff VGs put away their inadequate "flat-earth" paradigms and understand the need for a "round-earth" VNPS paradigm here and elsewhere.

The primary reason I see for mentally constructing a fifth conceptual sector of society is that *volunteer groups* (usually small member benefit groups with relatively fewer paid-staff hours per year vs. volunteer hours) *and their activities have much in common with each other and have little in common with any work organization including paid-staff VGs.* Volunteer VGs and paid-staff VGs have some voluntary altruism in common. But large paid-staff VGs, such as Harvard University and the Smithsonian Institution, have more in common with larger corporations and even government agencies than with GAs. Insofar as the general field of "organization research" deals with nonprofits (and this is to a very minor extent), only paid-staff nonprofits tend to be considered (see the otherwise excellent recent review book of such general organization research by Hall, 1996). Work organizations are virtually the only type of organizations considered in such mainstream research on organizations more generally. Volunteer organizations, including GAs, are essentially ignored.

Our present situation is perhaps analogous to differentiating between the Third World's and the Fourth World's socioeconomic development. Sometimes, the broader Third World concept is sufficient to highlight differences between developing countries and advanced industrial societies (Horowitz, 1972). But at other times, it is useful to distinguish between two levels of underdevelopment because the Third World concept "combines apples and oranges" in some important ways. As an example, the Third World nation of Costa Rica is *much* more developed than the Fourth World nation of Burkina Faso on numerous dimensions.

There are intermediary stages of VGs such as associations that have paid staff of one or a few full-time equivalent (1,700 hours per year) workers with a roughly similar amount of time put in by pure volunteer members. Many churches are common examples. Estimating the precise amount of work/activity time put in by volunteers for a given association or paid-staff nonprofit is difficult in any event. Thus, sometimes the appropriate classification is "balanced volunteer/paid-staff VG" or simply "mixed VG."

USING A BALANCED ROUND-EARTH
PARADIGM OF THE VNPS

The "mental discovery of America" among Europeans (Zerubavel, 1992) took more than two centuries after Columbus's first voyage to the New World. The "mental discovery of the round-earth VNPS" so far has taken more than three decades. This "discovery" still is taking place among scholars and leaders of the VNPS, let alone among the general public. Our Columbus or Amerigo Vespucci for the VNPS probably was Richard Cornuelle, who seems to have invented the VNPS concept in his 1965 book, *Reclaiming the American Dream*, calling the VNPS the "independent sector."

By the late 1980s, Van Til (1988) was suggesting in his *Mapping the Third Sector* a four-sector perspective of society (as I prefer), further breaking the voluntary nonprofit sector itself into "public-regarding or charitable [nonmember benefit] associations" versus "membership benefit associations" (p. 87). O'Neill's (1989) book *The Third America* included an empirical overview of both nonmember service and mutual benefit nonprofits listed with the Internal Revenue Service (IRS). My round-earth paradigm sketched in this book goes further, showing the hitherto neglected massive size of GAs in the aggregate in American society.

The mental discovery of the VNPS still is going on and is in its early stages historically with regard to the empirical mapping of the VNPS in the United States and elsewhere. My own attempt at a first round-earth VNPS magnitudes empirical map in Chapter 2 surely will be superseded soon by better round-earth maps with more complete and reliable data than were available to me. This is all the more true for other aspects of the round-earth paradigm as sketched in Chapter 10, on which I lack good data entirely (e.g., deviant VGs, social movement VGs).

I hope that the next version of a round-earth VNPS map is based on at least one high-quality, massive, representative, random sampling, quantitative study of the VNPS and especially GAs in the United States. I outlined broadly such a hypothetical but much-needed study in Chapter 2. The need for this study is the most important conclusion that I reach in this book about *needed research*. It will permit careful comparison and contrast of volunteer and paid-staff VGs, a top research priority given the work in this book.

For *narrow* purposes of understanding or comparing elite, larger, paid-staff, wealthier, older, nonmember benefit nonprofits, the Independent Sector-type flat-earth paradigms and corresponding maps will do (Hodgkinson and Weitzman, 1996b; Hodgkinson et al., 1992). Similarly, for narrow purposes of understanding or comparing smaller, volunteer-run, poorer, younger, member benefit, associational form nonprofits such as GAs, my own earlier co-authored chapter on the United States (Smith and Baldwin, 1974b) was a fairly good flat-earth empirical description of the magnitudes of the "associational subsector" of U.S. society a quarter-century ago. That partial perspective is essentially updated and expanded to a round-earth perspective in Chapter 2 here. I also give complementary data, where available, for paid-staff nonprofit organizations, program volunteering, youth program volunteering, and informal volunteering data. I use circa 1990 as an illustrative recent date, lacking underlying data and resources to bring all my statistics up to a more recent date. My circa 1990 data give a general idea of my findings in relation to the findings of flat-earth researchers, and that is my key point, not specific absolute magnitudes.

An adequate, round-earth, broad-view empirical map of the VNPS must include both major VNPS segments or subsectors. For a broad understanding of the whole VNPS, the IRS data and the Independent Sector-type maps based on them are quite simply very incomplete and *never* have been adequate. Similar incompleteness and inadequacy are true of the previously cited chapter on associations and associational volunteers by myself and Baldwin (Smith and Baldwin, 1974b).

My current round-earth paradigm of the VNPS states that a complete and comprehensive map of our American (or any territory's) VNPS *must* include both paid-staff VGs and volunteer-run VGs; social movement VGs and status quo-oriented VGs; traditional nonmember service VGs and modern member benefit, self-help, and advocacy VGs; conventional and deviant VGs; very formalized/ incorporated/government-listed and merely semiformal/unincorporated groups; developed nation and underdeveloped nation VGs; religious and secular VGs; and so on (see my sketch of the round-earth paradigm in Chapter 10).

Figuring out what the big picture of the VNPS must include has taken me more than three decades. This has happened in part because my own initial interests were in associations as one narrow flat-earth segment of the VNPS. This is analogous to the probable situation of most nonprofit managers and many nonprofit researchers reading this who are mainly interested in paid-staff VGs. There is no problem with either type of research (or other specialized types of nonprofit research) as long as it is properly labeled as dealing with only a special part of the VNPS, not the whole VNPS. The same is true for other limited flat-earth approaches to nonprofit research.

ONE CONTRARIAN CONCLUSION: NO FINANCIAL CRISIS FOR THE VNPS AS A WHOLE

There is no broad financial crisis of the VNPS in the United States (or else-where, probably). What has happened is that paid-staff nonprofit, flat-earth VNPS scholars and leaders, also continuing to use their correlative traditional, nonmember service, flat-earth paradigm of the VNPS, have ignored the GAs and other volunteer groups in the VNPS and their massive numbers of associational volunteers in the United States and elsewhere. When the proverbial "shoe pinches their feet," they cry out on behalf of all the VNPS that matters in their narrow VNPS worldview—the paid-staff VGs of a traditional social service type.

With an adequate, comprehensive, round-earth VNPS paradigm, the familiar but erroneous views of the VNPS, as held by too many scholars and leaders, are subject to substantial or even radical changes. This type of cognitive or intellectual change occurs with any important scientific paradigm change, according to Kuhn (1962). Consider the notion that the VNPS is in a financial crisis because of privatization and decreasing government money for health and social welfare activities (Kramer et al., 1993; Leat, 1986; LeGrand and Robinson, 1986; Rekart, 1993; Smith and Lipsky, 1993).

With the new round-earth paradigm of the VNPS that I am suggesting, *there is no financial or autonomy crisis of VGs or the VNPS generally, either now or recently, in the United States or elsewhere. However, this perceived crisis might be, and probably is, true for paid-staff VGs in the United States and elsewhere as one very important segment of the whole VNPS.*

The scholars and leaders of paid-staff VGs who take this VNPS "crisis" position without proper qualification regarding the type of VGs to which they are referring are ignoring GAs and supralocal volunteer groups when they draw such a distorted conclusion. GAs and their associational volunteers are the largest part of the VNPS by several measures. They seem to be much more important in any society or territory for achieving and maintaining political pluralism, participatory democracy, and civil society. GAs depend on money only to a small extent; volunteer commitment and time are far more important to them. And GAs very rarely depend on *any external grant* (let alone contract) funding, whether from the government or from other funding organizations, at least in the United States.

Hence, the purported "financial crisis for the VNPS" as a whole in the United States or for the VNPS in other postindustrial/service/information societies simply *does not exist* when the GAs and their volunteers are included in the VNPS, as they clearly should be. The financial situation of the VNPS as a whole only *seems* like a total VNPS crisis to flat-earth VNPS scholars and leaders who ignore volunteer group phenomena. In metaphorical mapping terms, just because finances are terrible in Europe (e.g., for paid-staff VGs) does not mean that finances are necessarily also terrible in Asia or in the United States (for GAs or supralocal volunteer VGs) as other parts of the total round-earth VNPS map.

The financial "shoe" still pinches the paid-staff VGs, but we no longer are misled by a false social construction of reality into believing that the whole VNPS is in crisis. National paid-staff associations that depend mainly on dues for revenues are not in crisis either. However, program service volunteering is likely to be reduced because it often is associated with paid-staff VGs, which are suffering cutbacks in staff who can process and monitor such volunteers.

THE ROLE OF VOLUNTEER
GROUPS IN SOCIETY

The societal niche of GAs and supralocal volunteer groups is the unpaid expression of voluntary altruism, especially toward other members but also toward the larger society. They often involve serious leisure as defined by Stebbins (1996), but they are "amateur" leisure time pursuits, whatever their level of "seriousness" (Stebbins, 1979). They involve both egoistic and altruistic rewards, consistent with my definition of *voluntary altruism* in Chapter 1. And GAs have their downside (their negative aspects) as well as their positive side (Smith, 1995c, forthcoming a; Wuthnow, 1998, p. 170).

I hope that the careful reader will have a better appreciation for GAs and various types of supralocal volunteer groups as a result of this book. I do not see volunteer groups, including GAs, as replacements for work organizations— whether governments, businesses, or paid-staff VGs. Nor do I view work organizations as replacements for GAs or supralocal volunteer VGs. Both volunteer VGs and work organizations, along with households and families, have important contributions to make to human society, human satisfaction, and (sometimes even) human survival. That is why we find such groups in nearly every distinct human society larger than 100 people (Lenski et al., 1995).

We need a balanced interdisciplinary picture of the VNPS and of society more generally, not the continued dominance of various narrow, restricted, and distorted views based on the use of one or more flat-earth paradigms as reviewed in Chapter 10. If one's theory does not direct researcher attention to a certain phenomenon such as GAs, then empirical researchers seldom, if ever, will notice such "nonexistent groups" and related phenomena, any more than most social scientists notice angels or trolls. (No, I am not including the latter in my theoretical critique of nonprofit research.) That is why Hall's (1996) overview book on organizations ignores volunteer groups such as GAs. Theoretical paradigms guide empirical research when science and scholarship are working well in a certain area of research.

GAs are *not* some powerful cure-all for any problem in any society at any period of human history. However, GAs can be very powerful in their cumulative impact when writ large for a whole society, with impact on their members, their nonmembers, and (sometimes) their surrounding biophysical environments (Smith, 1997a). GAs are, thus, a power to be reckoned with individually, in local coalitions as well as in regional, national, or transnational federations.

One intrinsic limitation on the impact of GAs is the informal or semiformal style of their operations (Smith, 1992b). Another is the intermittent sense in which they may exist only "theoretically" between their actual meetings of various members. Also limiting GAs is the sense in which their GA volunteer roles usually are "secondary" for their members and leaders. This means that, relative to individuals' volunteer roles, most people tend to have much greater attitudinal and time commitments to paid jobs and to household/family roles as more "primary" in their lives.

Another important intrinsic limitation on GAs and supralocal volunteer associations is that they depend in a central way on direct in-person relationships for a large part of their success. This level of personal interaction limits the size of a high-impact GA to no more than roughly 50 analytical members (i.e., active volunteers out of the total "official membership"). GAs with larger numbers of analytical members will tend to become more bureaucratic, less informal, and (in various ways) less satisfying to analytical members, tending to gradually reduce the impact of the groups and sometimes their ability to continue operations. This bureaucracy problem can be partially avoided if a larger GA has "cells" or subgroups within it that permit closer personal interaction within these subgroups. An example is a GA in a Boston suburb (see Appendix C) with little paid staff (older high school students who are part-time referees) and about 800 members including parents of players. In this instance, the cells are the many teams and leagues of the sport involved.

High prevalence rates of GAs and supralocal voluntary associations tend to be seen by many theorists as fundamental to participatory democracy, political pluralism, and civil society as manifestations of positive social capital in a territory, usually a society (Berry, 1997, Chapter 6; Cohen, 1992; Etzioni, 1993; Gamwell, 1984; Green, 1993; Hirst, 1994; Horowitz, 1979; Olsen, 1982; Putnam, Leonardi, and Nanetti, 1993; Smith, 1998b; M. Smith, 1990; Tester, 1992; Walzer, 1983; Wolfe, 1985). However, some scholars view the proliferation of associations, especially national associations with political goals, as blocking democratic processes and mainly favoring the wealthy (Berry, 1997, Chapter 10; Greider, 1992; Kariel, 1981; Mills, 1956; Rauch, 1994; Schlozman, 1984; Schlozman and Tierney, 1986; M. Smith, 1990).

Societal insiders (Becker, 1963) have indeed tended to dominate GAs since the anthropological/historical origins of GAs perhaps 25 millennia ago (Anderson, 1973; Smith, 1997c). In this sense, political pluralism of some sort or another is more of an ideal than a reality, even in postindustrial societies (M. Smith, 1990). However, the situation of political and socioeconomic equality has been improving as a result of various social movements during the past 200 years or so (Smith and Associates, forthcoming).

GAs still offer societal outsiders one of the best *persisting* long-term ways in which to make participatory democracy and a civil society *more* real for them. The glass is partly full, not partly empty. Rebellions, revolutions, and coups are only short-term solutions for most societal outsider problems. Active and free

political pluralism of GAs and supralocal volunteer groups for outsiders constitute a long-term ideal that modern Western societies seem at least to be moving
toward. What other road is there in this age of recent devolution of Socialist and
Communist dictatorships? These recent Second World collective outbursts
(circa 1989-90) were perhaps as much a rejection of Communist/Socialist government *bureaucracies* as anything else. If so, people in such nations should be,
and seem to be (Hegyesi, 1992), more interested in GAs now than ever before in
a half-century or more.

THE NEW SOCIAL SCIENTIFIC DISCIPLINE
OF VOLUNTARY ACTION STUDIES: 50 TO
100 YEARS AWAY IN THE FUTURE

In 1971, with the help of some others (James Luther Adams, Burt R. Baldwin,
John Dixon, Richard D. Reddy, James Shultz, and Cynthia Wedel), I formed the
Association of Voluntary Action Scholars. This international (but mainly U.S.)
scholarly association has grown over the years and numbered more than 1,000
members at year-end 1999. It now has the name Association for Research on
Nonprofit Organizations and Voluntary Action (ARNOVA), holds annual con-
ferences attended by hundreds, and publishes its own journal (*Nonprofit and
Voluntary Sector Quarterly*). I give more description in Appendix A.

I wish to point out that there are parallels between voluntary action research
as a field of study and the fields of political science and economics in relation to
the major sectors of society. Economics studies the business sector, and neither
the sector nor the scientific discipline ever are likely to vanish. Political science
studies the government sector, and neither the sector nor the scientific discipline
ever are likely to vanish. Now that there is a fledgling discipline or at least an
interdisciplinary research field of voluntary action research focusing on the
VNPS, it is unlikely that either this sector or its research field ever will likely
vanish. In 50 or 100 years, the latter research field might be much larger and
stronger than anyone now can imagine, especially if what I forecast in the next
section comes true. In such a case, it might become a new social scientific "discipline" (Smith, forthcoming b; see also Block, 1987; Hall, 1999; Milofsky,
1996).

POLICY RECOMMENDATIONS

Space limitations preclude my providing extensive treatment of policy rec-
ommendations here, so I can sketch only a few of my ideas (Smith, 1997b).
First, it is crucial to preserve and enhance civil liberties for all VGs but particularly GAs. I think that there should be less monitoring of GAs by the IRS by raising the threshold of annual revenues for required registration from $5,000 to

$25,000 or $50,000. The threshold for annual reporting of finances (vs. mere registration) also should be raised from its current $25,000 to $100,000. External granting agencies should try to avoid the folly of making grants for regular operations to GAs in developed nations. If GAs cannot support themselves from internal resources and fund-raising events, then they probably should "exit." GAs come and go. The form remains.

External granting agencies should instead consider grants to paid-staff VGs or GAs that help GAs seek their individual goals. I have written recently about activities such as contributing to the infrastructure for GAs (Smith, 1997b). I have in mind high school evening courses, training workshops for leaders, practical manuals, and so on. More meeting space for GAs might be provided in communities low in such space.

More research on GAs needs to be generated, particularly comparing GAs to work organizations such as paid-staff VGs. Nonprofit academic centers at various universities should get more involved both in GA research and in the short-term nondegree teaching of GA leaders from their localities. The latter will involve recruiting part-time teachers who know about GAs, not just about paid-staff VGs.

PAST AND FUTURE TRENDS
IN VG PREVALENCE

A large amount of empirical data and theory suggests that the long-term *macro trend* in human society worldwide over the 10 recent millennia has been for increasing numbers and importance of both GAs and supralocal volunteer associations and other nonprofits (Smith, 1997c; Smith and Associates, forthcoming). Although quantitative data usually are lacking, there is empirical qualitative evidence for rising GA prevalence for human society in general over recent millennia in both absolute and relative terms such as GAs per thousand population or per capita. This long-term macro trend for human society still is generally in full vigor worldwide (Anderson, 1973; Ross, 1976; Smith, 1973c, 1997c; Smith and Associates, forthcoming).

A related long-term *meso trend* upward in both absolute and relative associational and other VG prevalence has been largely in force over the past few centuries in colonial and later democratic America (Ellis and Noyes, 1990; Finke and Stark, 1994; Hall, 1987b, 1992; O'Neill, 1989) as well as in many other nations (Boulding, 1953; Smith, 1997c). This process of GA prevalence growth over recent centuries seems to be very widespread and persistent. There are very few nations that have been properly studied in terms of GA prevalence that have not had GAs growing in prevalence (Smith and Associates, forthcoming), although quantitative data on GAs are scarce over these several centuries.

At the level of *micro trends* for all of human society during the past quarter-century, the worldwide trend still seems to be upward in prevalence, again both in absolute and relative terms. It is not yet clear to what extent transition specifically to a postindustrial/service/information society involves increased growth, a slowing of growth, a plateau, or a decline in associational prevalence. Putnam (1995) sees such a decline of GAs and other associations in the United States recently. My reading of relevant data available suggests that the *world* VG trend generally still has been upward (Salamon and Anheier, 1994; Smith, 1997c; Smith and Associates, forthcoming).

GA prevalence and participation dynamics suggest that there will be gradual growth in absolute and relative GA prevalence and participation during the next quarter-century for the entire world as well as for any specific nations making significant progress on industrialization or modernization (Smith, 1973c, 1997c). I suggest this same forecast for supralocal volunteer groups as well, fostered by better interpersonal mediated communications (Rheingold, 1993). This is an argument from underlying causation worldwide, not from actual data on associations in the United States or elsewhere, over which there is much controversy (Baumgartner and Walker, 1988; Lappé and DuBois, 1994; Putnam, 1995; T. Smith, 1990; Wuthnow, 1998, pp. 50-54, 76-77).

DETERMINANTS OF GA PREVALENCE GROWTH WORLDWIDE

There are three broad, interrelated, and underlying processes accounting for all three temporal GA prevalence trends as absolute (i.e., raw) numbers in human society as a whole: (a) population growth, (b) growing preindustrial societal complexity, and (c) growing societal industrialization and other elements of modernization, on average. All three processes are interrelated theoretically and empirically. Population growth rises greatly with the initial stages of industrialization but eventually tends to slow or reverse direction with more territorial complexity and modernization of a society and its individuals, especially in a postindustrial/service/information society. Societal industrialization is a further stage of increasing preindustrial societal complexity, as is postindustrial society.

Population Growth

As long as there is a significant general population increase in a territory, GA prevalence also will tend to increase to accommodate the associational interests of people in that territory. At the very least, I expect future worldwide growth of GAs and supralocal volunteer associations to likely continue at a moderate pace of about 1% to 2% per year. The driving force behind this baseline arithmetic growth of volunteer nonprofits is simply continued population growth in the vast majority of nations (Famighetti, 1997). GAs service people in communities, usually with relatively small numbers of members per GA (McPherson, 1983b). More people in any community or larger territory, thus, usually means that more GAs and more supralocal volunteer nonprofits will be formed in that territory, whether during the next few decades or the next few centuries. This also has been true during past centuries.

In a less developed nation, it is possible that the GA prevalence growth rate would be closer to 2% when the nation is in a stage of sharp industrialization and modernization, as when it is actively moving from an agrarian society to an industrial society. These projections assume that the international situation remains essentially stable, without one or more macro crises or major world dislocations such as thermonuclear war, ecological collapse, and some widespread plague. Nearly all of the latter crises would result in substantially diminished prevalence of GAs in the affected areas, sometimes in the whole world.

Growing Preindustrial Societal Complexity

Part of the long-term macro trend for increasing GA prevalence in human history has resulted from increasing preindustrial societal complexity. Nomadic hunting-and-gathering tribes have dominated most of human history on the planet (Lenski et al., 1995). When settled horticultural villages became widespread 10 millennia ago, GAs began to flourish in them as well (Anderson, 1973; Smith, 1997c). Large agrarian societies, such as ancient Greece and Rome, represented another increasing level of preindustrial societal complexity and saw a corresponding increase in GA prevalence, especially in urban areas (Kloppenborg and Wilson, 1996; Waltzing, 1895). Growing preindustrial societal complexity still is occurring in many contemporary developing nations, especially with the process of urbanization.

Growing Societal Industrialization and Modernization

The meso trend of increasing GA prevalence during the past two centuries or so has been, to an important degree, the result of industrialization and modernization. As Boulding (1953) has pointed out, the industrial revolution brought with it an "organizational revolution." I contend that this organizational revolution has included extensive growth in GA and supralocal association prevalence (Smith, 1973c). Available research confirms this contention (Smith, 1997c).

Industrialization, seen as widespread dependence on factories for production, is but one part of the larger modernization process of the past two centuries. Other aspects include growth of literacy and mass education, growth of mass media, increased urbanization, development of better transportation and communication networks, and so on. Not least of the aspects of modernization is the development of a democratic polity and freedom of association within it. The process of societal modernization brings with it individual psychosocial modernity for many people in a modernizing society (Inkeles and Smith, 1974). All of these aspects of modernization contribute to greater absolute GA prevalence and participation (Smith, 1973c; Smith and Associates, forthcoming).

It seems reasonable to also forecast some increasing *relative* associational prevalence (per capita or per thousand population), based on the gradually increasing average modernization of societies globally during future decades and the 21st century. Computer networking (the Internet) might provide an as yet unmeasured further boost to volunteer association prevalence, especially for people in the wealthier nations able to afford personal computers and the associated costs of using the Internet (Rheingold, 1993). Such volunteer groups have not been well studied given their only recent emergence from the use of the Internet.

EXPANSION OF VOLUNTARY ROLE CHOICES IN THE FUTURE, ESPECIALLY IN POSTINDUSTRIAL SOCIETIES

There is a broader process that is occurring as well. Most generally, ascriptive kinship, work organization, social class, religious, and citizen/resident roles are declining in importance generally in modern societies relative to voluntary/achieved and even ephemeral roles (Biddle, 1979; Linton, 1945; Zurcher, 1978) that include GA and volunteer program participation as subtypes. This broader process is a "forest" in which growth in GA and program volunteer participation is one of the "trees."

Several factors have combined, or will combine, to give most members of postindustrial, service, and information societies *more voluntary choices* about how they will spend their time doing what, where, and with whom—including individual choices affecting volunteer group activities and a variety of social roles.

The extended family will continue to break down (a) as a single household living unit and (b) as an emotionally close but somewhat spatially dispersed local kin network with frequent in-person interactions into (c) a highly dispersed kin network spatially in which both face-to-face and mediated interactions will be ever more guided by voluntary choice, personal preferences, and nonascriptive friendships as much as, or more than, direct kin ties (e.g., never seeing a particular sibling because one dislikes him or her [Degler, 1980]). Improved transportation of various types contributes to this kin dispersal trend. In the type "c" situation just noted, interacting with nonhousehold and especially long-distance kin becomes another part of the general activity pattern (Smith, 1994a; Smith, Macaulay, and Associates, 1980) that probably correlates significantly with other aspects of that pattern, especially non-kin friendship activity and neighboring.

The lessened necessity of taking (a) whatever work role one's same-sex parent had or, more recently, (b) whatever job is available at the moment as the concept of personally chosen jobs and careers has become more and more established, at least for men and gradually also for women in service/information societies. Careers for women become more possible when there are accepted corporate and professional maternity leaves, fairly widespread child care facilities, and diminishing (although still powerful) sexism (especially among men and women in modern societies). Increases in the percentage of people, especially women, receiving higher education is an important factor underlying the present trend.

There will be greater ability and desire to move more or less permanently or repeatedly from one part of one's initial national region to another, or even from one country to another. Migration from rural areas to urban areas is one very common long-distance move in the modernizing societies, and moves to other societies often also are related to occupational and wealth/income aspirations. Being able to make such long-distance and cultural moves in modern societies creates a whole new set of voluntary residence area choices and, thus, many accompanying life activity and role choices.

One's religious role will decline from being totally ascriptive throughout one's lifetime, based on the religion of one's parental family, to being more a matter of personal voluntary choice after one reaches the age of majority (usually 18 or 21 years in the United States). Even being religious at all becomes a voluntary choice in modern societies, unlike traditional societies in which "heretics" (atheists and "dissenters") sometimes were tortured or executed for these then grave "sins" (Lambert, 1992). Exercising personal preferences and voluntary choice in the realm of religion and religious roles first becomes more feasible in urban areas of agrarian societies, where some degree of freedom of religion begins to grow (Finke and Stark, 1994; Pennock and Chapman, 1969; Robertson, 1966). This freedom of religion tends to increase in industrial and postindustrial societies as an integral part of freedom of association in democratic polities.

There will be ever-increasing communication and transportation network development in nations all over the world at differing rates and with differing results for general population use. High-quality and cheap telephone service, cell phones, faxes, and e-mail are particularly important and increasing means of mediated communication in modern societies. Greater technological innovation worldwide will contribute to the present trend, binding us ever more into a "global village" based far more on voluntary choices and achieved roles and interests than on ascriptive roles including nationality/citizenship, race/ethnicity, and social class. As the communication and transportation links among nations increase in the modern world, individual preference- or value-based voluntary choices will lead to more transnational volunteer groups.

The present long-term growth in the absolute wealth of nations per capita (infla-tion adjusted), on average, and the dropping world prices for many types of technology connected with transportation, communications, computers, tele-phones, faxes, e-mail, cable, and satellite television will make the use of these communication systems far more prevalent within and across societies. With e-mail, the cost of sending a message to the other side of the world is the same to an individual user as the cost of sending that message to a next-door neighbor. From a few mass media (newspapers and later radio) with little individual choice in earlier industrial societies, modern information societies are moving toward far more voluntary choices regarding individual and very personal access preferences about means and content of communications.

Increasing life expectancy and declining age of retirement from the full-time labor force will combine to make more retirees in modern societies who also tend to live longer, on average. Hence, they have more noneconomic voluntary choices regarding all of their activities and roles than they did previously. Put another way, a greater percentage of one's adult life will be lived without the necessity of paid work in the future, owing to changing full-time paid work and retirement trends. One result will be more volunteering and involvement in GAs.

There will be a gradual decline of paid work (Rifkin, 1995) as productivity gains through automation and computers obviate the necessity of large numbers of jobs that were needed in the industrial society but that are not needed in the post-industrial/service/information society. Rifkin (1995) writes, "In the coming century, the market and public sectors are going to play an ever-reduced role in the day-to-day lives of human beings around the world. The power vacuum will likely be taken up either by the growth of an increasing outlaw subculture or by greater participation in the third sector" (p. 249). I add, *or both*. This will involve a reversal of the trend toward increasing work hours seen by Schor (1993) dur-ing the 1970s and 1980s in the United States, in disagreement with others.

There will be continued growth of cultural pluralism (multiculturalism) as reflected in many more voluntary choices for cultural and subcultural identifi-cations in the form of activities and roles. The information society, and the Inter-net in particular as a part of such postindustrial society, permits its participants to conceal their racial, ethnic, religious, national, regional, economic, gender, political, and other statuses and roles if they wish. This permits Internet interactions among people to be liberated pluralistically by the technology involved. At the same time, one can foster and expand one's ascriptive role identifications, such as race/ethnicity/culture, insofar as one wishes on the Internet by focusing one's personal preferences on the appropriately chosen cultural or subcultural Web sites, bulletin boards, and discussion groups. But the assimilation of immigrants in America in the past suggests that most of them will want their families to be assimilated through their children or their children's children into their adopted nation (Alba, 1990; Steinberg, 1981). As Schlesinger (1993, p. 138) points out, the problem is to accomplish *e pluribus unum* ("from many, one") in the United States by fostering both pluralistic diversity *and* some common Western values such as individual freedom, political democracy, and human rights. Growth of antidiscrimination laws supports pluralistic diversity in some postindustrial societies such as the United States.

Declining illiteracy/innumeracy and increasing formal education levels, on average, in many nations and in the world population as a whole will contribute to voluntary choices by introducing children and youths to the range of roles and activity choices available to them, based on what people have done in the past or elsewhere. Such increased formal education also will contribute to more use of the printed media, including newspapers and magazines, which similarly introduce readers to many new ideas, roles, activities, and choices more generally. As suggested earlier, increasing educational levels are especially important in allowing more choice of occupational roles. Higher educational levels also are strongly associated with more GA membership and volunteering (Smith, 1994a).

A growing proportion of world society will become psychosocially modern in people's values, beliefs, attitudes, desires, and activities (Inkeles and Smith, 1974; Smith, 1995b) as a result of modernizing experiences in formal education, in factories, as mass media users, and as participants in other modern settings (e.g., effective corporations) that require psychosocially modern individuals. These experiences will continue to create such people in a causal feedback process over the coming decades and century. As a result, more individuals in world society and in specific modernizing societies will develop more varied ideas, interests, and preferences that lead to people making more individual choices about activities and roles that are not necessary in traditional societies where custom is the main determinant of these matters.

There will be ever more widespread knowledge of and dependence on English of one type or another for international communication, including on the Internet.

A global village requires a common language, and English is that language at present, whether a first, second, or third language for individuals. This will happen informally through the Internet as participants simply find that they can communicate better in a common language across nationalities and language barriers. This growing knowledge of English will contribute, in a feedback process over time, to better quality transnational communications and to better intranational communications and relationships in multilanguage nations (e.g., India) as well.

Marriage is ever more a voluntary arrangement between the people to be married. During earlier times in most societies, marriage was arranged by the parents of each member of the couple. Limiting economic factors, such as dowries and bride prices, are not present in modern societies. Growing ease of divorce in most postindustrial nations makes exit from a given marriage role ever more feasible, however painful for the parties and children involved. "Living together" without marriage has been growing in frequency as an even more voluntary alternative to traditional marriage.

Micro, meso, and macro trends of growth in absolute GA prevalence, in GAs per capita, in GA variety, and in supralocal volunteer groups are likely to continue, as will the trend for more program service volunteering. This will continue to occur, even in advanced postindustrial societies, as one part of the larger trend from collective ascribed roles to more individualized, personally chosen, and achieved roles (Biddle, 1979; Linton, 1945; Nadel, 1957, p. 36).

The forgoing trends and "social forces" together contrast markedly with the much more limited and ascriptive role pressures and activity choices for people in most *preindustrial* societies for whom kinship roles of various types were central; for whom nearly all work and religion roles were handed down from parent to child; for whom a marriage partner for life was chosen by one's parents; and for whom there was no question of leaving one's tribe, village, or nation. In fact, exile in a preliterate society was tantamount to death for the person involved because humans are social animals who can exist over the long term only as interdependent members of residential and work groups (Durkheim, 1964; Lenski et al., 1995).

In recent *agrarian* societies (in which raising crops and animals is the principal work of the society), ascriptive roles also have weakened somewhat. Such societies offered in the past, and still offer now where present today, *some* weakening of kinship bonds, a significant expansion of work role opportunities for males in urban areas relative to their parents, some weakening of religious role ascriptiveness in urban areas, and very modest changes in the importance of territorial/residence/citizen roles.

In many major agrarian societies (Lenski et al., 1995), such as ancient Rome and ancient China, there were stark differences in their members' ascriptive role "pressures" compared to those in industrial and postindustrial societies. Slavery, bond service, and serfdom were widespread practices in older agrarian societies. Peasant agriculturalist parents generally had children with similar work roles, although highly differentiated by gender. In the skilled trades, the sons of master craftsmen usually carried on with the family traditions in the specific trades. Only wealthy men of property, themselves descended from wealthy men of property, could be full citizens and vote. Women could not own anything valuable (e.g., real estate) and, hence, could not vote until very recently in historical terms.

THE VOLUNTARY CENTURY AND VOLUNTEER MILLENNIUM: THE ADVENT OF *HOMO VOLUNTAS*

If my forgoing analysis is correct, then the 21st century and the new millennium might be more the time of volunteers, voluntary choices, and voluntary roles in life for more individuals than ever before in human history. The well-known futurist, John Naisbitt, forecast a variety of trends for the 1980s that involved GAs in one way or another—increasing self-help, decentralization, participatory democracy, and networking (Naisbitt, 1982). These still are active trends in Western nations and (to some degree) elsewhere, especially in non-Western developed nations.

More recently, Naisbitt and Aburdene (1990) forecast some additional relevant trends for the 1990s and the initial decades of the new millennium. One trend is a religious revival for the third millennium that will involve paid-staff nonprofits as well as GAs, in my terms. The second is "the triumph of the individual" (p. 322). The latter involves many subtrends that clearly speak to the prevalence of GAs and supralocal volunteer groups based on voluntary individual preferences. The authors state, "Stripped down to the individual, one can build community, the free association of individuals" (p. 324). They are referring in part to the further development of communication technologies such as the Internet, fax machines, and cellular telephones that will permit individuals to contact each other as part of a global network based on personal interests and preferences as well as, or instead of, being based on ascriptive personal roles.

When seen from the standpoint of centuries and millennia, enormous changes already have occurred on the central life dimension of ascriptiveness versus voluntary choice of roles, relationships, and activities by the individual for the individual but often with others. Further change in the relative prevalence of voluntary roles versus ascriptive roles is likely, as is change in the amount of time per day, week, or year spent in these roles. The ascriptive/

traditional roles will tend to continue to decline, and the voluntary/achieved roles will increase in both relative and absolute terms.

Voluntary choices based on personal preferences and interests are more and more becoming the basis for time spent, roles played, and human interactions among specific individuals. Many such voluntary choices are analytically similar in nature to more narrow choice of a GA or volunteer program that matches one's interests and is present in or near the community in which one lives. Technologically mediated but relatively interactive communications of the types noted here will lead to a great increase in the prevalence of supralocal "virtual" volunteer groups whose members might seldom or never meet in person but that nonetheless are satisfying as voluntary individual choices are made regarding how to spend time interacting with like-minded people.

The 1800s can be seen as the century of *industrial society* and the 1900s as the century of the *information/service society* in the most developed nations. The new century could very well see the further development of the *society of free voluntary choice by the individual*—the society of individuals participating in voluntary activities, roles, and groups as *non-spatially bound, common-interest, voluntary communities of their choice*. In such "volunteer communities" of varying sizes and breadth of territorial bases (or really none at all on the Internet in the spatial sense), people will tend to develop and retain more of their individuality and uniqueness. But they will correspondingly gain outcomes such as more territorial/societal/international participation, pluralism, and diversity.

I term this general outcome the *voluntary society,* following the innovative use of Shultz (1972), as promoted by various professionals of the Center for a Voluntary Society (including its second director, John Dixon, and the first director, James Shultz) for which I was the director of research from 1970 to 1974.

Our species, more generally, still is *Homo Sapiens,* but we also have become distinctively *Homo Faber* (object-making or crafts people [Tilgher, 1958; Tyrrell, (1951) 1969]) and *Homo Ludens* (playing or recreating people [Huizenga, 1955]). The typical resident of a future, still more voluntary, society can be termed *Homo Voluntas* (the volunteer person). This person will be molded by his or her voluntary society in such a way that making numerous voluntary choices about roles and activities nearly every day seems more commonplace and "natural." This is partially true for many people today, especially youths and the peripatetic retired.

The trade-off between work and play, including the serious play of volunteering (Stebbins, 1996), will more often become resolved in terms of "play." This will tend to be the net result as the population ages (on average), as actual retirement ages creep downward, and as the average length of life span increases modestly. I argue that greater length of "adolescence" and of "retirement" or quasi-retirement counteracts opposite forces such as increased working hours per capita (Schor, 1993) during the past 20 years in the United States. One has to look at the whole picture, not just the picture for paid workers alone or for generalizing such paid work hours per capita. I believe that actual leisure hours for retired people, those semi-retired/part-time in the labor force, and full-time workers in the labor force should be studied separately and compared to make for better generalization of "paid work time."

Ecce Homo voluntas—"Behold the volunteer species" or "volunteer person." These somewhat awkward terms are necessary to make each synonym distinct from the everyday concept of a person who is a volunteer for a GA or volunteer service program today. The volunteer person of the future will make many more voluntary choices of roles and activities both in leisure (including volunteering as now understood) and in paid work and self/family maintenance activities.

APPENDIX A

Description of the (Largely North American) Association for Research on Nonprofit Organizations and Voluntary Action

Nonprofit organizations and voluntary action is a growing field of interdisciplinary and interprofessional study. This field began formally in the United States in 1971 when the Center for a Voluntary Society provided seed money through grants to Boston College and part of my paid time as director of research at the center to pursue my idea of developing an academic association for this field. James Shultz, the first director of the center, and later John Dixon, the second director, were instrumental in making these resources available. Those who find congenial the "resource mobilization" perspective on social movement origins and growth (McCarthy and Zald, 1977) will note the parallel here for a nonmovement.

Burt R. Baldwin and Richard D. Reddy, initially as graduate students of mine at Boston College and later as colleagues at their own colleges (Central Connecticut State University and State University of New York at Fredonia, respectively), were of tremendous help to me in getting the new association, the Association of Voluntary Action Scholars (AVAS), formed and going.

Eugene D. White, Jr., the first office manager and later executive officer of AVAS, also was virtually indispensable in helping get AVAS going during the first few years. More of this history of the field can be found in "Researching Volunteer Associations and Other Nonprofits: An Emergent Interdisciplinary Field and Potential New Discipline" (Smith, forthcoming b).

Concerted research on nonprofit organizations and voluntary action, applied and scholarly, is a field of study that is, thus, a bit more than 25 years old (Smith, 1993a, 1995e). AVAS, which since has become the Association for Research on Nonprofit Organizations and Voluntary Action (ARNOVA), has published its journal for more than 25 years. This *Journal of Voluntary Action Research,* now *Nonprofit and Voluntary Sector Quarterly* (*NVSQ*), was the first journal of its kind anywhere focused totally on voluntary action and nonprofit organizations (Smith, 1972a, 1972b).

In 1977, Yale University formed the Program on Non-Profit Organizations (PONPO) as the first university-based research center of its kind in the world. The two entities represented different streams of interest—voluntary action versus nonprofit organizations—that remained separate during the early years. The two traditions were unified, and the journal and organization were renamed in 1989 and 1990, respectively. In 1993, ARNOVA formed a new partnership with PONPO that assumed joint sponsorship of *NVSQ* under Carl Milofsky as editor-in-chief. When Steven Rathgeb Smith became editor-in-chief in 1998, the *NVSQ* headquarters location transferred to the University of Washington and the PONPO connection ended. At about the same time, in 1993 the Center on Philanthropy at Indiana University–Purdue University at Indianapolis began to house ARNOVA headquarters, which previously had been located at Boston College, Pennsylvania State University, Tufts University, and Washington State University. This involved a substantial annual support grant from the center to ARNOVA in addition to space.

ARNOVA is an independent, multidisciplinary, multiprofessional society whose mission is to foster research, both applied and theory oriented, on nonprofit organizations, philanthropy, citizen participation, and voluntary action. Our annual conference provides opportunities for independent scholars and thoughtful practitioners from diverse disciplines and service industries to interact as a community of scholars. More than 500 people participated in the 1999 conference including about 100 non-U.S. participants from 22 nations on four continents and Australia (my computation from 1999 list of participants).

ARNOVA is committed to building nonprofit research as a recognized field of study; remaining a neutral open forum for sound scholarship and research-related activities undertaken by scholars, practitioners, academic centers, and foundations; nurturing new scholars; and defining a common core of learning that constitutes the special field of study.

For more then two decades, ARNOVA's annual conferences have grown in size, diversity, and contribution to knowledge. ARNOVA received more than 500 proposals for the 1999 conference in Arlington, Virginia, up from 125 in 1991, and the number of conference participants has increased correspondingly. The membership of more than 1,000 independent scholars and practitioners at the end of 1999 has grown by more than 100% during the past five years (Anita Plotinsky, personal communication, November 6, 1999). ARNOVA continues to play a groundbreaking role in increasing the depth of knowledge about the nonprofit sector and voluntary action.

The phenomena on which *NVSQ* is focused are substantial in the United States and elsewhere, as Chapter 2 demonstrates. The variety of individual non-profits includes Harvard University, Northwestern Memorial Hospital (Chicago), the American National Red Cross, the Audubon Society, the Ford Foundation, the National Association of Social Workers, a local Girl Scouts troop, a local Parent-Teacher Association, a local Alcoholics Anonymous group, a local youth soccer league, and so on. This field has as much distinctiveness as do the economic and government sectors, for the groups we study have a very different structure than do governments and businesses. Nonprofits are not tied to people's voting or taxes in any territory, nor do they seek to distribute profits (indeed, by definition, they cannot distribute any excess revenues to members, their boards, or "owners"). Moreover, nonprofits or VGs are the main organized expression of voluntary altruism in society, along with service volunteer programs.

In addition to this growth within the United States, changes in the former Communist bloc and in less wealthy nations have produced growing interest in nonprofit organizations, voluntary action, and problems of civil society world-wide. ARNOVA always has included many Canadians as well as Americans. Elsewhere, there are many members from the United Kingdom as well as a sprinkling of members from Australia, New Zealand, Israel, continental Europe, Latin America, and elsewhere. At the end of 1999, there were members from 55 countries (ARNOVA, 1999). Although the international community of scholars recently founded an International Society for Third Sector Research, ARNOVA has been an international association from its inception, and *NVSQ* continues to publish occasional articles from around the world.

For many years, *NVSQ* has noted in each issue that the journal is interested in research papers on "voluntarism, citizen participation, philanthropy, and non-profit organizations." Interested readers of the present book who are not members of ARNOVA might, if interested, inquire of the headquarters office in Indianapolis about a brochure and information on various publications, confer-ences, and other services. Conferences usually are held in October or Novem-ber, rotating around the country haphazardly and sometimes meeting in other nations (Canada and the United Kingdom so far). One-page paper proposals are submitted in the spring and are peer-reviewed by a conference program committee. Journal subscriptions should be made through the Indianapolis office. (Please ask your library to subscribe as well.)

The current ARNOVA address is as follows:

> Dr. Anita Plotinsky
> Executive Director, ARNOVA
> Indiana University Center on Philanthropy
> 550 West North Street, Suite 301
> Indianapolis, IN 46202-3162
>
> Phone: (317) 684-2120
> Fax: (317) 684-2128
> E-mail: exarnova@iupui.edu
> Web: www.arnova.org

APPENDIX B

Creating a Local Nonprofit Sampling Frame Including Grassroots Associations: An American Example

Standard sampling texts (Henry, 1990; Jaeger, 1984; Yates, 1981) say little or nothing about the special problems of sampling semiformal groups and organizations such as nonprofits (defined in Chapter 1) that are nowhere fully listed. The Internal Revenue Service (IRS) registration lists of nonprofits in the United States are very biased and incomplete (Dale, 1993; Gronbjerg, 1989, 1994; Smith, 1997d; see also Chapter 2), contrary to what many researchers seem to believe. The IRS lists include primarily larger and nonreligious nonprofits. Religious groups (including churches) with any level of revenues and nonreligious groups with revenues under $5,000 per year at present do not have to register, and most do not (see Chapter 2). With $25,000 revenues per year, a nonprofit must file a Form 990 annual report. Nonregistered nonprofits in the United States include *most* nonprofits, which usually are small and volunteer run (Smith, 1997d; see also Chapter 2).

Given IRS records as a source for larger nonprofits, often with paid staff, the core of the nonprofit sampling problem is the small volunteer nonprofits. Omitting them makes a quite incomplete sample of nonprofits in any territory. Standard sampling procedures tell us to create a sampling frame (complete list) of nonprofits in a territory when none exists (Jaeger, 1984, p. 6; Yates, 1981, p. 63). One may *start* with IRS-registered nonprofits in an area, but one must go on from there to create a more complete sampling frame if one wishes to generalize to all nonprofits, not just large paid-staff nonprofits. Gronbjerg's (1989) article on creating a sampling frame for a metropolitan area for paid-staff public benefit nonprofits is a rare and welcome contribution. She shows that the IRS-listed nonprofits are only about half of the total even for such larger and public benefit nonprofits (see also Dale, 1993; Gronbjerg, 1994).

This appendix suggests how such a sample could be even more complete by including *volunteer* nonprofits (mainly grassroots associations [GAs]) as well as paid-staff nonprofits (Smith, 1981) and by including *member benefit* groups as well as nonmember benefit groups—all of which are nonprofits (Smith, 1991, 1993b; see also Chapters 1 and 2). Once one has such a sampling frame, either random or systematic sampling of the list will produce a sample of nonprofits that one can study and generalize from to the larger total of nonprofits in the territory. Very few studies have done this.

For many years, researchers studying voluntary associations have been studying the numbers of associations (volunteer nonprofits) in smaller communities (Babchuk and Edwards, 1965; Laskin and Phillett, 1965; Warriner and Prather, 1965). The usual method of identifying such associations has been to seek local lists and to content analyze the local newspaper, if present. Some general fieldwork has accompanied this. In the best-known U.S. instance of full-scale ethnographic fieldwork with special interest in associations in a town (Warner and Lunt, 1941), a much higher frequency of associations per 1,000 population was found than in most other studies (Smith, 1997d; Smith and Baldwin, 1974b, p. 281; see also Chapter 2), indicating that such fieldwork might be the method of choice for maximum completeness without concern for cost.

The problem is the completeness versus cost trade-off. It is very labor intensive and, hence, costly to find GAs on a community, even when starting with a major existing list. Most GAs are not in the IRS tax-exempt list, as noted earlier. A locality (e.g., city, town, county) in the United States may or may not have a good existing list. Hence, there is no reliable "single source" for a reasonably complete nonprofit list in most localities.

A MULTIMETHOD COMPREHENSIVE SAMPLING FRAME CREATION STRATEGY FOR NONPROFITS

The aim of the present multimethod strategy is to improve the completeness of the nonprofit sampling frame over use of lists and newspapers without using (very expensive) full-scale ethnography. The following are the elements of the multimethod strategy. Although developed for use in smaller communities, the approach also can be used for cities or even nations as territories.

Strategy 1: Key General Lists of Nonprofits

Find and use any existing general lists or directories of nonprofits in the community. Such lists might be kept by the town clerk, the mayor's or city manager's office, the chamber of commerce, the public library, or some organization interested in promoting business and tourism in the community. These days, the list might be computerized in larger localities. For states and nations (and occasionally counties and larger cities), there might be directories of nonprofits of all types or of a certain type of nonprofit. In the United States, for example, there is the *Encyclopedia of National Associations* (Jaszczak and Sheets, 1997). For Chicago, Gronbjerg (1989, p. 68) used a metropolitan Chicago social service directory as her third most productive source of paid-staff nonprofits. Hungary has a law requiring all GAs and other nonprofits to register with the government (Kuti, 1998), and most GAs may be included in this registration. France has a similar law, probably with similar results (Lanfant, 1976).

The problem with single lists purporting to be comprehensive is that they almost invariably are *not* comprehensive. The town clerk in one town I studied produced as "comprehensive" a list of fewer than 10% of the nonprofit organizations I later found in the town using the present comprehensive strategy. In another town, the list produced by a locality promotion/tourism organization was about 80% complete relative to the result of the comprehensive strategy. One cannot be sure about where some supposedly comprehensive list falls on a continuum of completeness until and unless the more comprehensive strategy is used at least in part. However, one can use as a rough guide the knowledge that about 30 nonprofits per 1,000 population usually are present, more in smaller places (Smith, 1997d; see also Chapter 2). The large majority of these are GAs.

Obviously, when there are two or more lists, one creates a master list eliminating overlaps. I favor a small card file. Others might favor a computer file, even initially, especially in a larger locality. One must take care with nonprofit names and name changes to avoid duplicates. I found particular trouble with people calling a nonprofit by the city name (i.e., "Boston . . .") versus not doing so. It pays to cross-reference nonprofits with, and again without, locality names to deal with this problem of possible double listing.

Strategy 2: Local Mass Media

a. *Content analyze the local newspapers for mentions of nonprofit organizations.* If there is no newspaper exclusively serving the community, then try to find an area newspaper that has a special section on the community or other area of interest. If there are two or more local newspapers serving the area, then try to identify which one pays more attention to nonprofits. The right newspaper to use might *not* be the primary or larger circulation paper. In my research, weekly newspapers tended to give more coverage to GAs than do daily newspapers. Look for pages in the newspapers that specialize in volunteer group or nonprofit affairs. Occasionally, the person at the newspaper responsible for volunteer and nonprofit activities will have a card or computer file on nonprofits or associations specifically and will give you access to it. Often, this list, if present, is published at least once a year in the local newspaper.

Do not assume that all mentions of nonprofits in a newspaper are to be found on special association or group pages. By sampling pages and days of the week, one can identify additional groups through systematic sampling and content analysis. Be careful to list finally only those nonprofits that are in the community of focus; the boundaries of coverage geographically by a newspaper often are vague. Where territorial coverage of a nonprofit is unclear, this can be checked later by telephone in many cases. Consider a GA as located in whatever town has the largest plurality of members in that GA, irrespective of other evidence suggesting alternative locations. Content analyzing newspapers is labor intensive, but in the experience of myself and others, it is more efficient than full-scale ethnography and is quite effective, especially in identifying volunteer (rather than paid-staff) nonprofits.

b. *Find local or local-coverage radio stations and seek their records or copies of "public service announcements."* These public service announcements (PSAs) are brief announcements of nonprofit organization activities made over the air by station announcers reading notes or cards sent in by nonprofits, usually GAs. They are more frequent in smaller towns or cities than in larger cities. If you can find a box or basket of these PSA cards at a radio station, it can be very helpful, especially with contact people and addresses. There are fewer of these PSAs now than before the U.S. government deregulation of radio stations during the early 1980s, but they still can be a useful source of information on volunteer and other nonprofits.

Strategy 3: Telephone Directories

a. *Search the local yellow pages from the telephone company under categories that are likely to yield nonprofits.* For example, seek nonprofits under categories such as associations, churches, clubs, fraternal organizations, labor organizations, and social and human services.[1] The organizations so identified, like many others identified by other methods, need to be screened individually or on a sampling basis to determine whether they are in fact nonprofits. Businesses can work their way into some of these and other categories.

b. *Seek in the white (regular) pages of the telephone book for entities listed in all capital letters and/or boldface type, screening for nonprofits with addresses in the target community (in urban areas, single telephone books cover many localities).* In very large cities, one may sample pages systematically and use estimation procedures to determine how many additional nonprofits might be in one's frame. There will be many businesses appearing in this source. Most can be identified as businesses by their names and can be omitted (e.g., "Rudy's Cleaners"). Possible nonprofits should be included and later screened as noted earlier. This tactic is tedious and time-consuming but necessary.

Strategy 4: Government General Lists of Nonprofits

a. *Try to obtain a computerized listing of nonprofits in 501(c)(3) and 501(c)(4) categorizations from the IRS.* These now are generally available for a fee. If these cannot be obtained or afforded, then use the latest cumulative list of organizations issued by this source (U.S. Department of the Treasury, 1979, is an earlier version). Do not assume that this source is complete. It overlooks many smaller, newer, low-budget volunteer nonprofits and most religious nonprofits (Smith, 1997d).

b. *Try to obtain a computerized list of nonprofits from U.S. state authorities that register nonprofits as part of the state incorporation procedure.* Typically, this information is kept by the Office of the Secretary of State. Such lists seldom are published. Some states still keep the information on index cards, I am told. As with the IRS information, this type of nonprofit organization list overlooks many unincorporated, smaller, newer, low-budget, semiformal, or religious volunteer nonprofits.

c. *At the town or city hall, ask to see (or have a copy of) the list of tax-exempt nonprofit property on the tax rolls.* This list of organizations consists of the wealthier nonprofits that are able to own real property and often buildings to meet in and use as headquarters. Sometimes, counties in the United States might have similar or even broader lists.

d. *At the town or city hall or post office, ask about the full list of nonprofits that are entitled to have their own tax-exempt mailing bulk rate numbers.*

Strategy 5: Interviews

Extensive interviewing is quite expensive, especially if viewed from the perspective of number of new nonprofits identified per interview. Nonetheless, this approach has some special advantages in identifying smaller, more informal volunteer nonprofits in a locality.

a. *Using Strategies 3(a), 3(b), and 4(c), identify the likely public meeting places for nonprofits (especially volunteer nonprofits) in the community.* Then, seek information through telephone or in-person interviews on what groups actually have met there during the past 12 months. The latter process involves many telephone calls and some in-person visits to meeting sites. In larger places, this can be done on a sampling basis. Some examples of probable meeting places include churches and synagogues, libraries, schools, veterans organizations, historical societies, and fraternal organizations. Every nonprofit identified in Strategy 4(c) should be checked as a meeting place on a random sampling basis, if necessary. For schools, officials should be queried regarding both student and parent groups as well as volunteer programs. For churches, one should ask about church-related as well as nonmember groups meeting at the churches, differentiating integral from nonintegral church-related groups (Smith, 1996).

b. *Key informants in the locality (e.g., nonprofit leaders, local government leaders) can be interviewed regarding the nonprofits with which they are familiar or to which they belong.* Local leaders tend to belong to many more volunteer nonprofits than does the average person in the community and, hence, can be a richer source of new nonprofits per interview than can the average citizen. However, even if such leaders are sampled carefully, it is difficult to know how many nonprofits one still might be missing when finished with key informants.

c. *Interview a representative sample of community residents regarding nonprofits they know, either as a separate process or as part of the initial interviews you perform in the community for some other related purpose.* This method shows diminishing returns, but 30 to 50 interviews of this sort can be useful in smaller places (more in larger cities), if only to confirm data from other sources. This tactic can be most sensitive to smaller, poorer, newer, less formal GAs, unlike most other tactics. It is especially effective if done on a careful, representative area-sampling basis, as discussed by Gronbjerg (1989, pp. 77-78) and performed by McPherson (1982). The drawbacks of depending solely on this method are that it fractionates real nonprofit groups in the data collection process and generally substitutes a random member of any group as an informant in place of a leader who is a preferred informant. I believe that identifying the nonprofits first, sampling from a reasonably complete list, and then interviewing leaders (preferably two or more for each nonprofit) is methodologically preferable. Hence, I recommend the present community sampling and interviewing of individuals as an auxiliary rather than the central method.

Strategy 6: Special Lists

In addition to general lists, *one can find lists of specific types of nonprofits* such as in human resource directories, human services directories, "people's yellow pages" (alternative social change-oriented directories), information and referral service directories or card files/computer files, environmental group lists, health-related agency lists, arts and cultural organization lists, ethnic group/minority group lists, community/ethnic housing/economic development group lists, educational institution/group lists, church lists, foundation lists, and trade union lists (most of the forgoing types are taken from Gronbjerg, 1989). Also, one can obtain a list of groups participating in any major local celebrations, parades, and so on from the town or city hall or from the sponsoring organization, if not the local government. This source might be unavailable but is useful if present.

Gronbjerg (1989) suggests examining official registration and license listings, if any, for nonprofits; seeking grant and contract listings for several years from public agencies, foundations, and councils; and using membership lists from coalitions, networks, and task forces. These might turn up some volunteer-run groups as well as paid-staff nonprofits. For all or a sampling of local banks, one might be able to obtain a listing of accounts that are owned by nonprofit organizations, especially associations. The amount of the account usually is private, but the existence or name of the account might not be. This source is very useful but often is hard to obtain, especially in cities. One may similarly seek a list of post office boxes in a locality, some of which will be rented by nonprofits. One can try to obtain a complete list of nonprofit organization mailing permits from the post office. All of these special list procedures tend to be more haphazard in coverage and time-consuming to use than are the general lists. In European nations, lists of post office bank accounts might be available. Finally, lists of community nonprofits can be obtained from high schools and colleges that have community service programs and place students in volunteer work in these groups (Raskoff and Sundeen, 1998).

CLEANING THE DATA

For all of the forgoing strategies, attention must be given to eliminating duplicates with similar names because of typographical errors, mistakes of hearing or memory, incomplete names, and names that do or do not use a locality (or church, school, etc.) name as a preface (e.g., Lions Club vs. Boston Lions Club). One also must try to catch major name changes. For example, the Association of Voluntary Action Scholars changed its name to the Association for Research on Nonprofit Organizations and Voluntary Action several years ago; it should not be counted twice in any national count of U.S. nonprofits. One also must strive to eliminate "dead" nonprofits by seeking evidence of some activity, as by self-addressed return postcards. Businesses and government agencies also must be eliminated from the final list. This can be very difficult. In most cases the names are indicative, but not necessarily. For example, Council on Aging might be a government agency, or it might be a nonprofit; the name is not indicative. When names are not indicative, phone calls can help, but profit-seeking firms often do not like to admit to this status if they are trying to pass as nonprofits (Gronbjerg, 1989). Checking with the IRS or state corporation records can help, and for larger businesses, there are standard commercial directories such as Standard & Poor's (1999). Sometimes, the people to whom one speaks at a nonprofit are genuinely uncertain whether they are a nonprofit or a government agency. A discussion of the nonprofit's funding and tax filing status might clarify this; a nonprofit that depends on a single long-term government contract for most of its revenues might confuse its workers regarding government versus nonprofit status. Gronbjerg's (1989, pp. 65-67) comments should be consulted on all of this.

OTHER COUNTRIES

There is not a great deal of literature on identifying and counting nonprofits elsewhere any more than there is in the United States. Salamon and Anheier (1994; see also Salamon, Anheier, and Associates, 1998) have made the largest and most systematic effort in this regard as part of their major project with many others. Even where smaller studies of towns or cities in other nations exist, they often are sketchy in their descriptions of how sampling frames were created (Drake, 1972; Koldewyn, 1984, 1986). Yet the meager literature extant suggests that the methods suggested here have some applicability beyond the United States.

In some countries, such as France (Lanfant, 1976; Meister, 1972a) and Malaysia (Douglas, 1972), existing official registries (Strategy 4) of volunteer associations at one government level or another greatly facilitate creating a sampling frame. In such nations, the first priority strategy becomes the use of good general government lists (lists far more complete than those in the United States). Even in these countries, however, supplementary methods must be used for completeness (Lanfant, 1976). When systematic government registry is lacking or very incomplete (as in the United States), other systematic sources might permit creation of a reasonable sampling frame using methods suggested earlier. For example, Meister (1972a) used an annual post office list of postal bank accounts (Strategy 6) to identify most associations in Geneva, Switzerland. However, this source omits smaller groups without such accounts and groups with accounts held in the names of treasurers rather than in the names of the groups. In Birmingham, England, Newton (1975) found his more than 4,000 associations using general and special lists (Strategies 1 and 6). Hatch (1980), studying social and environmental service associations in three towns/cities in England, successfully used methods similar to Strategies 1 and 2.

Societal parameters will affect both the prevalence of volunteer nonprofits and the problem of creating a sampling frame that properly includes them. Most important are freedom of association and assembly. If these are denied, as in totalitarian states, then GAs usually are few or are controlled by the government (blurring sector distinctions). GAs that exist independently tend to be underground and are, hence, very hard to find. In democratic societies with functioning civil liberties, GAs tend to be much more frequent per 1,000 population and easier to study in principle, although they are more resource-consuming to study because of their larger numbers. Freedom of religion and lack of a state church has a similar effect on general civil liberties, as do greater societal decentralization, social heterogeneity, and population size: There is a greater prevalence of GAs, making them easier to study but requiring more resources (Smith, 1973c; Smith and Baldwin, 1983).

CONCLUSION

A comprehensive sampling frame for nonprofits in a community can be created by combining the results of a variety of strategies. It is useful to keep track of which independent sources mention which nonprofits, computing overall percentage estimates of completeness. Special attention is given here to including member benefit nonprofits (vs. only nonmember benefit nonprofits) and volunteer nonprofits or GAs (vs. only paid-staff nonprofits), which often are ignored in spite of their collective importance (Smith, 1997a). *Failure to include volunteer-run nonprofits results in underestimating the true number of nonprofits in a territory by at least a factor of 5 times and quite possibly 10 times*—a gross underestimate (see Chapter 2). The result sought here is a sampling frame for nonprofits in a community that is more truly representative of the actual population of nonprofits, so that research generalizations based on samples from it can be more valid and reliable. The strategies used can be adapted for larger places, in some cases seeking data on a sampling basis rather than on a comprehensive census basis.

Multiple method strategies for creating a nonprofit sampling frame with special attention to the inclusion of volunteer nonprofits have shown promise when used outside the United States. However, much research effort is involved in creating a good sampling frame, even in societies where there is some registration of associations. Just as those who study paid-staff nonprofits tend to ignore volunteer nonprofits, those studying volunteer nonprofits tend to ignore paid-staff nonprofits in the United States and elsewhere. These two important segments of the nonprofit sector need to be sampled together in a comprehensive fashion if one desires to generalize about nonprofits.

Each of the various strategies noted here has its advantages and disadvantages. Strategy 1, general lists, has the advantage of simplifying one's work if a fairly complete list can be located. However, it might be very incomplete indeed, as is an IRS nonprofit listing for an area (Dale, 1993; Gronbjerg, 1989, 1994). Strategy 2, mass media sources, gives a lot of fine detail but is very time-consuming. It omits smaller and less publicly visible nonprofits. Strategy 3, telephone directories, also is time-consuming but is the easiest way in which to identify religious groups systematically missing from some other sources such as the IRS nonprofit listings. Strategy 4, government lists/data, can be easy but costly to access and tends to be very biased toward wealthier and more established nonprofits. Strategy 5, interviews, is strongly favored by some for its coverage of smaller nonprofit groups and for its potential randomness and generalizability. However, it is expensive and insufficient for studying any given group well because it does not let one speak to many nonprofit leaders directly. Strategy 6 has a haphazard quality to it and does not permit good estimation of what nonprofits are missing. However, if done fairly systematically, it is part of a good comprehensive strategy and can be relatively inexpensive.

I recommend that researchers in the United States use the suggested strategies in the order presented, going as far as resources will permit. I further recommend that research resources be spread over several, and preferably all, of the six strategies noted rather than being concentrated in one or two strategies (as others have done). This permits cross-checking the data from different sources and will yield a better estimate of how good any given source is. Statistically, the greater the overlap of two or more reasonably independent sources of information on existing nonprofits, the better these sources are and the fewer additional nonprofits are likely to be "out there" unnoticed. The less overlap there is, the poorer the sources are and the more nonprofits are likely to be missing from one's composite list.[2] More resources are needed to create a reasonable sampling frame in a big city than in a small town, but there are economies of scale in regard to some methods (e.g., long lists might cost about the same to obtain as do short ones) but not others (e.g., use of telephone directories, although sampling them will help limit costs).

Overall, the multistrategy approach seems superior to any single source, if only because multiple sources permit a more reliable estimate of the number of nonprofits *missing* from one's sampling frame. Multiple strategies also increase one's confidence in the existence of any given nonprofit in one's final composite list if its existence is suggested by two or more independent sources. Generalizations about the nonprofit sector should be based on valid and reasonably representative samples, not heavily biased ones such as IRS listings in the United States. We have gone past the initial stage of research on nonprofits when scholars could be forgiven for their use of convenient but inadequate data such as IRS listings. Higher standards of representativeness and completeness of sampling now must apply.

Notes

1. Other categories that often include nonprofits are abortion alternatives, abortion services, adoption services, alcohol information and treatment centers, art instruction and schools, arts organizations and information, athletic organizations, birth control information centers, chambers of commerce, child care centers, clinics, consumer cooperative organizations, cooperative organizations, credit unions, environmental-conservation and ecology organizations, family planning information centers, foundations, hospices, hospitals, humane societies, libraries (can be nonprofits even though they are funded by local government), mental health services, museums, nursing homes, professional organizations, religious organizations, rest homes, retirement homes, retreat facilities, schools (all types), senior citizen service organizations, veterans' and military organizations, youth organizations and centers.

2. In a personal communication, a statistician colleague (Paul Holland) suggested that a rough estimate of the completeness of a sampling frame or composite list (as in making a complete census) can be estimated as the product of the total number of elements in two independently derived lists used to create that frame, all divided by the number of overlapping elements present in both lists. When two such independent lists overlap completely, the composite list from the two sources is estimated as complete. When there is no overlap of such lists, the estimated larger universe of elements is estimated as infinite (dividing by zero) or at least very large. Usually, lists of similar things from a given territory have some overlap, and the estimate of the total universe of elements is finite but larger than one's composite list. By taking the number of elements in one's composite list divided by the estimate of the larger universe from the list overlap, one can compute the current extent of completeness of one's composite list. Two or more independent lists can be combined, and successive approximations of the total universe can be computed using subsequent independent lists/sources. This approach is very useful in creating a local nonprofit sampling frame because it gives a reasonable, if rough, estimate of how well one is doing and when it might be reasonable to stop one's sampling frame work (e.g., stopping with an estimated 80% or 90% completeness). If one is seeking to create a sampling frame or census of a specific type of nonprofit, then one should overlap "purified" lists that are thought by inspection of their names to deal with the purposive type of nonprofit of interest. If a list obtained from somewhere already is "pure" in the sense of containing, say, only health nonprofits or only self-help GAs, then no further purification might be necessary. However, if one obtains a broader list of nonprofits for the territory of concern, then the non-health-related or non-self-help-related groups would have to be deleted to get a purified list, which can then be overlapped with other independent lists of that same type of nonprofit entity. The resulting estimate of the nonprofit universe refers to that purposive type only, not to all nonprofits in the given territory.

APPENDIX C

Methodology of the Smith One-Suburb Study

The site of this study was a small, middle-class bedroom suburb of Boston with a population between 10,000 and 20,000. The town was chosen because preliminary inquiry suggested that there was a wide variety of both nonmember and member benefit nonprofits present and because of geographical convenience for fieldwork.

The first phase of the fieldwork involved creating a sampling frame of all the nonprofit voluntary groups in town (see Appendix B). This included tactics such as consulting the town clerk for a list of groups; obtaining the list of nonprofit tax-exempt properties in town; asking managers of meeting places in town about groups that met there; talking to church, school, and library leaders about their affiliated groups and other groups that met there; examining the white and yellow pages of local telephone directories; and talking to initial interviewees about groups they knew in town.

As the list of groups lengthened, I made telephone calls to groups that looked as though they might be businesses or parts of the local government, verifying their status. Sometimes, I was misled until a later point of contact. Occasionally, there were duplicates that I had to catch, owing to similar but different names given by different informants for the same group (e.g., Couples Club vs. Mr. and Mrs. Club).

The initial focus of the research was on the differences between public and member benefit groups. Thus, soon after I started on the sampling frame, I began to try to classify the groups as public versus private benefit in nature. I quickly found that I needed a middle category of mixed benefit groups for either uncertainty or verified mixture of aims. I made calls to a number of mixed benefit groups so as to verify proper classification. No attempt was made to call all mixed category groups. Groups also were classified as probable paid staff (at least one hour per week) or probable without paid staff. This low threshold of paid staff status reflects the generally small size and income of local groups. Such a threshold did not turn out to be meaningful in the data analysis, so that I now recommend a threshold of roughly one full-time equivalent in a grassroots association (GA) (see Chapters 1 and 2).

Using the sampling frame as it existed about a week before the start of interviewing, a stratified sample was drawn as follows. A total of 19 groups were randomly selected, if available, from each of the three group type categories (public benefit, mixed, and member benefit), and each set of 19 was further stratified into 12 without paid staff and 7 with some paid staff (at least one hour per week). Because of difficulties in ascertaining accurate classification on initial contact and the desire not to discard interviews once conducted, the final sample of groups looked like Appendix Table C-1. In the category that has only 10 all-volunteer public benefit groups, there were no more in town to sample.

When a group leader was interviewed who indicated facts suggesting that the group belonged in a different category, the group was transferred there, even though this had some negative effect on the stratified random sample. The aim was to obtain a sample that varied in purposive type and, to some extent, in paid-staff presence while being as random as one could make it under the circumstances of time and effort. No attempt is made to weight the sampling categories according to the size of the categories in the total sampling frame. Some disguised examples for the various sampling categories are as follows:

All-volunteer public benefit:	Group to help an established nonprofit organization operate
Some paid-staff public benefit:	Foundation
All-volunteer mixed benefit:	Parent group helping students in some way (fund-raising)
Some paid-staff mixed benefit:	Student group that significantly involves both personal and public benefit
All-volunteer member benefit:	Non-school-based youth sports group
Some paid-staff member benefit:	Trade union

Interviews were the primary means of data collection—partly qualitative, partly quantitative. There was a slight preponderance of quantitative over

APPENDIX TABLE C-1 Sampled Groups by Categories ($N = 59$)

	Public Benefit	Mixed	Member Benefit
All-volunteer	10	13	14
Some paid staff	7	6	9
Total	17	19	23

open-ended or qualitative questions in the interview schedule, but unplanned qualitative questions that were not in the interview occasionally were pursued. The interviews were made with a sample of 59 GA leaders in town and lasted about an hour (median = 60 minutes). The leaders were the top officials of their respective groups, with the exception of two rather leaderless groups. Sometimes, one of two co-leaders was interviewed, but never both. The leaders were chosen because they were the current official leaders of groups that fell into the GA sample.

A total of 198 nonprofits were identified circa 1991. A nonprofit was identified by me at that time as a group (Smith, 1967) with a nondistribution constraint (Hansmann, 1980), autonomous of government (Salamon, 1992), reasonably autonomous of other groups (Smith, 1994b), and not based mainly on kinship or marriage (Smith, 1991). Legal incorporation, let alone Internal Revenue Service registration as 501(c)(3) or 501(c)(4), was unnecessary for inclusion because these are legal/administrative distinctions, not reasonable aspects of analytical social science definition. They are important distinctions but are far too limiting when studying volunteer-managed nonprofits. Semiformal groups (Smith, 1992b), as well as more formal organizations, were allowed into the sample for inclusiveness. This meant that member boundaries did not have to be clear and the leadership structure could be loose, but a unique and "proper" name was required. To be counted in the sampling frame, a nonprofit also had to have a plurality of its members thought to be living in the suburb, according to the leader's estimate.

References

Abbott, Andrew. 1988. *The System of Professions*. Chicago: University of Chicago Press.

Abel, Emily K. 1986. "The Hospice Movement: Institutionalizing Innovation." *International Journal of Health Services* 16:71-85.

Abell, Peter. 1989. "Games in Networks: A Sociological Theory of Voluntary Associations." *Rationality and Society* 1:258-82.

Ablon, J. 1981. "Dwarfism and Social Identity: Self-Help Group Participation." *Social Science and Medicine B* 15:25-30.

Adler, Margot. 1986. *Drawing Down the Moon*. Rev. ed. Boston: Beacon.

Adler, N. and K. Matthews. 1994. "Health Psychology: Why Do Some People Get Sick and Some Stay Well?" *Annual Review of Psychology* 45:229-59.

Adler, Peter. 1981. *Momentum: A Theory of Social Action*. Beverly Hills, CA: Sage.

Ahlbrandt, R. S., Jr. 1984. *Neighborhoods, People, and Community*. New York: Plenum.

Ahrne, Goran. 1992. "Outline of an Organizational Theory of Society." *Protosoziologie* 3:52-60.

Akers, Ronald and Frederick L. Campbell. 1970. "Size and Administrative Component in Occupational Associations." *Pacific Sociological Review* 13:241-51.

Alba, Richard. 1990. *Ethnic Identity: The Transformation of White America*. New Haven, CT: Yale University Press.

Aldrich, Howard. 1979. *Organizations and Environments*. Englewood Cliffs, NJ: Prentice Hall.

Alexander, Jeffrey C. 1987. "The Social Requisites for Altruism and Voluntarism: Some Notes on What Makes a Sector Independent." *Sociological Theory* 5:165-71.

Alinsky, S. D. 1969. *Reveille for Radicals*. New York: Vintage Books.

Allen, Susan M., Vincent Mor, John A. Fleishman, and John D. Piette. 1995. "The Organizational Transformation of Advocacy: Growth and Development of AIDS Community-Based Organizations." *AIDS and Public Policy Journal* 10:48-59.

Allen, William S. 1984. *The Nazi Seizure of Power*. New York: Franklin Watt.

Almond, Gabriel A. and Sidney Verba. 1963. *The Civic Culture: Political Attitudes and Democracy in Five Nations*. Princeton, NJ: Princeton University Press.

Amis, William D. and Samuel E. Stern. 1974. "A Critical Examination of Theory and Functions of Voluntary Associations." *Journal of Voluntary Action Research* 3:91-99.

Anderson, Joan B. and J. A. Colombo. 1988. "Christian Base Communities and Grassroots Development." *Journal of Behavioral Economics* 17:97-112.

Anderson, Robert T. 1964. "Voluntary Associations in Hyderabad." *Anthropological Quarterly* 37:175-90.

———. 1973. "Voluntary Associations in History: From Paleolithic to Present Times." Pp. 9-28 in *Voluntary Action Research: 1973,* edited by David H. Smith. Lexington, MA: Lexington Books.

Anheier, Helmut K. 1987. "Indigenous Voluntary Associations, Nonprofits, and Development in Africa." Pp. 416-33 in *The Nonprofit Sector,* edited by Walter W. Powell. New Haven, CT: Yale University Press.

Anheier, Helmut K. and W. Seibel. 1990. *The Third Sector: Comparative Studies of Nonprofit Organizations.* New York: Aldine de Gruyter.

Antze, P. 1976. "The Role of Ideologies in Peer Psychotherapy Organizations: Some Theoretical Considerations and Three Case Studies." *Journal of Applied Behavioral Science* 12:323-46.

Appel, Willa. 1983. *Cults in America.* New York: Holt.

Ardrey, R. 1966. *The Territorial Imperative.* New York: Dell.

Argyris, Chris. 1960. *Understanding Organizational Behavior.* Homewood, IL: Dorsey.

Association for Research on Nonprofit Organizations and Voluntary Action. 1999. *ARNOVA Membership Directory.* Indianapolis, IN: ARNOVA.

Auslander, Gail K. and Howard Litwin. 1988. "Sociability and Patterns of Participation: Implications for Social Service Policy." *Journal of Voluntary Action Research* 17:25-37.

Austin, D. M. 1991. "Community Context and Complexity of Organizational Structure in Neighborhood Organizations." *Administration and Society* 22:516-31.

Austin, D. M. and Cynthia Woolever. 1992. "Voluntary Association Boards: A Reflection of Member and Community Characteristics?" *Nonprofit and Voluntary Sector Quarterly* 21:181-93.

Azrin, N. H., T. Flores, and S. J. Kaplan. 1975. "Job Finding Club: A Group Assisted Program for Obtaining Employment." *Behavior Research and Therapy* 13:17-27.

Babchuk, N. and A. Schmidt. 1976. "Voluntary Associations, Social Change, and Racial Discrimination: An Analysis of Means and Ends." *Journal of Voluntary Action Research* 5:65-74.

Babchuk, Nicholas and John N. Edwards. 1965. "Voluntary Associations and the Integration Hypothesis." *Sociological Inquiry* 35:149-62.

Babchuk, Nicholas, Ruth Marsey, and C. W. Gordon. 1960. "Men and Women in Community Agencies: A Note on Power and Prestige." *American Sociological Review* 25:399-403.

Badelt, Christoph. 1987. "Altruismus, Egoismus, und Rationalitat" (Altruism, Egoism, and Rationality in Economics). *Kölner Zeitschrift für Soziologie und Sozialpsychologie* (Suppl. 28): 54-72.

———. 1989. "Government Versus Private Provision of Social Services: The Case of Austria." Pp. 152-76 in *The Nonprofit Sector in International Perspective,* edited by Estelle James. New York: Oxford University Press.

Bailey, Darlyne and Karren E. Grochau. 1993. "Aligning Leadership Needs to the Organizational Stage of Development: Applying Management Theory to Nonprofit Organizations." *Administration in Social Work* 17:23-45.

Bailey, R., Jr. 1974. *Radicals in Urban Politics.* Chicago: University of Chicago Press.

Baltzell, E. Digby. [1958] 1979. *Philadelphia Gentlemen: The Making of a National Upper Class.* Philadelphia: University of Pennsylvania Press.

Bania, Neil, Elizabeth H. Katona, and Jenny Keiser-Ruemmele. 1995. "The Development of State-Level Nonprofit Databases." *Nonprofit Management and Leadership* 5:317-25.

Barber, Benjamin R. 1984. *Strong Democracy: Participatory Politics for a New Age.* Berkeley: University of California Press.

Barber, Bernard. 1987. "Participation and Mass Apathy in Associations." In *Studies in Leadership*, edited by Alvin W. Gouldner. New York: Garland.

Barker, Eileen. 1984. *The Making of a Moonie*. New York: Blackwell.

Barker, Roger G. and Paul V. Gump. 1964. *Big School, Small School: High School Size and Student Behavior*. Stanford, CA: Stanford University Press.

Barton, Allen H. 1961. *Organizational Measurement*. New York: College Entrance Examination Board.

Batson, C. D. 1991. *The Altruism Question*. Hillsdale, NJ: Lawrence Erlbaum.

Bauer, Rudolph. 1990. "Voluntarism, Nongovernmental Organizations, and Public Policy in the Third Reich." *Nonprofit and Voluntary Sector Quarterly* 19:199-214.

Bauman, Paul. 1994. "Book Groups: Informal and Innovative Adult Learning." *Journal of Adult Education* 22:31-41.

Baumgartner, F. R. and J. R. Walker. 1988. "Survey Research and Membership in Voluntary Associations." *American Journal of Political Science* 32:908-28.

Beal, George M. 1956. "Additional Hypotheses in Participation Research." *Rural Sociology* 21:249-56.

Bearman, Peter and Kevin Everett. 1993. "The Structure of Social Protest, 1961-1983." *Social Networks* 15:171-200.

Beattie, M. 1990. *Codependents' Guide to the Twelve Steps*. New York: Simon & Schuster.

Becker, Howard S. 1963. *Outsiders: Studies in the Sociology of Deviance*. New York: Free Press.

Belyaeva, Nina. 1992. "The Independent Sector in the USSR: Formation, Purposes, and Effects." Pp. 349-71 in *The Nonprofit Sector in the Global Community*, edited by Kathleen D. McCarthy, Virginia A. Hodgkinson, Russy D. Sumariwalla, and Associates. San Francisco: Jossey-Bass.

Ben-Ner, A. and T. Van Hoomissen. 1990. "The Growth of the Nonprofit Sector in the 1980s: Facts and Interpretation." *Nonprofit Management and Leadership* 1:99-116.

———. 1991. "Nonprofit Organizations in the Mixed Economy: A Demand and Supply Analysis." *Annals of Public and Cooperative Economics* 62:519-50.

Ben-Zadok, Efraim and Leonard Kooperman. 1988. "Voluntary Associations in West Africa: A Political Perspective." *Community Development Journal* 23:74-85.

Bender, Eugene I. 1986. "The Self-Help Movement Seen in the Context of Social Development." *Journal of Voluntary Action Research* 15:77-84.

Bennett, James T. and Thomas J. DiLorenzo. 1989. *Unfair Competition: The Profits of Nonprofits*. New York: Hamilton.

———. 1994. *Unhealthy Charities: Hazardous to Your Health and Wealth*. New York: Basic Books.

Berger, P. L. and T. Luckmann. 1967. *The Social Construction of Reality*. Garden City, NY: Anchor Books.

Berry, Jeffrey M. 1997. *The Interest Group Society*. 3rd ed. New York: Addison-Wesley Longman.

Berry, Jeffrey M., Kent E. Pourtney, and Ken Thomson. 1993. *The Rebirth of Urban Democracy*. Washington, DC: Brookings Institution.

Bestor, Theodore C. 1985. "Tradition and Japanese Social Organization: Institutional Development in a Tokyo Neighborhood." *Ethnology* 24:121-35.

Biddle, Bruce J. 1979. *Role Theory*. New York: Academic Press.

Bielefeld, Wolfgang. 1992. "Funding Uncertainty and Nonprofit Strategies in the 1980s." *Nonprofit Management and Leadership* 2:381-401.

Bielefeld, Wolfgang and John J. Corbin. 1996. "The Institutionalization of Nonprofit Human Service Delivery: The Role of Political Culture." *Administration & Society* 28:362-89.

Billis, David. 1993a. *Organising Public and Voluntary Agencies*. London: Routledge and Kegan Paul.

———. 1993b. "Sector Blurring and Nonprofit Centers: The Case of the United Kingdom." *Nonprofit and Voluntary Sector Quarterly* 22:241-57.

Billis, David and Howard Glennerster. 1994. "Human Service Nonprofits: Towards a Theory of Comparative Advantage." Paper presented at the annual conference of the Association for Research on Nonprofit Organizations and Voluntary Action, San Francisco, October.

Bishop, Jeff and Paul Hoggett. 1986. *Organising Around Enthusiasms.* London: Comedia.

Blackstock, Nelson. 1976. *COINTELPRO: The FBI's Secret War on Political Freedom.* New York: Vintage Books.

Blair, Karen J. 1994. *The Torchbearers: Women and Their Amateur Arts Associations in America.* Bloomington: Indiana University Press.

Blau, Judith R., Kenneth C. Land, and Kent Redding. 1992. "The Extension of Religious Affiliation: An Explanation of the Growth of Church Participation in the United States." *Social Science Research* 21:329-52.

Blau, Peter M. and W. R. Scott. 1962. *Formal Organizations.* San Francisco: Chandler.

Block, Stephan R. 1987. "The Academic Discipline of Nonprofit Organization Management." Ph.D. dissertation, University of Colorado, Denver.

Blum, A. and I. Ragab. 1985. "Developmental Stages of Neighborhood Organizations." *Social Policy* 15:21-28.

Blumberg, Rhoda L. 1991. *Civil Rights: The 1960s Freedom Struggle.* Rev. ed. New York: Twayne.

Bodanske, E. A. 1972. "Training Design for Volunteers in Juvenile Court Services." *Volunteer Administration* 6:42-48.

Boles, Jacqueline. 1985. "The Administration of Voluntary Associations: A Course for the '80s." *Teaching Sociology* 12:193-207.

Boles, Janet K. 1994. "Local Feminist Policy Networks in the Contemporary American Interest Group System." *Policy Sciences* 27:161-78.

Boli, John. 1992. The Ties That Bind: The Nonprofit Sector and the State in Sweden." Pp. 240-53 in *The Nonprofit Sector in the Global Community,* edited by K. D. McCarthy, V. A. Hodgkinson, R. D. Sumariwalla, and Associates. San Francisco: Jossey-Bass.

Bolle de Bal, M. 1989. "At the Center of the Temple: An Experience of Reliance, or the Tribe Rediscovered." *Societies* 24:11-13.

Bolton, Elizabeth B. 1991. "Developing Local Leaders: Results of the Structured Learning Experience." *Journal of the Community Development Society* 22:119-43.

Bond, Meg A. and James G. Kelly. 1983. "Social Support and Efficacy in Advocacy Roles: A Case Study of Two Women's Organizations." *Issues in Mental Health Nursing* 5:173-92.

Booth, Alan. 1972. "Sex and Social Participation." *American Sociological Review* 37:183-93.

Borkman, Thomasina. 1976. "Experiential Knowledge: A New Concept for the Analysis of Self-Help Groups." *Social Services Review* 50:445-56.

Borst, D. and P. J. Montana. 1977. *Managing Nonprofit Organizations.* New York: AMACOM.

Boulding, Kenneth E. 1953. *The Organizational Revolution.* New York: Harper.

———. 1973. *Economy of Love and Fear: A Preface to Grants Economics.* Belmont, CA: Wadsworth.

Bowen, William G., Thomas I. Nygren, Sarah E. Turner, and Elizabeth A. Duffy. 1994. *The Charitable Nonprofits.* San Francisco: Jossey-Bass.

Boyte, Harry C. 1980. *The Backyard Revolution: Understanding the New Citizen Movement.* Philadelphia: Temple University Press.

———. 1984. *Community Is Possible: Repairing America's Roots.* New York: Harper Colophon.

Bradburn, N. M. 1969. *The Structure of Psychological Well-Being.* Chicago: Aldine.

Bradburn, N. M. and D. Caplovitz. 1965. *Reports on Happiness.* Chicago: Aldine.

Bradshaw, C., S. Soifer, and L. Gutierrez. 1994. "Toward a Hybrid Model for Effective Organizing in Communities of Color." *Journal of Community Practice* 1:25-41.

Bradshaw, Pat, Vic Murray, and Jacob Wolpin. 1992. "Do Nonprofit Boards Make a Difference? An Exploration of the Relationships Among Board Structure, Process, and Effectiveness." *Nonprofit and Voluntary Sector Quarterly* 21:227-49.

Breault, M. and M. King. 1993. *Inside the Cult.* New York: Penguin.

Bremner, Robert H. 1960. *American Philanthropy.* Chicago: University of Chicago Press.

Brill, H. 1971. *Why Organizers Fail: The Story of a Rent Strike.* Berkeley: University of California Press.

Brilliant, Eleanor. 1990. *The United Way.* New York: Columbia University Press.

Broadbridge, Adelina and Suzanne Horne. 1996. "Volunteers in Charity Retailing: Recruitment and Training." *Nonprofit Management and Leadership* 6:255-70.

Brody, E. 1996. "Agents Without Principals: The Economic Convergence of the Nonprofit and For-Profit Organizational Forms." *New York Law School Law Review* 40:457-536.

Brokensha, David. 1974. " 'Maximum Feasible Participation' (U.S.A.)." *Community Development Journal* 9:17-27.

Brown, Diane R., Lawrence E. Gary, Angela D. Greene, and Norweeta G. Milburn. 1992. "Patterns of Social Affiliation as Predictors of Depressive Symptoms Among Urban Blacks." *Journal of Health and Social Behavior* 33:242-53.

Brown, Eleanor. 1999. "Assessing the Value of Volunteers." *Nonprofit and Voluntary Sector Quarterly* 28:3-17.

Brown, Lawrence A. and Susan G. Philliber. 1977. "The Diffusion of a Population-Related Innovation: The Planned Parenthood Affiliate." *Social Science Quarterly* 58:215-28.

Brown, Richard D. 1973. "The Emergence of Voluntary Associations in Massachusetts, 1760-1830." *Journal of Voluntary Action Research* 2:64-73.

Browne, William P. 1988. *Private Interests, Public Policy, and American Agriculture.* Lawrence: University of Kansas Press.

Bruce, Ian. 1994. *Meeting Need: Successful Charity Marketing.* Hempel Hempstead, UK: ICSA Publishing.

Brudney, Jeffrey L. 1990. *Fostering Volunteer Programs in the Public Sector.* San Francisco: Jossey-Bass.

Brudney, J. L. and M. M. Brown. 1990. "Training in Volunteer Administration: Assessing the Needs of the Field." *Journal of Volunteer Administration* 9:21-28.

Bruyn, Severyn T. 1977. *The Social Economy: People Transforming American Business.* New York: John Wiley.

Bryman, Alan. 1996. "Leadership in Organizations." Pp. 276-92 in *Handbook of Organization Studies,* edited by S. R. Clegg, C. Hardy, and W. Nord. London: Sage.

Bryman, Alan, David Gillingswater, and Ian McGuinness. 1992. "Decision-Making Processes in Community Transport Organisations: A Comparative Case Study of Service Providers." *Voluntas* 3:71-87.

Burns, James M. 1978. *Leadership.* New York: Harper & Row.

Burt, Sandra. 1990. "Canadian Women's Groups in the 1980's: Organizational Development and Policy Influence." *Canadian Public Policy* 16:17-28.

Burwell, N. Yolanda. 1995. "Lawrence Oxley and Locality Development: Black Self-Help in North Carolina, 1925-1928." *Journal of Community Practice* 2:49-69.

Bush, Richard. 1992. "Survival of the Nonprofit Spirit in a For-Profit World." *Nonprofit and Voluntary Sector Quarterly* 21:391-410.

Bushee, Frederick A. 1945. "Social Organization in a Small City." *American Journal of Sociology* 51:217-26.

Butler, R. and D. Wilson. 1990. *Managing Voluntary and Nonprofit Organisations.* London: Routledge.

Cable, Sherry and Beth Degutis. 1997. "Measurement Outcomes of Local Mobilizations." *Current Sociology* 45:121-35.

Caplow, Theodore. 1957. "Organizational Size." *Administrative Science Quarterly* 1:484-505.

———. 1964. *Principles of Organizations.* New York: Harcourt Brace Jovanovich.

Carden, Maren L. 1969. *Oneida: Utopian Community to Modern Corporation.* Baltimore, MD: Johns Hopkins University Press.

Carr, Gordon. 1975. *The Angry Brigade.* London: Gollancz.

Carter, April. 1974. *Direct Action and Liberal Democracy.* New York: Harper Torchbooks.

Carver, J. 1997. *Boards That Make a Difference: A New Design for Leadership in Nonprofit and Public Organizations.* 2nd ed. San Francisco: Jossey-Bass.

Caserta, M. S. and D. A. Lund. 1993. "Intrapersonal Resources and the Effectiveness of Self-Help Groups for Bereaved Older Adults." *The Gerontologist* 33:619-29.

Caulkins, D. D. 1976. "A Note on the Prevalence of Voluntary Associations in Two Norwegian Provinces." *Journal of Voluntary Action Research* 5:155-59.

Chan, Cristina and Sonali Rammohan. 1999. *Flying Under the Radar: The Significant Work of All-Volunteer Organizations.* San Francisco: Support Center for Nonprofit Management/NDC.

Chapin, F. S. and John E. Tsouderos. 1956. "The Formalization Process in Voluntary Associations." *Social Forces* 34:342-44.

Charles, Jeffrey A. 1993. *Service Clubs in American Society: Rotary, Kiwanis, and Lions.* Urbana: University of Illinois Press.

Chatfield, C. 1992. *The American Peace Movement.* New York: Twayne.

Chesler, M. A. 1991. "Mobilizing Consumer Activism in Health Care: The Role of Self-Help Groups." *Research in Social Movements Conflicts and Change* 13:275-305.

Chesler, Mark A., Barbara Chesney, and Benjamin Gidron. 1990. "Israeli and U.S. Orientations Toward Self-Help Groups for Families in Crisis." *Nonprofit and Voluntary Sector Quarterly* 19:251-63.

Chinman, Matthew J. and Abraham Wandersman. 1999. "The Benefits and Costs of Volunteering in Community Organizations: Review and Practical Implications." *Nonprofit and Voluntary Sector Quarterly* 28:46-64.

Chrislip, David E. and Carl E. Larson. 1994. *Collaborative Leadership.* San Francisco: Jossey-Bass.

Christian, Jim. 1980-81. "Using 'Outside Resource People' in Community-Based Organizations." *Journal of Alternative Human Services* 6:15-19.

Chutis, Laurie Ann. 1983. "Special Roles of Mental Health Professionals in Self-Help Group Development." *Prevention in Human Services* 2:65-73.

Clark, Elmer T. 1937. *The Small Sects in America.* Rev. ed. New York: Abingdon Press.

Clark, John. 1991. *Democratizing Development: The Role of Voluntary Organizations.* West Hartford, CT: Kumarian Press.

Clark, Peter B. and James Q. Wilson. 1961. "Incentive Systems: A Theory of Organizations." *Administrative Science Quarterly* 6:129-66.

Clary, E. G. 1987. "Social Support as a Unifying Concept in Voluntary Action." *Journal of Voluntary Action Research* 16:58-68.

Clawson, Mary A. 1989. *Constructing Brotherhood: Class, Gender, and Fraternalism.* Princeton, NJ: Princeton University Press.

Cnaan, Ram A. 1991. "Neighborhood-Representing Organizations: How Democratic Are They?" *Social Service Review* 65:614-34.

Cnaan, Ram A., Femida Handy, and Margaret Wadsworth. 1996. "Defining Who Is a Volunteer: Conceptual and Empirical Considerations." *Nonprofit and Voluntary Sector Quarterly* 25:364-83.

Coakes, Sheridan J. and Brian J. Bishop. 1996. "The Experience of Moral Community in a Rural Community Context." *Journal of Community Psychology* 24:108-17.

Cohen, Jean L. 1992. *Civil Society in Political Theory.* Cambridge: MIT Press.

Cohen, Mark W. and Robert O. Ely. 1981. "Voluntary Associations as Resources for Neighborhood Problem-Solving." *Journal of Voluntary Action Research* 10:40-48.

Coleman, W. 1988. *Business and Politics: A Study of Collective Action.* Montreal: McGill-Queen's University Press.

Commission on Private Philanthropy and Public Needs. 1975. *Giving in America: Toward a Stronger Voluntary Sector.* Washington, DC: CPPPN.

Connors, Tracy D. 1988. *The Nonprofit Organization Handbook.* 2nd ed. New York: McGraw-Hill.

Conrad, W. R., Jr. and W. E. Glenn. 1983. *The Effective Voluntary Board of Directors.* Rev. ed. Athens, OH: Swallow Press.

Conway, M. M. 1991. *Political Participation in the United States.* 2nd ed. Washington, DC: Congressional Quarterly Press.

Cook, Annabel K., Robert E. Howell, and Ivan L. Weir. 1985. "Rural Leadership Programs and Changing Participation of Men and Women in Public Affairs." *Journal of the Community Development Society* 16:41-56.

Cook, Constance E. 1984. "Participation in Public Interest Groups: Membership Motivations." *American Politics Quarterly* 12:409-30.

Coombs, Gary. 1973. "Networks and Exchange: The Role of Social Relationships in a Small Voluntary Association." *Journal of Anthropological Research* 29:96-112.

Cope, T. and D. V. Kurtz. 1980. "Default and the Tanda: A Model Regarding Recruitment for Rotating Credit Associations." *Ethnology* 19:213-31.

Cornes, R. and T. Sandler. 1989. *The Theory of Externalities, Public Goods, and Club Goods.* Cambridge, UK: Cambridge University Press.

Cornuelle, Richard. 1965. *Reclaiming the American Dream.* New York: Vintage Books.

Corsino, Louis. 1985-86. "Campaign Organizations, Social Technology, and Apolitical Participation." *New Political Science* 14:141-55.

Coston, Jennifer. 1998. "A Model and Typology of Government-NGO Relationships." *Nonprofit and Voluntary Sector Quarterly* 27:358-82.

Coston, Jennifer M., Terry L. Cooper, and Richard A. Sundeen. 1993. "Response of Community Organizations to the Civil Unrest in Los Angeles." *Nonprofit and Voluntary Sector Quarterly* 22:357-73.

Covey, Herbert C., Scott Menard, and Robert J. Franzese. 1992. *Juvenile Gangs.* Springfield, IL: Charles C Thomas.

Cox, Craig. 1994. *Storefront Revolution: Food Co-ops and the Counterculture.* New Brunswick, NJ: Rutgers University Press.

Cress, Daniel M. 1997. "Nonprofit Incorporation Among Movements of the Poor: Pathways and Consequences for Homeless Social Movement Organizations." *Sociological Quarterly* 38:343-60.

Cress, Daniel M., J. Miller McPherson, and Thomas Rotolo. 1997. "Competition and Commitment in Voluntary Memberships: The Paradox of Persistence and Participation." *Sociological Perspectives* 40:61-79.

Crowder, N. L. and V. A. Hodgkinson. n.d. *Academic Centers and Programs Focusing on the Study of Philanthropy, Voluntarism, and Not-for-Profit Activities.* 3rd ed. Washington, DC: Independent Sector.

Cullinan, A. L. 1992. "The Impact of a Self-Help Group on Nurses and Their Dying Patients." Pp. 97-104 in *Self-Help: Concepts and Applications,* edited by Alfred H. Katz, Hannah L. Hedrick, Daryl H. Isenberg, and Associates. Philadelphia: Charles Press.

Curtis, James E. 1971. "Voluntary Association Joining: A Cross-National Comparative Note." *American Sociological Review* 36:872-80.

Curtis, James E., Steven D. Brown, Ronald D. Lambert, and Barry J. Kay. 1989. "On Lipset's Measurement of Voluntary Association Affiliation Differences Between Canada and the United States." *Canadian Journal of Sociology* 14:383-89.

Curtis, James E., Edward Grabb, and Douglas Baer. 1992. "Voluntary Association Membership in Fifteen Countries: A Comparative Analysis." *American Sociological Review* 57:139-52.

Curtis, Lynn A. 1987. "The Retreat of Folly: Some Modest Replications of Inner-City Success." *Annals of the American Academy of Political and Social Science* 494:71-89.

Cutler, Neal E. 1980. "Toward an Appropriate Typology for the Study of the Participation of Older Persons in Voluntary Associations." *Journal of Voluntary Action Research* 9:9-19.

———. 1981-82. "Voluntary Association Participation and Life Satisfaction: Replication, Revision, and Extension." *International Journal of Aging and Human Development* 14:127-37.

Cutler, S. J. 1976. "Membership in Different Types of Voluntary Associations and Psychological Well-Being." *The Gerontologist* 16:335-39.

Dale, H. 1993. "On Estimating the Size of the Non-Profit Sector in the U.S. Economy." *Voluntas* 4:183-89.

Daniels, Arlene K. 1988. *Invisible Careers: Women Civic Leaders From the Volunteer World.* Chicago: University of Chicago Press.

Danziger, J. N. 1983. "Group Influence in American County Politics." *Local Government Studies* 9:67-82.

Daraul, Arkon. 1965. *Secret Societies.* London: Tandem Books.

Davidson, H. 1979. "Development of a Bereaved Parents Group." Pp. 80-94 in *Self-Help Groups for Coping With Crisis,* edited by M. Lieberman, L. Borman, and Associates. San Francisco: Jossey-Bass.

Davies, J. C. I. 1966. *Neighborhood Groups and Urban Renewal.* New York: Columbia University Press.

Davis, J. A. and T. W. Smith. 1989. *The General Social Survey, 1972-1989: Cumulative Codebook.* Chicago: National Opinion Research Center.

Davis, James A. 1961. *Great Books and Small Groups.* New York: Free Press.

Davis-Smith, Justin. 1993. *Volunteering in Europe.* London: Volunteer Centre.

Dawkins, R. 1976. *The Selfish Gene.* New York: Oxford University Press.

Deacon, D. and P. Golding. 1991. "The Voluntary Sector in 'the Information Society': A Study in Division and Uncertainty." *Voluntas* 2:69-88.

Degler, Carl. 1980. *At Odds: Women and the Family in America From the Revolution to the Present.* New York: Oxford University Press.

DeGrazia, Alfred. 1957. *Grassroots Private Welfare.* New York: New York University Press.

Delgado, Gary. 1986. *Organizing the Movement: The Roots and Growth of ACORN.* Philadelphia: Temple University Press.

Delworth, Ursula, Marv Moore, Julie Millick, and Patrick Leone. 1974. "Training Student Volunteers." *Personnel and Guidance Journal* 53:57-61.

DeTocqueville, Alexis. [1845] 1945. *Democracy in America.* 2 vols. New York: Knopf.

DeVall, W. B. and Joseph Harry. 1975. "Associational Politics and Internal Democracy." *Journal of Voluntary Action Research* 4:90-97.

Devereux, Edward C., Jr. 1960. "Springdale and Its People." *Journal of Social Issues* 16 (4): 7-15.

DiMaggio, P. and W. W. Powell. 1983. "The Iron Cage Revisited: Institutional Isomorphism and Collective Rationality in Organizational Fields." *American Sociological Review* 82:147-60.

DiMaggio, Paul J. and Helmut K. Anheier. 1990. "The Sociology of Nonprofit Organizations and Sectors." *Annual Review of Sociology* 16:137-59.

Domhoff, G. W. 1974. *The Bohemian Grove and Other Retreats.* New York: Harper & Row.

———. 1983. *Who Rules America Now?* New York: Simon & Schuster.

Douglas, James. 1987. "Political Theories of Nonprofit Organizations." Pp. 43-54 in *The Nonprofit Sector,* edited by Walter W. Powell. New Haven, CT: Yale University Press.

Douglas, Stephen A. 1972. "Voluntary Associational Structure in Malaysia: Some Implications for Political Participation." *Journal of Voluntary Action Research* 1:24-37.

Dow, Greg K. and F. T. Juster. 1985. "Goods, Time, and Well-Being: The Joint Dependence Problem." Pp. 1-18 in *Time, Goods, and Well-Being,* edited by F. T. Juster and F. P. Stafford. Ann Arbor: University of Michigan Press.

Drabek, T. E. 1986. *Human System Responses to Disaster: An Inventory of Sociological Findings.* New York: Springer.

Drake, George F. 1972. "Social Class and Organizational Dynamics: A Study of Voluntary Associations in a Colombian City." *Journal of Voluntary Action Research* 1 (3): 46-52.

Droghe, D., P. Arnston, and R. Norton. 1986. "The Social Support Function in Epilepsy Self-Help Groups." *Small Group Behavior* 17:139-63.

Drucker, Peter F. 1990. *Managing the Non-Profit Organization.* New York: HarperCollins.

DuBow, Fred and Aaron Podolofsky. 1982. "Citizen Participation in Crime Prevention." *Human Organization* 41:307-14.

Duck, S. W. 1988. *Handbook of Personal Relationships.* Chichester, UK: Wiley.

Durkheim, Emile. 1964. *The Division of Labor in Society.* New York: Free Press.

Ehrlich, Blake. 1965. *Resistance: France, 1940-1945.* Boston: Little, Brown.

Elkin, Frederick. 1978. "Voluntary Associations at Different Territorial Levels." Paper presented at the Ninth World Congress of the International Sociological Association, Uppsala, Sweden, August.

Elkind, Pamela D. 1992. "Active Members in Nuclear Repository Issues Organizations: A Demographic Research Note." *Nonprofit and Voluntary Sector Quarterly* 21:95-104.

Ellis, Susan J. and Katherine H. Noyes. 1990. *By the People: A History of Americans as Volunteers.* Rev. ed. San Francisco: Jossey-Bass.

Emerick, Robert E. 1989. "Group Demographics in the Mental Health Patient Movement: Group Location, Age, and Size as Structural Factors." *Community Mental Health Journal* 25:277-300.

———. 1991. "The Politics of Psychiatric Self-Help: Political Factions, Interactional Support, and Group Longevity in a Social Movement." *Social Science and Medicine* 32:1121-28.

Emrick, C. D., J. S. Tonigan, H. Montgomery, and L. Little. 1993. "Alcoholics Anonymous: What Is Currently Known?" Pp. 41-76 in *Research on Alcoholics Anonymous: Opportunities and Alternatives,* edited by B. S. McCrady and W. R. Miller. New Brunswick, NJ: Center on Alcohol Studies.

Eriksson-Joslyn, K. 1973. "A Nation of Volunteers: Participatory Democracy or Administrative Manipulation?" *Berkeley Journal of Sociology* 74:159-81.

Esman, M. J. and N. T. Uphoff. 1984. *Local Organizations: Intermediaries in Local Development.* Ithaca, NY: Cornell University Press.

Estey, Martin. 1981. *Unions.* 3rd ed. San Diego: Harcourt Brace Jovanovich.

Etzioni, Amitai. 1961. *A Comparative Analysis of Complex Organizations.* New York: Free Press.

———. 1972. "The Untapped Potential of the Third Sector." *Business and Society Review* 1:39-44.

———. 1993. *The Spirit of Community: Rights, Responsibilities, and the Communitarian Agenda.* New York: Crown.

Etzioni, Amitai and Pamela Doty. 1976. "Profit in Not-for-Profit Corporations: The Example of Health Care." *Political Science Quarterly* 91:433-53.

Evers, Adalbert. 1995. "Part of the Welfare Mix: The Third Sector as an Intermediate Area." *Voluntas* 6:159-82.

Executive Office of the President and Office of Management and the Budget. 1987. *Standard Industrial Classification Manual.* Washington, DC: Office of Management and the Budget.

Fagan, Jeffrey. 1987. "Neighborhood Education, Mobilization, and Organization for Juvenile Crime Prevention." *Annals of the American Academy of Political and Social Science* 494:54-70.

Famighetti, Robert, ed. 1997. *World Almanac and Book of Facts, 1997.* Mahwah, NJ: World Almanac Publishers.

Farcau, Bruce W. 1994. *The Coup: Tactics in the Seizure of Power.* Westport, CT: Praeger.

Farrow, D. L., E. R. Valenzi, and B. M. Bass. 1980. "A Comparison of Leadership and Situational Characteristics Within Profit and Nonprofit Organizations." *Proceedings of the Academy of Management* 5:334-38.

Feld, Werner J., Robert S. Jordan, and Leon Hurwitz. 1994. *International Organizations.* 3rd ed. Westport, CT: Praeger.

Ferguson, Charles W. 1937. *Fifty Million Brothers: A Panorama of American Lodges and Clubs.* New York: Farrar, Straus & Giroux.

Fernandez, Roberto M. 1991. "Structural Bases of Leadership in Intraorganizational Networks." *Social Psychology Quarterly* 54:36-53.

Ferree, M. M. and B. B. Hess. 1995. *Controversy and Coalition: The New Feminist Movement.* Rev. ed. New York: Twayne.

Ferris, James M. 1993. "The Double-Edged Sword of Social Service Contracting: Public Accountability Versus Nonprofit Autonomy." *Nonprofit Management and Leadership* 3:363-76.

Fine, Gary A. and Lori Holyfield. 1996. "Secrecy, Trust, and Dangerous Leisure: Generating Group Cohesion in Voluntary Organizations." *Social Psychology Quarterly* 59:22-38.

Finke, R. and R. Stark. 1994. *The Churching of America.* New Brunswick, NJ: Rutgers University Press.

Finks, P. D. 1984. *The Radical Vision of Saul Alinsky.* New York: Paulist Press.

Finlinson, Rachel. 1995. "A Survey of Grassroots Advocacy Organizations for Nursing Home Residents." *Journal of Elder Abuse and Neglect* 7:75-91.

Fischer, C. S. 1982. *To Dwell Among Friends: Personal Networks in Town and City.* Chicago: University of Chicago Press.

Fisher, James C. and Kathleen M. Cole. 1993. *Leadership and Management of Volunteer Programs; A Guide for Volunteer Administrators.* San Francisco: Jossey-Bass.

Fisher, Julie. 1984. "Development From Below: Neighborhood Improvement Associations in the Latin American Squatter Settlements." *Studies in Comparative International Development* 19:61-85.

———. 1993. *The Road From Rio: Sustainable Development and the Nongovernmental Movement in the Third World.* Westport, CT: Praeger.

———. 1998. *Nongovernments: NGOs and the Political Development of the Third World.* West Hartford, CT: Kumarian Press.

Fisher, Robert. 1994. *Let the People Decide: Neighborhood Organizing in America.* Rev. ed. New York: Twayne.

Fiske, F. M. 1973. "The Elks: An American Ideology." *Journal of Voluntary Action Research* 2:135-47.

Flanagan, Joan. 1984. *The Successful Volunteer Organization.* Chicago: Contemporary Books.

Fletcher, Leonard P. 1985. "The Limitations of Management and the Decline of Friendly Societies in Trinidad and Tobago." *Journal of Voluntary Action Research* 14:30-44.

Foot, Michael R. D. 1976. *Resistance.* London: Methuen.

Fortmann, Louise. 1985. "Seasonal Dimensions of Rural Social Organization." *Journal of Development Studies* 21:377-89.

Freeman, David M. 1989. *Local Organizations for Social Development.* Denver, CO: Westview.

Freeman, Jo. 1975. *The Politics of Women's Liberation.* New York: David McKay.

Freudenberg, Nicholas. 1984. "Citizen Action for Environmental Health: Report on a Survey of Community Organizations." *American Journal of Public Health* 74:444-48.

Freudenberg, Nicholas and Carol Steinsapir. 1991. "Not in Our Backyards: The Grassroots Environmental Movement." *Society and Natural Resources* 4:235-45.

Friedman, Robert R., Paul Florin, Abraham Wandersman, and Ron Meier. 1988. "Local Action on Behalf of Local Collectives in the U.S. and Israel: How Different Are Leaders From Members in Voluntary Associations?" *Journal of Voluntary Action Research* 17:36-54.

Frisby, Wendy. 1985. "A Conceptual Framework for Measuring the Organizational Structure and Context of Voluntary Leisure Service Organizations." *Society and Leisure* 8:605-13.

Frizzell, Alan and E. Zureik. 1974. "Voluntary Participation: The Canadian Perspective." Pp. 253-76 in *Voluntary Action Research: 1974,* edited by David H. Smith. Lexington, MA: Lexington Books.

Frohlich, Dieter. 1978. "Innerbetriebliche Arbeitssituation und Teilnahme an Freiwilligen Vereinigungen" (Work Experience and Participation in Voluntary Associations). *Zeitschrift für Soziologie* 7:56-71.

Fuller, Lon L. 1969. "Two Principles of Human Associations." Pp. 45-57 in *Voluntary Associations,* edited by J. R. Pennock and J. W. Chapman. New York: Atherton.

Gamson, William A. 1990. *The Strategy of Social Protest.* 2nd ed. Belmont, CA: Wadsworth.

Gamwell, Franklin I. 1984. *Beyond Preference: Liberal Theories of Independent Association.* Chicago: University of Chicago Press.

Gandhi, Raj S. 1978. "The Social Functions of Caste Associations and the Possibility of Their Transformation Into Voluntary Associations." Paper presented at the Ninth World Congress of the International Sociological Association, Uppsala, Sweden, August.

Garfield, Richard M. and Sten H. Vermund. 1986. "Health Education and Community Participation in Mass Drug Administration for Malaria in Nicaragua." *Social Science and Medicine* 22:869-77.

Gartner, Alan and Frank Riessman. 1984. *The Self-Help Revolution.* New York: Human Sciences Press.

Gaul, G. M. and N. A. Borowski. 1993. *Free Ride: The Tax Exempt Economy.* Kansas City, MO: Andrews and McMeel.

Gaylin, W., I. Glaser, S. Marcus, and D. J. Rothman. 1978. *Doing Good: The Limits of Benevolence.* New York: Pantheon Books.

George, John and Laird Wilcox. 1992. *Nazis, Communists, Klansmen, and Others on the Fringe: Political Extremism in America.* Buffalo, NY: Prometheus Books.

Gerlach, Luther P. and Virginia H. Hine. 1970. *People, Power, Change: Movements of Social Transformation.* Indianapolis, IN: Bobbs-Merrill.

Gidron, Benjamin, Ralph Kramer, and Lester Salamon. 1992. *Government and the Third Sector.* San Francisco: Jossey-Bass.

Gittell, Marilyn. 1980. *The Limits to Citizen Participation: The Decline of Community Organizations.* Beverly Hills, CA: Sage.

———. 1983. "The Consequences of Mandating Citizen Participation." *Policy Studies Review* 3:90-95.

Gittell, Marilyn and Teresa Shtob. 1980. "Changing Women's Roles in Political Volunteerism and Reform of the City." *Signs* 5 (Suppl.): 67-78.

Gjems-Onstad, Ole. 1990. "The Independence of Voluntary Organizations in a Social Democracy: Governmental Influences in Norway." *Nonprofit and Voluntary Sector Quarterly* 19:393-407.

Glaser, John S. 1994. *The United Way Scandal: An Insider's Account of What Went Wrong and Why.* New York: John Wiley.

Gold, D. B. 1971. "Woman and Volunteerism." Pp. 533-54 in *Woman in Sexist Society,* edited by Vivian Gornick and Barbara K. Moran. New York: Basic Books.

———. 1979. *Opposition to Volunteerism: An Annotated Bibliography.* Chicago: Council of Planning Librarians Bibliographies.

Gomez, Sergio. 1987. "Organizaciones Empresariales Rurales: Los Casos de Brasíl y de Chile" (Rural Employers' Organizations in Brazil and Chile). *Revista Paraguaya de Sociología* 24:17-32.

Gonyea, J. G. and N. M. Silverstein. 1991. "The Role of Alzheimer's Support Groups in Families' Utilization of Community Services." *Journal of Gerontological Social Work* 16:43-55.

Goodchilds, Jacqueline D. and John Harding. 1960. "Formal Organizations and Informal Activities." *Journal of Social Issues* 16 (4): 16-28.

Gora, JoAnn G. and Gloria M. Nemerowicz. 1985. *Emergency Squad Volunteers: Professionalism in Unpaid Work*. New York: Praeger.

Gordon, C. W. and Nicholas Babchuk. 1959. "Typology of Voluntary Associations." *American Sociological Review* 24:22-29.

Grabb, E. G. and J. E. Curtis. 1992. "Voluntary Associations Activity in English Canada, French Canada, and the United States: A Multivariate Analysis." *Canadian Journal of Sociology* 17:371-88.

Granovetter, M. S. 1974. *Getting a Job: A Study of Contacts and Careers*. Cambridge, MA: Harvard University Press.

Gray, George A. 1975. "Differential Effects of Temporal Constraints on Organizational Participation." *Pacific Sociological Review* 18:327-41.

Green, David G. 1993. *Reinventing Civil Society*. London: Institute of Economic Affairs, Health and Welfare Unit.

Greider, William. 1992. *Who Will Tell the People: The Betrayal of American Democracy*. New York: Simon & Schuster.

Grimso, A., G. Helgesen, and C. Borchgrevink. 1981. "Short-Term and Long-Term Effects of Lay Groups on Weight Reduction." *British Medical Journal* 283:1093-95.

Grindheim, Jan Erik and Per Selle. 1990. "The Role of Voluntary Social Welfare Organizations in Norway: A Democratic Alternative to a Bureaucratic Welfare State?" *Voluntas* 1:62-76.

Gronbjerg, Kirsten A. 1989. "Developing a Universe of Nonprofit Organizations: Methodological Considerations." *Nonprofit and Voluntary Sector Quarterly* 18:63-80.

———. 1993. *Understanding Nonprofit Funding*. San Francisco: Jossey-Bass.

———. 1994. "Using NTEE to Classify Non-Profit Organisations: An Assessment of Human Service and Regional Applications." *Voluntas* 5:301-28.

Gronbjerg, Kirsten A., M. H. Kimmick, and Lester M. Salamon. 1985. *The Chicago Nonprofit Sector in a Time of Government Retrenchment*. Washington, DC: Urban Institute.

Gronbjerg, Kirsten A. and Sheila Nelson. 1998. "Mapping Small Religious Nonprofit Organizations: An Illinois Profile." *Nonprofit and Voluntary Sector Quarterly* 27:13-31.

Gros, Dominique. 1986. "Les Acteurs des Luttes Urbaines" (Actors in Urban Conflicts). *Schweizerische Zeitschrift für Soziologie* 12:485-94.

Gross, A. E., B. S. Wallston, and I. M. Piliavin. 1980. "The Help Recipient's Perspective." Pp. 355-69 in *Participation in Social and Political Activities*, edited by David H. Smith, J. Macaulay, and Associates. San Francisco: Jossey-Bass.

Gummer, Burton. 1988. "The Hospice in Transition: Organizational and Administrative Perspectives." *Administration in Social Work* 12:31-43.

Gusfield, Joseph R. 1963. *Symbolic Crusade*. Urbana: University of Illinois Press.

Hage, Jerald. 1980. *Theories of Organizations*. New York: John Wiley.

Haines, Herbert H. 1984. "Black Radicalization and the Funding of Civil Rights, 1957-1970." *Social Problems* 32:31-43.

Hall, Leda M. and Melvin F. Hall. 1996. "Big Fights: Competition Between Poor People's Social Movement Organizations." *Nonprofit and Voluntary Sector Quarterly* 25:53-72.

Hall, Melvin F. 1995. *Poor People's Social Movement Organizations: The Goal Is to Win*. Westport, CT: Praeger.

Hall, Peter D. 1987a. "Abandoning the Rhetoric of Independence: Reflections on the Nonprofit Sector in the Post-Liberal Era." *Journal of Voluntary Action Research* 16:11-28.

———. 1987b. "A Historical Overview of the Private Nonprofit Sector." Pp. 3-26 in *The Nonprofit Sector,* edited by Walter W. Powell. New Haven, CT: Yale University Press.

———. 1990. "Conflicting Managerial Cultures in Nonprofit Organizations." *Nonprofit Management and Leadership* 1:153-65.

———. 1992. *Inventing the Nonprofit Sector and Other Essays on Philanthropy, Volunteerism, and Nonprofit Organizations.* Baltimore, MD: Johns Hopkins University Press.

———. 1999. "The Work of Many Hands: A Response to Stanley N. Katz on the Origins of the 'Serious Study' of Philanthropy." *Nonprofit and Voluntary Sector Quarterly* 28:522-34.

Hall, Richard H. 1972. *Organizations: Structures and Processes.* Englewood Cliffs, NJ: Prentice Hall.

———. 1996. *Organizations: Structures, Processes, and Outcomes.* 6th ed. Englewood Cliffs, NJ: Prentice Hall.

Hallenstvedt, A. 1974. "Formal Voluntary Associations in Norway." Pp. 213-27 in *Voluntary Action Research: 1974,* edited by David H. Smith. Lexington, MA: Lexington Books.

Halliday, Terence C. and Charles L. Cappell. 1979. "Indicators of Democracy in Professional Associations: Elite Recruitment, Turnover, and Decision Making in a Metropolitan Bar Association." *American Bar Foundation Research Journal* 4:699-767.

Hamilton, A. 1980. *An Exploratory Study of Therapeutic Self-Help Child Abuse Groups.* D.S.W. thesis, University of California, Los Angeles, School of Social Welfare.

Hamm, Mark S. 1993. *American Skinheads.* Westport, CT: Praeger.

Hammack, David C. and Dennis R. Young, eds. 1993. *Nonprofit Organizations in a Market Economy.* San Francisco: Jossey-Bass.

Handlin, Oscar. 1951. *The Uprooted.* New York: Grosset and Dunlop.

Handy, C. 1988. *Understanding Voluntary Organisations.* London: Penguin.

Hanks, M. 1981. "Youth, Voluntary Associations, and Socialization." *Social Forces* 60:211-23.

Hanks, Michael and Bruce K. Eckland. 1978. "Adult Voluntary Associations and Adolescent Socialization." *Sociological Quarterly* 19:481-90.

Hannan, Michael T. and John Freeman. 1977. "The Population Ecology of Organizations." *American Journal of Sociology* 82:929-64.

———. 1989. *Organizational Ecology.* Cambridge, MA: Harvard University Press.

Hansmann, Henry. 1980. "The Role of Nonprofit Enterprise." *Yale Law Journal* 89:835-901.

———. 1987. "Economic Theories of Nonprofit Organization." Pp. 27-42 in *The Nonprofit Sector,* edited by Walter W. Powell. New Haven, CT: Yale University Press.

Hardin, Garrett. 1977. *The Limits of Altruism: An Ecologist's View of Survival.* Bloomington: Indiana University Press.

Hargreaves, Alec G. 1991. "The Political Mobilization of the North African Immigrant Community in France." *Ethnic and Racial Studies* 14:350-67.

Harris, Ian M. 1984. "The Citizens Coalition in Milwaukee." *Social Policy* 15:27-31.

Harris, Margaret. 1998a. "Doing It Their Way: Organizational Challenges for Voluntary Associations." *Nonprofit and Voluntary Sector Quarterly* 27:144-58.

———. 1998b. *Organizing God's Work.* New York: St. Martin's.

Harrison, Paul M. 1960. "Weber's Categories of Authority and Voluntary Associations." *American Sociological Review* 25:231-37.

Hartman, William E., Marilyn Fithian, and Donald Johnson. 1991. *Nudist Society.* Rev. ed. Los Angeles: Elysium Growth Press.

Hartson, Louis D. 1911. "A Study of Voluntary Associations, Educational and Social, in Europe During the Period From 1100 to 1700." *Journal of Genetic Psychology* 18:10-30.

Hatch, Stephen. 1980. *Outside the State: Voluntary Organisations in Three English Towns*. London: Croom Helm.

Hatch, S. and I. Mocroft. 1979. "The Relative Costs of Services Provided by Voluntary and Statutory Organisations." *Public Administration* 41:397-405.

Hawkins, B. W., M. A. Steger, and J. Trimble. 1986. "How (Some) Community Organizations Adapt to Fiscal Strain." *Research in Urban Policy* 2:117-25.

Heckethorne, Charles W. 1965. *The Secret Societies of All Ages and Countries*. 2 vols. New Hyde Park, NY: University Books.

Hegyesi, Gabor. 1992. "The Revival of the Nonprofit Sector in Hungary." Pp. 309-22 in *The Nonprofit Sector in the Global Community*, edited by Kathleen D. McCarthy, Virginia A. Hodgkinson, Russy D. Sumariwalla, and Associates. San Francisco: Jossey-Bass.

Henderson, Paul and David N. Thomas. 1981. "Federations of Community Groups: The Benefits and Dangers." *Community Development Journal* 16:98-104.

Henry, Gary T. 1990. *Practical Sampling*. Newbury Park, CA: Sage.

Herman, R. and Associates. 1994. *The Jossey-Bass Handbook of Nonprofit Leadership and Management*. San Francisco: Jossey-Bass.

Herman, Robert D. and Richard D. Heimovics. 1991. *Executive Leadership in Nonprofit Organizations*. San Francisco: Jossey-Bass.

Herman, Robert D. and Jon Van Til, eds. 1989. *Nonprofit Boards of Directors: Analyses and Applications*. New Brunswick, NJ: Transaction Books.

Herman, Robert D., Edward Weaver, and Robert Heimovics. 1991. "Judgments of Nonprofit Organization Effectiveness." Paper presented at the annual conference of the Association for Research on Nonprofit Organizations and Voluntary Action, Chicago, October.

Herzberg, Frederick, Bernard Mausner, and Barbara Synderman. 1959. *The Motivation to Work*. New York: John Wiley.

Herzog, A. R. and J. N. Morgan. 1992. "Age and Gender Differences in the Value of Productive Activities: Four Different Approaches." *Research on Aging* 14:169-98.

Hill, M. S. 1985. "Patterns of Time Use." Pp. 133-76 in *Time, Goods, and Well-Being*, edited by F. T. Juster and F. P. Stafford. Ann Arbor: University of Michigan Press.

Hirsch, Barry T. and John T. Addison. 1986. *The Economic Analysis of Unions*. Boston: Allyn & Unwin.

Hirsch, Eric L. 1986. "The Creation of Political Solidarity in Social Movement Organizations." *Sociological Quarterly* 27:373-87.

Hirst, P. Q. 1994. *Associative Democracy: New Forms of Economic and Social Governance*. Amherst: University of Massachusetts Press.

Hochschild, A. R. 1983. *The Managed Heart: Commercialization of Human Feeling*. Berkeley: University of California Press.

Hodge, R. W. and D. J. Trieman. 1968. "Social Participation and Social Status." *American Sociological Review* 33:722-40.

Hodgkinson, V. A., J. Gorski, S. M. Noga, and E. B. Knauft. 1995. *Giving and Volunteering in the United States*, Vol. 2: *Trends in Giving and Volunteering by Type of Charity*. Washington, DC: Independent Sector.

Hodgkinson, Virginia A. and Christopher Toppe. 1991. "A New Research and Planning Tool for Managers: The National Taxonomy of Exempt Entities." *Nonprofit Management & Leadership* 1:403-14.

Hodgkinson, V. A. and M. S. Weitzman. 1984. *Dimensions of the Independent Sector: A Statistical Profile*. 1st ed. Washington, DC: Independent Sector.

———. 1992. *Giving and Volunteering in the United States: 1992 Edition*. Washington, DC: Independent Sector.

————. 1996a. *Giving and Volunteering in the United States: 1996 Edition*. Washington, DC: Independent Sector.

————. 1996b. *Nonprofit Almanac, 1996-1997*. San Francisco: Jossey-Bass.

Hodgkinson, V. A., M. S. Weitzman, and A. D. Kirsch. 1989. *From Belief to Commitment: The Activities and Finances of Religious Congregations in the United States*. Washington, DC: Independent Sector.

Hodgkinson, Virginia A., Murray S. Weitzman, Christopher M. Toppe, and Stephen M. Noga. 1992. *Nonprofit Almanac, 1992-1993*. San Francisco: Jossey-Bass.

Holland, T. P. 1988. "The Effectiveness of Non-Profit Organizations." *Journal of Applied Behavioral Science* 12:202-21.

Hollingshead, A. B. 1975. *Elmtown's Youth and Elmtown Revisited*. New York: John Wiley.

Holmes, Len and Margaret Grieco. 1991. "Overt Funding, Buried Goals, and Moral Turnover: The Organizational Transformation of Radical Experiments." *Human Relations* 44:643-63.

Horch, Heinz D. 1988. "Ressourcenzusammensetzung und Oligarchisierung freiwilliger Vereinigungungen" (Resource Structure and Oligarchic Tendencies in Voluntary Associations). *Kölner Zeitschrift für Soziologie und Sozialpsychologie* 40:527-50.

————. 1994. "Does Government Financing Have a Detrimental Effect on the Autonomy of Voluntary Associations? Evidence From German Sport Clubs." *International Review for the Sociology of Sport* 29:269-85.

Horowitz, Irving L. 1972. *Three Worlds of Development*. 2nd ed. New York: Oxford University Press.

————. 1979. "Beyond Democracy: Interest Groups and the Patriotic Core." *Humanist* 39:4-10.

Hougland, James G., Jr. 1979. "Toward a Participation-Based Typology of Voluntary Organizations." *Journal of Voluntary Action Research* 8:84-92.

Houle, Cyril O. 1989. *Governing Boards: Their Nature and Nurture*. San Francisco: Jossey-Bass.

Howe, Fisher. 1997. *The Board Member's Guide to Strategic Planning: A Practical Approach to Strengthening Nonprofit Organizations*. San Francisco: Jossey-Bass.

Howell, R. E., I. L. Weir, and A. K. Cook. 1987. *Development of Rural Leadership*. Battle Creek, MI: W. K. Kellogg Foundation.

Hrebenar, R. J. (1997) *Interest Group Politics in America*. 3rd ed. Armonk, NY: M. E. Sharpe.

Huang, Jui-Cheng and Peter Gould. 1974. "Diffusion in an Urban Hierarchy: The Case of Rotary Clubs." *Economic Geography* 50:333-40.

Hudson, James R. 1988. "Organized Groups, Land Use Decisions, and Ecological Theory." *Sociological Perspectives* 31:122-41.

Huizenga, Johan. 1955. *Homo Ludens*. Boston: Beacon.

Humphreys, Keith. 1997. "Individual and Social Benefits of Mutual Aid Self-Help Groups." *Social Policy* 27:12-19.

Humphreys, R. 1995. *Sin, Organized Charity, and the Poor Law in Victorian England*. New York: St. Martin's.

Hunter, Albert. 1993. "National Federations: The Role of Voluntary Organizations in Linking Macro and Micro Orders in Civil Society." *Nonprofit and Voluntary Sector Quarterly* 22:121-36.

Hunter, A. and S. Staggenborg. 1986. "Communities Do Act: Neighborhood Characteristics, Resource Mobilization, and Political Action by Local Community Organizations." *Social Science Journal* 23:169-80.

Hutchins, Francis G. 1973. *India's Revolution*. Cambridge, MA: Harvard University Press.

Hyland, Stanley E., Alicia Russell, and Fontaine Hebb. 1990. "Realigning Corporate Giving: Problems in the Nonprofit Sector for Community Development Corporations." *Nonprofit and Voluntary Sector Quarterly* 19:111-19.

Iannello, Kathleen P. 1992. *Decisions Without Hierarchy: Feminist Interventions in Organization Theory and Practice*. London: Routledge.

Ibsen, Bjarne. 1996. "Changes in Local Voluntary Associations in Denmark." *Voluntas* 7:160-76.

Inkeles, Alex and David H. Smith. 1974. *Becoming Modern.* Cambridge, MA: Harvard University Press.

Institute for Nonprofit Organization Management. 1995. *California Nonprofit Organizations, 1995.* San Francisco: University of San Francisco, Institute for Nonprofit Management.

Jacobs, Jeffrey. 1992-93. "A Community Organizing Case Study: An Analysis of CAP-IT's Strategy to Prevent the Location of a Toxic Waste Incinerator in Their Community." *International Quarterly of Community Health Education* 13:253-63.

Jacoby, Arthur and Nicholas Babchuk. 1963. "Instrumental and Expressive Voluntary Associations." *Sociology and Social Research* 47:461-71.

Jaeger, Richard M. 1984. *Sampling in Education and the Social Sciences.* New York: Longman.

James, Estelle. 1989. *The Nonprofit Sector in International Perspective.* New York: Oxford University Press.

Jaszczak, Sandra and Tara Sheets, eds. 1997. *Encyclopedia of Associations.* 32nd ed. Detroit, MI: Gale Research International.

Jeavons, T. H. 1992. "When the Management Is the Message: Relating Values to Management Practice in Nonprofit Organizations." *Nonprofit Management & Leadership* 2:403-17.

―――. 1994. "Ethics in Nonprofit Management: Creating a Culture of Integrity." Pp. 184-207 in *The Jossey-Bass Handbook of Nonprofit Leadership and Management,* edited by Robert Herman and Associates. San Francisco: Jossey-Bass.

Jenkins, J. Craig. 1977. "Radical Transformation of Organizational Goals." *Administrative Science Quarterly* 22:568-85.

Jenkins, J. Craig and Craig M. Eckert. 1986. "Channeling Black Insurgency: Elite Patronage and Professional Social Movement Organizations in the Development of the Black Movement." *American Sociological Review* 51:812-29.

Johnson, Alice K., Linda Ourvan, and Dennis R. Young. 1995. "The Emergence of Nonprofit Organizations in Romania and the Role of International NGOs." *Social Development Issues* 17:38-56.

Johnson, Paul E. 1990. "Unraveling in Democratically Governed Groups." *Rationality and Society* 2:4-34.

Johnstone, Ronald L. 1992. *Religion in Society: A Sociology of Religion.* 4th ed. Englewood Cliffs, NJ: Prentice Hall.

Jolicoeur, Pamela M. and Louis L. Knowles. 1978. "Fraternal Associations and Civil Religion: Scottish Rite Freemasonry." *Review of Religious Research* 20:3-22.

Jordan, W. K. 1960. *The Charities of London, 1480-1660: The Aspirations and Achievements of the Urban Society.* New York: Russell Sage Foundation.

Juster, F. T. 1985. "Conceptual and Methodological Issues Involved in the Measurement of Time Use." Pp. 19-31 in *Time, Goods, and Well-Being,* edited by F. T. Juster and F. P. Stafford. Ann Arbor: University of Michigan Press.

Kahaner, Larry. 1988. *Cults That Kill: Probing the Underworld of Occult Crime.* New York: Warner Books.

Kahn, Arleen and Eugene I. Bender. 1985. "Self-Help Groups as a Crucible for People Empowerment in the Context of Social Development." *Social Development Issues* 9:4-13.

Kalifon, S. Zev. 1991. "Self-Help Groups Providing Services: Conflict and Change." *Nonprofit and Voluntary Sector Quarterly* 20:191-205.

Kanter, Rosabeth M. 1972. *Commitment and Community: Communes and Utopias in Sociological Perspective.* Cambridge, MA: Harvard University Press.

Kanter, Rosabeth and Louis A. Zurcher, Jr. 1973. "Evaluating Alternatives and Alternative Valuing." *Journal of Applied Behavioral Science* 9:381-97.

Kaplan, Matthew. 1986. "Cooperation and Coalition Development Among Neighborhood Organizations: A Case Study." *Journal of Voluntary Action Research* 15:23-34.

Kariel, Henry. 1981. *The Decline of American Pluralism.* Stanford, CA: Stanford University Press.

Karl, Jonathan. 1995. *The Right to Bear Arms: The Rise of America's New Militias.* New York: HarperCollins.

Katz, Alfred H. 1961. *Parents of the Handicapped.* Springfield, IL: Charles C Thomas.

————. 1993. *Self-Help in America: A Social Movement Perspective.* New York: Twayne.

Katz, Alfred H. and Eugene I. Bender. 1976. *The Strength in Us: Self-Help Groups in the Modern World.* New York: New Viewpoints/Franklin Watts.

Kay, Richard. 1994. "The Artistry of Leadership: An Exploration of the Leadership Process in Voluntary Not-for-Profit Organizations." *Nonprofit Management and Leadership* 4:285-300.

Kellerhals, J. 1974. "Voluntary Associations in Switzerland." Pp. 231-50 in *Voluntary Action Research: 1974,* edited by David H. Smith. Lexington, MA: Lexington Books.

Kelly, J. R. (1996) *Leisure.* Boston: Allyn & Bacon.

Kendall, Jeremy and Martin Knapp. 1995. "A Loose and Baggy Monster." Pp. 66-95 in *An Introduction to the Voluntary Sector,* edited by J. Davis-Smith, C. Rochester, and R. Hedley. London: Routledge.

Kennedy, M. and K. Humphreys. 1994. "Understanding Worldview Transformation in Mutual Help Groups." *Prevention in Human Services* 11:181-98.

Kephart, William M. and William W. Zellner. 1994. *Extraordinary Groups.* 5th ed. New York: St. Martin's.

Kerri, J. N. 1972. "An Inductive Examination of Voluntary Association Functions in a Single-Enterprise-Based Community." *Journal of Voluntary Action Research* 1 (2): 43-51.

Kikulis, Lisa M., Trevor Slack, and Bob Hinings. 1992. "Institutionally Specific Design Archetypes: A Framework for Understanding Change in National Sport Organizations." *International Review for the Sociology of Sport* 27:343-70.

Kilbane, Sally C. and John H. Beck. 1990. "Professional Associations and the Free Rider Problem: The Case of Optometry." *Public Choice* 65:181-87.

Kimmel, Michael S. 1990. *Revolution: A Sociological Interpretation.* Philadelphia: Temple University Press.

King, C. Wendell. 1956. *Social Movements in the United States.* New York: Random House.

King, David C. and Jack L. Walker. 1992. "The Provision of Benefits by Interest Groups in the United States." *Journal of Politics* 54:394-426.

Klandermans, Bert. 1989. "Introduction: Leadership and Decision-Making." *International Social Movement Research* 2:215-24.

Klausen, Kurt K. 1995. "On the Malfunction of the Generic Approach in Small Voluntary Associations." *Nonprofit Management and Leadership* 5:275-90.

Klausen, Kurt Klaudi and Per Selle. 1996. "The Third Sector in Scandinavia." *Voluntas* 7:99-122.

Kleidman, Robert. 1994. "Volunteer Activism and Professionalism in Social Movement Organizations." *Social Problems* 41:257-76.

Kloppenborg, John and Stephen Wilson. 1996. *Voluntary Associations in the Graeco-Roman World.* New York: Routledge.

Knauft, E. B., R. A. Berger, and S. Gray. 1991. *Profiles of Excellence: Achieving Success in the Nonprofit Sector.* San Francisco: Jossey-Bass.

Knight, Stephen. 1984. *The Brotherhood: The Secret World of the Freemasons.* London: Dorset.

Knoke, David. 1982. "Political Mobilization by Voluntary Associations." *Journal of Political and Military Sociology* 10:171-82.

————. 1986. "Associations and Interest Groups." *Annual Review of Sociology* 12:1-21.

————. 1988. "Incentive in Collective Action Organizations." *American Sociological Review* 53:311-29.

————. 1989. "Resource Acquisition and Allocation in U.S. National Associations." *International Social Movement Research* 2:129-54.

————. 1990a. "Networks of Political Action: Toward Theory Construction." *Social Forces* 68:1041-63.

————. 1990b. *Organizing for Collective Action: The Political Economies of Associations.* New York: Aldine de Gruyter.

Knoke, David and Richard E. Adams. 1987. "The Incentive Systems of Associations." *Research in the Sociology of Organizations* 5:285-309.

Knoke, David and D. Prensky. 1984. "What Relevance Do Organization Theories Have for Voluntary Organizations?" *Social Science Quarterly* 65:3-20.

Knoke, David and James R. Wood. 1981. *Organized for Action: Commitment in Voluntary Associations.* New Brunswick, NJ: Rutgers University Press.

Knowles, Malcolm. 1973. "Motivation in Volunteerism: Synopsis of a Theory." *Journal of Voluntary Action Research* 1 (2): 27-29.

Koldewyn, Phillip. 1984. "Voluntary Associations in Neuquen, Argentina." *Journal of Voluntary Action Research* 13:38-54.

————. 1986. "Mexican Voluntary Associations: A Community Study." *Journal of Voluntary Action Research* 15:46-64.

Kraft, Michael E. and Ruth Kraut. 1985. "The Impact of Citizen Participation on Hazardous Waste Policy Implementation: The Case of Clermont County, Ohio." *Policy Studies Journal* 14:52-61.

Kramer, Ralph M. 1979. "Voluntary Agencies in Four Welfare States." *Administration in Social Work* 3:397-407.

————. 1984. *Voluntary Agencies in the Welfare State.* Berkeley: University of California Press.

————. 1987. "Voluntary Agencies and the Personal Social Services." Pp. 240-57 in *The Nonprofit Sector,* edited by Walter W. Powell. New Haven, CT: Yale University Press.

Kramer, Ralph M., Hakon Lorentzen, Willem Melief, and Sergio Pasquinelli. 1993. *Privatization in Four European Countries.* Armonk, NY: M. E. Sharpe.

Krause, Elliott A. 1996. *Death of the Guilds: Professions, States, and the Advance of Capitalism, 1930 to the Present.* New Haven, CT: Yale University Press.

Kraybill, D. and P. Pellman-Good, eds. 1992. *The Perils of Professionalization.* Scottsdale. AZ: Herald Press.

Kronus, Carol L. 1977. "Mobilizing Voluntary Associations Into a Social Movement: The Case of Environmental Quality." *Sociological Quarterly* 18:267-83.

Kuhn, Thomas S. 1962. *The Structure of Scientific Revolutions.* Chicago: University of Chicago Press.

Kunz, Jennifer and Phillip R. Kunz. 1995. "Social Support During the Process of Divorce: It Does Make a Difference." *Journal of Divorce and Remarrriage* 24:111-19.

Kurtz, Linda F. 1990. "The Self-Help Movement: Review of the Past Decade of Research." *Social Work With Groups* 13:101-15.

Kuti, Eva. 1998. "Letter to David Horton Smith." *Nonprofit and Voluntary Sector Quarterly* 27:90-92.

Lacy, Virginia P. 1971. "Political Knowledge of College Activist Groups: SDS, YAF, and YD." *Journal of Politics* 33:840-45.

Lamb, Curt. 1975. *Political Power in Poor Neighborhoods.* New York: John Wiley.

Lambert, Joseph M. 1891. *Two Thousand Years of Gild Life.* Hull, UK: A. Brown.

Lambert, Malcolm. 1992. *Medieval Heresy: Popular Movements From the Gregorian Reform to the Reformation.* 2nd ed. Oxford, UK: Blackwell.

Lancourt, Jane. 1979. *Confront or Concede: The Alinsky Citizen Action Organizations.* Lexington, MA: D. C. Heath.

Landsberger, Henry. 1972a. " 'Maximum Feasible Participation': Working Class and Peasant Movements as a Theoretical Model for the Analysis of Current U.S. Movements of Poor and Minority Groups." *Journal of Voluntary Action Research* 1 (3): 25-41.

———. 1972b. "Trade Unions, Peasant Movements, and Social Movements as Voluntary Action." Pp. 135-58 in *Voluntary Action Research: 1972,* edited by David H. Smith, Richard D. Reddy, and Burt Baldwin. Lexington, MA: Lexington Books.

Lanfant, Marie-Françoise. 1976. "Voluntary Associations in France." *Journal of Voluntary Action Research* 5:192-207.

Lappé, Frances M. and Paul M. DuBois. 1994. *The Quickening of America.* San Francisco: Jossey-Bass.

Larsen, E. Nick. 1992. "The Politics of Prostitution Control: Interest Group Politics in Four Canadian Cities." *International Journal of Urban and Regional Research* 16:169-89.

Laskin, R. and S. Phillett. 1965. "An Integrative Analysis of Voluntary Associational Leadership and Reputational Influences." *Sociological Inquiry* 35:176-85.

Lavigne, Yves. 1994. *Hell's Angels.* New York: Carol.

Lavoie, F., T. Borkman, and B. Gidron. 1994. *Self-Help and Mutual Aid Groups: International and Multicultural Perspectives.* New York: Haworth.

Lawson, R. 1983. "Origins and Evolution of a Social Movement Strategy: The Rent Strike in New York City, 1904-1980." *Urban Affairs Quarterly* 18:371-95.

Leat, Diana. 1986. "Privatization and Voluntarization." *Quarterly Journal of Social Affairs* 2:285-320.

———. 1993. *Managing Across Sectors: Similarities and Differences Between For-Profit and Voluntary Non-Profit Organisations.* London: City University Business School.

LeGorreta, Judith L. and Dennis R. Young. 1986. "Why Organizations Turn Nonprofit: Lessons From Case Studies." Pp. 196-204 in *The Economics of Nonprofit Institutions,* edited by Susan Rose-Ackerman. New York: Oxford University Press.

LeGrand, Julian and Ray Robinson. 1986. *Privatisation and the Welfare State.* London: Allen & Unwin.

Leighley, Jan. 1996. "Group Membership and the Mobilization of Political Participation." *Journal of Politics* 58:447-63.

Lenski, Gerhard, Patrick Nolan, and Jean Lenski. 1995. *Human Societies.* 7th ed. New York: McGraw-Hill.

Levine, M. and A. Levine. 1970. *A Social History of the Helping Services.* New York: Appleton-Century-Crofts.

Levitt, Theodore. 1973. *The Third Sector: New Tactics for a Responsive Society.* New York: AMACOM.

Lieberman, M. A. and L. R. Snowden. 1994. "Problems in Assessing Prevalence and Membership Characteristics of Self-Help Group Participants." Pp. 32-49 in *Understanding the Self-Help Organization,* edited by T. J. Powell. Thousand Oaks, CA: Sage.

Lieberman, M. A. and L. Videka-Sherman. 1986. "The Impact of Self-Help Groups on the Mental Health of Widows and Widowers." *American Journal of Orthopsychiatry* 56:435-49.

Limerick, Brigid and Tracy Burgess-Limerick. 1992. "Volunteering and Empowerment in Secondary Schools." *Nonprofit and Voluntary Sector Quarterly* 21:19-37.

Lin, Nan, Alfred Dean, and Walter M. Ensel. 1986. *Social Support, Life Events, and Depression.* New York: Academic Press.

Lincoln, James R. 1977. "The Urban Distribution of Voluntary Organizations." *Social Science Quarterly* 58:472-80.

Lindgren, H. E. 1987. "The Informal-Intermittent Organization: A Vehicle for Successful Citizen Protest." *Journal of Applied Behavioral Science* 23:397-412.

Linton, Ralph. 1945. *The Cultural Background of Personality.* New York: Appleton-Century-Crofts.

Lipset, Seymour M., Martin A. Trow, and James S. Coleman. 1956. *Union Democracy*. Glencoe, IL: Free Press.

Lipset, Seymour M. and Sheldon S. Wolin. 1965. *The Berkeley Student Revolt*. Garden City, NY: Doubleday.

Lissner, Jorgen. 1972. *The Politics of Altruism: A Study of the Political Behavior of Voluntary Development Agencies*. Geneva, Switzerland: Lutheran World Federation.

Little, Kenneth. 1965. *West African Urbanization: A Study of Voluntary Associations in Social Change*. Cambridge, UK: Cambridge University Press.

Litwak, Eugene. 1961. "Voluntary Associations and Neighborhood Cohesion." *American Sociological Review* 26:258-71.

Lofland, John. 1996. *Social Movement Organizations: A Guide to Insurgent Realities*. New York: Aldine de Gruyter.

Lofland, John and Michael Jamison. 1984. "Social Movement Locals: Modal Member Structures." *Sociological Analysis* 45:115-29.

Logan, John R. and Gordana Rabrenovic. 1990. "Neighborhood Associations: Their Issues, Their Allies, and Their Opponents." *Urban Affairs Quarterly* 26:68-94.

Lohmann, Roger A. 1989. "And Lettuce Is Non-Animal: Toward a Positive Economics of Voluntary Action." *Nonprofit and Voluntary Sector Quarterly* 18:367-83.

———. 1992. *The Commons: New Perspectives on Nonprofit Organizations and Voluntary Action*. San Francisco: Jossey-Bass.

Longair, M. S. 1996. *Our Evolving Universe*. Cambridge, UK: Cambridge University Press.

Longdon, Bill, Jim Gallacher, and Tony Dickson. 1986. "The Community Resources Project and the Training of Activists." *Community Development Journal* 21:259-69.

Longley, Lawrence D., Herbert A. Terry, and Erwin G. Krasnow. 1983. "Citizen Groups in Broadcast Regulatory Policy-Making." *Policy Studies Journal* 12:258-70.

Lozier, J. 1976. "Volunteer Fire Departments and Community Mobilization." *Human Organization* 35:345-54.

Lubove, Roy. 1965. *The Professional Altruist: The Emergence of Social Work as a Career*. Cambridge, MA: Harvard University Press.

Luloff, A. E., W. H. Chittenden, E. Kriss, S. Weeks, and L. Brushnett. 1984. "Local Voluntarism in New Hampshire: Who, Why, and at What Benefit?" *Journal of the Community Development Society* 15:17-30.

Lundberg, George, Mirra Komarovsky, and Mary A. McInerny. 1934. *Leisure: A Suburban Study*. New York: Columbia University Press.

Luza, Radomir V. 1989. *The Resistance in Austria, 1938-1945*. Minneapolis: University of Minnesota Press.

Lynd, Robert S. and Helen M. Lynd. 1929. *Middletown*. New York: Harcourt Brace.

Lynn, P. and J. Davis-Smith. 1991. *The 1991 National Survey of Voluntary Activity in the UK*. York, UK: Joseph Rowntree Foundation.

Lyons, Arthur. 1988. *Satan Wants You: The Cult of Devil Worship in America*. New York: Mysterious Press.

MacKeith, J. 1993. *NGO Management: A Guide Through the Literature*. London: Centre for Voluntary Organisation.

MacLeod, David I. 1983. *Building Character in the American Boy: The Boy Scouts, YMCA, and Their Forerunners, 1870-1920*. Madison: University of Wisconsin Press.

Maeyama, Takashi. 1979. "Ethnicity, Secret Societies, and Associations: The Japanese in Brazil." *Comparative Studies in Society and History* 21:589-610.

Magrass, Yale R. 1986. "The Boy Scouts, the Outdoors, and Empire." *Humanity and Society* 10 (1): 37-57.

Majone, Giandomenico. 1984. "Professionalism and Nonprofit Organizations." *Journal of Health Politics, Policy, and Law* 8:639-59.

Makela, Klaus. 1994. "Rates of Attrition Among the Membership of Alcoholics Anonymous in Finland." *Journal of Studies on Alcohol* 55:91-95.

Mancho, S. 1982. "Role of Associations as Regards Second-Generation Migrants, Especially From the Point of View of Maintaining Cultural Links With the Country of Origin." *International Migration* 20:85-101.

Mandle, Jay R. and Joan D. Mandle. 1989. "Voluntarism and Commercialization in Basketball: The Case of Trinidad and Tobago." *Sociology of Sport Journal* 6:113-24.

Manes, Christopher. 1990. *Green Rage: Radical Environmentalism and the Unmaking of Civilization.* Boston: Little, Brown.

March, James G. and Herbert A. Simon. 1958. *Organizations.* New York: John Wiley.

Marquez, Benjamin. 1990. "Organizing the Mexican American Community in Texas: The Legacy of Saul Alinsky." *Policy Studies Review* 9:355-73.

Marshall, Mac and Alice Oleson. 1996. "MADDer Than Hell." *Qualitative Health Research* 6:6-22.

Marullo, Sam. 1988. "Leadership and Membership in the Nuclear Freeze Movement: A Specification of Resource Mobilization Theory." *Sociological Quarterly* 29:407-27.

Marullo, Sam, R. Pagnucco, and J. Smith. 1996. "Frame Changes and Social Movement Contraction: U.S. Peace Movement Framing After the Cold War." *Sociological Inquiry* 66:1-28.

Maslow, A. 1954. *Motivation and Personality.* New York: Harper & Row.

Mason, David E. 1984. *Voluntary Nonprofit Enterprise Management.* New York: Plenum.

————. 1996. *Leading and Managing the Expressive Dimension.* San Francisco: Jossey-Bass.

Maton, K. I. 1988. "Social Support, Organizational Characteristics, Psychological Well-Being, and Group Appraisal in Three Self-Help Group Populations." *American Journal of Community Psychology* 16:53-77.

Maton, K. I. and D. A. Salem. 1995. "Organizational Characteristics of Empowering Community Settings: A Multiple Case Study Approach." *American Journal of Community Psychology* 23:631-56.

Matson, Floyd W. 1990. *Walking Alone and Marching Together: A History of the Organized Blind Movement in the United States, 1940-1990.* Baltimore, MD: National Federation of the Blind.

Mausner, J. S., S. C. Benes, and I. W. Gabrielson. 1976. "Study of Volunteer Ambulance Squads." *American Journal of Public Health* 66:1062-68.

Mayhew, B. H., J. M. McPherson, T. Rotolo, and L. Smith-Lovin. 1995. "Sex and Race Homogeneity in Naturally Occurring Groups." *Social Forces* 74:15-52.

McAdam, Doug. 1982. *Political Process and the Development of Black Insurgency, 1930-1970.* Chicago: University of Chicago Press.

————. 1983. "Tactical Innovation and the Pace of Insurgency." *American Sociological Review* 48:735-54.

McAdam, Doug and David A. Snow. 1997. *Social Movements.* Los Angeles: Roxbury.

McCarthy, John D., David W. Britt, and Mark Wolfson. 1991. "The Institutional Channeling of Social Movements by the State in the United States." *Research in Social Movements, Conflicts and Change* 13:45-76.

McCarthy, John D. and Mayer N. Zald. 1977. "Resource Mobilization and Social Movements: A Partial Theory." *American Journal of Sociology* 82:1212-41.

McCarthy, Kathleen D., Virginia A. Hodgkinson, Russy D. Sumariwalla, and Associates, eds. 1992. *The Nonprofit Sector in the Global Community.* San Francisco: Jossey-Bass.

McGuire, Steve. 1996. "Baseball: Political Economy Would Like to Say 'It Ain't So'." *Humanity and Society* 20:87-93.

McKenzie, Evan. 1994. *Privatopia.* New Haven, CT: Yale University Press.

McMurtry, Steven L., F. Ellen Netting, and Peter M. Kettner. 1991. "How Nonprofits Adapt to a Stringent Environment." *Nonprofit Management and Leadership* 1:235-52.

McNamie, Stephan J. and Kimberly Swisher. 1985. "Neighborhood Decentralization and Organized Citizen Participation." *Sociological Focus* 18:301-12.

McPherson, J. M. 1982. "Hypernetwork Sampling: Duality and Differentiation Among Voluntary Organizations." *Social Networks* 3:225-50.

———. 1983a. "An Ecology of Affiliation." *American Sociological Review* 48:519-32.

———. 1983b. "The Size of Voluntary Organizations." *Social Forces* 61:1044-64.

———. 1988. "A Theory of Voluntary Organization." Pp. 42-76 in *Community Organizations,* edited by Carl Milofsky. New York: Oxford University Press.

McPherson, J. M., Pamela Popielarz, and Sonja Drobnic. 1992. "Social Networks and Organizational Dynamics." *American Sociological Review* 57:153-70.

McPherson, J. M. and James Ranger-Moore. 1991. "Evolution on a Dancing Landscape: Organizations and Networks in Dynamic Blau Space." *Social Forces* 70:19-42.

McPherson, J. M. and Thomas Rotolo. 1996. "Testing a Dynamic Model of Social Composition: Diversity and Change in Voluntary Groups." *American Sociological Review* 61:179-202.

McPherson, J. M. and Lynn Smith-Lovin. 1982. "Women and Weak Ties: Differences by Sex in the Size of Voluntary Organizations." *American Journal of Sociology* 87:883-904.

———. 1986. "Sex Segregation in Voluntary Associations." *American Sociological Review* 51:61-79.

Mehta, Prayag. 1987. "Organising for Empowering the Poor." *Man and Development* 9 (3): 49-59.

Meister, Albert. 1972a. "A Comparative Note on the Prevalence of Voluntary Associations in Geneva and Paris." *Journal of Voluntary Action Research* 1 (3): 42-45.

———. 1972b. *Vers un Sociologie des Associations* (Toward a Sociology of Associations). Paris: Les Editions Ouvrieres.

Melton, J. G. 1990. *Cults and New Religions: Sources for the Study of Nonconventional Religious Groups in 19th and 20th Century America.* New York: Garland.

Mentzer, Marc S. 1993. "The Leader Succession-Performance Relationship in a Non-Profit Organization." *Revue Canadienne de Sociologie et d'Anthropologie/Canadian Review of Sociology and Anthropology* 30:191-204.

Messinger, Sheldon. 1955. "Organizational Transformation: A Case Study of a Declining Social Movement." *American Sociological Review* 20:3-10.

Michels, Robert. [1911] 1968. *Political Parties.* New York: Free Press.

Middleton, Melissa. 1987. "Nonprofit Boards of Directors: Beyond the Governance Function." Pp. 141-53 in *The Nonprofit Sector,* edited by Walter W. Powell. New Haven, CT: Yale University Press.

Miller, Henry and Connie Phillip. 1983. "The Alternative Service Agency." Pp. 779-91 in *Handbook of Clinical Social Work,* edited by A. Rosenblatt and D. Waldfogel. San Francisco: Jossey-Bass.

Miller, Robert W. 1986. "Expanding University Resources in Support of Volunteer Development: Evaluation of a Pilot Effort." *Journal of Voluntary Action Research* 15:100-15.

Mills, C. W. 1956. *The Power Elite.* New York: Oxford University Press.

Milofsky, Carl. 1987. "Neighborhood-Based Organizations: A Market Analogy." Pp. 277-95 in *The Nonprofit Sector,* edited by Walter W. Powell. New Haven, CT: Yale University Press.

———, ed. 1988a. *Community Organizations: Studies in Resource Mobilization and Exchange.* New York: Oxford University Press.

———. 1988b. "Structure and Process in Community Self-Help Organizations." Pp. 183-216 in *Community Organizations,* edited by Carl Milofsky. New York: Oxford University Press.

———. 1996. "The End of Nonprofit Management Education." *Nonprofit and Voluntary Sector Quarterly* 25:277-82.

Milofsky, Carl and Stephen D. Blades. 1991. "Issues of Accountability in Health Charities: A Case Study of Accountability Problems Among Nonprofit Organizations." *Nonprofit and Voluntary Sector Quarterly* 20:371-93.

Milofsky, Carl and Albert Hunter. 1994. "Where Nonprofits Come From: A Theory of Organizational Emergence." Paper presented at the annual conference of the Association of Researchers on Nonprofit Organizations and Voluntary Action, Berkeley, CA, October.

Milofsky, Carl and Frank P. Romo. 1988. "The Structure of Funding Arenas for Neighborhood-Based Organizations." Pp. 217-42 in *Community Organizations,* edited by Carl Milofsky. New York: Oxford University Press.

Minde, K., N. Shosenberg, P. Marton, J. Thompson, J. Ripley, and S. Burns. 1980. "Self-Help Groups in a Premature Nursery: A Controlled Evaluation." *Journal of Pediatrics* 96:933-40.

Minnis, Mhyra S. 1952. "Cleavage in Women's Organizations." *American Sociological Review* 18:47-53.

Mirvis, Philip H. 1992. "The Quality of Employment in the Nonprofit Sector: Employee Attitudes in Nonprofits Versus Business and Government." *Nonprofit Management and Leadership* 3:23-41.

Moberg, David O. 1983. "Compartmentalization and Parochialism in Religious and Voluntary Action Research." *Review of Religious Research* 24:318-21.

Moen, Phyllis, Donna Dempster-McClain, and Robin M. Williams, Jr. 1992. "Successful Aging: A Life-Course Perspective on Women's Multiple Roles of Health." *American Journal of Sociology* 97:1612-38.

Mok, Bong Ho. 1988. "Grassroots Organizing in China: The Residents' Committee as a Linking Mechanism Between the Bureaucracy and the Community." *Community Development Journal* 23:164-69.

Moller, Valerie, Theresa Mthembu, and Robin Richards. 1994. "The Role of Informal Clubs in Youth Development: A South African Case Study." *Journal of Social Development in Africa* 9:5-29.

Moore, P. 1978. "People as Lawyers: Lay Advocacy and Self-Help in the Legal System." *British Journal of Law and Society* 1:121-32.

Morgan, David L. and Duane F. Alwin. 1980. "When Less Is More: School Size and Student Social Participation." *Social Psychology Quarterly* 43:241-52.

Morgan, J. N., R. F. Dye, and J. N. Hybels. 1977. "Results From Two National Surveys of Philanthropic Activity." Pp. 157-323 in *Research Papers,* Vol. 1, edited by the Commission on Private Philanthropy and Public Needs. Washington, DC: U.S. Department of the Treasury.

Morrison, D. 1970. *Farmers' Organizations and Movements.* East Lansing: Michigan State University, Agricultural Experiment Station.

Moyer, Mel. 1984. *Managing Voluntary Organizations.* Toronto: York University Press.

Moynihan, D. P. 1970. *Maximum Feasible Misunderstanding: Community Action in the War on Poverty.* New York: Free Press.

Mudimbe, V. Y., ed. 1996. *Open the Social Sciences: Report of the Gulbenkian Commission on the Restructuring of the Social Sciences.* Stanford, CA: Stanford University Press.

Muehlbauer, Gene and Laura Dodder. 1983. *The Losers: Gang Delinquency in an American Suburb.* New York: Praeger.

Mueller, Marnie W. 1975. "Economic Determinants of Volunteer Work by Women." *Signs* 1:325-38.

Mulford, Charles L. and Gerald E. Klonglan. 1972. "Attitude Determinants of Individual Participation in Organized Voluntary Action." Pp. 251-76 in *Voluntary Action Research: 1972,* edited by David H. Smith, Richard D. Reddy, and Burt R. Baldwin. Lexington, MA: Lexington Books.

Mulford, Charles L. and Mary A. Mulford. 1980. "Interdependence and Intraorganizational Structure for Voluntary Organizations." *Journal of Voluntary Action Research* 9:20-34.

Murray, V. and B. Tassie. 1994. "Evaluating the Effectiveness of Nonprofit Organizations." Pp. 303-24 in *The Jossey-Bass Handbook on Nonprofit Leadership and Management,* edited by R. Herman and Associates. San Francisco: Jossey-Bass.

Nadel, S. F. 1957. *The Theory of Social Structure.* London: Cohen & West.

Naisbitt, John. 1982. *MEGATRENDS.* New York: Warner.

Naisbitt, John and Patricia Aburdene. 1990. *MEGATRENDS 2000.* New York: William Morrow.

Nall, Frank C. I. 1967. "National Associations." Pp. 276-313 in *The Emergent American Society,* Vol. 1, edited by W. L. Warner. New Haven, CT: Yale University Press.

Newman, William H. and Harvey Wallender. 1978. "Managing Not-for-Profit Enterprises." *Academy of Management Review* 3:23-31.

Newton, Kenneth. 1975. "Voluntary Organizations in a British City: The Political and Organizational Characteristics of 4,264 Voluntary Associations in Birmingham." *Journal of Voluntary Action Research* 4:43-62.

Nielsen, Waldemar. 1979. *The Endangered Sector.* New York: Columbia University Press.

Nikolov, Stephan E. 1992. "The Emerging Nonprofit Sector in Bulgaria: Its Historical Dimensions." Pp. 333-48 in *The Nonprofit Sector in the Global Community,* edited by Kathleen D. McCarthy, Virginia A. Hodgkinson, Russy D. Sumariwalla, and Associates. San Francisco: Jossey-Bass.

Nolt, Steven M. 1992. *A History of the Amish.* Intercourse, PA: Good Books.

Nownes, A. J. and G. Neeley. 1996. "Public Interest Group Entrepreneurship and Theories of Group Mobilization." *Political Research Quarterly* 49:119-46.

Obinne, Chukwudi P. 1994. "A Strategy for Agricultural Progress and Socio-Economic Upliftment: Federation of Farmers' Associations of Nigeria." *Community Development Journal* 29:40-46.

O'Connell, Brian. 1983. *America's Voluntary Spirit.* New York: Foundation Center.

———. 1984. *The Board Members Book.* New York: Foundation Center.

O'Neill, Michael. 1989. *The Third America: The Emergence of the Nonprofit Sector in the United States.* San Francisco: Jossey-Bass.

———. 1994. "Philanthropic Dimensions of Member Benefit Organizations." *Nonprofit and Voluntary Sector Quarterly* 23:3-20.

O'Neill, Michael and D. R. Young. 1988. *Educating Managers of Nonprofit Organizations.* New York: Praeger.

Oliver, Pamela. 1983. "The Mobilization of Paid and Volunteer Activists in the Neighborhood Movement." *Research in Social Movements, Conflicts and Change* 5:133-70.

Olsen, Marvin E. 1982. *Participatory Pluralism.* Chicago: Nelson-Hall.

Olson, Mancur. 1965. *The Logic of Collective Action: Public Goods and the Theory of Groups.* Cambridge, MA: Harvard University Press.

Onyx, Jenny and Madi Maclean. 1996. "Careers in the Third Sector." *Nonprofit Management and Leadership* 6:331-45.

Orora, John H. O. and Hans B. C. Spiegel. 1981. "Harambee: Self-Help Development Projects in Kenya." Pp. 93-103 in *Volunteers, Voluntary Associations, and Development,* edited by David H. Smith and Frederick Elkin. Leiden, Netherlands: E. J. Brill.

Ortmeyer, D. L. and D. Fortune. 1985. "A Portfolio Model of Korean Household Sector Saving Behavior." *Economic Development and Cultural Change* 33:575-99.

Oster, Sharon M. 1992. "Nonprofit Organizations as Franchise Operations." *Nonprofit and Voluntary Sector Quarterly* 2:223-38.

———. 1995. *Strategic Management for Nonprofit Organizations: Theory and Cases.* New York: Oxford University Press.

Ostrander, Susan A. 1984. *Women of the Upper Class.* Philadelphia: Temple University Press.

———. 1995. *Money for Change.* Philadelphia: Temple University Press.

Ouchi, William G. and Alan L. Wilkins. 1985. "Organizational Culture." *Annual Review of Sociology* 11:457-83.

Pakulski, Jan. 1986. "Leaders of the Solidarity Movement: A Sociological Portrait." *Sociology* 20:64-81.

Palisi, Bartolomeo. 1985. "Voluntary Associations and Well-Being in Three Metropolitan Areas: Cross-Cultural Evidence." *International Journal of Comparative Sociology* 22:265-88.

Palisi, Bartolomeo J. and Bonni Korn. 1989. "National Trends in Voluntary Association Membership: 1974-1984." *Nonprofit and Voluntary Sector Quarterly* 18:179-90.

Panet-Raymond, Jean. 1987. "Community Groups in Quebec: From Radical Action to Voluntarism for the State?" *Community Development Journal* 22:281-86.

————. 1989. "The Future of Community Groups in Quebec: The Difficult Balance Between Autonomy and Partnership With the State." *Canadian Social Work Review/Revue Canadienne de Service Social* 6:126-35.

Paradis, Adrian A. 1994. *Opportunities in Nonprofit Organization Careers.* Lincolnwood, IL: VGM Career Horizons.

Payne, Raymond. 1954. "An Approach to the Study of Relative Prestige of Formal Organizations." *Social Forces* 32:244-47.

Pearce, Jone L. 1982. "Leading and Following Volunteers: Implications for a Changing Society." *Journal of Applied Behavioral Science* 18:385-94.

————. 1993. *Volunteers: The Organizational Behavior of Unpaid Workers, London U.* London: Routledge.

Pedalini, Livia M., Sueli G. Dallari, and Rosemary Barber-Madden. 1993. "Public Health Advocacy on Behalf of Women in Sao Paolo: Learning to Participate in the Planning Process." *Journal of Public Health Policy* 14:183-97.

Pennock, J. R. and John W. Chapman. 1969. *Voluntary Associations, Nomos XI.* New York: Atherton.

Perkins, Kenneth B. 1989. "Volunteer Firefighters in the United States: A Descriptive Study." *Nonprofit and Voluntary Sector Quarterly* 18:269-77.

Perkins, Kenneth B. and Darryl G. Poole. 1996. "Oligarchy and Adaptation to Mass Society in an All-Volunteer Organization: Implications for Understanding Leadership, Participation, and Change." *Nonprofit and Voluntary Sector Quarterly* 25:73-88.

Perlman, Janice E. 1976. "Grassrooting the System." *Social Policy* 7:4-20.

Perlmutter, Felice D. 1982. "The Professionalization of Volunteer Administration." *Journal of Voluntary Action Research* 11:97-107.

Perlstadt, Harry. 1975. "Voluntary Associations and the Community: The Case of Volunteer Ambulance Corps." *Journal of Voluntary Action Research* 4:85-89.

Perlstadt, Harry and Lola J. Kozak. 1977. "Emergency Medical Services in Small Communities: Volunteer Ambulance Corps." *Journal of Community Health* 2:178-88.

Perrow, Charles. 1961. "The Analysis of Goals in Complex Organizations." *American Sociological Review* 26:854-66.

————. 1970. "Members as Resources in Voluntary Organizations." Pp. 93-101 in *Organizations and Clients,* edited by William R. Rosengren and Mark Lefton. Columbus, OH: Merrill.

Perry, Charles R. 1996. "Corporate Campaigns in Context." *Journal of Labor Research* 17:329-43.

Pestoff, V. A. 1977. *Voluntary Associations and Nordic Party Systems.* Stockholm, Sweden: Stockholm University.

Pfeffer, Jeffrey and Gerald Salancik. 1978. *The External Control of Organizations.* New York: Harper & Row.

Picardie, Justine. 1988. "Secrets of the Oddfellows." *New Society* 83:13-15.

Piliavin, J. A. and H-W. Charng. 1990. "Altruism: A Review of Recent Theory and Research." *Annual Review of Sociology* 16:27-65.

Pillai, R. 1993. "Crisis and the Emergence of Charismatic Leadership in Groups: An Experimental Investigation." *Journal of Applied Social Psychology* 26:543-62.

Piven, Frances F. and Richard A. Cloward. 1979. *Poor People's Movements*. New York: Vintage Books.

Podolofsky, Aaron and F. DuBow. 1981. *Strategies for Community Crime Prevention*. Springfield, IL: Charles C. Thomas.

Politser, Peter E. and Mansell Pattison. 1980. "Social Climates in Community Groups: Toward a Taxonomy." *Community Mental Health Journal* 16:187-200.

Popielarz, Pamela A. and J. Miller McPherson. 1995. "On the Edge or In Between: Niche Position, Niche Overlap, and the Duration of Voluntary Association Memberships." *American Journal of Sociology* 101:698-720.

Poulton, Geoff. 1988. *Managing Voluntary Organisations*. Chichester, UK: Wiley.

Powell, Thomas J. 1994. *Understanding the Self-Help Organization*. Thousand Oaks, CA: Sage.

Powell, Walter W. 1987. *The Nonprofit Sector*. New Haven, CT: Yale University Press.

Prestby, John E. and Abraham Wandersman. 1985. "An Empirical Exploration of a Framework of Organizational Viability: Maintaining Block Organizations." *Journal of Applied Behavioral Science* 21:287-305.

Prestby, John E., Abraham Wandersman, Paul Florin, Richard Rich, and David Chavis. 1990. "Benefits, Costs, Incentive Management, and Participation in Voluntary Organizations: A Means to Understanding and Promoting Empowerment." *Journal of Community Psychology* 18:117-49.

Putnam, Robert D. 1995. "Bowling Alone: America's Declining Social Capital." *Journal of Democracy* 6:65-78.

Putnam, Robert D., Robert Leonardi, and Rafaella Y. Nanetti. 1993. *Making Democracy Work: Civic Traditions in Modern Italy*. Princeton, NJ: Princeton University Press.

Quarrick, Gene. 1989. *Our Sweetest Hours: Recreation and the Mental State of Absorption*. Jefferson, NC: McFarland.

Randon, Anita and Perri 6. 1994. "Constraining Campaigning: The Legal Treatment of Non-Profit Policy Advocacy Across 24 Countries." *Voluntas* 5:27-58.

Raskoff, Sally and Richard A. Sundeen. 1998. "Youth Socialization and Civic Participation: The Role of Secondary Schools in Promoting Community Service in Southern California." *Nonprofit and Voluntary Sector Quarterly* 27:66-87.

Rauch, Jonathan. 1994. *Demosclerosis: The Silent Killer of American Government*. New York: Times Books.

Reavis, Dick J. 1995. *The Ashes of Waco*. New York: Simon & Schuster.

Reck, Franklin M. 1951. *The 4-H Story*. Chicago: National 4-H Service Committee.

Rein, Martin. 1966. "The Transition From Social Movement to Organization." Pp. 17-22 in *The Government of Associations*, edited by William A. Glaser and David L. Sills. Totowa, NJ: Bedminster Press.

Reitzes, Donald C. and Dietrich C. Reitzes. 1984. "Alinsky's Legacy: Current Applications and Extensions of His Principles and Strategies." *Research in Social Movements, Conflicts and Change* 6:31-55.

Rekart, Josephine. 1993. *Public Funds, Private Provision: The Role of the Volunteer Sector*. Vancouver: University of British Columbia Press.

Revenson, Tracey A. and Brian J. Cassel. 1991. "An Exploration of Leadership in a Medical Mutual Help Organization." *American Journal of Community Psychology* 19:683-98.

Rheingold, Howard. 1993. *The Virtual Community*. New York: HarperCollins.

Rich, Richard C. 1980. "Dynamics of Leadership in Neighborhood Organizations." *Social Science Quarterly* 60:570-87.

Richan, W. 1992. "The Alternative Agency as an Active Learner: A Case Study." *Social Work* 37:406-10.

Richardson, James T. 1979. "The Evolution of a Jesus Movement Organization." *Journal of Voluntary Action Research* 8:93-111.

Rietschlin, John C. 1996. "On the Contribution of Community to Psychological Well-Being: The Importance of Incorporating Group Membership Into Stress Research." Unpublished master's thesis, University of Western Ontario.

Rifkin, Jeremy. 1995. *The End of Work.* New York: Putnam.

Riger, Stephanie. 1983. "Vehicles for Empowerment: The Case of Feminist Movement Organizations." *Prevention in Human Services* 3:99-117.

Riiskjaer, Søren and Klaus Nielsen, 1987. Financial Dependence and Organizational Autonomy: The Ecology of Voluntary Sport in Denmark. *International Review for the Sociology of Sport* 22:193-208.

Robbins, Diana. 1990. "Voluntary Organizations and the Social State in the European Community." *Voluntas* 1:98-128.

Robertson, D. B. 1966. *Voluntary Associations: A Study of Groups in Free Societies.* Richmond, VA: John Knox Press.

Robinson, B. and M. G. Hanna. 1994. "Lesson for Academics From Grassroots Community Organizing: A Case Study—The Industrial Areas Foundation." *Journal of Community Practice* 1:63-94.

Robinson, J. 1990. "The Changing Focus of the Hub Club." *The Boston Globe,* March 27, pp. 25, 36.

Robinson, John P. 1977. *How Americans Use Their Time.* New York: Praeger.

———. 1985. "The Validity and Reliability of Diaries Versus Alternative Time Use Measures." Pp. 33-62 in *Time, Goods, and Well-Being,* edited by F. T. Juster and F. P. Stafford. Ann Arbor: University of Michigan Press.

Rochford, E. B., Jr. 1985. *Hare Krishna in America.* New Brunswick, NJ: Rutgers University Press.

Rock, Paul. 1988. "On the Birth of Organisations." *L.S.E. Quarterly* 2:123-53.

Rodin, J. and P. Salovey. 1989. "Health Psychology." *Annual Review of Psychology* 40:533-79.

Rogers, David L., Ken H. Barb, and Gordon L. Bultena. 1975. "Voluntary Association Membership and Political Participation: An Exploration of the Mobilization Hypothesis." *Sociological Quarterly* 16:305-18.

Romanofsky, Peter. 1973. "Professionals Versus Volunteers: A Case Study of Adoption Workers in the 1920's." *Journal of Voluntary Action Research* 2:95-101.

Ronan, Colin A. 1991. *The Natural History of the Universe.* New York: Macmillan.

Rose, Arnold M. 1954. *Theory and Method in the Social Sciences.* Minneapolis: University of Minnesota Press.

———. 1955. "Voluntary Associations Under Conditions of Competition and Conflict." *Social Forces* 34:159-63.

———. 1960. "The Impact of Aging on Voluntary Associations." Pp. 666-97 in *Handbook of Social Gerontology,* edited by C. W. Tibbitts. Chicago: University of Chicago Press.

Rose-Ackerman, S. 1980. "United Charities: An Economic Analysis." *Public Policy* 28:323-50.

———, ed. 1986. *The Economics of Nonprofit Institutions.* New York: Oxford University Press.

———. 1990. "Competition Between Non-Profits and For-Profits: Entry and Growth." *Voluntas* 1:13-25.

Rosenbloom, R. A. 1981. "The Neighborhood Movement: Where Has It Come From? Where Is It Going?" *Journal of Voluntary Action Research* 10:4-26.

Rosenstone, Steven J. and John M. Hansen. 1993. *Mobilization, Participation, and Democracy in America.* New York: Macmillan.

Ross, Jack C. 1976. *An Assembly of Good Fellows: Voluntary Associations in History.* Westport, CT: Greenwood.

Ross, Robert J. 1977. "Primary Groups in Social Movements: A Memoir and Interpretation." *Journal of Voluntary Action Research* 6:139-52.

Rothschild-Whitt, J. 1979. "The Collectivist Organization." *American Sociological Review* 44:509-27.

Rousseau, Cecile. 1993. "Community Empowerment: The Alternative Resources Movement in Quebec." *Community Mental Health Journal* 29:535-46.

Rubin, Hank, Laura Adamski, and Stephen R. Block. 1989. "Toward a Discipline of Nonprofit Administration: Report From the Clarion Conference." *Nonprofit and Voluntary Sector Quarterly* 18:279-86.

Rudney, Gabriel. 1987. "The Scope and Dimensions of Nonprofit Activity." Pp. 55-64 in *The Nonprofit Sector,* edited by Walter W. Powell. New Haven, CT: Yale University Press.

Rudwick, Elliott. 1972. "CORE: The Road From Interracialism to Black Power." *Journal of Voluntary Action Research* 1:12-19.

Rudy, D. R. 1986. *Becoming Alcoholic: Alcoholics Anonymous and the Reality of Alcoholism.* Carbondale: Southern Illinois University Press.

Rummel, R. J. 1994. *Death by Government.* New Brunswick, NJ: Transaction Publishers.

Sabatier, Paul A. and Susan M. McLaughlin. 1990. "Belief Congruence Between Interest Group Leaders and Members: An Empirical Analysis of Three Theories and a Suggested Synthesis." *Journal of Politics* 52:914-35.

Sagarin, Edward. 1969. *Odd Man In: Societies of Deviants in America.* Chicago: Quadrangle Books.

Saidel, Judith R. 1989. "Dimensions of Interdependence: The State and Voluntary Sector Relationship." *Nonprofit and Voluntary Sector Quarterly* 18:335-47.

Salamon, Lester M. 1987. "Of Market Failure, Voluntary Failure, and Third-Party Government: Toward a Theory of Government-Nonprofit Relations in the Modern Welfare State." *Journal of Voluntary Action Research* 16:29-49.

———. 1992. *America's Nonprofit Sector.* New York: Foundation Center.

———. 1993. "The Nonprofit Almanac: What Are the Issues?" *Voluntas* 4:163-72.

Salamon, Lester and Alan J. Abramson. 1982. *The Federal Budget and the Nonprofit Sector.* Washington, DC: Urban Institute.

Salamon, Lester M., D. M. Altschuler, and J. Myllyluoma. 1990. *More than Just Charity: The Baltimore Area Nonprofit Sector in a Time of Change.* Baltimore, MD: Johns Hopkins University, Institute for Policy Studies.

Salamon, Lester and Helmut K. Anheier. 1992a. "In Search of the Non-Profit Sector I: The Question of Definitions." *Voluntas* 3:125-51.

———. 1992b. "In Search of the Non-Profit Sector II: The International Classification of Non-Profit Organisations." *Voluntas* 3:125-52.

———. 1994. *The Emerging Sector.* Baltimore, MD: Johns Hopkins University, Institute for Policy Studies.

———. 1997. *Defining the Nonprofit Sector.* Manchester, UK: Manchester University Press.

Salamon, L. M., H. K. Anheier, and Associates. 1998. *The Emerging Sector Revisited: A Summary.* Baltimore, MD: Johns Hopkins University, Center for Civil Society Studies.

Salipante, Paul F. and Karen Golden-Biddle. 1995. "Managing Traditionality and Strategic Change in Nonprofit Organizations." *Nonprofit Management and Leadership* 6:3-20.

Salomon, K. 1986. "The Peace Movement: An Anti-Establishment Movement." *Journal of Peace Research* 23:115-27.

Saltman, Juliet. 1973. "Funding, Conflict, and Change in an Open-Housing Group." *Journal of Voluntary Action Research* 2:216-23.

Samuelson, Paul A. and William D. Nordhaus. 1995. *Economics.* 15th ed. New York: McGraw-Hill.

Savery, Lawson and Geoffrey Soutar. 1990. "Community Attitudes Toward Trade Union Effectiveness." *Australian Bulletin of Labour* 16:77-89.

Schaefer, Richard T. 1980. "The Management of Secrecy: The Ku Klux Klan's Successful Secret." Pp. 161-77 in *Secrecy: A Cross-Cultural Perspective,* edited by Stanton R. Petit. New York: Human Sciences Press.

Schafer, C. L. 1979. "How National Associations Help Local Chapters." *Association Management* 24:67-71.

Scherer, Ross. 1972. "The Church as a Formal Voluntary Organization." Pp. 81-108 in *Voluntary Action Research: 1972,* edited by David H. Smith, Richard D. Reddy, and Burt Baldwin. Lexington, MA: Lexington Books.

Schlesinger, Arthur M., Jr. 1993. *The Disuniting of America: Reflections on a Multicultural Society.* New York: Norton.

Schlesinger, Arthur M., Sr. 1944. "Biography of a Nation of Joiners." *American Historical Review* 50:1-25.

Schlozman, Kay. 1984. "What Accent the Heavenly Chorus? Political Equality in the American Pressure System." *Journal of Politics* 46:1006-32.

Schlozman, Kay and J. Tierney. 1986. *Organized Interests and American Democracy.* New York: Harper & Row.

Schmidt, Alvin J. 1973. *Oligarchy in Fraternal Organizations: A Study in Organizational Leadership.* Detroit, MI: Gale Research International.

Schmidt, Alvin J. and Nicholas Babchuk. 1972. "Formal Voluntary Groups and Change Over Time: A Study of Fraternal Associations." *Journal of Voluntary Action Research* 1:46-55.

Schondel, Connie, Kathryn Boehm, Jared Rose, and Alison Marlowe. 1995. "Adolescent Volunteers: An Untapped Resource in the Delivery of Adolescent Preventive Health Care." *Youth & Society* 27:123-35.

Schor, Juliet B. 1993. *The Overworked American.* New York: Basic Books.

Schuppert, Gunnar F. 1991. "State, Market, Third Sector: Problems of Organizational Choice in the Delivery of Public Services." *Nonprofit and Voluntary Sector Quarterly* 20:123-36.

Schwab, Reiko. 1995-96. "Bereaved Parents and Support Group Participation." *Omega* 32:49-61.

Schwartz-Shea, P. and D. D. Burrington. 1990. "Free Riding, Alternative Organization, and Cultural Feminism: The Case of Seneca Women's Peace Camp." *Women and Politics* 10:1-37.

Scott, Anne F. 1991. *Natural Allies: Women's Associations in American History.* Urbana: University of Illinois Press.

Scott, J. C., Jr. 1957. "Membership and Participation in Voluntary Associations." *American Sociological Review* 22:315-26.

Scott, William A. 1965. *Values and Organizations: A Study of Fraternities and Sororities.* Chicago: Rand McNally.

Seeley, John R., Buford H. Junker, and Wallace R. Jones, Jr. 1957. *Community Chest: A Case Study in Philanthropy.* Toronto: University of Toronto Press.

Selle, P. and B. Øymyr. 1992. "Explaining Changes in the Population of Voluntary Organizations: The Roles of Aggregate and Individual-Level Data." *Nonprofit and Voluntary Sector Quarterly* 21:147-79.

Sharma, Manoj and Gayatri Bhatia. 1996. "The Voluntary Community Health Movement in India: A Strengths, Weaknesses, Opportunities, and Threats (SWOT) Analysis." *Journal of Community Health* 21:453-64.

Sharp, Elaine B. 1981. "Organizations, Their Environments, and Goal Definition: An Approach to the Study of Neighborhood Associations in Urban Politics." *Urban Life* 9:415-39.

Sharp, Gene. 1973. *The Politics of Nonviolent Action.* Boston: Porter Sargent.

Shenhar, Yehouda, Wesley Shrum, and Sigal Alon. 1994. " 'Goodness' Concepts in the Study of Organizations: A Longitudinal Survey of Four Leading Journals." *Organization Studies* 15:753-76.

Shultz, James. 1972. "The Voluntary Society and Its Components." Pp. 25-38 in *Voluntary Action Research: 1972,* edited by David H. Smith, Richard D. Reddy, and Burt R. Baldwin. Lexington, MA: Lexington Books.

Sidjanski, Dusan. 1974. "Interest Groups in Switzerland." *Annals of the American Academy of Political and Social Science* 413:101-23.

Sills, David L. 1957. *The Volunteers: Means and Ends in a National Organization.* Glencoe, IL: Free Press.

———. 1968. "Voluntary Associations: Sociological Aspects." Pp. 363-76 in *The International Encyclopedia of the Social Sciences,* Vol. 16, edited by David Sills. New York: Macmillan.

Simon, John G. 1987. "The Tax Treatment of Nonprofit Organizations: A Review of Federal and State Policies." Pp. 67-98 in *The Nonprofit Sector,* edited by Walter W. Powell. New Haven, CT: Yale University Press.

Simpson, Richard L. and William H. Gulley. 1962. "Goals, Environmental Pressures, and Organizational Characteristics." *American Sociological Review* 27:344-51.

Sims, Patsy. 1997. *The Klan.* 2nd ed. Lexington: University Press of Kentucky.

6, Perri and Diana Leat. 1997. "Inventing the British Voluntary Sector by Committee: From Wolfenden to Deakin." *Non-Profit Studies* 1:33-45.

Skocpol, Theda. 1992. *Protecting Soldiers and Mothers.* Cambridge, MA: Harvard University Press.

Smiley, Charles W. 1975. "Reality, Social Work, and Community Organization." *Community Development Journal* 10:162-65.

Smith, Bradford. 1992. "The Use of Standard Industrial Classification (SIC) Codes to Classify the Activities of Nonprofit, Tax-Exempt Organizations." Working Paper No. 19, University of San Francisco, Institute for Nonprofit Organization Management.

Smith, Bradford, Sylvia Shue, and Joseph Villarreal. 1992. *Asian and Hispanic Philanthropy.* San Francisco: University of San Francisco Press.

Smith, Constance and Anne Freedman. 1972. *Voluntary Associations: Perspectives on the Literature.* Cambridge, MA: Harvard University Press.

Smith, David H. 1964. "Psychological Factors Affecting Participation in Formal Voluntary Organizations in Chile." Ph.D. dissertation, Harvard University.

———. 1966. "A Psychological Model of Individual Participation in Formal Voluntary Organizations: Application to Some Chilean Data." *American Journal of Sociology* 72:249-66.

———. 1967. "A Parsimonious Definition of 'Group': Toward Conceptual Clarity and Scientific Utility." *Sociological Inquiry* 37:141-67.

———. 1972a. "The Journal of Voluntary Action Research: An Introduction." *Journal of Voluntary Action Research* 1:2-5.

———. 1972b. "Major Analytical Topics of Voluntary Action Research: An Introduction." *Journal of Voluntary Action Research* 1:6-19.

———. 1972c. "Organizational Boundaries and Organizational Affiliates." *Sociology and Social Research* 56:494-512.

———. 1972d. "Ritual in Voluntary Associations." *Journal of Voluntary Action Research* 1:39-53.

———. 1973a. "The Impact of the Voluntary Sector on Society." Pp. 387-99 in *Voluntary Action Research: 1973,* edited by David H. Smith. Lexington, MA: Lexington Books.

———. 1973b. *Latin American Student Activism.* Lexington, MA: Lexington Books.

———. 1973c. "Modernization and the Emergence of Voluntary Organizations." Pp. 49-73 in *Voluntary Action Research: 1973,* edited by David H. Smith. Lexington, MA: Lexington Books.

———. 1974. *Voluntary Action Research: 1974.* Lexington, MA: Lexington Books.

———. 1975. "Voluntary Action and Voluntary Groups." *Annual Review of Sociology* 1:247-70.

———. 1977. "The Role of the United Way in Philanthropy." Pp. 1093-1108 in *Research Papers, Sponsored by the Commission on Private Philanthropy and Public Needs,* Vol. 2, Part 2, edited by Commission on Private Philanthropy and Public Needs. Washington, DC: Government Printing Office.

———. 1978. "The Philanthropy Business." *Society* 15:8-15.

———. 1981. "Altruism, Volunteers, and Volunteerism." *Journal of Voluntary Action Research* 10:21-36.

———. 1984. "Churches Are Generally Ignored in Contemporary Voluntary Action Research: Causes and Consequences." *Journal of Voluntary Action Research* 13:11-18.

———. 1986a. "Outstanding Local Voluntary Organizations in the 1960's: Their Distinguishing Characteristics." *Journal of Voluntary Action Research* 15:24-35.

———. 1986b. "Social Movement: A Voluntary Group Definition." Pp. 153-58 in *Proceedings of the 1986 Annual Meeting of the Association of Voluntary Action Scholars.* College Park: Pennsylvania State University.

———. 1990. "Voluntary Inter-Cultural Exchange and Understanding Groups: The Roots of Success in U.S. Sister City Programs." *International Journal of Comparative Sociology* 31:177-92.

———. 1991. "Four Sectors or Five? Retaining the Member Benefit Sector." *Nonprofit and Voluntary Sector Quarterly* 20:137-50.

———. 1992a. "National Nonprofit, Voluntary Associations: Some Parameters." *Nonprofit and Voluntary Sector Quarterly* 21:81-94.

———. 1992b. "A Neglected Type of Voluntary Nonprofit Organization: Exploration of the Semi-Formal, Fluid Membership Organization." *Nonprofit and Voluntary Sector Quarterly* 21:252-70.

———. 1993a. "The Field of Nonprofit and Voluntary Action Research: Then and Now." *Nonprofit and Voluntary Sector Quarterly* 22:197-200.

———. 1993b. "Public Benefit and Member Benefit Nonprofit, Voluntary Groups." *Nonprofit and Voluntary Sector Quarterly* 22:53-68.

———. 1994a. "Determinants of Voluntary Association Participation and Volunteering: A Literature Review." *Nonprofit and Voluntary Sector Quarterly* 23:243-63.

———. 1994b. "The Rest of the Nonprofit Sector: The Nature, Magnitude, and Impact of Grassroots Associations in America." Paper presented at the annual conference of the Association of Researchers on Nonprofit Organizations and Voluntary Action, Berkeley, CA, October.

———. 1995a. "Churches Are Mainly Member Benefit Nonprofits, Not Public Benefit Nonprofits." Paper presented at the annual conference of the Association of Researchers on Nonprofit Organizations and Voluntary Action, Cleveland, OH, November.

———. 1995b. "Democratic Personality." Pp. 941-43 in *The Encyclopedia of Democracy,* Vol. 3, edited by Seymour M. Lipset. Washington, DC: Congressional Quarterly Press.

———. 1995c. "Deviant Voluntary Groups: Ideology, Accountability, and Subcultures of Deviance in Nonprofits." Paper presented at the annual conference of the Association of Researchers on Nonprofit Organizations and Voluntary Action, Cleveland, OH, November.

———. 1995d. "Improving Classification of Nonprofits: Some Comments on the NTEE and ICNPO." Unpublished manuscript, Boston College.

———. 1995e. "Some Challenges in Nonprofit and Voluntary Action Research." *Nonprofit and Voluntary Sector Quarterly* 24:99-101.

———. 1996. "Improving the International Classification of Nonprofit Organizations." *Nonprofit Management and Leadership* 6:317-24.

———. 1997a. "Grassroots Associations Are Important: Some Theory and a Review of the Impact Literature." *Nonprofit and Voluntary Sector Quarterly* 26:269-306.

———. 1997b. "Grassroots Associations: The Lost Non-Profit World." *Chronicle of Philanthropy,* September 18, pp. 44-45.

———. 1997c. "The International History of Grassroots Associations." *International Journal of Comparative Sociology* 38:1-28.

———. 1997d. "The Rest of the Nonprofit Sector: Grassroots Associations as the Dark Matter Ignored in Prevailing 'Flat-Earth' Maps of the Sector." *Nonprofit and Voluntary Sector Quarterly* 26:114-31.

―――. 1998a. "Material vs. Personal Resource Attraction Systems for Local All-Volunteer Groups." Paper presented at the annual conference of the Association of Researchers on Nonprofit Organizations and Voluntary Action, Seattle, WA, November.

―――. 1998b. "Negative Social Capital and Deviant Voluntary Groups." Paper presented at the Michigan State University International Conference on Social Capital, East Lansing, MI, April.

―――. 1999a. "The Effective Grassroots Association, Part 1: Organizational Factors That Produce Internal Impact." *Nonprofit Management and Leadership* 9:443-56.

―――. 1999b. "The Effective Grassroots Association: II. Organizational Factors That Produce External Impact." *Nonprofit Management and Leadership* 10:103-16.

―――. Forthcoming a. *Organizations on the Fringe: Understanding Deviant Nonprofits as Part of a Round-Earth Paradigm of the Voluntary Nonprofit Sector.*

―――. Forthcoming b. "Researching Volunteer Associations and Other Nonprofits: An Emergent Interdisciplinary Field and Potential New Discipline. *American Sociologist* 30.

―――. Forthcoming c. *Volunteer Participation: A Round-Earth Paradigm of Individual Involvement in the Voluntary Nonprofit Sector.*

Smith, David H. and Associates. Forthcoming. *The World History and Geography of Associations and Other Nonprofits: A Theoretical Approach.*

Smith, David H. and Burt R. Baldwin. 1974a. "Parental Influence, Socioeconomic Status, and Voluntary Organization Participation." *Journal of Voluntary Action Research* 3:59-66.

―――. 1974b. "Voluntary Associations and Volunteering in the United States." Pp. 277-305 in *Voluntary Action Research: 1974,* edited by David H. Smith. Lexington, MA: Lexington Books.

―――. 1983. "Voluntary Organization Prevalence in the States of the USA: Presentation and a Test of the Revised Smith Model." Pp. 50-62 in *International Perspectives on Voluntary Action Research,* edited by David H. Smith and Jon Van Til. Washington, DC: University Press of America.

Smith, David H., Burt R. Baldwin, and Eugene D. White. 1988. "The Nonprofit Sector." Pp. 1.3-1.15 in *The Nonprofit Organization Handbook,* edited by Tracy D. Connors. New York: McGraw-Hill.

Smith, David H. and Michael Dover. Forthcoming. *Concepts and Terminology for Nonprofit and Voluntary Sector Studies.*

Smith, David H. and F. Elkin. 1981. *Volunteers, Voluntary Organizations, and Development.* Leiden, Netherlands: E. J. Brill.

Smith, David H., Jacqueline Macaulay, and Associates. 1980. *Participation in Social and Political Activities.* San Francisco: Jossey-Bass.

Smith, David H., R. D. Reddy, and B. R. Baldwin. 1972a. "Types of Voluntary Action: A Definitional Essay." Pp. 159-95 in *Voluntary Action Research: 1972,* edited by David H. Smith, Richard D. Reddy, and Burt R. Baldwin. Lexington, MA: Lexington Books.

―――. 1972b. *Voluntary Action Research: 1972.* Lexington, MA: Lexington Books.

Smith, David H. and Richard D. Reddy. 1973. "The Impact of Voluntary Action on the Volunteer/Participant." Pp. 169-237 in *Voluntary Action Research: 1973,* edited by David H. Smith. Lexington, MA: Lexington Books.

Smith, David H., Mary Seguin, and Marjorie Collins. 1973. "Dimensions and Categories of Voluntary Organizations/NGOs." *Journal of Voluntary Action Research* 2:116-20.

Smith, David H. and C. Shen. 1996. "Factors Characterizing the Most Effective Nonprofits Managed by Volunteers." *Nonprofit Management and Leadership* 6:271-89.

Smith, David H. and Jon Van Til, with the collaboration of Dan Bernfeld, Victor Pestoff, and David Zeldin. 1983. *International Perspectives on Voluntary Action Research.* Washington, DC: University Press of America.

Smith, David H. and J. Malcolm Walker. 1977. "Higher Education Programs for Volunteer Administrators." *Volunteer Administration* 10:1-9.

Smith, L. M. 1975. "Women as Volunteers: The Double Subsidy." *Journal of Voluntary Action Research* 4:119-36.

Smith, M. J. 1990. "Pluralism, Reformed Pluralism, and Neopluralism: The Role of Pressure Groups in Policy-Making." *Political Studies* 37:302-22.

Smith, Steven R. and Michael Lipsky. 1993. *Nonprofits for Hire*. Cambridge, MA: Harvard University Press.

Smith, Tom W. 1990. "Trends in Voluntary Group Membership: Comments on Baumgartner and Walker." *American Journal of Political Science* 34:646-61.

Snyder, Eldon E. 1970. "Longitudinal Analysis of Social Participation in High School and Early Adulthood Voluntary Associational Participation." *Adolescence* 5:79-88.

Soen, D. and P. de Comarmond. 1971. "Savings Associations Among the Bamileke: Traditional and Modern Cooperation in South-West Cameroon." *Journal de la Societé des Africanistes* 2:189-201.

Soysal, Yasemin N. 1994. *Limits of Citizenship: Migrants and Postnational Membership in Europe*. Chicago: University of Chicago Press.

Speer, Paul W. and Joseph Hughey. 1996. "Mechanisms of Empowerment: Psychological Processes for Members of Power-Based Community Organizations." *Journal of Community and Applied Social Psychology* 6:177-87.

Spencer, Metta. 1991. "Politics Beyond Turf: Grassroots Democracy in the Helsinki Process." *Bulletin of Peace Proposals* 22:427-35.

Spergel, Irving A. 1995. *The Youth Gang Problem*. New York: Oxford University Press.

Staggenborg, Suzanne. 1989. "Stability and Innovation in the Women's Movement: A Comparison of Two Movement Organizations." *Social Problems* 36:75-92.

Stallings, R. A. and E. Quarantelli. 1985. "Emergent Citizen Groups and Emergency Management." *Public Administration Review* 9:67-82.

Stallings, Robert A. 1973. "Patterns of Belief in Social Movements: Clarifications from an Analysis of Environmental Groups." *Sociological Quarterly* 14:465-80.

Standard & Poor's. 1999. *Standard & Poor's Register of Corporations, Directors, and Executives*. New York: Standard & Poor's Corporation.

Stanton, Esther. (1970) *Clients Come Last: Volunteers and Welfare Organizations*. Beverly Hills, CA: Sage.

Stark, Rodney. 1994. *Sociology*. Belmont, CA: Wadsworth.

Stark, Rodney and Charles Y. Glock. 1968. *American Piety: The Nature of Religious Commitment*. Berkeley: University of California Press.

Starkweather, D. B. 1993. "Profit Making by Nonprofit Hospitals." Pp. 105-37 in *Nonprofit Organizations in a Market Economy,* edited by David C. Hammack and Dennis R. Young. San Francisco: Jossey-Bass.

Starr, Frederick. 1991. "The Third Sector in the Second World." *World Development* 19:65-71.

Stebbins, Robert A. 1979. *Amateurs*. Beverly Hills, CA: Sage.

———. 1996. "Volunteering: A Serious Leisure Perspective." *Nonprofit and Voluntary Sector Quarterly* 25:211-24.

Steers, Richard M. 1975. *Motivation and Work Behavior*. New York: McGraw-Hill.

Stein, Arlene J. 1986. "Between Organization and Movement: ACORN and the Alinsky Model of Community Organizing." *Berkeley Journal of Sociology* 31:93-115.

Steinberg, Richard. 1987. "Nonprofit Organizations and the Market." Pp. 118-38 in *The Nonprofit Sector,* edited by Walter W. Powell. New Haven, CT: Yale University Press.

———. 1990. "Labor Economics and the Nonprofit Sector: A Literature Review." *Nonprofit and Voluntary Sector Quarterly* 19:151-69.

Steinberg, Stephen. 1981. *The Ethnic Myth: Race, Ethnicity, and Class in America*. Boston: Beacon.

Steinman, Richard and Donald M. Traunstein. 1976. "Redefining Deviance: The Self-Help Challenge to the Human Services." *Journal of Applied Behavioral Science* 12:347-61.

Stephenson, Tamara. 1973. "Internal Structure of a Voluntary Political Organization: A Case Study." *Journal of Voluntary Action Research* 2:240-43.

Stewman, Shelby. 1988. "Organizational Demography." *Annual Review of Sociology* 14:173-202.

Stinson, T. F. and J. M. Stam. 1976. "Toward an Economic Model of Vountarism: The Case of Participation in Local Government." *Journal of Voluntary Action Research* 5:52-60.

Stoecker, Randy. 1993. "The Federated Frontstage Structure and Localized Social Movements: A Case Study of the Cedar-Riverside Neighborhood Movement." *Social Science Quarterly* 74:56-68.

Stubblefield, Harold and Leroy Miles. 1986. " Administration of Volunteer Programs as a Career: What Role for Higher Education?" *Journal of Voluntary Action Research* 15:4-12.

Sugden, R. 1984. "Reciprocity: The Supply of Public Goods Through Voluntary Contributions." *The Economic Journal* 94:772-87.

Suler, J. 1984. "The Role of Ideology in Self-Help Groups." *Social Policy* 14:29-36.

Suler, J. and E. Bartholemew. 1986. "The Ideology of Overeaters Anonymous." *Social Policy* 16:48-53.

Sulloway, Frank J. 1996. *Born to Rebel: Birth Order, Family Dynamics, and Creative Lives.* New York: Pantheon.

Swanson, James M. 1974. "Non-Governmental Organizations in the USSR, 1958-1973." Pp. 69-86 in *Voluntary Action Research: 1974,* edited by David H. Smith. Lexington, MA: Lexington Books.

Tannenbaum, Arnold S. 1961. "Control and Effectiveness in a Voluntary Organization." *American Journal of Sociology* 67:57-77.

Tester, Keith. 1992. *Civil Society.* London: Routledge.

Thielen, Gary L. and Dennis L. Poole. 1986. "Educating Leadership for Effecting Community Change Through Voluntary Associations." *Journal of Social Work Education* 22:19-29.

Thompson, A. M., III. 1993. "Volunteers and Their Communities: A Comparative Analysis of Volunteer Fire Fighters." *Nonprofit and Voluntary Sector Quarterly* 22:155-66.

———. 1995. "The Sexual Division of Leadership in Volunteer Emergency Medical Service Squads." *Nonprofit Management and Leadership* 6:55-66.

Thompson, K. 1980. "Organizations as Constructors of Social Reality." In *Control and Ideology in Organizations,* edited by G. Salamon and K. Thompson. Cambridge: MIT Press.

Thomson, Randall J. and David Knoke. 1980. "Voluntary Associations and Voting Turnout of American Ethnoreligious Groups." *Ethnicity* 7:56-69.

Tilgher, Adriano. 1958. *Homo Faber: Work Through the Ages.* Chicago: Regnery.

Tilly, Charles. 1978. *From Mobilization to Revolution.* Reading, MA: Addison-Wesley.

Timperly, Stuart R. and Michael D. Osbaldeston. 1975. "The Professionalization Process: A Study of an Aspiring Occupational Organization." *Sociological Review* 23:607-27.

Tobias, H. J. and C. E. Woodhouse. 1985. "Revolutionary Optimism and the Practice of Revolution: The Jewish Bund in 1905." *Jewish Social Studies* 47:135-50.

Torres, C. C., M. Zey, and W. A. McIntosh. 1991. "Effectiveness in Voluntary Organizations: An Empirical Assessment." *Sociological Focus* 24:157-74.

Traunstein, Donald M. 1984. "From Mutual Aid Self-Help to Professional Service." *Social Casework* 65:622-27.

Traunstein, Donald M. and Richard Steinman. 1973. "Voluntary Self-Help Organizations: An Exploratory Study." *Journal of Voluntary Action Research* 2:230-39.

Trojan, Alf, Edith Halves, Hans-Wilhelm Wetendorf, and Randolph Bauer. 1990. "Activity Areas and Developmental Stages in Self-Help Groups." *Nonprofit and Voluntary Sector Quarterly* 19: 263-78.

Trow, Donald B. and David H. Smith. 1983. "Correlates of Volunteering in Advocacy Planning: Testing a Theory." Pp. 95-104 in *International Perspectives on Voluntary Action Research,* edited by David H. Smith and Jon Van Til. Washington, DC: University Press of America.

Truant, Cynthia M. 1979. "Solidarity and Symbolism Among Journeymen Artisans: The Case of Compagnonnage." *Comparative Studies in Society and History* 21:214-26.

Tsouderos, John E. 1955. "Organizational Change in Terms of a Series of Selected Variables." *American Sociological Review* 20:206-10.

Tuckman, Howard P. and Cyril F. Chang. 1991. "A Methodology for Measuring the Financial Vulnerability of Charitable Nonprofit Organizations." *Nonprofit and Voluntary Sector Quarterly* 20:445-60.

Turner, Sarah E., Thomas I. Nygren, and William G. Bowen. 1993. "The NTEE Classification System: Tests of Reliability/Validity in the Field of Higher Education." *Voluntas* 4:73-94.

Tyrrell, George N. M. [1951] 1969. *Homo Faber: A Study of Man's Mental Evolution.* London: Methuen.

Unger, Aryeh L. 1974. *The Totalitarian Party: Party and People in Nazi Germany and Soviet Russia.* Cambridge, UK: Cambridge University Press.

Unger, Donald G. and Abraham Wandersman. 1983. "Neighboring and Its Role in Block Organizations: An Exploratory Report." *American Journal of Community Psychology* 11:291-300.

Unterman, Israel and Richard H. Davis. 1982. "The Strategy Gap in Not-for-Profits." *Harvard Business Review* 60:30-40.

U.S. Bureau of the Census. 1993. *Statistical Abstract of the United States: 1993, 113th Edition.* Washington, DC: U.S. Department of Commerce.

U.S. Department of the Treasury. 1979. *Cumulative List of Organizations.* Washington, DC: U.S. Department of the Treasury, Internal Revenue Service.

Vaillancourt, François and Micheline Payette. 1986. "The Supply of Volunteer Work: The Case of Canada." *Journal of Voluntary Action Research* 15:45-56.

Van Harberden, P. and T. Raymakers. 1986. "Self-Help and Government Policy in the Netherlands. *Journal of Voluntary Action Research* 15:24-32.

Van Til, Jon. 1987. "The Three Sectors: Voluntarism in the Changing Political Economy." *Journal of Voluntary Action Research* 16:50-63.

———. 1988. *Mapping the Third Sector: Voluntarism in a Changing Social Economy.* New York: Foundation Center.

Van Til, Jon and J. Carr. 1994. "Defining the Nonprofit Sector." Paper presented at the annual conference of the Association for Research on Nonprofit Organizations and Voluntary Action, Berkeley, CA, November.

Vaux, Alan. 1988. *Social Support: Theory, Research, and Intervention.* New York: Praeger.

Verba, S., K. L. Schlozman, and H. E. Brady. 1995. *Voice and Equality: Civic Voluntarism in American Politics.* Cambridge, MA: Harvard University Press.

Verba, Sidney and Norman H. Nie. 1972. *Participation in America.* New York: Harper & Row.

Vidich, Arthur J. and Joseph Bensman. 1968. *Small Town in Mass Society.* Rev. ed. Princeton, NJ: Princeton University Press.

Wade, Robert. 1975. "Ruralism as a Way of Life? Stratification and Voluntary Associations in a Tuscan Village." *Sociologia Ruralis* 15:245-58.

Wagner, A. 1991. "On Sharing: A Preface to an Economic Theory of Voluntary Action." *Nonprofit and Voluntary Sector Quarterly* 20:359-70.

Walker, J. Malcolm. 1975. "Organizational Change, Citizen Participation, and Voluntary Action." *Journal of Voluntary Action Research* 4:4-22.

———. 1983. "Limits of Strategic Management in Voluntary Organizations." *Journal of Voluntary Action Research* 12:39-56.

Waltzing, Jean P. 1895. *Etude Historique sur les Corporations Professionelles Chez les Romains Depuis les Origines Jusqu la Chute de L'Empire D'Occident.* Louvain, Belgium: Paters.

Walzer, M. 1983. *Spheres of Justice: A Defense of Pluralism and Equality.* New York: Basic Books.

Warner, W. K. 1972. "Major Conceptual Elements of Voluntary Associations." Pp. 71-80 in *Voluntary Action Research: 1972,* edited by David H. Smith, Richard D. Reddy, and Burt Baldwin. Lexington, MA: Lexington Books.

Warner, W. K. and William B. Heffernan. 1967. "Benefit-Participation Contingency in Voluntary Farm Organizations." *Rural Sociology* 32:139-53.

Warner, W. L. 1949. *Democracy in Jonesville.* New York: Harper.

Warner, W. L. and P. S. Lunt. 1941. *The Social Life of a Modern Community.* New Haven, CT: Yale University Press.

Warren, Roland. 1967. "The Interorganizational Field as a Focus for Investigation." *Administrative Science Quarterly* 12:396-419.

Warren, Roland L., Stephen M. Rose, and Ann F. Bergunder. 1974. *The Structure of Urban Reform.* Lexington, MA: Lexington Books.

Warriner, Charles K. and Jane E. Prather. 1965. "Four Types of Voluntary Associations." *Sociological Inquiry* 35:138-48.

Watson, Paula D. 1994. "Founding Mothers: The Contributions of Women's Organizations to Public Library Development in the United States." *Library Quarterly* 64:233-69.

Weber, Max. 1947. *The Theory of Social and Economic Organization.* Glencoe, IL: Free Press.

———. 1952. *The Protestant Ethic and the Spirit of Capitalism.* New York: Scribner.

———. 1972. "Max Weber's Proposal for the Sociological Study of Voluntary Associations." *Journal of Voluntary Action Research* 1:20-23.

Weed, Frank J. 1989. "The Impact of Support Resources on Local Chapter Operations in the Anti-Drunk Driving Movement." *Sociological Quarterly* 30:77-91.

Weightman, Judith. 1983. *Making Sense of the Jonestown Suicides.* New York: Edwin Mellen.

Weisbrod, Burton A. 1977. *The Voluntary Nonprofit Sector: An Economic Analysis.* Lexington, MA: Lexington Books.

———. 1988. *The Nonprofit Economy.* Cambridge, MA: Harvard University Press.

———. 1992. "Tax Policy Toward Nonprofit Organizations: A Ten Country Survey." Pp. 29-50 in *The Nonprofit Sector in the Global Community: Voices From Many Nations,* edited by K. D. McCarthy, V. A. Hodgkinson, R. A. Sumariwalla, and Associates. San Francisco: Jossey-Bass.

Weitzman, M. S. 1983. *Measuring the Number of Hours Spent and Dollar Value of Volunteer Activity of Americans.* Washington, DC: Independent Sector.

Wenocur, S., R. V. Cook, and N. L. Steketee. 1984. "Fund-Raising at the Workplace." *Social Policy* 14:55-60.

Wertheim, Edward G. 1976. "Evolution of Structure and Process in Voluntary Organizations: A Study of 35 Consumer Food Cooperatives." *Journal of Voluntary Action Research* 5:4-15.

Whitmore, Elizabeth, Harry W. Snappington, J. Lin Compton, and Jennifer C. Green. 1988. "Adult Learning Through Participation in Rural Community Groups." *Journal of Voluntary Action Research* 17:55-69.

Whitson, David and Donald Macintosh. 1989. "Rational Planning vs. Regional Interests: The Professionalization of Canadian Amateur Sport." *Canadian Public Policy* 15:436-39.

Widmer, Candace. 1985. "Why Board Members Participate." *Journal of Voluntary Action Research* 14:8-23.

———. 1991. "Board Members' Perceptions of Their Roles and Responsibilities." In *Collaboration: The Vital Link Across Practice, Research, and the Disciplines,* edited by Association for Research on Nonprofit Organizations and Voluntary Action. Pullman, WA: ARNOVA.

Wiewel, Wim and Nicholas C. Rieser. 1989. "The Limits of Progressive Municipal Economic Development: Job Creation in Chicago, 1983-1987." *Community Development Journal* 24:111-19.

Wilderom, C. P. M. and J. B. Miner. 1991. "Defining Voluntary Groups and Agencies Within Organization Science." *Organization Science* 2:366-78.

Willerman, Ben and L. Swanson. 1953. "Group Prestige in Voluntary Organizations: A Study of College Sororities." *Human Relations* 6:57-77.

Williams, Constance. 1986. "Improving Care in Nursing Homes Using Community Advocacy." *Social Science and Medicine* 23:1297-1303.

Wilson, Bryan R. 1970. *Religious Sects: A Sociological Study.* London: Weidenfeld & Nicolson.

Wilson, David C. 1992. "The Strategic Challenges of Cooperation in British Voluntary Organizations: Toward the Next Century." *Nonprofit Management and Leadership* 2:239-54.

Wilson, John. 1980. "Voluntary Associations and Civil Religion: The Case of Freemasonry." *Review of Religious Research* 22:125-36.

Wineburg, Robert J. 1992. "Local Human Service Provision by Religious Congregations: A Community Analysis." *Nonprofit and Voluntary Sector Quarterly* 21:107-18.

Wish, N. B. 1993. "Colleges Offering More Nonprofit Graduate Programs." *Non-Profit Times,* June, pp. 22-23.

Wittig, Michele A. and Joseph Schmitz. 1996. "Electronic Grassroots Organizing." *Journal of Social Issues* 52 (1): 53-69.

Wolch, J. 1990. *The Shadow State: Government and Voluntary Sector in Transition.* New York: Foundation Center.

Wolfe, J. D. 1985. "A Defense of Participatory Democracy." *Review of Politics* 47:370-89.

Wolfenden Committee. 1978. *The Future of Voluntary Organisations.* London: Croom Helm.

Wolke, H. 1991. *Wilderness on the Rocks.* Tucson, AZ: Ned Ludd.

Wolozin, H. 1975. "The Economic Role and Value of Volunteer Work in the United States: An Exploratory Study." *Journal of Voluntary Action Research* 4:23-42.

Wood, James R. 1981. *Leadership in Voluntary Organizations.* New Brunswick, NJ: Rutgers University Press.

Wortman, Max S., Jr. 1981. "A Radical Shift From Bureaucracy to Strategic Management in Voluntary Organizations." *Journal of Voluntary Action Research* 10:62-81.

Wright, C. R. and H. H. Hyman. 1958. "Voluntary Association Memberships of American Adults: Evidence From National Sample Surveys." *American Sociological Review* 23:284-94.

Wrong, Dennis H. 1961. "The Oversocialized Concept of Man in Modern Sociology." *American Sociological Review* 26:183-93.

Wuthnow, Robert. 1990. "Religion and the Voluntary Spirit in the United States: Mapping the Terrain." Pp. 3-21 in *Faith and Philanthropy in America,* edited by Robert Wuthrow, Virginia Hodgkinson, and Associates. San Francisco: Jossey-Bass.

———. 1994. *Sharing the Journey: Support Groups and America's New Quest for Community.* New York: Free Press.

———. 1998. *Loose Connections: Joining Together in America's Fragmented Communities.* Cambridge, MA: Harvard University Press.

Yamazaki, H. and M. Miyamoto. 1988. *Trade Associations in Business History.* Tokyo: University of Tokyo Press.

Yanitskiy, Oleg N. 1992. "Razvitie Ekologicheskikh Dvizheniy na Zapade i Vostoke Evropy" (The Development of the Ecological Movement in the West and East of Europe). *Sotsiologicheskie Issledovaniya* 19:32-39.

Yates, Frank. 1981. *Sampling Methods for Censuses and Surveys.* 4th ed. London: Charles Griffin.

York, Alan and Esther Zychlinski. 1996. "Competing Nonprofit Organizations Also Collaborate." *Nonprofit Management and Leadership* 7:15-27.

Young, Dennis R. 1983. *If Not for Profit, for What?* Lexington, MA: D. C. Heath.

———. 1987. "Executive Leadership in Nonprofit Organizations." Pp. 167-79 in *The Nonprofit Sector,* edited by Walter W. Powell. New Haven, CT: Yale University Press.

———. 1989. "Local Autonomy in a Franchise Age: Structural Change in National Voluntary Associations." *Nonprofit and Voluntary Sector Quarterly* 18:101-17.

Young, Dennis R., Neil Bania, and Darlyne Bailey. 1996. "Structure and Accountability: A Study of National Nonprofit Associations." *Nonprofit Management and Leadership* 6:347-66.

Young, Dennis R., Robert M. Hollister, Virginia A. Hodgkinson, and Associates. 1993. *Governing, Leading, and Managing Nonprofit Organizations: New Insights From Research and Practice.* San Francisco: Jossey-Bass.

Young, R. C. and Olaf E. Larson. 1965. "The Contribution of Voluntary Organizations to Community Structure." *American Journal of Sociology* 71:178-86.

Yuchtman, Ephraim and Stanley Seashore. 1967. "A System Resource Approach to Organizational Effectiveness." *American Sociological Review* 32:891-903.

Zablocki, B. 1981. *Alienation and Charisma: A Study of Contemporary Communes.* New York: Free Press.

Zakour, Michael J., D. F. Gillespie, M. W. Sherraden, and C. L. Streeter. 1991. "Volunteer Organizations in Disasters." *Journal of Volunteer Administration* 9:18-28.

Zald, Mayer N. 1970. *Organizational Change; The Political Economy of the YMCA.* Chicago: University of Chicago Press.

Zald, Mayer N. and R. Ash. 1966. "Social Movement Organizations: Growth, Decline, and Change." *Social Forces* 44:327-40.

Zald, Mayer N. and Michael A. Berger. 1978. "Social Movements in Organizations: Coup d'état, Insurgency, and Mass Movements." *American Journal of Sociology* 83:823-61.

Zald, Mayer N. and Patricia Denton. 1983. "From Evangelism to General Service: The Transformation of the YMCA." *Administrative Science Quarterly* 8:214-34.

Zellner, William W. 1995. *Countercultures.* New York: St. Martin's.

Zerubavel, E. T. 1992. *The Mental Discovery of America.* New Brunswick, NJ: Rutgers University Press.

Zhou, Xueguang. 1993. "Unorganized Interests and Collective Action in Communist China." *American Sociological Review* 58:54-73.

Zimmerman, M. A. 1995. "Psychological Empowerment: Issues and Illustrations." *American Journal of Community Psychology* 23:581-99.

Zimmerman, M. A. and J. Rappaport. 1988. "Citizen Participation, Perceived Control, and Psychological Empowerment." *American Journal of Community Psychology* 16:725-50.

Zipf, George K. 1949. *Human Behavior and the Principle of Least Effort.* Reading, MA: Addison-Wesley.

Zipps, M. and H. Z. Levine. 1984. "Roundup: Volunteer Experience a Plus on a 'Résumé'." *Personnel* 61;40-42.

Zurcher, Louis A., Jr. 1978. "Ephemeral Roles, Voluntary Action, and Voluntary Associations." *Journal of Voluntary Action Research* 7:65-74.

Index

AUTHOR'S NOTE: GA = Grassroots Association; VG = Voluntary Group = Nonprofit group/
entity; VNPS= Voluntary Nonprofit Sector.

About the Author

David Horton Smith has been a Professor of Sociology at Boston College since 1976 and was Associate Professor there from 1968 to 1976. He currently is on a leave of absence from the university.

Born and raised in the Los Angeles Area, he received his B.A. from the University of Southern California (1960) magna cum laude in three major departments/fields: philosophy, psychology, and sociology. He was elected to the Phi Beta Kappa and Phi Kappa Phi honorary societies, and on graduation he received a National Science Foundation Graduate Fellowship and a Woodrow Wilson Honorary Fellowship. His M.A. (1962) and Ph.D. (1965) in sociology were received from Harvard University in the interdisciplinary Department of Social Relations.

He was the founder and first president of the Association for Research on Nonprofit Organizations and Voluntary Action (ARNOVA), the first interdisciplinary and interprofessional association in the field (1971), and he was the founder and first editor of its journal *Nonprofit and Voluntary Sector Quarterly* (1972). He spent the period from 1971 to 1974 in Washington, D.C., as research director for a nonprofit concerned with voluntarism (the Center for a Voluntary Society) that supported his work in founding ARNOVA through Boston College. He has published more than 100 articles and book chapters on nonprofit and voluntary action research and has written or edited eight earlier books in the field. His major books include *Voluntary Action Research: 1972, 1973,* and *1974* (a three-volume series), *Participation in Social and Political Activities* (1980), and *International Participation in Voluntary Action Research* (1983, edited with Jon Van Til).

He was the recipient of the first ARNOVA Lifetime Achievement Award for Distinguished Contribution to Nonprofit and Voluntary Action Research (1993). Recently, he has been the founding chair of the new Community/Grassroots Associations Section of ARNOVA.